MANAGING MARKETING LINKAGES

Text, Cases, and Readings

Frank V. Cespedes

The Center for Executive Development

Prentice Hall, Upper Saddle River, New Jersey 07458

Library of Congress Cataloging-in-Publication Data
Cespedes, Frank V., (date)
    Managing marketing linkages / Frank V. Cespedes.
        p. cm.
    ISBN 0–13–234923–X
    1. Marketing.   2. Marketing—Case studies.   3. Business planning.
    I. Title.
    HF5415.C45   1996
    658.8—dc20   95–20173
                                                                              CIP

Acquisitions editor: *David Borkowsky*
Editorial/production supervision: *Kim Gueterman*
Cover designer: *Bruce Kenselaar*
Buyer: *Vincent Scelta*

© 1996 by Prentice-Hall, Inc.
Simon & Schuster/A Viacom Company
Upper Saddle River, New Jersey 07458

Case material of the Harvard Graduate School of Business Administration is made
possible by the cooperation of business firms and other organizations which may
wish to remain anonymous by having names, quantities, and other identifying
details disguised while maintaining basic relationships. Cases are prepared as the
basis for class discussion rather than to illustrate either effective or ineffective
handling of an administrative situation.

Printed in the United States of America
10   9   8   7   6   5   4   3   2   1

ISBN 0-13-234923-X

Prentice-Hall International (UK) Limited, *London*
Prentice-Hall of Australia Pty. Limited, *Sydney*
Prentice-Hall of Canada Inc., *Toronto*
Prentice-Hall Hispanoamericana, S.A., *Mexico*
Prentice-Hall of India Private Limited, *New Delhi*
Prentice-Hall of Japan, Inc., *Tokyo*
Simon & Schuster Asia Pte. Ltd., *Singapore*
Editora Prentice-Hall do Brasil, Ltda., *Rio de Janeiro*

For Bonnie Costello

Contents

Part III SERVICE MARKETS 215

Part IV BUILDING AND MAINTAINING CUSTOMER RELATIONSHIPS 317

About the Author

Frank V. Cespedes is a managing partner at The Center for Executive Development in Cambridge, Massachusetts, where he provides management education and consulting services to companies in North America, South America, Europe, and Asia. Cespedes was a member of the Harvard Business School faculty for 15 years, where he specialized in marketing, organizational design, and strategy implementation, developed and taught various courses in the MBA program, and also led the Strategic Marketing Management program for senior executives. He is the author of numerous articles and six books, including *Concurrent Marketing: Integrating Product, Sales, and Service, Organizing and Implementing the Marketing Effort* and *Going to Market: Distribution Systems for Industrial Products*.

Preface

In recent years, companies around the world have dramatically altered their management philosophies and processes in areas such as production, operations, physical distribution, and customer service. Such changes inevitably affect marketing tasks and challenges. This book concerns a central aspect of marketing organization: interactions among product, sales, and service units. It focuses on these key customer-contact groups as a means of generating analyses and discussions of: (a) market factors that affect the organization and management of these increasingly intertwined activities; (b) what companies in different market environments are doing to manage these marketing linkages; and (c) the wider organizational implications in areas ranging from strategy development, on the one hand, to tactical sales management issues, on the other.

The book is aimed at advanced students of marketing and at managers whose responsibilities include cross-functional activities among marketing groups as well as between these groups and other parts of the company. Although the book provides a detailed look at product, sales, and service tasks in a variety of business settings, it is not another introduction to product management, sales management, or service management. Topics such as product life-cycle strategies, sales skills, and service operations are discussed within the framework of the readings and case studies. But the focus is on the interaction of external market factors and internal organizational linkages required to develop and maintain profitable customer relationships.

The book includes an introductory chapter and twelve case studies. The introduction explains the growing importance of the topic for management theory and practice, the conceptual structure of the cases included, and the organization of the book. Each of the four parts of the book is introduced by an overview article.

The case studies are unique in that they cover interactions among these marketing units in a variety of business-to-business, consumer, and services markets. By contrast, nearly all existing case studies and much of marketing literature focus either on product management or sales management or service operations in isolation from the other activities. But, as these field cases and readings illustrate, business process redesign initiatives and other developments in many industries are forcing new interdependencies and interactions among these groups, making a purely functional approach decreasingly relevant to students and practitioners. This book can give its readers insights on how new marketing requirements can be managed better within the context of overall business strategy.

ACKNOWLEDGMENTS

My greatest thanks go to the many executives of the companies highlighted in the case studies. They generously donated their time and trust. I also gratefully acknowledge the financial support of the Division of Research at the Graduate School of Business Administration, Harvard University. Thanks are also due to my research assistants during this period: Marie Bell and Laura Goode.

During the research effort for this book, I benefited from the advice and insights of a number of people inside and outside academia. I especially want to thank Dr. John Cady of The Center for Executive Development, Professor Daniel Dunn of Northeastern University, Professor Joel Goldhar of the Illinois Institute of Technology, Professor Stephen Greyser of Harvard Business School, Stephen Haeckel of IBM, John Lewis of Procter & Gamble, Alan J. McMillan of Regis McKenna, Inc., Kathleen Mocniak of Leaf, Inc., Professor John Quelch of Harvard Business School, Professor Richard Reizenstein of the University of Tennessee, Professor Benson Shapiro of Harvard Business School, Henry Smith of Becton Dickinson and Company, Professor Frederick Webster of Dartmouth University, Professor Brown Whittington of Emory University, and Professor Lawrence Wortzel of Boston University.

Finally, I thank David Borkowsky and Kim Gueterman at Prentice Hall for their professionalism and help with the manuscript.

Frank V. Cespedes

Cambridge, Massachusetts

Introduction

In most companies, the interdependent activities of the sales, product management, and customer service groups are the major ways in which the firm interacts with customers. This book concerns this core aspect of organization. It can help students and executives better understand and manage the internal linkages that ultimately build or destroy external relationships with customers.

The book consists of case studies and, in addition to this introduction, readings about different aspects of the topic. The cases illustrate market factors that affect interactions among sales, product management, and customer service groups; allow for inter- and intra-industry comparisons; and provide useful perspectives on the dynamics of managing marketing linkages within different structures and systems. The readings augment the learning from the case discussions. Each considers certain aspects of the topic in a different market environment, discusses field research concerning the topic, and suggests frameworks useful in analyzing the issues raised by the case studies.

Together, the case studies and the readings are intended for management students, scholars, and practitioners who want to learn more about how and why coordination among these marketing units is increasingly important and complex for many firms; about the similarities and differences in the nature of coordination requirements across the markets examined; and about the costs and benefits of different approaches to managing these marketing linkages.

IMPORTANCE OF THE TOPIC FOR MANAGEMENT THEORY AND PRACTICE

Because of their central role in customer acquisition and retention, marketing interactions always have wider organizational and management implications. Similarly, the materials here have relevance for both marketing theory and practice.

Place in the Literature

In terms of marketing scholarship, this book can help to address a gap in the literature, provide needed empirical studies of marketing and sales organization, and act as an input to future research in this area.

A substantial literature now discusses the interfaces between marketing and other functions (Wind, 1981; Ruekert and Walker, 1987; and Lim and Reid, 1992, provide literature reviews and discussions of marketing's interactions with other functions). But little attention has been devoted to key linkages that are typically *within* the marketing function in many firms. This lack of attention is noteworthy when one considers a repeated assumption and assertion in marketing theory: the inevitable interactions among marketing-mix variables (product, price, promotion, and distribution) and, therefore, the importance of "coordinated marketing" within, as well as beyond, the boundaries of the firm. As editions of a leading textbook (Kotler, 1991) have emphasized:

> Coordinated marketing means two things. First, the various marketing functions—sales force, advertising, product management, marketing research, and so on—must be coordinated among themselves [and] from the customer's point of view. Second, marketing must be well coordinated with other company departments. . . . For this reason, the marketing concept requires the company to carry out internal marketing as well as external marketing. In fact, internal marketing must precede external marketing.

Yet, despite recognition of the importance of these linkages, no systematic effort has been made to identify the dimensions of required coordination among these groups, the factors that affect their interactions in the development and delivery of customer value, or how students and managers can usefully diagnose relevant issues and options in managing these relationships.

In the industrial marketing area, the most relevant literature concerns new product introductions. These studies indicate that one-third to one-half of all new industrial products fail to meet the firm's goals (Cooper and Kleinschmidt, 1991; Kortge, 1989), and consistently point to management of the product launch—and, in particular, the hand-off from product management to sales and service groups—as a key determinant of new product success or failure (Cooper, 1979; Choffray and Lilien, 1984; Link, 1987; Mahajan and Wind, 1991). But beyond indicating the importance of these organizational linkages, the literature has not examined the factors affecting interactions between industrial product, sales, and service units.

In the area of consumer goods and services, the most relevant literature concerns the management of sales promotions. In this process, it is typically the manufacturer's sales force that must convince the retail trade to sponsor a promotion for the brand and to purchase the required inventory. Studies of promotion success have found that sales force support and execution are either just as important as (Curhan and Kopp, 1988), or even more important than (Hardy, 1986), promotion incentive levels to consumers. The most complete study to date notes that "a better understanding is required about how the individual promotions designed by each product manager are integrated with the promotion plans of all the other products sold by the company or divisional sales force" (Quelch, 1989). But the only direct examination of this interface (Dubinsky, Barry, and Kerin, 1981) is now some years old, has found little input from sales into product promotion development, and may simply be obsolete in light of subsequent industry developments documented in the cases in this book and in other recent studies of consumer marketing (McClaughlin and Rao, 1991).

The materials in this book therefore make a number of contributions relevant to marketing theory. The case studies outline typical interdependencies that affect planning and execution of marketing tasks; the readings provide frameworks for considering integration requirements and barriers at marketing interfaces; and both document specific company contexts for scholars and practitioners interested in improving linkages among these groups.

This last comment is relevant to another contribution. Despite a voluminous literature about selling, studies of how field sales activities are actually organized are surprisingly scarce, while analyses of the relationships between sales tasks and other components of organization are even rarer. As the authors of a recent study note, "the empirical literature on marketing organization is limited in both scope and number of investigations. Nowhere does one find an overview of how marketing activities within companies are organized" (Tull et al., 1991). Hence, these materials provide a needed "thick description" of key components of marketing organization, illustrating institutional and competitive contexts needed for understanding initiatives with these joint marketing tasks in different business environments.

Such an investigation seems especially timely at this point. Recent discussions in both academic (Glazer, 1991) and business journals (McKenna, 1991) about the changing role of marketing have rightly focused on the implications of new production capabilities, information sources, supply chain arrangements, shorter product life cycles, changing trade channels, and other factors present in the cases in this book. The major theme in these discussions is that these forces mean the withering away of the traditional marketing function in corporations and especially "the death of the salesman" in favor of network organizations and/or various strategic alliances. But, without better understanding of how companies actually organize their primary customer-contact activities and the implementation issues generated by market developments, these predictions remain largely armchair speculations. We must know more about what companies are allegedly abandoning before we can credibly delineate "the" future of marketing. As a thoughtful discussion of this topic emphasizes, "more careful analysis is needed of the forces reshaping the marketing function at both the corporate and SBU levels [and] marketers need to get into companies and examine the multiple new forms marketing is taking. . . . Marketing is more than an economic optimization problem; it is a central component of the guidance system of the firm and we need to understand its functioning in much richer detail" (Webster, 1992).

Relevance to Practice

Although there is little scholarly literature about these marketing linkages, the relevance of the topic to current and future managers is clear. The marketing trade press frequently highlights this topic (for recent examples, see Carpenter, 1992; Konrath, 1992; Vieira, 1992), while broader management publications also indicate its salience for firms around the world (Ohbora, Parsons, and Riesenbeck, 1992; Sullivan, 1990).

This practitioner literature tends to offer three types of advice to managers: (1) simply encourage "more communication" between sales, product management, and customer service managers; (2) align their incentives by paying all these groups the same way; and (3) recognize that it is not great products or effective selling but great service that will motivate customers to beat a path to your door. But, as the case studies in this book indicate, there are many complications that arise when companies attempt to act on this advice, other important factors that affect processes among these marketing groups, and useful alternative approaches available to managers.

Beyond the marketing area, moreover, the materials are also relevant to executives concerned with the development and implementation of corporate strategies in a changing competitive landscape. The significance of shorter product life cycles and "time-based competition" (Stalk and Hout, 1990) is by now a familiar theme in the management literature, which emphasizes how companies compete via faster product development (Wheelwright and Clark, 1992), mass customization of diverse product offerings (Pine, 1993), and innovative supply chain arrangements (Davis, 1993; Fincke and Goffard, 1993). But little attention has been given to the impact of such developments on downstream marketing, sales, and customer service activities, where responsibility for implementation of these initiatives usually resides.

One result, experienced by a number of firms in recent years, is the realization that there is only limited utility in shortening product-development cycles, improving product quality, and investing in interlinked manufacturing-distribution systems if, in its downstream activities, the firm's marketing system cannot handle or (as in some cases in this book) actively resists a greater variety of products, services, and markets. Among other things, this book indicates how these aspects of competition are reshaping marketing requirements and forcing firms to rethink traditional roles and responsibilities in order to create qualitatively different linkages among their sales, product management, and customer service personnel.

STUDYING THE CASE STUDIES

The cases in this book are not intended to provide a comprehensive inventory of all the issues embedded in this topic. But the cases were developed to cover a range of industries, firm contexts, products, buying situations, and markets. They provide a relevant sample for thinking about important interrelationships that affect organizational requirements, and managerial skills, in marketing.

It is useful to consider the range of business situations covered here. Two dimensions along which the cases can be categorized involve: (1) the nature of the customer and, in particular, whether the selling firm's ultimate customer is an individual or another business organization; and (2) the nature of the firm's offering to those customers and, in particular, whether it is composed primarily of "tangible" goods or "intangible" services. The first distinction has traditionally delineated consumer versus industrial (or business-to-business) marketing courses in management education (Fern and Brown, 1984), and the second has traditionally distinguished services marketing from either consumer or industrial marketing contexts (Bateson, 1989).

Along these dimensions, the case materials align as follows:

		Nature of Product Offering	
		"Tangible" Goods	"Intangible" Services
Nature of Customer	Individual	Case 4 Case 5 Case 6	Case 7 Case 8 Case 10
	Organization	Case 1 Case 2 Case 3 Case 11 Case 12	Case 7 Case 8 Case 9 Case 10 Case 12

Part of what we learn by studying these cases, however, are the limitations of these traditional ways of categorizing marketing efforts. It is not simply that some companies represented here (such as MCI and American Mobile Satellite Corporation) sell both to consumers and other business organizations, or that the consumer goods firms must now take into account other business organizations (for example, different classes of retail trade) in their traditionally end-user focused marketing programs. What we see in these cases is how market and competitive developments are increasing the services content of buyer-seller exchanges in both industrial and consumer markets. One result at these firms, and others around the world, is that marketing programs now revolve around offerings composed of tangible product *and* service support *and* ongoing information services that must be established and maintained both before and after the sale. In turn, effective development and implementation of such programs requires the participation of all the various groups responsible for managing an integrated product-service-information package. Each has an indispensable role to play in the creation and delivery of customer value.

Another relevant dimension for categorizing the cases is the company contexts represented. Borrowing a distinction from the organizational design literature (Mintzberg, 1979), we can describe the companies either as *"bureaucracies"* (generally older and bigger companies with established hierarchies and divisions of labor, formalized procedures and communication channels in their organizations, and a functional grouping of tasks) or as *"adhocracies"* (generally younger and/or smaller companies with looser divisions of labor, few established formal procedures and communication channels in their organizations, and relatively fluid functional boundaries). This distinction should be viewed in terms of a spectrum, rather than as a mutually exclusive contrast. But, along these dimensions of organization, the case materials align as follows:

"BUREAUCRACIES"	"ADHOCRACIES"
Becton Dickinson	AMSC
Hewlett-Packard	Astra/Merck
IBM	Dendrite
Packaged Products Company	MCI
Pepsi-Cola	MEM

Moving between the two types of firms is instructive. Many students, and an influential stream of thought in the management literature (e.g., Peters, 1992), often assume that the coordination issues considered here are a problem endemic to "big stovepiped bureaucracies," not smaller or younger firms with fluid, "entrepreneurial" cultures. But the cases indicate how these issues also arise, with different opportunities and constraints, in adhocratic companies. In addition, the cases allow us to examine in some detail both the potential applicability and the limitations of much current conventional wisdom about how managers should deal with these issues via cross-functional teams, about the abolition of distinct divisions of labor, and about various informal communication processes aimed at promoting teamwork.

Other relevant dimensions to consider in studying the cases concern the nature of the joint marketing tasks that are the focus of many specific decisions in the cases. The first reading in this book outlines a way of thinking about typical interdependencies among sales, product management, and customer service groups in firms. In terms of that framework, the cases illustrate issues involved in managing joint tasks at key marketing interfaces.

PRODUCT MANAGEMENT ◄──► SALES MANAGEMENT ISSUES
CONCERNING:

- Market Analyses, Product Development, Product Positioning
   —AMSC, IBM (A), MEM, Pepsi, PPCo
- Customer Communications, Promotions, Pricing
   —Astra/Merck, HP, MCI, MEM
- Account Selection, Account Management
   —AMSC, Astra/Merck, BD, PPCo

**SALES MANAGEMENT ◄──► SERVICE MANAGEMENT ISSUES
CONCERNING:**

- Applications Development, Channel Management, Account Management
  —AMSC, Dendrite, IBM (B), MCI, Pepsi
- Physical Distribution, Installation/Merchandising, Post-Sale Service
  —BDD, Dendrite, HP, PPCo

For each set of decisions, the relevant cases span business-to-business, consumer, and services marketing contexts. This provides opportunities for useful comparisons concerning the dynamics of interactions between these marketing units in relation to different elements of the marketing mix.

Because integrating these marketing activities takes time and resources, moreover, managers must make choices about where and how to attempt appropriate linkages. As well as focusing on specific decisions, the cases also illustrate different approaches to managing required linkages as well as a variety of strategic, measurement, and staffing issues inherent in different approaches.[1] The cases can be categorized in terms of their emphasis on one or more of the following:

STRUCTURAL LINKAGES

- Headquarters Liaison Units: IBM (A), PPCo
- Field Marketing Specialists: HP, MCI

RESEARCH/INFORMATION/ACCOUNT MANAGEMENT SYSTEMS

- Market Research: Dendrite, PPCo
- Market Segmentation Criteria: Astra/Merck, IBM (B)
- Multifunctional Account Teams: Astra/Merck, BD

MANAGEMENT PROCESSES

- Career Paths: BDD, MCI, Pepsi
- Training & Development: BDD, PPCo
- Informal Communication Channels: AMSC, MEM, MCI

These opportunities to compare and contrast the dynamics of similar issues in different market environments and different company conditions can help both current and future managers develop a skill that is increasingly important in today's global marketplace: the ability to recognize patterns of cause-and-effect while avoiding false analogies. In an era of rapid changes in management and marketing practice, which is nevertheless prone toward sweeping generalizations about the allegedly unvarying components of organizational excellence, developing this ability remains a prime task of education for judgment.

---

[1]A comprehensive discussion of these issues is available in Frank V. Cespedes, *Concurrent Marketing: Integrating Product, Sales, and Service* (Boston: Harvard Business School Press, 1995).

ORGANIZATION OF THE BOOK

The cases are grouped into four sections with each section introduced by an overview article. Each case finds management facing one or more challenges in the external marketplace that require rethinking and perhaps reorganization of internal marketing alignments.

Part I concerns companies in business-to-business markets. The introductory reading for that section discusses factors that are changing marketing requirements for many industrial suppliers, and suggests a framework for analyzing both the interdependencies and barriers that typically characterize relations among sales, product management, and customer service groups in industrial firms. The first case in the book concerns a seemingly straightforward decision: should the head of marketing at a medical products firm hire another marketing manager and, if so, what should this person do? Examining this decision, however, opens up an array of strategic, industry analysis, measurement, and broader human resource management issues that are often implicit in marketing organization decisions. The other cases in this section concern IBM, and provide a unique look at the internal marketing issues confronting this firm as it struggles to deal with a rapidly changing external marketplace for its products and services.

Part II concerns companies in consumer goods markets. The introductory reading discusses the factors that are altering conventional distinctions between marketing strategy and sales implementation in these markets, the implications for required interactions between brand marketing and sales management groups at consumer goods firms, and what some firms are doing to manage these new requirements. The cases in this section look at product introduction decisions at three different types of consumer marketers. Pepsi-Cola's Fountain Beverage Division sells that firm's beverage products to consumers through bottlers and other institutional customers. Packaged Products Company is a snack foods company that sells its products to consumers through a variety of trade channels. MEM is a manufacturer and marketer of men's and women's fragrances that reach consumers primarily through department stores, mass merchandisers, and drug stores.

Part III concerns service markets and the services component of marketing programs. The introductory reading provides frameworks useful for analyzing key components of customer service and the dynamics of customer retention in different business situations. The cases in this section concern three commercial service companies: two provide telecommunications services and another provides information services to clients. In each case, the seemingly tactical issue of sales-service coordination is found to have much wider strategic importance for each firm.

Part IV integrates the learning and perspectives from the previous cases by focusing on the raison d'être of marketing: how to build and maintain profitable customer relationships. The introductory reading for that section explains how and why the nature of selling and account management is changing at many companies. The factors discussed in industrial, consumer, and services markets mean that selling now often involves a team effort, involving the bundling of different product lines (the products often made by different divisions and sold from different locations) to customers that demand a customized product-service package. The cases in this section concern companies confronting these account management requirements in an industry undergoing revolutionary changes: health-care products and services. Astra/Merck Group is a unique start-up in this industry, and its strategy is based on the ability to integrate and customize its product, sales, and service capabilities for customers. Managers at Hewlett-Packard's Imaging Systems Division must consider how distribution channel decisions affect account management capabilities, and product-sales-service interactions, for that firm's products. The final case in the book brings us back to the first company we examined, Becton Dickinson, but from a very different perspective. Here, the decision is whether and how this firm should pursue cross-divisional marketing efforts at key accounts, a decision that raises many of the issues considered separately in other cases in the book. In turn, these issues are at the heart of challenges facing many other firms that must align their various customer-contact activities without diluting necessary expertise and accountability among their functional units.

REFERENCES

BATESON, JOHN E. G. (1989), *Managing Services Marketing* (Hinsdale, IL: The Dryden Press).

CARPENTER, PHILIP (1992), "Bridging the Gap Between Marketing and Sales," *Sales & Marketing Management* 144 (March), 29–31.

CHOFFRAY, JEAN, and GARY L. LILIEN (1984), "Strategies Behind the Successful Industrial Product Launch," *Business Marketing* 17 (March), 82–94.

COOPER, ROBERT G. (1979), "The Dimensions of Industrial New Product Success and Failure," *Journal of Marketing* 43 (Summer), 93–103.

COOPER, ROBERT G., and ELKO J. KLEINSCHMIDT (1991), "New Product Processes at Leading Industrial Firms," *Industrial Marketing Management* 20 (2), 137–147.

CURHAN, RONALD C., and ROBERT J. KOPP (1988), "Obtaining Retailer Support for Trade Deals," *Journal of Advertising Research* 26 (3), 54–66.

DAVIS, TOM (1993), "Effective Supply Chain Management," *Sloan Management Review* 34 (Summer), 35–46.

DUBINSKY, ALAN J., THOMAS E. BARRY, and ROGER A. KERIN (1981), "The Sales-Advertising Interface in Promotion Planning," *Journal of Advertising* 4 (Winter), 35–41.

FERN, EDWARD F., and JAMES R. BROWN (1984), "The Industrial/Consumer Marketing Dichotomy," *Journal of Marketing* 48 (Spring), 68–77.

FINCKE, ULRICH, and EDWIN GOFFARD (1993), "Customizing Distribution," *The McKinsey Quarterly* (1), 115–131.

GLAZER, RASHI (1991), "Marketing in an Information-Intensive Environment," *Journal of Marketing* 55 (October), 1–19.

HARDY, KENNETH G. (1986), "Key Success Factors for Manufacturers' Sales Promotions in Package Goods," *Journal of Marketing* 50 (July), 13–23.

KONRATH, JILL (1992), "Why New Products Fail," *Sales & Marketing Management* 144 (November), 48–56.

KORTGE, G. DEAN (1989), "Reducing the New Product Failure Rate," *Industrial Marketing Management* 18 (4), 301–306.

KOTLER, PHILIP (1991), *Marketing Management*, 7th ed. (Englewood Cliffs, NJ: Prentice Hall).

LIM, JEEN-SU, and DAVID A. REID (1992), "Vital Cross-Functional Linkages with Marketing," *Industrial Marketing Management* 21 (2), 159–165.

LINK, PETER L. (1987), "Keys to New Product Success and Failure," *Industrial Marketing Management* 16 (2), 109–118.

MAHAJAN, VIJAY, and JERRY WIND (1991), "New Product Models: Practice, Shortcomings, and Desired Improvements," Report No. 91-125 (Cambridge, MA: Marketing Science Institute).

MCCLAUGHLIN, EDWARD W., and VITHALA R. RAO (1991), *Decision Criteria for New Product Acceptance: The Role of Trade Buyers* (Westport, CT: Quorum).

MCKENNA, REGIS (1991), "Marketing Is Everything," *Harvard Business Review* 69 (January–February), 65–79.

MINTZBERG, HENRY (1979), *The Structuring of Organizations* (Englewood Cliffs, NJ: Prentice Hall).

OHBORA, TATSUO, ANDREW PARSONS, and HAJO RIESENBACK (1992), "Alternate Routes to Global Marketing," *The McKinsey Quarterly* (3), 52–74.

PETERS, THOMAS J. (1992), "Rethinking Scale," *California Management Review* 35 (Fall), 7–29.

PINE, B. JOSEPH (1993), *Mass Customization: The New Frontier in Business Competition* (Boston, MA: Harvard Business School Press).

QUELCH, JOHN A. (1989), *Sales Promotion Management* (Englewood Cliffs, NJ: Prentice Hall).

RUEKERT, ROBERT W., and ORVILLE WALKER (1987), "Marketing's Interactions with Other Functional Units," *Journal of Marketing* 51 (January), 1–19.

STALK, GEORGE, and THOMAS M. HOUT (1990), *Competing Against Time: How Time-Based Competition Is Reshaping Global Markets* (New York: The Free Press).

SULLIVAN, RAWLIE R. (1990), "New Trends in Business-to-Business Sales Require Interdynamic Integration," *Review of Business* 12 (Summer), 25–32.

TULL, DONALD S., BRUCE E. COOLEY, MARK R. PHILLIPS, and HARRY S. WATKINS (1991), "The Organization of Marketing Activities of American Manufacturers," Report No. 91-126 (Cambridge, MA: Marketing Science Institute).

VIEIRA, JERRY (1992), "How to Bridge the Gap Between the Marketing Department and the Sales Force," *Business Marketing* 25 (January), 63–64.

WEBSTER, FREDERICK E. (1992), "The Changing Role of Marketing in the Corporation," *Journal of Marketing* 56 (October), 1–17.

WHEELWRIGHT, STEVEN, and KIM B. CLARK (1992), *Revolutionizing Product Development* (New York: The Free Press).

WIND, YORAM (1981), "Marketing and Other Business Functions," *Research in Marketing* 5 (Greenwich, CT: JAI Press), 237–264.

PART I

Business-to-Business Markets

Industrial Marketing: Managing New Requirements

An industrial products firm recently held a meeting for senior managers to discuss marketing strategy and implementation. An outside facilitator, who led a discussion about improving marketing effectiveness, encouraged participants to list the key issues facing the firm. The blackboard in the meeting room was soon filled with two lists:

Salespeople say:

- "Marketing people do not spend enough time in the field. They don't take specific customer complaints seriously enough. Marketing needs to establish a system for better field communications."
- "Marketing should be more demanding with R&D and manufacturing to alter product designs and production schedules."
- "Biggest frustration to our sales reps is lack of timely information."
- "Sales reps' compensation should not be penalized for price erosion. . . . That's a product issue out of our control."

Marketing people say:

- "Salespeople are always asking for information that they have already received. We spend much effort gathering and writing up product and competitive information, send out that information, and reps call a week later for the same information. . . . This takes time away from other important tasks we have."

Frank V. Cespedes, "Industrial Marketing: Managing New Requirements," *Sloan Management Review* 35, 3 (Spring 1994), 45–60.

- We are underresourced: too many chiefs and not enough implementation people."
- "Our success depends on fulfilling customer expectations for tomorrow, not just today."
- "Sales is happy to criticize, rather than accept responsibility and suggest constructive improvements."

These comments reflect the changing tasks these managers face. Salespeople in this firm need more information, more often, from more marketing managers, as sales tasks involve more customized product-service packages at accounts. Conversely, marketing's complaints about "too many chiefs and not enough implementation people" reflect a situation in which product managers must work with more functional areas (and especially with field sales and service), even as cost-reduction pressures shrink staff support resources. Also, while sales generates more customized orders and complains about marketing's seeming inability to alter product designs and production schedules, marketing managers respond that "our company now has highly automated manufacturing operations, making design and other product changes a complex process." Hence, marketing rightly evaluates these requests with more than sales' often account-specific specifications in mind.

Especially for industrial firms, these interactions can be costly. Studies indicate that as many as one-half of new industrial products fail to meet business goals and consistently point to the management of the product launch—and, in particular, the hand-off from product management to sales and service groups—as key to new product success or failure.[1] But little effort has been made to identify the dimensions of required coordination among these marketing groups, organizational factors that affect their interactions, or how managers can usefully diagnose relevant options.

This article focuses on the interface between sales and service, and especially between sales and product management. Based on research at computer, telecommunications, and medical equipment firms (see the Appendix for details of the study), it first discusses why managing marketing interfaces is increasingly important and complex at many industrial firms. It then outlines typical interdependencies and organizational barriers that affect the planning and execution of these activities. It concludes by evaluating the strengths and vulnerabilities of initiatives aimed at improving links between the marketing groups.

NEW MARKETING REQUIREMENTS

Factors affecting the marketing units include changes in what many industrial firms sell (the nature of the product offering), to whom they sell it

[1]For pertinent studies of industrial product introductions, see: J. Choffray and G. Lilien, "Strategies behind the Successful Industrial Product Launch," *Business Marketing* 17 (1984): 82–94; R. Cooper and E. Kleinschmidt, "New Product Processes at Leading Industrial Firms," *Industrial Marketing Management* 20 (1991): 137–147; J. Konrath, "Why New Products Fail," *Sales & Marketing Management* 144 (1992): 48–56; and V. Mahajan and J. Wind, "New Product Models: Practice, Shortcomings, and Desired Improvements" (Cambridge, Massachusetts: Marketing Science Institute, Report 91–125, 1991).

(market fragmentation), how they sell it (supply chain management requirements), and under what product life-cycle conditions they sell it.

Nature of the Product Offering

Industrial marketing programs increasingly involve a combination of tangible products, service support, and ongoing information services both before and after the sale.[2] Development and execution of such programs require the participation of the various marketing groups responsible for managing product, service, and actual sale.

A salient example is "systems integration" in the computer business. Many computer vendors are positioning themselves as a single point of contact for integrated systems, with the vendor (often with third parties) providing a combination of hardware, software, training, and other services tailored to the customer's business goals. In effect, the seller acts as a general contractor in managing system design, installation, maintenance, and, in some cases, ongoing operation of installed systems. The seller's offering to customers is ultimately the ability to coordinate its own product, sales, and service activities smoothly. One executive noted, "The real product is our company itself, and most of my job is to act as an information broker: I try to make my company transparent to the customer and the customer's requirements transparent to relevant product and service units in my company."

Similar requirements now face firms in many industrial markets. At medical equipment firms, group purchasing arrangements among hospitals have increased buyers' knowledge of terms and conditions among potential suppliers. An executive explained how this affected suppliers' marketing programs:

> Basic services in our business now include on-time delivery, damage-free goods, and efficient order-inquiry routines. Value-added services in our business include custom-designed product labeling, customized quality programs, dedicated order-entry specialists, extended warranty plans, and new services in areas such as waste management and safety programs. Value-added services build the relationship and sustain our pricing structure; and we've found that cost-effective development and provision of these services require a multifunctional approach among product, sales, and service personnel in different divisions.

For the customer, these services are growing portions of the value added by a supplier. For the supplier, closer product-sales-service linkages are more important as its offer in the marketplace becomes a changing product-service-information mix that must reflect more segmented opportunities.

[2]Developments tending toward a merging of manufacturing and service businesses have been discussed from various perspectives. For example, see: J. Gershuny and I. Miles, *The New Service Economy* (London: Pinter, 1983); M. Piore and C. Sabel, *The Second Industrial Divide* (New York: Basic Books, 1984); J. B. Quinn et al., "Technology in Services: Rethinking Strategic Focus," *Sloan Management Review*, Winter 1990, pp. 79–87; and R. Norman and R. Ramírez, "From Value Chain to Value Constellation," *Harvard Business Review*, July–August 1993, pp. 65–77.

Market Fragmentation

Phrases like "micro-marketing" and "mass customization" have become perhaps too familiar in recent years. Managers risk losing sight of what is competitively distinctive about these developments versus what is fundamentally old wine in new bottles.

What is *not* new is the fact of customer differences and niche marketing. Industrial product applications have long been tailored to various customer groups that employ the same core product for different uses. What *is* new is the extent and necessity of such segmentation due to the tools now available for tracking differences in many markets. Commercial customers are more diverse in terms of vertical applications and geography, yet more able (via their internal information systems) to coordinate purchasing requirements across heretofore separate buying centers. Conversely, the sellers' information search costs associated with locating these differences are also lower and, in many product categories, worth more to the industrial marketer in a slow-growth economy.

A manager at a telecommunications firm noted, "We can no longer target broad industry categories for our products. Value and profits no longer reside, for example, in 'financial service' applications, but in more specific products aimed at commercial banks versus brokerage firms versus community financial institutions." Similarly, a computer executive described a market evolution common to many other industrial businesses:

> Twenty years ago, we provided the hardware and the specifications for a broad application, and the customer's MIS department provided the specific solution. But, over the past two decades, the industry has grown and fragmented. At each stage of the value chain, specialists have arisen, while buying is more influenced by end users at accounts. Segmentation becomes more important.

In responding to more diverse segments, product variety often expands significantly. Most of the firms I studied increased the number of items they assigned to product managers by 50 percent or more during the past decade—findings in keeping with studies of product variety in other industrial markets.[3] This affects sales and service requirements as well as the need for links among product, sales, and service groups. Managers noted headquarters' difficulty in responding to market fragmentation on a centralized basis. Field sales and service personnel are often *better* informed about customer requirements (and an account's willingness to pay for an application or line extension) than upper management or headquarters product managers can be. But field personnel, responding to local conditions, are often less able to ensure scale economies or consistency in company dealings across segments. One executive commented, "Our central marketing issue is simply stated and difficult to manage: we need to decentralize and empower lower levels in the organization, while maintaining a coordinated customer interface."

[3]For data concerning product variety, see: S. Wheelwright and K. Clark, *Revolutionizing Product Development* (New York: Free Press, 1992), chapter 1.

Supply Chain Management

Competitive bidding has historically dominated buyer-seller negotiations for many industrial products. The buyer's primary objective was to minimize nominal price by working with a large vendor base (to ensure supply continuity and increase buyer power), making frequent shifts in the amount of business it gives to each supplier (to limit supplier power and signal "discipline"), and conducting arm's-length, transaction-oriented negotiations through annual contract renewals and rebidding.[4] But total quality concepts focus on ways to reduce reject rates, improve cycle times, and decrease inventory throughout the supply chain. From this perspective, the cost and time for monitoring many suppliers of a product—largely "hidden" costs in the competitive bidding model—become visible and significant, while the means for improving information and product flows along the supply chain often motivate closer relations with fewer supply sources. Major industrial customers such as Allied-Signal, Ford, GM, Motorola, Texas Instruments, and Xerox have cut the number of suppliers they use by 20 percent to 90 percent during the past decade and have demanded new supply-chain arrangements from those they continue to do business with.[5]

One goal is to optimize the total cost-in-use of doing business with a vendor. Customers' cost-in-use components fall into three groups (see **Table 1**). Supply-chain initiatives seek to lower these costs and increase the vendor's ability to develop and sustain value-based pricing policies that reflect total system benefits for customers. Implementation of this concept affects companies in at least two ways. First, this sales strategy emphasizes customizing product mix, delivery, handling, and other supply-chain activities to customers' operating characteristics. This increases the required interactions between the vendor's product and sales personnel.

Second, this approach requires closer coordination of sales and service, since important account management tasks involve just-in-time delivery, special field-engineering resources, and order-fulfillment factors that service units often execute. For example, a service executive explained how this approach places more pressure on the accuracy of sales forecasts, "Inaccurate forecasts mean greater transportation, warehousing, and inventory carrying costs. So it makes sense that we be involved in administering the forecasts. I don't think of them as forecasts anymore; it's a management planning tool." Further, key elements of service in industrial markets often vary by type of customer and, for a customer, across different phases of the order cycle and account relationship.[6] Understanding these differences and activating relevant alignments along the vendor's supply chain become

[4]E. R. Corey, *Procurement Management: Strategy, Organization, and Decision Making* (Boston: CBI Publishing Company, 1978).

[5]J. Emshwiller, "Suppliers Struggle to Improve Quality as Big Firms Slash Their Vendor Rolls," *Wall Street Journal*, 16 August 1991, p. B1.

[6]For more on this topic, see: F. Cespedes, "Once More: How Do You Improve Customer Service?," *Business Horizons*, March–April 1992, pp. 58–67. For an excellent discussion of wider cross-functional issues implicated in supply-chain initiatives, see: H. Lee and C. Billington, "Managing Supply Chain Inventory: Pitfalls and Opportunities," *Sloan Management Review*, Spring 1992, pp. 65–73.

TABLE 1 Customers' Cost-in-Use Components

Acquisition Costs	+	Possession Costs	+	Usage Costs	=	Total Cost-in-Use
Price		Interest cost		Field defects		
Paperwork cost		Storage cost		Training cost		
Shopping time		Quality control		User labor cost		
Expediting cost		Taxes and insurance		Product longevity		
Cost of mistakes in order		Shrinkage and obsolescence		Replacement costs		
Prepurchase product evaluation costs		General internal handling costs		Disposal costs		

part of the selling process. This places more emphasis on product-sales-service coordination in order to design products with supply-chain requirements in mind.

Product Life Cycles

As in many other markets, product life cycles at the companies I examined had shortened in recent years.[7] A computer executive commented, "Until the 1980s, our business was like the old automobile business—five-year model changes. Product management utilized these time horizons and then performed basic market research, did relevant financial projections, and worked to get other functions to buy into a product plan. [But] market changes make the results obsolete way before the end date." At telecommunications firms, deregulation and merging of voice and data technologies have had a similar impact on product life cycles, while hospital cost-control legislation and new safety concerns have accelerated life cycles for medical products.

These developments have made the notion of "time-based competition" common in the management literature of the 1990s, which emphasizes faster product development and linked manufacturing-distribution systems. But there has been little attention paid to the impact on downstream marketing activities, where responsibility for the customer's implementation of these initiatives still resides. One computer firm decreased product development cycles by 67 percent between 1986 and 1990. But for the salespeople, the new products meant learning new technologies, establishing relationships with different decision makers in reseller and end-user organizations, confronting different buying processes, seeking more information and support from product managers and service personnel—in short, developing new ways of marketing that were perceived as "alien" to traditional revenue-generation routines. The firm eventually realized that there is limited utility in shortening product-development cycles and investing millions in flexible

---

[7]For data concerning product life cycles in various industrial product categories, see: C. J. Easingwood, "Product Life Cycle Patterns for New Industrial Products," *R&D Management* 18 (1988): 22–32; and C. F. von Braun, "The Acceleration Trap," *Sloan Management Review*, Fall 1990, pp. 49–58.

manufacturing if the firm's marketing system cannot handle or (as in some companies) actively resists a greater variety of products, services, and segments.

Hence, even as other factors increase the amount of required coordination among these marketing groups, shorter product life cycles decrease the time available for establishing and assimilating the relevant coordination mechanisms.

MARKET REQUIREMENTS AND MARKETING INTERDEPENDENCIES

Market changes require changes in marketing programs. But without understanding the issues that traditional organizational alignments generate, change is less likely to be purposeful. **Figure 1** indicates tasks often associated with product, sales, and customer service groups at industrial firms. Where the responsibility for each task resides varies among companies. Together, however, these groups are responsible for tasks that move from market and competitive analysis, through the activities associated with the marketing mix (product policy, pricing, promotion, and distribution), to the provision of pre- and post-sale services. As **Figure 1** suggests, these tasks are best viewed as a continuum of activities where one unit has primary responsibility for tasks whose achievement is affected by another group's plans and actions.

Inherent in this alignment is the interlinked nature of their responsibilities. **Figure 2** emphasizes the mutual dependencies and information flows.

Product Management ... Sales Management ... Customer Service

- Market Research
    - Competitive Analysis
        - Product Development
            - Product Positioning
                - Advertising/Consumer Communications
                    - Packaging
                        - Promotions
                            - Pricing
                                - Account Selection
                                    - Personal Selling
                                        - Channel Management
                                            - Account Management
                                                - Applications Development
                                                    - Physical Distribution
                                                        - Installation/Merchandising
                                                            - After-Sale Service(s)

FIGURE 1   A Continuum of Marketing Tasks

The product, market, supply chain, and life-cycle factors discussed above make the timely exchange of this information more complex *and* more crucial for marketing effectiveness. But most industrial firms differentiate these activities so that expertise in (and accountability for) some subset of the continuum outlined in **Figure 1** can be developed and maintained. In the firms I studied (as at other industrial firms), product managers' core responsibilities included creating strategies, developing plans, and managing budgets and programs for one or more of the firm's products.[8] Field sales was responsible, in varying proportions, for five types of activities: contacting customers directly, working with orders, working with resellers, servicing the product and/or account, and managing information to and from the seller and buyer. Customer service personnel were involved in pre- and post-sale activities that affected product programs and sales tasks (e.g., product demonstrations, installation, customer training, field repair, and inventory management services).

[8]For data on responsibilities of industrial product and sales personnel, see: R. Eccles and T. Novotny, "Industrial Product Managers: Authority and Responsibility," Industrial Marketing Management 13 (1984): 71–76; and W. Moncrief, "Selling Activity and Sales Position Taxonomies for Industrial Sales Forces," Journal of Marketing Research 23 (1986): 261–270.

Product Management ... Field Sales ... Customer Service

Market strategies and plans
Market research data and analysis
Product literature, displays, etc.
Pricing analyses and policies

Sales forecasts and results
Customer feedback on:
• Current products
• New products
Information on:
• Buying behavior
• Competitive activity

Sales strategies and plans
Account-specific goals and activities
Formal sales terms and conditions
"Promises" made during selling process

Pre-sale service support:
• Demonstrations
• Order fulfillment
• Installation
Post-sale service support:
• Customer training
• Maintenance, repair, warranty
• Merchandising support

FIGURE 2   Typical Interdependencies along the Continuum

What issues affect the daily give-and-take between marketing groups with more interdependencies yet distinct roles in customer-contact efforts? My research indicates that three factors are especially important: (1) the layering of priorities that characterizes each group's *hierarchy of attention*; (2) *measurement systems* that help to enforce these priorities; and (3) *information flows* that affect the data each unit tracks, the role of the data, and the measurements that influence each unit's priorities.

Hierarchies of Attention

The marketing units differed in their priorities and the resource allocation patterns that flowed from these priorities. These are differences in their "hierarchy of attention"—i.e., what each group takes for granted as part of its daily work versus what it considers as nice to have or discretionary in its allocation of attention and effort.[9] In particular, product management's focus on its assigned products often clashes with sales' and service's responsibilities for multiple products at multiple accounts. One result is explicit conflict partly due to implicit disagreements about what constitutes "success" in performing a marketing activity. Managers in each area may agree that success is ultimately defined by "the customer." But the groups that are jointly responsible for customer satisfaction perceive the customer differently.

Consider product introductions. At a telecommunications firm, one product group ran a promotional blitz to generate field enthusiasm for its product. But another product manager noted that, due to this campaign, "I just can't compete for sales reps' attention," and redirected her efforts to telemarketing and reseller channels—distribution components not prominent in her original plans and where channel support required redesigning many product features. At a computer firm, product and sales managers typically disagreed about the timing of new product announcements. Sales preferred delaying announcements as long as possible because, as one sales executive explained, "Once a new product announcement is made, customers stop buying the current generation of products while they evaluate the new technology. The result can be stalled sales and quota-crushing delays." But product managers preferred to announce new products as early as possible to build customer attention and train service personnel well in advance of actual introduction.

These marketing units also differed in their time horizons. In each firm, ongoing product-line development was a key product management responsibility, and, as a product manager at a medical equipment firm noted,

---

[9]What I here call "hierarchies of attention" is analogous to what some have labeled organizational "routines" or "thought worlds": the patterns of activity that characterize different subgroups in a firm, that shape the assumptions and marketplace interpretations of each group, and that in turn become the "genes" of a firm's repertoire of capabilities. For a discussion of organizational routines, see: R. Nelson and S. Winter, *An Evolutionary Theory of Economic Change* (Cambridge, Massachusetts: Harvard University Press, 1982), chapter 5. For a discussion of the various "thought worlds" that characterize groups typically involved in industrial product development activities, see: D. Dougherty, "Interpretive Barriers to Successful Product Innovation in Large Firms," *Organization Science* 3 (1992): 179–202.

"Crucial development decisions must be made years before introduction, and the consequences of those decisions linger for years afterward. Meanwhile, budgeting procedures at the customers contacted by sales and service rarely allow them to look long term in assessing their needs." Moreover, product managers implicitly competed for the firm's available development resources. This provided an incentive to "stretch" a proposed product's applicability across multiple segments to justify budget requests and drive development resources in one direction—a finding consistent with previous studies of marketing budgeting procedures.[10]

With their focus on specific accounts, however, sales personnel had different time horizons and priorities. Even as product managers tried to stretch a product's applicability across customer groups as part of the selling firm's capital budgeting process, sales managers often tried to specify product requirements more narrowly in terms of buying processes at assigned accounts. A common result was the complaint of one sales manager at a medical products firm, "Salespeople know customer interests [but] we sometimes introduce products that product managers are successful in attaining from other functions, not what my customer wants."

Measurement Systems

Quotas, performance appraisals, and bonuses for salespeople at the companies I studied focused primarily on sales volume. Product management measures focused on annual profit contribution for assigned products. Customer service metrics varied but typically involved both "customer satisfaction" (measured via customer surveys and/or customer retention) and cost efficiencies in providing relevant services. These varying metrics raise a number of issues at marketing interfaces.

In four firms, multiple product groups went to market via a pooled salesforce. The firms apportioned selling expenses to product units during the marketing planning process. A manager explained, "P&L product managers view the apportionment as a fixed cost [during the relevant budgeting cycle], and then push for as much sales attention as possible to their product line." An example is a computer firm, where profit and pricing responsibility resided with each product group, while sales earned credit toward quotas and bonuses via a point system based on sales volume of individual products at list price (i.e., before netting out any discounts granted to customers). During annual negotiating sessions, sales managers and product managers set product point allocations. One executive described the process:

> Product managers essentially lobbied [sales] to place more points on their particular product line in the annual sales compensation plan, and the negotiations usually centered on the allowable price discounts. Since the larger, better established lines had more room to

[10]See M. Cunningham and C. Clark, "The Product Management Function in Marketing," *European Journal of Marketing* 9 (1975): 129–149; and N. Piercy, "The Marketing Budgeting Process," *Journal of Marketing,* October 1987, pp. 45–59.

move in this regard, the tendency was to place disproportionate emphasis on established hardware products and less on newer products, especially software and services. We knew something was wrong when, for three years running, 75 percent of field reps made their point targets while the corporation missed its annual revenue and profit goals.

Another issue concerns the impact of different measurement systems on account-management tasks. Every company in this sample had established a key account program for cross-selling at important customers. But prevailing metrics often made it difficult for account managers to orchestrate the selling company's product and pricing package. An executive explained:

> Sales and product see the world differently: a customer might be interested in a package of products, yet each product unit is primarily interested in its product line and resistant to altering price or terms and conditions for the sake of the package. But industrial customers are looking for productivity improvements and a vendor provides those improvements with a system, not individual products.

Conversely, salesforce metrics affect product development and service requirements. At a computer firm that sells mainframe and mid-range systems, an executive in the mid-range business explained the impact of revenue-based sales compensation policies on product policy. The firm sold mainframes through the direct salesforce, while mid-range systems required comarketing efforts between direct and reseller channels. To generate more field attention for its line, mid-range product management had for years skewed development priorities toward larger, higher-priced systems that provided more revenue for direct selling efforts. But one result was that, as a manager remarked, "We neglected the growing low end of this market, left ourselves open to more competitors, and generated pre- and post-sale service requirements that exceeded our resellers' capabilities."

Information Flows

The marketing units also differed in the types of data each unit tracked, the role and use of that data, and (in the majority of the firms I studied) the hardware and software systems for disseminating information among the groups.

Product managers viewed data about pertinent products and markets (defined as segments across geographical boundaries) as their highest information priorities. Sales managers sought data about geographically defined markets and specific accounts and resellers within those markets. Service managers needed data about both products and accounts but in different terms from the data categories most salient to product and sales units. As in many companies, accounting systems tracked costs and other information primarily by product categories, rather than customer or channel categories. One result was often a gap between the aggregate data most meaningful to product planning activities and the disaggregate data meaningful to account- or region-specific sales and service activities.[11]

How these marketing units used the information also differed. Product managers need detailed data relevant to product development, costing, and pricing decisions. They make formal presentations a part of their firms' planning processes, more so than sales or service managers do. Hence, compatibility with the *selling* firm's budgeting and planning vocabulary is an important criterion of useful data for product managers. By contrast, compatibility with multiple *buying* vocabularies and data categories are more important to sales managers. Also, the less formal and often time-constrained context of sales calls means that "a few key points" are an important criterion of useful information for sales personnel. Service's responsibilities make detailed data about product specifications and delivery requirements important. But in contrast to priorities in product or sales units, compatibility with customers' technical or logistical vocabularies are the criteria for useful service information.

These differing data uses can create organizational "transmission problems." Across the companies I studied, the most common field complaint about information flows was the lack of timely information. One sales manager explained, "'Timely' means data relevant to current selling efforts. The information is not useful if it arrives too late to be used in our customers' budgeting cycles." Product managers in this firm provided the complementary perspective, "We spend considerable effort gathering and writing up product and competitive information, send out that information, and reps call a week later for the same information. [For product managers], this takes time away from other important things." Such comments reflect different cycles of information use. Industrial product managers must typically gather and present data to and from a variety of internal departments. At one company, charting a product's competitive price and share for annual planning purposes meant soliciting data from more than twenty countries as well as finance, warehousing, and sales departments. By contrast, the timing of sales' and service's information needs is irregular, less capable of being scheduled, and generated (in sales' eyes at least) by an "urgent" customer need.

Finally, information technology also affected marketing interactions and output. At most of the companies in my sample, the hardware and software used for disseminating information among the units had become fragmented. Meanwhile, customer activities required the integration of data captured by multiple, often technically incompatible systems. For example, at the telecommunications firms, competition for commercial customers increasingly focused on developing and selling network applications. In both firms, software and marketing expenses began to surpass annual facilities expenses. But both firms also encountered the following situation: their product, sales, and service units used different information systems and means to categorize expense data, resulting in a number of inconsistent and money-losing bids for commercial business. At a computer firm where sales and product units utilized different information systems, salespeople can-

---

[11]For a discussion of the gaps between accounting data and the types of information sought by managers in various functional areas, see: S. M. McKinnon and W. J. Bruns, Jr., *The Information Mosaic* (Boston: Harvard Business School Press, 1992).

didly admitted that they often shaped orders to *avoid* cross-product orders because of the time-consuming internal interactions involved. In turn, this limited the company's presence in important systems integration markets.

More generally, fragmented information systems mean that the groups meet to discuss customer-related issues on a reactive rather than proactive basis, and each group arrives with ideas based on different data sources. In practice, it is difficult to coordinate under such circumstances.

COMPETENCY TRAPS

The traditional alignment of industrial marketing roles and responsibilities assumes a sequential process in which sales and service execute product

TABLE 2   Typical Differences among Marketing Groups at Industrial Firms

	Product Management	Field Sales	Customer Service
Hierarchy of Attention	Operate across geographies, with specific product responsibilities.	Operate within geographical territories, with specific account responsibilities.	Operate within geographies, with multiple product and account responsibilities.
Time Horizons Driven by:	Product development and introduction cycles. Internal budgeting processes.	Selling cycles at multiple accounts. External buying processes.	Product installation/maintenance cycles. Field service processes.
Measurement Systems	Performance measures based on profit-and-loss and market-share metrics.	Performance measures based primarily on annual, quarterly, or monthly sales volume.	Measures vary, but typically "customer satisfaction" and cost efficiencies.
Information Flows			
Data Priorities:	Aggregate data about products and markets (defined in terms of segments).	Disaggregate data about geographical markets, specific accounts, and pertinent resellers.	Disaggregate data about product usage at accounts.
Key Data Uses:	Role of data makes compatibility with seller's planning and budgeting categories a criterion of useful information.	Role of data makes compatibility with buyers' categories a criterion of useful information; "timely" data as a function of varied selling cycles at assigned accounts.	Role of data makes compatibility with relevant technical vocabularies a criterion of useful information.

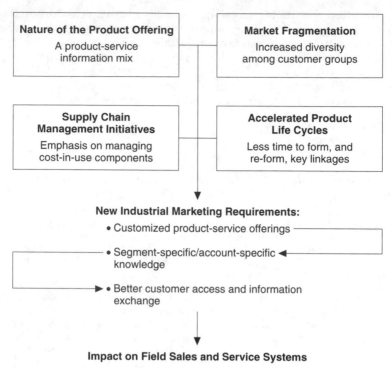

FIGURE 3   "Domino Effect" of Market Factors

management's plans (see **Table 2**). But market developments are changing their coordination requirements. As outlined in **Figure 3**, there is a "domino effect" inherent in the market factors discussed earlier in this article, which place more emphasis on a firm's ability to customize product-service packages for more diverse customer groups. This places more value on the ability to generate and maintain timely segment- and account-specific knowledge throughout the marketing organization. In turn, this places new requirements on field sales and service systems because, in most industrial firms, this is where primary responsibility for customer access and information exchange resides.

In many companies, the result is a misfit between market developments and the organizational capabilities needed for effective marketing. Product, sales, and service units must synchronize their activities in a context in which each unit's window on the external environment, its metrics and time horizons, and its information flows differ. Each unit adopts routines that accelerate the performance of its own subset of customer-contact responsibilities. Provided these routines support using procedures with the highest potential for customer satisfaction, this specialization is advantageous. But in most busy organizations, the routines themselves soon are treated as fixed. The result is too often a series of "competency traps" in which each group is unwittingly "fighting the last war"—i.e., developing and executing marketing programs relevant to a previous stage of product-market competition.[12] Further, each unit's established procedures keep the firm from gaining experience with new procedures. Other alignments may be more appropriate to changing market conditions. But competency is associated with the information flows supporting the metrics that complement the hierarchy of attention at each marketing unit.

MANAGING NEW REQUIREMENTS

How can managers avoid competency traps? How can they think about the options involved in coordinating these marketing units? A first step is to recognize the organizational issues that typically impede coordination among the groups. Because integrating their activities takes time and resources, however, the next step involves choices about where and how to attempt links along the continuum of tasks outlined in **Figure 1**.

At the companies I studied, major initiatives fell into three categories: an emphasis on headquarters *structural* devices, such as formal liaison units; changes in field marketing *systems*, such as multifunctional account teams; and alterations in broader management *processes*, including new career paths and training programs. These categories are neither exhaustive nor mutually exclusive. Most firms utilized a variety of linkage mechanisms among, and in addition to, those discussed here. Moreover, the initiatives are themselves interdependent: new headquarters structures without supporting field implementation systems, or new account-management systems without the appropriate human resources and wider organizational processes, have limited impact. But these initiatives were the most widely used, and, at different firms, each frequently represented the "platform" on which management hoped to build complementary mechanisms for improving product-sales-service integration. Further, the emphasis on each set of initiatives differed for companies in different business environments. Next I evaluate the environment, benefits, and key issues associated with each approach.

Liaison Units

One dimension along which industrial firms differ is the relative complexity of product technology and how dynamic the technology is. When product technology is complex and fast-changing, coordinating mechanisms need to ensure that product, sales, and service units work together on aspects of marketing plans and programs while maintaining distinct expertise in product development and account management tasks. In my sample, the computer firms dealt with the most complex and fast-changing technology. In these firms, product development required concentrated technical expertise and sales or customer input far in advance of introduction, while effective product introductions required sales and service to identify the specific product-service combinations that compose a customer solution in the field.

[12]B. Levitt and J. G. March, "Organizational Learning," *Annual Review of Sociology* 14 (1988): 319–340.

In these firms, formal liaison units were common. Located at headquarters, their focus was on "upstream" interactions between product management and field sales and service units in developing marketing plans and during the introduction phase of product programs. One executive explained:

> We must accelerate our time to market. Also, customers want integrated solutions. That means forging closer working relationships between our labs, field sales, and product management groups to make sure customer requirements are known early in product development. Differences must be resolved more quickly, and [the liaison units] are intended to expedite this process and surface any problems earlier in the development-to-introduction cycle.

One benefit of establishing such units is that they signal the importance of product-sales-service collaboration in companies where these activities have traditionally been in separate departments, each with its own hierarchy of attention. Without a dedicated liaison unit, informal methods of managing their interactions are often too time-consuming (in a rapidly changing marketplace) or simply ineffective because other units view attempts by product, sales, or service personnel to alter their plans as inappropriate infringements on their domain. This is true whether or not the company conforms to popular conceptions of bureaucracy. An executive at a computer firm known for its informal culture of empowerment noted:

> We are a company with few official channels. But when product managers tried to alter sales plans, or when a sales vice president lobbied for a product modification, they were seen as meddling in the other group's business and without understanding the tradeoffs involved. Important changes weren't made even though more people spent more time in meetings. Despite our distaste for structure, we found we needed an official liaison group.

Usually staffed by sales as well as product personnel, liaison units also help to shape product plans and promotions with field realities in mind. They provide a specific decision-making mechanism in an environment where important tradeoffs and marketing information increasingly reside at the interfaces *among* product, sales, and service groups, rather than *within* each area. At one firm, the liaison unit had a limited budget to fund the development priorities that field groups identified. The unit head explained how this affected product-sales interactions:

> In a technically complex category, each product unit works for years on its line, and the natural tendency is to provide the state-of-the-art configuration. But the result is often a product with costs too high to support a competitive price or too late to capture important first-mover advantages. Our role is to increase the market tension in the development process.
>
> For example, we believed a new low-end product, at a certain price point, would be an important addition to our line. We then informed

the relevant product manager that her group could have $X million and a certain time frame to spend on this project. She responded with a figure of $2X million and a longer development schedule, and our response was that we would take our funds to another product group to get the work done. Her reaction was, "We'll look again at our assumptions and get back to you." We finally compromised on the time and money involved. The process forces a healthy prioritization of time and resources.

Another benefit is that liaison units can make increasingly segmented customer requirements salient earlier, and higher, in planning processes. Some managers stressed an analogy with quality initiatives: such units, an executive commented, help to "make visible issues that cut across product and sales groups, just as quality circles helped to build awareness of the cross-functional requirements of quality management." A manager in one liaison unit explained that, at planning sessions, "My role is to inject industry or other vertical market applications criteria into what would otherwise be investment decisions guided by product categories." Another liaison unit altered traditional product development processes to take explicit account of the interplay between product features and the requirements of selling and servicing customers through indirect distribution channels.

Liaison units represent another management layer with attendant costs in salaries, support systems, and overhead. As a result, such units require a critical mass in the firm's product portfolio and sales base to be economically viable. Thus, they tend to be established in larger companies where the additional management layer can be a mixed blessing for speedy marketing decision making.

Further, liaison units usually face a constant challenge from line managers in product, sales, and service, who often perceive them as staff interlopers rather than integrators. In practice, these units tend to be the focus of many contentious negotiations. This may be inherent in their role, which must balance consistent product strategies with customized channel and service requirements—or, as one liaison manager commented, "We sit in the middle between product management's development and manufacturing concerns and the field's selling and service concerns, and we don't "own" resources on either side. So, information, personal relations, and judicious use of top management become paramount management tools."

To develop credibility and influence, these units need managers with broad organizational contacts and current knowledge of changing product and field realities. This presents a staffing challenge in many industrial firms. Experienced managers are often reluctant to take a position with no direct line authority. And, to keep contacts and knowledge current, these units typically rotate personnel frequently. The head of one liaison unit noted:

In staffing, you need a balance between "short-timers" and "long-termers." Rotating twelve- to eighteen-month assignments keep our field contacts and information current; on the other hand, our development process is lengthy, and it takes time and continuity [to] understand the product strategy, develop trust in the development groups, and master the complexity of product introductions. My staff is about 80 percent short-timers and 20 percent long-termers.

This is a difficult balance to achieve, and the danger with this amount of rotation is that other managers will see those in the liaison unit as "always learning what their job is." But when balance is achieved, these units provide a way to capture and disseminate learning about important marketing-interface activities and to combine one group's product-technology perspectives with others' channel-account perspectives.

Multifunctional Account Teams

Another important dimension distinguishing industrial firms is their coordination requirements for managing customer relationships. At one end of a spectrum, a firm may sell one product with one application to an account. At the other end are companies selling multiple products with multiple applications among multiple sites of an account, each interdependent in terms of the vendor's selling and/or service activities. In the latter situation, important account management tasks require the alignment of multiple areas of expertise at both the buyer and the seller.

The medical products firms in my sample encountered this requirement at multihospital chains and group purchasing organizations (GPOs). Both are intended to increase buyer power, and, during the past decade, most U.S. hospitals have established affiliations with chains or GPOs. These organizations purchase across the seller's product line and choose vendors on the basis of specialized services in addition to price (e.g., logistical support, special order-entry systems, or ongoing reports about product usage in various hospital departments). In providing these services, the medical products suppliers in my study instituted multifunctional account teams for selected customers.

These teams comprise individuals from product marketing, sales, service, and often manufacturing, logistics, MIS, and other functions. Unlike the liaison units described above, the focus is rarely on product development activities but, rather, on interactions for cost-effective implementation of services that cut across the seller's product groups, sales territories, and business units. Hence, this approach differs from traditional account-management programs in two ways. First, the nature of buyer-seller exchange places a premium on effective supply chain management and the team's primary responsibility involves reducing the spectrum of cost-in-use components outlined in **Table 1**. One executive commented:

> Traditional account management—where a salesperson coordinates the seller's resources—works when you're providing a solution for a customer in a discrete functional area. That's project management, and good salespeople are good project managers. But in our industry, the value added is in providing solutions that cut across our customers' functions and our own product, selling, distribution, and service activities. That's program management and requires a different approach.

Second, because of this emphasis, the account manager in such situations is not necessarily someone from sales, because core tasks involve integration of product bundles, pre- and post-sales services, stocking and other logistics arrangements, and ongoing information exchange about evolving product use and applications. At one firm, the manager of a multifunctional team for a buying group was a finance executive, partly because new MIS and distribution links between the buyer and seller make payment terms a way to increase sales to this account *and* a way to protect the seller's pricing structure in response to increasingly cost-conscious buyers.

One benefit of this coordinating mechanism is that it can focus information flows on the ultimate source of revenues and profits: the customer. The multifunctional team becomes a way of dealing, on an account-specific basis, with the information "transmission problems" noted earlier. At industrial firms, product managers typically have the product-profitability data, knowledge of planned product introductios, and other information necessary to customize profitably a company's product-service package. But sales and service personnel have the accrued local knowledge necessary to know what specific customers value in each area of supply-chain activity. This approach facilitates exchange of information at the account level.

Another benefit is the impact on business planning. Salespeople at major customers are often the first to recognize emerging market problems and opportunities. But they often lack the means to respond with more than tactical (usually, price-sensitive) programs. One reason is that, without this approach, sales efforts lack the cross-functional perspective required to manage cost in use. Also, with traditional account-management systems, sales and service efforts on behalf of individual product groups hamper the vendor's ability to track and manage its true marketing costs at an account, while obscuring the service value that it often *does* provide to customers that purchase across the product line. A senior executive at a medical products firm commented:

> Traditionally, we categorized customers by the amounts bought from different product groups. That's the way we were organized, but not the way markets act. Our total costs and benefits with a hospital or GPO were large but "hidden" because sales were spread across product groups. We have the broadest line in the category (which facilitates customer ordering and usage), a broad distribution network (which makes inventory management easier to handle and plan), and our sales and service personnel provide extensive end-user training and other services not explicitly costed out in our contracts. Accounts will focus on price and ignore these services unless there's a coordinated approach on our part.

Key issues in managing multifunctional teams are team staffing, decision-making processes, and account selection. This approach may spur integration at the account level, but wider functional reporting relationships usually remain intact. Hence, when resources are allocated, the lines of authority are often unclear. One firm required more than a dozen senior executive signatures to approve team initiatives with accounts. Another firm allocated account-team funding by product group, raising concerns in each group about "who works for whom" when account behavior and product-group goals did not coincide. One manager remarked:

> When we established a multifunctional partnership with [account Z], people here were thrilled. But that account recently decided to source one of our product categories from a competitor. That product group is outraged. "Partnering" often connotes across-the-board agreement to many managers, and that's unrealistic. We have many common goals and conflicts with this account. And the tradeoffs differ for individual product and sales units in our firm.

Multifunctional teams also raise human resource challenges. Team members from different functions rotate even as the team seeks to build continuity and relationships with customers. Product, service, and other personnel often resist what they see as a "sales" assignment. Conversely, many salespeople, accustomed to working on their own, often lack the skills and temperament for operating in teams.

Finally, this approach generates many transaction-specific investments for sellers. Some firms require major IS investments to provide on-line order entry, automated stock replenishment, and other supply-chain services to accounts. One manager explained:

> Which customers don't become multifunctional partners? That's a tough issue. Inevitably, other accounts want the customized services that account X is getting. And if we don't give that service, one of our competitors will. Also, many of the product-sales-service linkages required to implement the concept are specific to an account, and the benefits for individual product and sales units in our company differ widely by account. I'm not sure the customer incurs the same switching costs we do.

These factors ultimately emphasize the importance of rigorous account selection in linking functions. The successful multifunctional teams at these firms shared certain characteristics: (1) initiation of the approach at top levels of both buyer and seller firms; (2) a buyer who buys across the seller's product line; and (3) customers seen as influential and leading edge in some aspect of product applications or supply-chain management, so that the seller's investments yielded benefits at other accounts.

Career Paths and Training Programs

In many high-tech industrial firms, career paths in product management and sales diverge sharply. Product managers have undergraduate technical degrees, are increasingly recruited from MBA programs, and rotate among product lines as preparation for a potential general management position. Salespeople usually have much less technical training, and their career paths keep them in a given sales territory for some time so that account relationships are not severed. Rarely do the twain meet. In other industrial firms, career paths in sales versus service are the mirror image of the product-sales situation in high-tech firms. Sales is the "fast track" up the management hierarchy, while service personnel accrue "time in territory" experience with end users and distributors.

Hence, beyond changes in structure and account teams, companies have tried to develop managers experienced on "both sides" of marketing interfaces. In my sample, this was especially true at telecommunications firms, for reasons related to their business environment. During the 1980s, after the development of fiber optics and new network software, these firms provided many new voice/data/messaging service combinations. The same software also allowed commercial customers to track patterns of telecommunications use in their organizations more easily and precisely. The result was to increase dramatically the range of potential product-market applications and shift the basis of competition to product packages tailored to customer specifications that differ by industry, size of company, and region. One executive explained:

> A key company asset is the shared network, and that means headquarters product management must understand the interrelationships implicated by each product introduction or modification. The complexity of this increases as software-based services become a bigger part of the products we offer. Similarly, in a high fixed-cost service operation, sales and service personnel confront a quickly expanding product line and must deal with more groups in pre- and post-sales activities that affect our shared asset.

Thus, coordinating mechanisms in these firms must address a situation in which adapting a core asset requires local knowledge that is unavailable (or too costly to gather and keep current) at headquarters levels, but in which using shared resources efficiently also requires central oversight to ensure that field activities support companywide operating and marketing objectives (e.g., capacity utilization and consistent product positioning and pricing).

To address this situation, the telecommunications firms have altered career tracks to provide more cross-functional mobility for product, sales, and service managers. This includes expanding the length and type of field sales exposure required for product management positions and creating new positions. One firm established field marketing specialists (FMS), mid-level product and sales managers who, after eighteen to twenty-four months in this position, were slotted for senior line positions in the core product or sales organization. Unlike the liaison units described earlier, FMSs are assigned to field regions, but, unlike the multifunctional account team initiatives, their focus is on a subset of the firm's product line, not on a specific customer. FMSs have two roles: (1) to increase learning (and comfort level) with new selling and service requirements (FMSs work with sales and service managers on applications identification, product demonstrations, and installation) and (2) to coordinate these field activities with headquarters product units. FMSs are a way for a product group to "sell" field managers on a new initiative. Conversely, FMSs negotiate with product groups for the product modifications and engineering resources needed locally.

At another telecommunications firm, the customer service engineers (CSEs) were at customer locations more frequently than the salespeople and were important to customer retention and revenue growth in the installed base. Yet, an executive explained, "CSEs are technical people who don't like to think of themselves as selling, even though that's what they're implicitly doing. Conversely, many sales reps worry about account control; their attitude is, 'No one can do this at my account as well as I can.'" The company now provides joint training for salespeople and CSEs and has realigned its reward system to provide a new-revenue bonus that sales and service personnel at an account share. In addition, sales and service reps now evaluate ech other on a questionnaire that ranks performance in such areas as "quick response" and "contribution to customer satisfaction." Customers complete these questionnaires, managers to whom the sales and service reps report review them, and sales and service personnel assigned to the same account meet biannually to explain their evaluations. A manager noted, "These discussions are a considerable benefit in a business where, for good logistical reasons, the sales rep is dedicated to a select group of accounts, but these customers are among dozens that clamor for the service rep's attention."

One benefit of these initiatives is better awareness of another unit's operating conditions, constraints, and contributions. Managers with product and sales experience, for example, are more likely to develop marketing programs that reflect their reciprocal requirements. One interviewee, who became a product manager after a decade in sales, noted, "In sales, I had no appreciation for what product marketing does. In sales, there are identifiable wins and losses, but 80 percent of product management is invisible to salespeople—and essential to effective selling."

More generally, these assignments help to buidl what an observer called the "thick informal networks one finds wherever multiple leadership initiatives work in harmony. . . . Too often these networks are fragmented: a tight network exists inside the marketing group and inside R&D but not across the two departments."[13] Similarly, a study of multinational firms found that cross-country career paths create a "verbal information network . . . which results in [coordination] that is personal yet decentralized," allowing local discretion within the context of companywide policies.[14] Likewise, product-sales-service career paths provide bridges across the differing information flows described earlier and complement any formal liaison positions. With training programs, these assignments can also develop what one executive called "system savvy. Most managers are 'good citizens' who want to do what is right for the firm, not just their area. But they're often unaware of the impact of their decisions on other parts of an interdependent business system. Our joint training programs and career rotation aim at disseminating this savvy."

However, the management issues raised by this approach are formidable. In many industrial firms, joint training programs usually entail additional training beyond the still-required functional training in product management, sales, and service tasks. So, beyond incremental expenses, therefore, people are spending more time in training and less on "core" ac-

[13]J. P. Kotter, *A Force for Change* (New York: Free Press, 1990), p. 92.

[14]A. Edstrom and J. R. Galbraith, "Transfer of Managers as a Coordination and Control Strategy in Multinational Organizations," *Administrative Science Quarterly* 22 (1977): 251.

tivities; some firms view this as unnecessary or infeasible in a cost-conscious environment in which they are not adding marketing personnel.

Similarly, these career paths entail multiyear time horizons for the company and the individuals involved, plus a willingness to assume inherent career risks, since most managers have risen to their positions by acquiring functional expertise. Cross-functional career paths tend to build skill bases that are more company-specific than do functionally oriented careers. In Japanese firms, while cross-functional rotations and training programs are common, they are traditionally complemented by "lifetime employment" patterns, promotions based on seniority, and, historically, social pressures on managers who seek to switch employers. As a result, Japanese firms have had more assurance that a competitor will not reap returns on long-term investments in cross-functional careers, while individual managers have less incentive to develop a career via expertise in one area and more incentive to develop cross-functional skills at a single firm.[15] These wider corporate and social conditions rarely pertain at Western companies. Hence, at the firms I studied, training and career path initiatives were limited to a few managers who often encountered obstacles because most careers in their organizations proceeded according to a different paradigm.

CONCLUSION

Firms utilize other initiatives in addition to those I discuss here. Managers interested in improving linkages among product, sales, and service units should not focus on identifying only one preferred approach. Rather, after analyzing how market factors affect marketing interdependencies in their firms, managers should focus on those areas and actions that, within their business context, are likely to provide the best returns on time-consuming and expensive coordination efforts.

Table 3 summarizes the focus, environment, and key management issues associated with each initiative I discuss. By highlighting the implementation issues, Table 3 emphasizes an important challenge facing firms in this aspect of their marketing efforts. "Coordination" is a value-laden term with positive connotations. Especially before making tradeoffs and allocating resources, managers' espoused support for coordination is now the "politically correct" attitude. But, as this article indicates, coordination comes at a cost, and each approach is implicitly a choice about the kinds of ongoing issues a firm must monitor and manage.

Further, the conflicts I discuss partly reflect the continuing need for specialized expertise in each marketing unit. Such expertise is important for achieving the in-depth knowledge, scale and scope economies, and ongoing efficiencies in each unit that remain important aspects of industrial marketing efforts. Hence, the goal in managing new marketing requirements should not be to eradicate differences between these groups or to assert that

---

[15]See M. Aoki, "Ranking Hierarchy as an Incentive Scheme," in *Information, Incentives, and Bargaining in the Japanese Economy* (Cambridge, England: Cambridge University Press, 1988), chapter 3; and K. Koike, "Skill Formation Systems: Japan and U.S.," in *The Economic Analysis of the Japanese Firm*, ed. M. Aoki (New York: North-Holland Press, 1984), pp. 63–73.

TABLE 3   Coordinating Mechanisms in Different Marketing Environments

	Formal Liaison Units	Multifunctional Account Teams	Career Paths and Training Programs
Focus	Facilitate product-sales-service interactions in the development of product marketing plans and during product introduction.	Product-sales-service interactions concerning specialized services at key accounts.	Product-sales and sales-service interactions concerning various customization activities of shared assets.
Most Common Marketing Environment			
Product:	Complex, fast-changing technology; long lead times between product development and actual introduction to market(s).	Importance of cost-in-use and supply chain management activities in purchase criteria for multiple product offerings from vendor.	Product value and pricing tied to applications tailored to different customer groups; applications development/installation requires adaptation of a core asset.
Market:	Multiple products flowing through common channels of distribution.	Large, multilocation accounts that generate many transaction-specific investments by the seller.	Headquarters product marketing programs require ongoing modifications and local field sales and service knowledge of varied segments; efficient use/positioning of shared asset requires central oversight of local field activities.
Key management issues	Costs, credibility, and staffing of liaison units.	Account selection criteria, accountability, impact of wider organizational processes on staffing and decision making.	Costs, time, and impact on individual managers.

"everybody is responsible for customer satisfaction." In most busy organizations, what everyone is responsible for in theory, nobody is responsible for in practice. Rather, the managerial issue is how to link, efficiently and effectively, knowledge, resources, and varying sources of customer value that are necessarily located across different marketing units in many industrial firms. In considering the initiatives I discuss, managers must keep this distinction in mind, while recognizing that, without appropriate linkages among these groups, their firms increasingly encounter two other types of costs.

One cost is fragmentation at the company-customer interface. The market factors outlined in **Figure 3** mean that effective marketing management at industrial firms requires developing and executing customer solutions across internal product, sales, and service units. But the differences outlined in **Table 2** tend to direct funding, time, attention, and efforts within, rather than across, these units. The result is too often a partial solution, with limited customer value and usually negative competitive consequences.

The other cost is more subtle. The issues discussed in this article rarely mean total paralysis in interactions among product, sales, and service units. Managers needing to "get product out the door" will forge agreements sooner or later. But the nature of these agreements is unlikely to maximize customer value, and the process itself can be harmful. One executive, commenting on interactions between product and sales managers in her company, articulated the implicit cost, "We spend so much time bargaining, and the result is that we often unintentionally reward managers for their negotiating skills, not for problem solving or customer-oriented performance."

APPENDIX

The study involved 125 personal interviews at six industrial firms: two computer firms, two telecommunications companies, and two medical equipment suppliers. At participating companies, the focus was on business units where product management, sales, and customer service activities are primary responsibilities of various managers within the business unit's marketing function. In 1992, sales of these business units ranged from $100 million to more than $1 billion.

At each company, I conducted interviews with managers on both sides of each sales interface and, when present, with formal liaison managers between sales and product management or service units, as well as selected managers in areas such as R&D, MIS, and market research. Other data included internal company documents that interviewees supplied, personal observation while attending company meetings, and customer calls with field sales and service personnel.

The unstructured interviews averaged ninety minutes. Interviewees received a list of the research questions in advance. Thus, most interviews focused on one or more of the following questions (depending on the responsibilities of the interviewee): (1) What are the major issues facing your area in interactions with product management/sales/service?; (2) What factors determine the relative importance of coordination with each group, the tasks that must be coordinated, and the kinds of conflicts or opportunities that arise?; (3) What mechanisms exist in your firm for managing these joint tasks?; (4) In practice, how do things most often "get done" at these sales interfaces—i.e., what are the informal as well as formal means for managing interactions across these marketing units?

Case 1

Becton Dickinson Division: Marketing Organization

In June 1990, Gary Cohen, Director of Marketing for the Becton Dickinson Division (BDD) of Becton Dickinson and Company (BD), was reviewing the current alignment of roles and responsibilities in BDD's marketing department. Mr. Cohen noted:

> Like most medical products manufacturers, we are facing ongoing price pressures associated with tighter health-care reimbursement procedures as well as many new requirements in our traditional markets. So, it's important that we keep our marketing efforts aligned with current customers' evolving needs and continue to provide superior value in our division's core product areas.
>
> At the same time, a number of potential new products and services may soon be vital aspects of the business. These developments are driven by important trends, and some represent new markets, significant technological change, opportunities, and threats. They may also mean

This case was prepared by Professor Frank V. Cespedes and Research Associate Laura Goode as the basis for class discussion rather than to illustrate either effective or ineffective handling of an administrative situation. Certain company data, while useful for discussion purposes, have been disguised.

developing new marketing skills, programs, and partnerships not currently a big part of our department's activities.

I want to be proactive in meeting these developments rather than play catch-up a few years from now. How do we organize to handle effectively our existing business while building the capabilities required for new business developments?

COMPANY BACKGROUND

BD manufactured and marketed a range of products for use by health care professionals, medical research institutions, industry, and the general public. Net sales in 1989 were $1.8 billion (see **Exhibit 1**), with non–U.S. sales representing 40% of the total. The company was organized into two product sectors—Medical (59% of 1989 sales) and Diagnostic (41%)—with 19 operating divisions (each with profit responsibility and most with their own manufacturing, marketing, sales, and service resources) and the international sector. BDD was a division in the Medical sector and, in terms of personnel and sales volume, the largest division at BD.

In BD's 1989 annual report, management noted: "Our strategic response to the industry trends of cost containment, changing patterns of purchasing and delivery of health care, and internationalization is to continue to build our competitive advantage through technological innovation. This allows us to differentiate our products on the basis of superior performance, and to enhance our reputation as a worldwide quality leader."

Becton Dickinson Division

Mr. Robert Flaherty, president of BDD since 1985, had previously run VACUTAINER Systems, another BD division. Reporting to Mr. Flaherty were executives heading the division's Sales, Manufacturing, Marketing, M.I.S., Human Resources, R&D, and Quality Assurance functions as well as a controller and a general manager for Technique Products (see **Exhibit 2**).

In Sales, Mr. Robert Jones managed an organization aligned geographically by region, each headed by a Regional Sales Manager (RSM), who in turn managed a District Manager and 7–12 sales representatives, most of whom sold the full line of BDD products. Also reporting to Mr. Jones were: a Director of Contract Sales, responsible for contract terms established directly with large hospitals or buying groups as well as two senior sales representatives designated as Managers of National Accounts; a Market Manager for sales training, sales promotions, and communications to the sales force; and a Manager of Sales Administration & Services, responsible for sales analyses and general sales administrative tasks including order processing.

BDD's products were sold to hospitals, laboratories, other manufacturers (OEM sales), the government, and a variety of alternate care providers. Except for OEM and government segments, virtually all sales were made through distributors. Unless otherwise indicated, all hospital, nonhospital, and distributor accounts within a territory were the responsibility of the field sales rep. Key users of BDD's products in the hospital setting were nurses, pharmacists, and physicians such as radiologists and anesthesiologists. Product preferences in nonhospital settings were influenced by product adoptions at hospitals.

In the hospital market, BDD salespeople called on hospital accounts to negotiate pricing and other terms-and-conditions for orders. Their chief contact was typically the director of purchasing and/or materials management at hospitals. Other important buying influencers called on by salespeople were the director of Nursing, director of Pharmacy, and the director of Central Supply, who often administered and dispensed supply products across various hospital departments. In addition, salespeople also promoted their products with the hospital's Standards Committee, Product Evaluation Committee, and director of Infection Control.

After negotiating terms with BDD, hospital accounts selected a distributor for order fulfillment. Distributors typically received from BDD a commission for stocking and delivery of product; but in recent years, many hospitals had entered into a second round of negotiations with distributors in order to bargain down further their product acquisition costs. As a result, distributors often relinquished part of their commission from the supplier in order to get or retain hospital business. BDD salespeople called on distributors to monitor inventory and stocking levels, help with specific sales situations, and (as one manager noted) "maintain our share of mind with the distributors; this is particularly important for nonhospital customers, since we do not make many direct calls in that large but fragmented market." Some distributors focused on hospital accounts and some on nonhospital segments; most of BDD's distributors sold to both.

Commenting on the typical usage situation for BDD products, Mr. Cohen noted:

> Syringes and needles are used in many different hospital departments. In fact, of hospital supplies, only IV solutions are used in as many different areas. This tends to increase the decision-making power of the hospital's Purchasing department, because no single group of users has the final say for a big order. Purchasing personnel often believe that hypodermics are "commodities," because Purchasing is not always familiar with specific needs and applications in various departments or with the many other devices that hypodermics must be compatible with in the hospital setting. However, this situation also means that our installed base has some protection, because conversions in this product category involve so many different people and departments at hospitals.

In managing accounts, a key task for sales reps at hospitals was to conduct "in-service" training programs for all users when a hospital switched to a BDD product. With marketing support, this process required the rep to demonstrate proper product usage and to educate nurses, physicians, and other end-users on BDD products. A marketing manager commented that, "Done well, in-service builds our relationships and brand image with important influencers at accounts. Done poorly, it makes future sales to that account more difficult." A sales manager noted:

> Product conversions in our category are traumatic for hospitals and their employees, and any conversion won't hold if the in-service is not handled well. Our products, and especially our packaging, are different than our competitors', and that makes in-service important. New product introductions and, especially with needles, a heightened awareness of AIDS and other factors, also make in-service important. It must be handled patiently with every end-user, and that's a big task.

Sales compensation in the division involved a base salary and a commission portion that typically accounted for 20%–35% of the salesperson's total annual compensation. Commissions were based on two factors: regional performance in relation to budgeted sales goals, and the individual salesperson's achievement of sales goals on 12 designated "focus products." Salespeople also received a car, coverage of all normal business expenses, and generous fringe benefits.

Mr. Jones became vice president of Sales at BDD in 1985. He noted that:

> BDD sells the corporation's well-established, core products. For years, it was informally considered the "flagship" division in our company. But in the early 1980s, changes in our environment placed many new pressures on our operations. When I got here, most of my initial efforts were aimed at improving field morale and sales results in the new environment. My focus now, however, is on upgrading the skills of our sales force in the full use of "value added" selling of both our product and service capabilities in selected segments, and in developing in-depth field sales relationships beyond purchasing with decision influencers in various departments.

Products

BDD's major product lines are listed in **Exhibit 3. Hypodermic needles and syringes** represented more than half of BDD sales and a higher percentage of divisional operating income. BDD's market share in the hospital segment of the U.S. market for needles and syringes had increased over 10% in the past five years to about two-thirds of sales in this segment. Sherwood Medical accounted for most of the remainder and a new entrant, Terumo, for 1%.

With over 300 products, BDD's line was the broadest available and noted for excellence in the areas of needle sharpness, ease of use, and safety. In the past three years, moreover, BDD had introduced new product features such as a clearer syringe barrel and bolder scale for reading ease and dosage accuracy by end-users, sharper needles, and a syringe with a built-in sliding shield for maximum safety. These product improvements had required extensive capital investments in R&D, quality control, manufacturing capacity, and plant tooling and production processes. In addition, management cited the division's extensive U.S. distribution network, and its strong worldwide position, as reasons for its success in hypodermics.

An important element in BDD's strategy for hypodermics was what one executive termed "quality aggression." Since BD had vertically integrated into the production of most components, it could manufacture these products at especially demanding specifications and pioneer in product features which demanded a tight hold on quality.

During the 1980s, unit demand in the United States for hypodermics had grown at single digit rates. But government cost-containment legislation enacted in 1983 had caused selling prices for most medical products in the hospital market to decline. In addition, new forms of medication delivery systems (e.g., premixed delivery systems and controlled-release capsules) had the potential to decrease usage of hypodermic products.

Medical gloves, less than a fifth of BDD sales in 1989, accounted for about a quarter share of the vinyl glove market in the United States and less than 10% of the total vinyl/latex glove market. BDD sold its vinyl nonsurgical gloves to the hospital, alternate care, and government markets.

In recent years, medical personnel had become increasingly concerned with hand protection, and stricter FDA regulations had recently changed market priorities from fit and comfort to protective durability and strength. Management believed these trends supported BDD's historical emphasis on premium-priced, high-quality medical gloves. Nonetheless, in 1989, 65% of medical gloves sold worldwide were latex, and there was an oversupply of vinyl capacity. As a result, manufacturers of vinyl gloves faced a difficult selling environment.

Technique needles were specialized for use in anesthesia, biopsy, and radiology procedures, and were purchased by hospitals, alternate care facilities, and OEMs. This product category accounted for less than 10% of BDD sales in 1989, but BDD anticipated significant growth over the next few years due to a rapidly growing biopsy market.

Thermometry included glass and digital thermometers and accessories, and accounted for less than 10% in 1989 divisional sales. A pioneer with a long-standing reputation for quality, BDD maintained a leading share of the glass thermometer market. But thermometry had been rapidly moving toward electronic products in recent years. Hence, BDD's strategy was to focus on the higher-priced, specialty applications for glass thermometers at hospitals and alternate care facilities as well as selected growth opportunities for digital thermometers.

In 1989, the approximately 6,000 short-term hospitals in the United States accounted for a majority of BDD's hypodermic business. Mr. Cohen noted:

> Our best customers buy on value for a broad range of applications. An important marketing task is identifying such customers and develop-

ing appropriate product and service programs. An important sales task is learning to sell our value (versus our lower-priced competitors) by maintaining and developing our presence with the hospital bench people—i.e., the people in various departments who actually use our products, care about the quality of what they use, and complain to hospital administrators if they do not get the product they want.

The nonhospital market included physicians' offices, nursing homes, health maintenance organizations, veterinarians, and outpatient centers. There were about 550,000 nonhospital sites in the United States in 1990. The nonhospital segment was growing, both in terms of sales volume and number of facilities. Further, this segment typically delivered higher margins than hospitals, since average selling prices tended to be higher in alternate care sites. However, this was a relatively fragmented market segment.

The OEM market was primarily composed of medical equipment manufacturers and custom-kit packers that included syringes and needles in procedure trays and other kits for sale to hospitals. OEM accounts represented less than 10% of BDD's hypodermic business.

The government market included all government-operated hospitals (e.g., veterans' hospitals), clinics, pharmacies and agencies. Contract awards in this segment were typically made through a formal bid process and awarded to the low bidder meeting government specifications. This segment also represented less than 10% of BDD's hypodermic business.

Market Trends

In 1983, a change in how the U.S. government reimbursed hospitals for Medicare patients (40% of all hospital patient days) affected the entire health care industry. Previously, hospitals had been reimbursed for all costs incurred in serving those patients. The 1983 legislation mandated a prospective-payment approach based on "diagnosis-related groups" (DRGs). Payment to a hospital was based on national and regional costs for each DRG, not on the individual hospital's costs. Moreover, the average costs were continually updated so that, as hospitals improved their cost performance, they were subject to stricter DRG-related payment limits.

During the 1980s, the impact was dramatic. Hospital admissions fell, the average length of a patient's hospital stay declined, and hospital profit margins decreased. In 1990, over 75% of hospitals surveyed expected to lose money on their Medicare patient load.

By 1990, the number of hospital beds in the United States had declined slightly to about one million. In their place, a variety of smaller, short-term health care facilities had proliferated. In addition, some hospitals were diversifying into outpatient surgical centers, rehabilitation centers, home health services, and other forms of nonhospital treatment. In 1984, in-patient services had represented more than 80% of total hospital revenues; by 1988, it accounted for 74% and was projected to drop to 68% in 1991. A related development was increased concern among employers and insurers about the costs of health insurance. Many health plans encouraged employees to shorten their hospital stays and to shun more expensive in-patient treatment in favor of outpatient care.

These trends affected health care products manufacturers. First, hospitals placed increased pressures on manufacturers to lower prices while reducing their supplies inventories. Medical supplies accounted for 10%–15% of a hospital's total operating costs, while the order processing and logistical expenses associated with supplies made up another 10%–15%. (Labor costs usually accounted for at least 60% of hospital costs.) A BDD salesperson noted, "just-in-time delivery is a very important concept for hospital materials managers. Hypodermics typically account for less than 5% of the total supplies volume purchased by a hospital. But it's a key product line with high visibility among nurses, doctors, and their patients. Hospitals order hypodermics frequently, and most have a standing weekly order with one or more distributors for needles and syringes."

Second, purchasing decisions had changed. Mr. Cohen noted that, "In the past, the hospital's director of nursing was often the key decision maker in our product category. But cost containment has increased the influence and power of the purchasing department."

Third, the formation of group purchasing organizations (GPOs) and multihospital chains had accelerated. Both were intended to increase the purchasing power of hospitals for equipment and supplies and, by 1990, most hospitals belonged to chains and/or buying groups. In these arrangements, purchases were handled centrally; but individual hospitals were often free to accept or reject the terms negotiated on a specific item by the central buying group.

Fourth, during the 1980s, the incidence of AIDS patients had increased the medical community's concern with product quality and safety, especially in categories where accidents involving skin puncture were not uncommon (e.g., needles).

Competition

BDD competed primarily with two other firms: Sherwood Medical, predominantly a U.S. competitor, and Terumo, a global competitor.

Sherwood Medical, a division of American Home Products, represented about 10% of the sales of its parent company, which manufactured and sold a variety of health care products, many of which competed with other BD divisions. Sherwood's main emphasis was the hospital market, but it also sold to the dental, consumer and industrial sectors.

Sherwood's primary line was known as Monoject, and its key differentiating feature was its packaging: each Monoject needle/syringe was self-contained in plastic package. However, as a BDD marketing manager noted, "Sherwood's packaging is both its strength and potential weakness. Many users like their package, but it also yields more waste material for hospitals than competing brands." Another BDD manager noted that, "In its latest annual report, American Home Products emphasized the importance of being a low-cost producer in this business, and outlined plans for a $125 million program to develop state-of-the-art production, distribution, and warehouse facilities by late 1992."

Terumo Corporation, with 1988 sales of $715 million, sold over 1,000 health care products worldwide. About 27% of the corporation's sales were from injection systems (including hypodermics), 26% from pharmaceuticals, 17% from blood transfusion equipment, and the remainder from a variety of clinical testing systems. Terumo had been selling health care products in the United States since 1974. But as its U.S. general manager noted in a trade-press interview, "Until recently, it wasn't a serious effort. We had some products and we sold them where we could." In 1989, however, a corporate restructuring and a $75 million investment in a new U.S. manufacturing facility were, according to this manager, "Symbolic of the serious commitment Terumo is making in the U.S. market. In 1988, Terumo imported from Japan about 70% of the products it sold here; today (late 1989), it manufactures about 65% of its products here and expects to increase that to 90% within two years." In outlining these plans, Terumo's U.S. general manager also noted that:

> If we're going to be a major player [in the United States], it's important to establish our name as a quality company with a large part of the market. And what products are more widely used than needles and syringes? The biggest advantage BD and Sherwood have is the sheer momentum of the thousands of people who use their products. A syringe is so fundamental to what a nurse or doctor does that it becomes part of them, like a watch or wedding ring, and many won't even think of changing until someone comes in and does a selling job on them. But this market is too large, and the customer base too broad, to be satisfied by two players.

Terumo's first U.S. plant was built to focus on hypodermics. But plans called for construction of two additional U.S. plants with capacity to manufacture other products such as catheters, specimen collection, and other lines also sold by various BD divisions.

Terumo, both in the United States and abroad, followed a low-price strategy. As part of its U.S. marketing effort, moreover, Terumo had created special distributor incentive programs which, depending upon a distributor's commitment to the line, offered guaranteed margins of around 15% regardless of actual market or bid prices with a hospital or buying group. Terumo's distributor margins for alternate-care business were not guaranteed but, as with other suppliers, were reported to be 25%–40%. Terumo had less intensive U.S. distribution than BDD.

According to a standard industry research source, average unit selling prices for hypodermic syringes in the hospital market were:

	FY 1988 Index	FY 1990 Index
Average market price	100	100
BDD	100	100
Sherwood	101	101
Terumo	85	86

BDD MARKETING ORGANIZATION

In the early 1980s, BDD's marketing department had been organized along traditional product-management lines. Each product manager had P&L responsibility for his or her line in all market segments, and each reported to one of three Group Product Managers (Hypodermics, Technique Products, Gloves), who in turn reported to a Director of Marketing. In 1985, this structure was modified to make Hypodermics a separate business unit, but the product focus remained. Within Hypodermics, there were three product managers (Needles/Syringes, Sharps Collectors, and Pharmacy Products), each with P&L responsibility.

During this period, new divisional management established a task force to examine sales and marketing. The task force held meetings to discuss ways of improving organizational effectiveness. Below are representative comments from the division's sales managers:

Marketing people do not spend adequate time in the field. They don't take customer complaints seriously enough. Marketing people will call salespeople for information, but then the marketing manager often gets upset when these same sales reps call the marketing manager for product information and help. Marketing needs to establish a system for better field communications.

Marketing should be more demanding with manufacturing and R&D to alter product designs, meet production schedules, or alter schedules when necessary. We sometimes introduce products that marketing is successful in attaining from other functions, not what the customer wants.

Sales gets plenty of excellent product literature. But most other communications from marketing come through the "grapevine" or informal discussions. The biggest frustration to sales reps is lack of timely information. We do not track our sales to end-users or track concrete results of promotional programs. So, in a cost-conscious environment, we can't justify the programs and Finance can shoot holes in what we're doing because we lack the facts.

Our compensation system is not geared for the current environment. Reps should not be penalized for price erosion.

Following are representative comments from the division's marketing managers:

Sales reps are quick to phone for information they have already received. We spend considerable effort gathering and writing up product and competitive information, and reps call in a week later for the same information. Also, when reps come to headquarters for sales training, it's clear that many haven't read the product-release memos. This takes time away from other things.

We are under-resourced: too many chiefs and not enough implementation people to help deal with sales, manufacturing, finance and customer service. Top management points to long-term changes in the environment, and we agree; but our personal success depends on fulfilling expectations for tomorrow.

Marketing offers tools for sales, but there's no accountability to ensure that sales uses the tools. Being outsold by competition is never cited as the reason for an unsuccessful program; sales is happy to criticize rather than make efforts to suggest improvements.

In 1987, Marketing was reorganized along market-management lines. Mr. Cohen (a product manager in the previous organization and a market manager after the 1987 reorganization) noted that the change was made for a number of reasons: "Cost containment in hospitals was driving more rapid growth in nonhospital sectors due to shorter hospital stays, more outpatient referrals, and other practices. We needed to develop programs especially tailored to these segments. Also, some product managers (especially in the core hypodermic business) found it increasingly difficult to manage adequately across all the division's markets as buying groups became more prominent in the hospital market, as new alternate care sites proliferated, and as the division began to introduce new products and new product/service features." Four market manager positions were created (Hospital, Alternate Care, Pharmacy, and Safety/OEM/Dental), with specific product lines attached to each position but with some product overlaps between markets as well. In this organization, P&L goals were established by product and then allocated to each market manager according to the segment or trade channel each was responsible for.

In 1989, Mr. Cohen became BDD's Director of Marketing and reorganized the department along program/product management lines. He described the current organization (see **Exhibit 4**) as follows: "At the beginning of the year, we identify key strategic objectives as part of the divisional planning process. Program management responsibilities are then created to address each objective and to develop specific programs."

In the current structure, each Product Manager had responsibility for various assignments as well as budgets and sales goals for individual products and programs. Product assignments tended to cut across individual program assignments. For example, while Ms. Higgins was the Senior Product Manager for Hypodermic Programs, Ms. Ferro in National Account Services, Mr. Short (responsible for the Hospital Market), and Mr. Sutton (responsible for Distributor Programs) also had individual sales and profit objectives for the hypodermic line as part of their SOPs (standard of performance). Also in the SOPs of all Product Managers was budget and implementation responsibility for assigned programs. Mr. Cohen noted that "These program objectives and implementation plans are established at the start of the year, and used in performance appraisals. Simultaneous product and program responsibilities does make it sometimes difficult to measure each person's discrete impact and achievements. But I believe this structure fits the facts of our business and allows us to achieve focused responsibility for programs that reflect specific opportunities and threats in a fast-changing environment." He added that other organizational considerations were his desire to align the strengths and aspirations of individual marketing personnel with formal responsibilities, and the goal of having both previous sales and marketing experiences represented in the department.

What follows is a more detailed description of the roles and responsibilities in the BDD marketing organization as of June 1990.

• **Ms. Laureen Higgins, senior product manager for Hypodermic Programs,** had worked for six years in marketing positions in BD's Consumer Products division and had gained much experience in consumer promotions and advertising. Her main responsibility was to launch and coordinate end-user advertising programs for BDD's hypodermic product line. She was responsible for ad planning, concept development, direct mail, contests, and sales force education regarding the use of these materials. Ms. Higgins described BDD's advertising objectives:

> Our primary objective is to maintain and build awareness among end-users as to how BDD's hypodermic products and services differ from competitors. Our prices are higher, and our ads emphasize our quality, ancillary services and support, and our general value as a supplier. I am currently looking at how to promote BDD to current users of our products. This is a new approach for us, but my research indicates that many end-users only learn of our advantages after having switched to a competitor's line and then experiencing problems.

Ms. Higgins' other major responsibility was gathering and disseminating competitive information, and she had recently assumed responsibility for a "Hot Line" and monthly newsletter, both designed to facilitate worldwide hypodermic sales efforts and communication.

The "Hot Line" was a telephone exchange where sales reps reported information about competitive threats or opportunities at hospital accounts as well as feedback and suggestions concerning products, promotions, distributors, or other marketing activities. Conversely, Ms. Higgins provided the sales reps with information and advice when they requested assistance in dealing with a competitive threat related to hypodermics. She noted that "the Hot Line keeps me closer to current field activities and market developments. Before, competitive information was buried in the Monthly Management Reports and other reports. By the time I had dug out this information, it was often too late to deal with the actual field situation.

Now, reps are more apt to call since they know we can respond quicker." Data from the Hot Line also serves as an input to the monthly newsletter. Ms. Higgins checked sales rep reports with external sources and, along with data gathered from industry research services, published a newsletter distributed to about 50 people throughout BD, including sales managers in various divisions, corporate executives, and international general managers.

Ms. Higgins also had P&L responsibility for Allergist Syringes, a small but growing BDD line sold to doctors' offices. Ms. Higgins noted that "Gary gave me this line because I was already familiar with allergist products from my experience in Consumer Products."

Ms. Higgins said that in her previous product management position she had "complete responsibility for a product from start to finish and I always felt I knew the total story about that line. But in BDD, we have three marketing managers dealing with different customers of a common product line: distributors, hospitals, and (in my case) end-users. This creates overlaps that I'm still learning to manage. For example, my ad programs cut across all the division's market segments, and I must work hard at interfacing with those managers to gather data and buy-in about the campaigns. Sometimes we're not sure where one job ends and another begins. But the strengths of this structure are that everyone in marketing has broad exposure to a variety of issues, and the program responsibilities allow Gary to make good use of people's individual skills and abilities."

- **Mr. Robert Short, senior product manager for the Hospital Market**, had been in sales with BD for 19 years before accepting his current position in October 1989. He had three major responsibilities: forecasting, hospital conversion programs, and product development.

Forecasting sales involved tracking inventory and sales movement through distributors, OEMs, and government. Mr. Short explained that "I am concerned both with units sold and average selling price because prices and competition vary significantly in each segment." Mr. Short obtained data from various sources. In the hospital segment, most business was transacted via distributor rebates and hospital buying group contracts. BDD typically negotiated unit prices with hospitals or buying groups which were lower than those paid to BDD by distributors. The difference was then rebated by BDD to distributors upon receipt of an invoice. This process permitted the tracking of sales by product to specific hospitals or buying groups. However, no such mechanism currently existed for tracking sales to nonhospital accounts.

Another source was the division's sales force. Although there were no formal forecasting forms completed by BDD reps, Mr. Short was able to obtain "important bits and pieces" through informal discussions with sales reps, "many of whom I know from my years in the field." In addition, reps completed a monthly Management Report documenting competitive activity at their accounts. This form was sent to Regional Sales Managers and then to divisional headquarters. However, Mr. Short used this information as a "check on broad market conditions, not forecasting; these reports tend to be too general and distilled for the latter purpose."

Hospital conversion programs involved the management of "in-service" training programs for all end-users of BDD products. Mr. Short explained that "my role is to develop and disseminate tools that make our salespeople more efficient during in-service. My previous sales experience is an advantage here. I know what details are important and can establish credibility with busy people in the field."

Product development involved work with multifunctional teams (8 at the time of this case study) that examined aspects of product development ranging from new product research and existing product modifications to worldwide standardization of divisional product codes and numbering systems. The functional areas represented were R&D, Inventory Control, Manufacturing, and Product Management represented by Mr. Short. Product development also involved extensive interaction with customer segments and Mr. Short coordinated these meetings, field tests, and feedback sessions. He also noted that "I get several calls weekly from sales reps looking for a new product or a product modification to respond to a specific customer request or segment opportunity, such as a syringe with a different plunger for infant applications. The sales force supplies 60%–70% of our product development ideas. Our core products have many applications, making it difficult to identify common market needs. Also, our division has highly automated manufacturing operations, making any design or other product changes a complex and expensive process."

At BDD, Mr. Short had worked in four different sales territories before becoming RSM in Atlanta. He noted: "When I was in Sales, I had no appreciation for what Marketing does. In Sales, there are identifiable wins and losses, but 80% of what Marketing managers do is invisible. Much of my time is spent responding to special requests or attending meetings or gathering information required for decisions and effective sales efforts. On the other hand, with two decades of sales experience, I realize that field Sales can realistically focus on only a few strategic areas and programs at any one time. But Marketing managers tend to proliferate lots of ideas, programs, and segments."

• **Mr. Greg Sutton, senior product manager for Distributor Programs**, was responsible for developing BDD's distributor programs. Ten distributors accounted for a significant percentage of BDD sales volume, and these included large national and regional organizations such as Baxter Corporation's Hospital Supply Division (the largest U.S. distributor of health-care products), General Medical Corporation, Owens & Minor, Inc., and Durr Fillauer Medical, Inc. Many of BDD's distributors (including its largest) also sold competitors' products as well as products sold by other BD divisions.

Mr. Sutton administered the division's Advantage Distributor Program, which offered distributors an incentive package based on three factors: a distributor's unit sales versus the previous year, hospital versus non-hospital sales volume, and the number of hypodermic product lines carried by the distributor. Mr. Sutton also had product management responsibilities for BDD's line of nursing home syringes and alternate care syringes, segments where BDD had few dedicated sales reps and where distributor support was crucial.

• **Ms. Peggy Ferro, product manager for National Account Services**, had started at BDD in field sales in 1985 and, in 1988, moved to marketing. In early 1989, she became responsible for National Account Services and for the division's Pharmacy Products line. Ms. Ferro noted that the latter represented a small percentage of sales but was a "developmental assignment that's initiating me into core product management tasks."

Ms. Ferro was a liaison between marketing and BDD's three National Account Managers (NAMs) responsible for sales efforts to large hospital buying groups. She had recently developed a program targeted at BDD's top 30 groups. "The goal," explained Ms. Ferro, "is to educate and convince these customers of the importance of BDD's services and product offerings. This means gathering and presenting facts that demonstrate how, despite higher prices, our total cost-in-use for hospital accounts is often much lower than competitors. Another goal is to improve our standing in the contract renewal process. Typical contracts with groups are three years in duration, and in the past we began to focus on renewal only weeks or months before expiration. I'm instituting a quarterly review with the NAMs so that we're more proactive in segmenting account needs, buying influences, competitive threats, and service opportunities."

Ms. Ferro also helped to develop and make presentations to national accounts. As buying groups became important in the 1980s, marketing input became a more important aspect of selling, according to Ms. Ferro. "I saw this happening during my time in Sales. More formal presentations to big hospitals required more facts about many different matters in addition to price and product. Part of my job is to gather, analyze and position all this data for the NAMs, and this involves working across other product and market segments in the organization."

The NAMs were veteran salespeople whose responsibilities included working with BDD territory and distributor sales reps in selling and servicing their assigned accounts. In the past, Ms. Ferro noted, NAMs were often reluctant to allow Marketing personnel to deal with their customers or take an active role in account management activities. "Their relationships with customers are of long duration, and they rightly feel that their efforts are an important reason we have the market shares we have today. Also, the NAMs hear about any problems at these accounts, and their incentive compensation is tied to sales results at these accounts. In the past, few marketing personnel had previous sales experience; part of my job is building this link with our account managers and demonstrating how Marketing input can help selling efforts."

- **Mr. Roger Hankin, product manager for Safety Systems**, had been in his current position since joining BDD in early 1988. He had an MBA from the University of Chicago, and had worked several years as a product manager for a large firm in the printing industry. Mr. Hankin noted that he had come to BDD "without any working knowledge of the health-care industry, and Gary designed my current position with this in mind. Whereas most other marketing managers here have responsibility for programs organized by channel, market, or function—as well as profit responsibility for multiple product lines—I focus only on one product line and so can thoroughly learn one piece of the business. At the same time, Safety Systems is a group of products that cuts across all our channels, exposing me to a variety of purchasing processes, distributors, and market needs. Safety Systems also involves much interaction with BDD sales reps, product managers in other BD divisions, and people from various external groups."

Mr. Hankin was responsible for products and services that facilitated the storage and disposal of hypodermics at their point of use and, in particular, helped to reduce the incidence of accidental exposure. Currently, this involved primarily two products (Sharps Collectors and Safety Lok), which together accounted for less than 10% of 1989 divisional sales.

Sharps Collectors were containers for used needles and blades ("sharps"). Traditionally, used sharps were transported from the point of use to a centralized storage and disposal site in a hospital or alternate care facility. But as safety concerns increased, many hospitals and some nonhospital accounts wanted specialized containers installed in each room where sharps were used. BDD sought to emphasize its education programs and training services and to encourage an increase in overall levels of safety compliance at accounts.

Safety Lok was an innovative needle-and-syringe combination. It could be used as a normal syringe, but a movable shield slid forward to cover the needle after injection; hence, no recapping was required and needlesticks were virtually eliminated. Safety Lok had been introduced in 1988 at unit prices five times that of BDD's standard syringes. But, by mid-1990, Safety Lok's average selling price was 2.5 times that of BDD's standard needles and syringes. BDD had targeted this product category for significant growth in 1990.

The Safety Systems line did not have as high a market share as most other BDD products. An estimated 9%–12% of hospital employees were involved annually in needlestick accidents, and certain diseases were transmitted through puncture wounds including hepatitis, malaria, and AIDS. The latter was of special concern due to the increasing numbers of HIV-positive people. A 1988 study, for example, estimated that one in sixteen emergency room patients in the United States were HIV-positive, a dramatic increase over previous years.

Hankin developed educational programs for safety products. These programs were used by the sales reps to instruct end-users. He noted that "I essentially compete with the other product/program managers for the sales force's time and attention, and my line is new and different. I work hard at developing sales relationships by returning phone calls from the field as quickly as possible and, when possible, working with reps on any safety problems or issues at an account. But this is not easy with a large, full-line, geographically dispersed sales force." Hankin also noted that, in 1990, Sharps Collectors and Safety Lok became part of the dozen "focus products" highlighted in the sales compensation plan, and "this obviously helps a lot. Of course, I must set realistic targets for the reps or the bonus goal becomes meaningless. But having focus-product status increases attention and effort." Mr. Hankin also established volume-based pricing guidelines for his products. These pricing policies were given to RSMs, who explained them to field reps.

When a marketing manager wanted to offer an incentive program, he or she had to "sell" the idea to Mr. Cohen and divisional management. Such funds came from a divisional sales promotional budget and were allocated at the start of the year. In 1990, Mr. Hankin had won approval for a contest concerning Sharps Collectors: sales reps received $1 for every sale of a new unit and, at the end of a six-month period, the rep with the most volume received a trip to a resort. Mr. Hankin believed that this contest had helped to increase sales of Sharps Collectors during the first half of 1990.

• **Mr. John Kao, manager of Marketing Research**, had joined BD in 1971, after receiving an MBA degree from Columbia University, and held a variety of market research positions. Mr. Kao noted: "We now focus much more closely on specific hospitals' needs, problems, opportunities and buying patterns. We rely less on traditional research activities such as marketwide surveys, focus groups, and aggregate purchase studies. This reflects our recognition that BDD must develop new products and applications, and offer many new services that are often account-specific."

Mr. Kao spent time traveling with BDD sales reps. He described a recent example: "To assess the potential for a new product, I asked certain reps to identify accounts that are using this product (developed by another firm), and we spoke with users about applications and experiences. Sales reps are not trained to ask the right questions and get the kind of information from users that is necessary for product development purposes. This is especially true with unfamiliar products or applications."

MARKET DEVELOPMENTS

Mr. Cohen believed any organizational decision should consider various factors likely to affect BDD's market position. One factor was the continuing impact of cost-containment in the division's core hospital market. Mr. Cohen commented:

As hospital purchasing personnel and buying groups become more influential, there is the threat that our core product categories will be viewed as "commodities." Countering that perception has meant new product, service, price, promotional, and delivery approaches. It may also mean forging new marketing alliances with other divisions and with complementary suppliers outside the company.

A second factor was competition in the hospital market:

In different ways, both Sherwood and Terumo have become more aggressive in their marketing efforts. This has further increased price and margin pressures. Although we gained market share in the past year, for example, our net income did not increase proportionately. Are we organized to deal effectively with these ongoing buyer and competitive developments in our major market?

A third factor was the increasing importance of nonhospital/alternative-care markets:

All estimates indicate that nonhospital treatment should account for larger proportions of health-care activity during the next decade. But we're staffed to manage our base business where the majority of sales volume is to hospital customers. In addition, the nonhospital market, while growing fast, is also fragmented and composed of many different types of health-care facilities.

A fourth factor was new technologies. In 1990, for example, one large company was test-marketing a product that allowed health-care workers to pierce IV sets with blunt, plastic insertion tips into special rubber injection sites on the IV. The result was a "needleless" means of delivering certain medication. One estimate indicated that, if successful, such a product could substitute for up to 10% of hypodermic needle sales within two years. Mr. Cohen noted:

In one form or another, such products are likely to become increasingly common, since fears of accidental needlesticks are an important issue in hospitals. But this situation can also open up opportunities in what has been a mature market, if we become an active participant. As a full-line supplier with broad distribution, we can save our customers time and worry in this area (e.g., concerns about training, delivery, compatibility with different sizes of syringes). But this will require closer linkages between R&D, Manufacturing, Marketing and Sales to develop, introduce, and build business for any such initiatives.

A fifth factor was increased market interest in new product/service arrangements:

Our initiatives in Safety Systems are an example. Developing and marketing these products requires a high service component. We need to reeducate doctors, nurses, and hospital housekeeping personnel about sharps disposal processes; and the hospitals, already under severe cost pressures, must provide data, access, resources, feedback and high-level support. We want to position ourselves as consultants and partners with our hospital customers in this area. But, thus far, adoption of the new safety products has been slower than expected.

A related development concerned medical waste disposal. U.S. hospitals generated over two million tons of waste annually, 10% of which was considered infectious by the Environmental Protection Agency. Estimates indicated that waste disposal had become two to three times more expensive for the average hospital between 1988 and 1990. In many instances, product acquisition costs were lower than the costs of disposal, especially for supply items. Mr. Cohen noted:

> The opportunity and threat is that the product/service package is being redefined. Disposal costs make customers more conscious of total cost-in-use; they may expect vendors to identify cost effective ways to dispose of infectious waste. Due to our broad line, we can offer product/service packages and forge external partnerships. But this takes time and attention.

Commenting on these factors, Mr. Cohen stated:

> The precise direction of each development is still unclear, but the impact of these factors will certainly be felt in our product categories. The marketing department is now dealing in some form with each of these factors, but the danger is that our organization will allow either new opportunities or current responsibilities to fall between the cracks. It's therefore important to prioritize attention and focus our limited resources on specific opportunities and threats.

Organizational Decisions

During the 1990 budgeting process, Mr. Cohen had obtained approval to hire an additional marketing manager. Budgeted costs for the potential hire (including salary, benefits, and expenses) were set at about $150,000. Mr. Cohen commented:

> At this point, adding another good person is attractive. But I want to be clear about the focus of this person's responsibilities, since an addition can impact other managers' responsibilities. I'll also need to spell out the kind of background, experience and skills a candidate (from inside or outside BDD) should possess.
>
> At the same time, continuing price pressures in our market mean continuing pressures to lower expenses. There's a good chance that, at some point in this fiscal year, we'll be asked to reduce marketing expenses. If so, I'd rather not make cuts in key areas after already incur-

ring the financial and other start-up costs of bringing on a new person. It's easier, and less disruptive to ongoing activities and personnel, to freeze a part of the budget not yet in place, such as the approved hire.

More generally, I want to know if we're structured to make optimal use of current personnel. Are the right people focusing on the right issues? Do any of these market developments warrant a reallocation of marketing responsibilities, or an additional person, at this point? If so, does the marketing organization require significant changes or will small modifications be sufficient?

EXHIBIT 1   Three-Year Summary of Selected Financial Data (thousands of dollars, except per share amounts)

		1989	1988	1987
Operations	Net sales	$1,811,456	$1,709,368	$1,462,882
	Gross profit margin	45.7%	46.5%	46.5%
	Income from continuing operations	158,002	148,856	139,946
	Earnings per share			
	—Continuing operations	4.00	3.69	3.30
	—Net income	5.40[a]	4.01	3.57
	Dividends per share	1.00	.86	.74
Financial position	Total assets	$2,270,130	$2,067,533	$1,891,478
	Current ratio	1.5	1.7	1.7
	Long-term debt	516,047	449,969	479,559
	Book value per share	27.99	24.33	21.62
Financial relationships	Income from continuing operations before income taxes			
	as a percent of sales	12.6%	12.1%	12.9%
	Return on total assets	14.0[b]	14.6	14.3[b]
	Return on equity	17.0[b]	17.8	16.0[b]
Additional data	Capital expenditures	$ 314,367	$ 272,538	$ 190,968
	Research and development expense	97,543	93,255	82,825
	Number of employees	18,800	20,600	19,900

Note: Earnings before interest expense and taxes as a percent of average total assets.
[a]Includes after-tax gain of $44,658, or $1.12 per share on the sale of Edmont subsidiary.
[b]Excludes gain on sale of Edmont and Endevco subsidiaries in 1989 and 1987 respectively.
Source: Company annual reports.

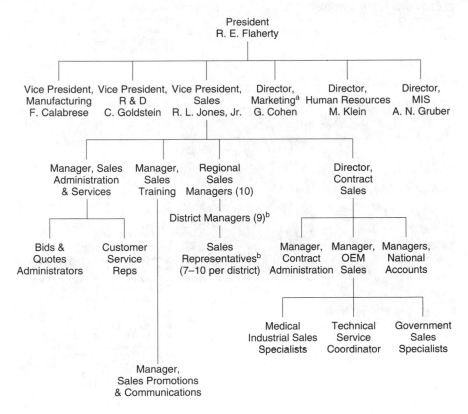

President
R. E. Flaherty

Vice President, Manufacturing — F. Calabrese

Vice President, R & D — C. Goldstein

Vice President, Sales — R. L. Jones, Jr.

Director, Marketing[a] — G. Cohen

Director, Human Resources — M. Klein

Director, MIS — A. N. Gruber

Manager, Sales Administration & Services

Manager, Sales Training

Regional Sales Managers (10)

Director, Contract Sales

District Managers (9)[b]

Bids & Quotes Administrators

Customer Service Reps

Sales Representatives[b] (7–10 per district)

Manager, Contract Administration

Manager, OEM Sales

Managers, National Accounts

Medical Industrial Sales Specialists

Technical Service Coordinator

Government Sales Specialists

Manager, Sales Promotions & Communications

[a]See Exhibit 4 for detailed marketing organization.

[b]Not all District Managers had supervisory responsibilities, and some field Sales Representatives reported directly to Regional Sales Managers.

EXHIBIT 2   Organization Chart

BECTON-DICKINSON DIVISION
Stanley Street
Rutherford, NJ 07070
201-460-2000

SERVES: **Physicians**
Nurses
Radiologists
Anesthesiologists
Pharmacists

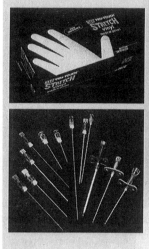

Becton-Dickinson Division is the market leader in the manufacture of high quality single-use products such as hypodermic syringes, needles and related products.

The Division is also a major manufacturer of vinyl medical gloves and your source for an expanding line of technique needles for use in various procedures, including biopsy, anesthesia, angiography and myelography.

Becton-Dickinson Division products include:

Hypodermic Products

B-D® Single-use Syringes and Needl
B-D Sharps Collectors
B-D Insulin and Allergy Syringes
B-D Pharmacy Products
B-D Reusable Syringes and Needles

Technique Products and Supplies

B-D Medical Gloves
B-D Anesthesia, Radiology, and
  Biopsy Needle Products
B-D Thermometry Products
ACE® Brand Bandages and Elastic
  Support Products
A-V® Fistula Needles

EXHIBIT 3

G. Cohen
Director of Marketing

L. Higgins Sr. Product Manager, Hypodermic Programs	G. Sutton Sr. Product Manager, Distributor Programs	R. Hankin Product Manager, Safety Systems
• End-User Advertising • Marketing Intelligence • Worldwide Hypodermic • Allergist Syringe	• BD Advantage Program • Easy Draw Syringe • Nursing Home Syringe • Alternate Care Syringe	• Sharps Collectors • Safety Lok Syringe • Solo Shot Syringe • Syringe Disposal

R. Short Sr. Product Manager, Hospital Market	M. Ferro Product Manager, National Accounts Service	J. Kao Manager, Marketing Research

• Hospital Conversion
  Programs
• Forecasting
• Product Development
• Packaging
	• National Accounts
	  Marketing
	• Hospital Advantage
	  Program
	• Multi-Divisional
	  Program
	• Pharmacy Products
		• Primary Research
		• Market Share
		  Reporting
		• Customer/Market
		  Analysis
		• Competitor Analysis

EXHIBIT 4   Marketing Organization

Case 2

IBM:
Assistant General Manager of Marketing (A)

In 1991, IBM was organized in five geographical groupings—IBM United States, IBM Canada, IBM Latin America, IBM Asia Pacific, and IBM Europe/Middle East/and Africa—each responsible for sales, service, and manufacturing operations in its geography. As part of a series of moves designed to decentralize decision-making in the company, "line of business" organizations (LOBs) were established in 1988 (see **Exhibit 1**). Each LOB was responsible for worldwide product development, expenses, and revenue goals for its products and services, as well as U.S. manufacturing operations. One industry journal commented:

> IBM's ability to execute depends in large measure on how well its LOBs coordinate with each other. LOBs are centered on specific product lines: Personal Systems (PS/2 and RT workstations), Application Business Systems (the AS/400 midrange family), Enterprise Systems (mainframe products), Technology Products (semiconductors), Programming Systems (Systems Application Architecture) [and Commu-

---

This case was prepared by Professor Frank V. Cespedes and Research Associate Laura Goode as the basis for class discussion rather than to illustrate either effective or ineffective handling of an administrative situation.

Copyright © 1992 by the President and Fellows of Harvard College. Harvard Business School case 9-592-066.

nication Systems (networking hardware and software)]. . . . U.S. Marketing & Services concentrates on selling and servicing the products made by the other lines of business. Each is under pressure to get products out faster. The company's stated goal is to cut product development time in half across the board, for both hardware and software.[1]

A senior IBM executive noted:

Establishing LOBs is designed to leverage our wide product line while focusing responsibilities closer to the customer. Each LOB has its own market analysis units, and development and manufacturing resources. Enter the complexity: there are many interdependencies among the LOBs. For example, Enterprise Systems, Application Business Systems, and Personal Systems rely on Programming Systems for databases and Communication Systems for networks. Within U.S. Marketing & Services is the Application Solutions LOB, whose mission is to provide customers with a unified solution by integrating offerings from among the other LOBs. Also, while each LOB has its own products and services, all share a common sales force organized by geography.

This case focuses on one mechanism utilized to facilitate coordination among the LOBs and between the LOBs and field marketing organizations: the position of Assistant General Manager of Marketing (AGMM). The case describes the origins and goals of the position, historical relations between product and marketing units at IBM, perspectives on the AGMM, and representative issues.

IMMEDIATE ORIGINS OF THE AGMM POSITION

In June 1986, IBM was finalizing plans to release a new product, the IBM 9370. The introduction had been scheduled for 1987. But, concerned that an impatient market was seeking competitive alternatives, Development wanted to release the product in the fall of 1986. In response, marketing managers cited a number of reasons why IBM should not release a major product in the fourth quarter. "Especially in our mainframe line," one manager noted, "product transitions are crucial. Once an announcement is made, many customers often stop buying the current generation of products while they decide whether to purchase the new technology. The result can be stalled sales and quota-crushing delays for individual marketing reps."

The conflict was escalated to IBM's Management Committee (MC), which agreed with Development. The introduction was scheduled for October 1986. However, the decision was not without costs. Field marketing plans established under the assumption of a 9370 introduction the following year had to be revised. The order process in place at the time of introduction

[1]J. Moad and S. Kerr, "How Line Managers Run the New IBM," *Datamation* (January 1, 1990), 30.

could accept only a limited set of product options. In addition, as one manager explained, when the product was introduced, "Some important marketing personnel were still miffed about the decision while many salespeople, working hard in the fourth quarter to make their annual numbers, did not attend the necessary training classes for the new product." While studies showed that the earlier release did slow the competitive activity that had concerned Development, sales results were less than anticipated in the original business plan for the 9370. One executive commented:

> IBM learned a lesson from this experience. Especially in mainframe product categories, we have close relations with installed-base customers and processes for determining product requirements. The problem was the implementation of our programs. The groups responsible for execution had conflicting priorities and opinions, and few mechanisms to resolve disagreements short of a last-minute intervention by the MC. As a result, with the 9370, we were initially trying to sell hardware without the total solutions in place.
>
> As we looked at our next major upcoming product release (the mid-range AS/400 line), we asked, "What did we learn from the 9370 experience and what should we do differently?" We decided we needed one group responsible for orchestrating the product introduction among the developers, the marketing managers in headquarters, field salespeople, and (especially for a mid-range product line) the industry/vertical-market specialists that have knowledge of required applications and important indirect channels of distribution.

In response, the MC appointed (about one year before the planned introduction date) William Grabe (a senior executive with significant marketing and product management experience) as project manager for the AS/400 release. He established a project team of 15 people, and assigned these individuals to manage various interfaces important to the product introduction, including with systems managers in the development lab, software developers in other units, industry specialists at headquarters, advertising and promotions personnel in relevant marketing organizations, and field sales personnel in the geographies.

In addition, a group of high-level executives from each of the major worldwide marketing and product development organizations met monthly to discuss coordination issues surrounding the pending announcement. One manager involved described the meetings as follows:

> With the backing of the MC, Bill could insist on having the key executives (no substitutes) from the relevant functions attend these meetings. Hence, once a month, we filled a room in Connecticut with about 40 people for an all-day shootout in which issues were surfaced, discussed and, over time, resolved. These meetings were sometimes contentious, but communications improved dramatically. Also, after the first meeting, key executives tended to bring along other important managers in their organizations, and so there was also an increase in

responsiveness for developing a given action plan before the next meeting.

One result is that we were able to focus a number of different product and marketing groups on core key success factors for the AS/400 line: providing a good and easy migration path for our installed base of S/36 and S/38 users; providing a variety of relevant software applications at the time of introduction (not some time afterwards); and providing field salespeople with literature and other forms of support for specific applications and target markets.

The AS/400 introduction in 1988 was a major success. IBM sold 25,000 AS/400s during the first quarter the product was available and, by the end of 1988, 98 of IBM's top 100 accounts either had an AS/400 pilot project underway or had one planned. One year after introduction, a survey found that, of accounts indicating an intention to purchase an AS/400 over the next two years, 57% were not replacing existing systems, suggesting that the product had opened-up new segments for IBM. Two years after introduction, an observer commented:[2]

> When IBM announced the Application System/400 line of midrange computers, it met with some skepticism. In an age of open systems, IBM was wagering a hefty chunk of its future on a proprietary midrange system. But, to everyone's surprise, the AS/400 has turned into one of Big Blue's hottest-selling products. In August (1989)—not a notoriously brisk sales month—IBM sold out of AS/400s, making it the biggest order month in the product's two-year history. . . . A consulting firm specializing in midrange machines estimates the total market for the AS/400 and related products at $10 billion annually. If this revenue belonged to a separate company, those numbers would make it the third largest U.S. IS supplier.

With the AS/400 introduction process as a recent example, the AGMM position was then established within each LOB as part of the 1988 corporate reorganization. One executive noted: "with 6–10 major product introductions annually, something like the AS/400 team had to be institutionalized and not formed on an ad hoc basis. But we also realized that, across LOBs, different development and marketing issues rightly take precedence. Therefore, with the exception of certain general guidelines, no one 'model' was proposed for this new position." In outlining the intended goals of the AGMM position, another executive explained:

> The AGMM in each LOB is the gearbox between the Marketing & Service organization (M&S) in each geographic area, the Application Solutions LOB, and the development lab. The AGMM represents the voice of the customer in its LOB, making sure that worldwide requirements are met. The job requires the ability to zero-in on a set of customers

[2]Mike Ricciuti, "IBM Entry Spans Midrange Gap," Datamation (November 1, 1990), 101–102.

while also taking a wide-angle view of the whole product line. Why the whole line? Because as we address more diverse markets, our solutions need clear positioning so they don't—or don't appear to—compete with each other. The job of differentiating belongs to the AGMM, as does the role of orchestrating announcements so that hardware, software, and other important elements come out together, as they did with the AS/400.

PRODUCT-MARKETING RELATIONS AT IBM

The liaison role at the heart of the AGMM position also involved a larger company context. Among the factors cited as relevant for understanding this role were: the process established in the 1960s and 1970s for managing product requirements and introductions; the impact of measurement systems; changes in customers' buying processes; and market segmentation and selection procedures.

System/360 and Product-Marketing Relations

A major turning point in IBM's history was the development of the System/360-series of computers in the mid-1960s. With the S/360, IBM introduced upward compatibility over a wide product line that shared a common operating system, a variety of common input/output devices across the line, and a single general-purpose line of equipment for a variety of commercial data-processing applications. These developments required IBM to become a vertically integrated manufacturer of computer systems, components, peripherals, and software. In addition, management decided to introduce all major S/360 products simultaneously in April 1965 so that customers would perceive the full impact of the new line. This meant that the many labs and plants involved in S/360 development had to coordinate closely in order to meet a rigorous schedule for product introductions.

The S/360 successfully consolidated IBM's position in general-purpose mainframe systems. But its development and market introduction required the total commitment of IBM's financial resources and a tumultuous series of internal efforts. After an internal review, top management instituted changes intended to assure the "functional excellence" of IBM activities. "With the 360 experience," one manager commented, "the notion of assuming start-to-finish responsibility for a product became a guiding philosophy at IBM. And since P&L responsibility throughout this period was lodged in the product units, the System Manager in the Development organizations became accountable. This meant the System Manager had final say over product requirements for his or her product and, in turn, this accountability encouraged them to want maximum control over their own resources and priorities."

In addition, IBM instituted a new "Phase Process" for reviewing product plans from concept development through specifications, production scheduling, announcement, and introduction. At each phase, the relevant functional groups involved were required to assent, dissent, and perhaps commit resources to the product plans that, in most cases, were driven by a given Development organization. "A key job in this process," noted one executive, "was the Product Forecaster, who reported in through the Finance and Planning function. During the 1970s, our business—at least at the high end—was like the automobile business: five-year model changes. Product Forecasters, each assigned to a product, utilized a 3- to 5-year time horizon and performed basic market research, did relevant financial projections, and then worked to get other functions to buy-into a product plan. This budgeting process served as a negotiating vehicle among key development, manufacturing, marketing, and finance executives." Another executive commented:

> The phase process was a serial procedure with built-in conflict. It was part of our contention management system where the basic assumption was that, by forcing "yes" or "no" positions at each phase, the best decision would evolve. However, marketing groups typically had to commit resources (and so had a real "voice") only at the announcement and introduction phases—after other important decisions about specifications had already been made. In fact, it was not uncommon during this process for marketing managers to be invited *out* of the meeting when the subject of pricing was discussed. Product managers, looking at P&L projections, were afraid that marketing managers, looking at product volume quotas, would always opt for lower prices. The result was a tug-of-war between product development and the channel, and this conflict escalated as our business grew, as new product lines from different development units were introduced, and as the total systems emphasis increased interdependencies among the product units.
>
> This background is an important dimension behind the establishment of the AGMM position. For sound competitive reasons, we want to cut our product development time in half and, in general, accelerate our time-to-market performance. Also, now that large customers have automated their obvious functions, they're looking for more. They want integrated solutions and unique services. That means forging closer working relationships between our Labs, M&S, and the AGMMs in the LOBs in order to make sure customer requirements are known early in product development.
>
> Then, we must manage the provision of these requirements faster and better. Our old rules based on contention management assumed that the best argument would eventually win out and that top management could sort-out the best argument in a timely manner. We can't afford that today. Differences must be resolved more quickly to assure timely delivery of solutions to selected customer segments. This is an important task for the AGMMs: they should expedite this

process and surface any problems earlier in the development-to-intro-duction cycle.

Measurement Issues

Another factor affecting Product and Field Marketing units was the metrics used to evaluate performance in each unit. Until 1990, product units were P&L centers, while marketing units looked to annual sales volumes and annual selling expense-to-revenue ratios (E/R) as key metrics. "In both cases," noted one executive, "managers' attention rapidly shifts to 'controllable' expenses—those that are in the individual manager's budget":

> For field marketing managers, the main controllable items are educa-tion and training, travel, and entertainment. But big hitters like salaries, facilities, telephone, and I/S services were essentially "fixed" at the local level by headcount. Hence, the focus on E/R caused many field marketing managers to cut back on training and some account-development activities. Meanwhile, headcount reductions through early retirement resulted in fewer marketing reps and systems engi-neers. And as IBM introduced many new products during the 1980s, this ultimately translated into complaints by product units about the field's lack of product knowledge and consequent inability to sell the new products.

In product units, a large portion of expenses reflected development costs. Once developed, variable manufacturing expenses for computer hardware were relatively small and, at IBM, a decreasing portion of product costs after investments in highly automated production facilities during the 1970s and 1980s. These production economics made volume sales a key goal for product units, as did the "apportionments" component of expenses for product P&L managers. Apportionments were essentially overhead ex-penses (including marketing expenses) allocated to product units by corpo-rate during the budgeting process. As one manager explained: "The tendency for the P&L product managers is to view the apportionment as an uncontrollable fixed expense, and then to push for as much marketing at-tention as possible to their product line. Investments that improved a prod-uct's serviceability or manufacturability ultimately showed up as variable cost reductions on the product manager's P&L. But with marketing ex-penses treated as part of a product unit's 'fixed costs,' there is an incentive for those managers to add product functions that increase the size of the po-tential market, but less incentive to make investments in product improve-ments or sales support that increase field marketing productivity."

Some managers believed this situation was exacerbated by the sales compensation system in place until 1988. Under the previous system, IBM marketing reps earned credit toward quotas, bonuses, and commissions via a "point" system based on an individual product's list price (i.e., before net-ting out any price discounts granted to the customer). Point allocations were set each fall during a series of negotiating sessions between M&S executives and the product LOBs who, at that time, had P&L responsibility and control over price discounting for their lines. One executive described the process as follows:

> Product managers essentially lobbied M&S to place more points on their particular product line in the annual sales compensation plan. An individual's negotiating skills could influence this process significantly and, since Marketing earned points based on list price, the negotiations usually centered on the allowable price discounts. Also, since the larger, better-established lines had more room to move in this regard, the tendency was to place disproportionate emphasis on established hardware products and less on newer products, especially software and services. The point system had a distinguished 50-year history at IBM. But we knew something was wrong when, for three years running (1986–1988), 75% of field reps made their point targets while the corporation missed its annual growth, revenue and profit goals.

In 1989, marketing quotas were changed and based on total customer revenue, regardless of the specific products sold. In addition, software, services, and "sell-through" revenues (i.e., sales made through dealers and other channel intermediaries) became explicit parts of marketing quotas. In 1990, the M&S organization became a profit center responsible for sales, service, and integration of all IBM products and services, while the LOBs became "cost and quality" centers for research, development, and manufacturing. Hence, key performance measures for LOB general managers were: Worldwide Program Profitability and Market Share, Schedule Integrity, Quality, and Morale.

One executive noted that part of the AGMM's role is to "help facilitate these changes, which generally place more power and responsibility in the field":

> In the past decade, IBM has improved manufacturing and service quality. Between 1986 and 1990 manufacturing cycle times in our plants were down by as much as 50%; the time to produce mainframes was reduced by 67% and installation time cut from a week to 16 hours; our mid-range business unit won the 1990 Baldrige quality competition; and we stipulated that any new product must exceed its predecessor in terms of measured reliability.
>
> But we haven't paid similar attention to marketing issues, and (like most companies) don't have goals or metrics for marketing matters such as the amount of training time a new product requires of users or the product's fit with our increasingly important indirect channels. Let me cite a small example. Apple computers come in bright, multicolored boxes that many dealers find attractive, and so display in their store windows or in piles in the shopping area. But our PC gets delivered in a nondescript box covered with shipping data, and often gets placed in the dealer's back room. While this has some impact on con-

sumer awareness and any point-of-purchase decision making, it shows up nowhere as a marketing, product development, manufacturing, or logistics metric.

We've made great strides in getting manufacturability and reliability issues considered early in the development process. Part of the AGMM's job is to make marketability issues visible and important earlier in development. If the end product does not fill a need, how well-built it may be is meaningless.

Changes in Acquisition Behavior

Until the late 1970s, most customers leased, rather than purchased, IBM equipment and software. Under these standard leasing (or "rental") agreements, customers could return equipment and cease rental payments with 30-days' notice. During the 1980s, IBM changed its pricing strategy to encourage purchase. As IBM's business grew, rental agreements required huge working capital investments on IBM's part. In addition, as more low-end products were introduced, the equipment became less expensive and so more amenable to up-front purchase.

This change affected marketing requirements. One manager explained:

> In the leasing environment, we were focused on growing the installed base. Headquarters research focused on understanding current customers' requirements; product development tended to focus on adding to the high end of the line with bigger and faster equipment; and field marketing became proficient at finding new applications for existing products and software and in selling additional capacity requirements. New users were a secondary priority for each group.
>
> But as buying moves to purchase, the field must sell major capital investments to a broader range of buyers and a complete solution, rather than an incremental sale that builds on the infrastructure already in place at an account. The enabling software and services become a bigger part of what the customers buy. In turn, this requires more and better market (as opposed to individual customer) information in order to develop these offerings for selected segments.

Another manager noted that "product development and sales both have a tendency to keep doing what they're doing by extending a given product life cycle as long as possible":

> For Development groups, a high-end line extension traditionally means growth of the installed base, minimal disruption to large accounts' existing software and support investments, and the ability to leverage past R&D efforts. For Sales, a high-end extension traditionally means more points, or revenue dollars, per sale. But new market opportunities often mean introducing a low-end, entry-level product to reach new buyers. AGMMs should, in my opinion, help to argue for

these entry-level products in the face of implicit fears by Development and Sales that this means trading down, or cannibalizing, installed-base business.

Market Segmentation and Market Selection

In a 1989 memorandum, "Being Market Driven" (see **Exhibit 2** for excerpts), John Akers outlined IBM's goal as being "the best at satisfying the needs and wants of customers in the markets we choose to serve." Many managers noted that the emphasis on market selection was significant. "Historically," one executive explained, "this company has excelled in R&D, manufacturing, and sales, but not in marketing defined as targeting certain customer groups and providing a coherently customized marketing mix for each group. We've long had processes for product development but no process aimed at clarifying market selection criteria." A number of reasons were cited for this situation. One manager commented:

Throughout the 1950s and 1960s, IBM's genius was to allay big customers' fears of computing by assuming product and service responsibility: leasing reduced purchase risk, our product groups focused on increasing power without sacrificing customers' sunk-cost investments in programming and fixed-cost investments in programmers, and our service policies protected these customers against downtime. At the time, few other vendors could duplicate our abilities across these pre- and post-sales activities. But one result is that, over time, we found ourselves committed to being everything to everyone, and never focused on market segmentation. Today, however, different parts of the computer industry's value chain—e.g., leasing, software, maintenance, value-added distribution—are served by hundreds of specialized organizations.

Another manager emphasized the impact of historical product policy:

There has always been a tension in this industry between generalists and specialists, between building a general-purpose platform and tailoring a platform designed for a specific vertical segment or application. The issue is how to balance the scale and scope economies of the generalist against the specialist's ability to focus and customize a solution. The issue used to revolve around hardware, but now it's increasingly a software development issue.

Over the past two decades, the industry has grown and fragmented. Also, MIS centers are swamped with work and more influenced by end users when making purchase and upgrade decisions. Hence, there is less value placed on the hardware per se, and more on a vendor's ability to act as a general contractor—that is, a vendor capable of taking on the technical and subcontracting risks of applications development. But no one can assume these risks for all types of customers. Market segmentation and selection become more important.

As explained in **Exhibit 2**, AGMMs, with the Application Solutions LOB and Marketing organizations in the geographies, were expected to take the lead in market segmentation and selection activities. Management expected this process, and the accompanying dialogue among the different groups involved, to help address an issue described by one executive in the following terms:

> It's not hard to get people to embrace the idea that "customer needs" are important in business. The hard part is acting on this belief via appropriate funding mechanisms and internal alignments. Providing a solution often means cutting horizontally across internal organizational boundaries such as LOBs, but our budgeting process drives funding and measurements vertically by internal unit such as LOB and geography. One result has been that we often provided 80% of many solutions, rather than 100% of a select number.
>
> The challenge in a technically complex, fast-moving business is aligning market owners and resource owners. Market owners are responsible for identifying wants and needs in terms of accounts, segments, industries, and geographies, and for developing appropriate channel skills and motivation. Resource owners are responsible for functional excellence in R&D, product development, manufacturing, and service. AGMMs occupy a crossroads position between development, marketing, and the industry/sector organizations. Their challenge is, among other things, to facilitate the convergence of these groups.

AGMM: ROLES AND RESPONSIBILITIES

Those appointed as AGMMs were all senior managers with 20 or more years of experience at IBM, generally in the following areas: 6–10 years as field marketing reps and then branch or division sales managers; 2–5 years as Product Line Planning Managers where the responsibilities included managing and negotiating production scheduling and other resources; and 4–6 years in senior marketing positions either at corporate headquarters or in the U.S. M&S organization. Each AGMM reported directly to the General Manager of the LOB, and each was measured on worldwide revenues of that LOB's product line.

As **Exhibit 3** indicates, the AGMMs had responsibility for their LOB's worldwide market strategy and market requirements. In addition, they worked with Development, Finance and Planning groups within their LOBs, and with industry and field groups in M&S, on product development issues, product introductions, and market support. **Exhibit 4** outlines AGMM interactions with other groups in performing these responsibilities.

Within the LOB, the AGMM was expected to work with the Development Labs and Finance & Planning (F&P) function in product planning. In most LOBs, both F&P and the Labs had long had sizeable staff groups responsible for product, market, and financial analyses. But, as one manager described it, "their concerns typically focus on product functional requirements and production forecasting, not with marketing issues or channel productivity concerns." AGMMs were also expected to interact with their counterparts at other LOBs concerning issues that affected multiple LOBs. One issue was networking of computers. One journal estimated that "62% of the largest U.S. companies use IBM's Systems Network Architecture (SNA) as the primary method for tying their computers together":[3]

> There are more than 50,000 data networks built on SNA. They run airline reservation systems, transfer funds, and coordinate vital corporate functions from inventory to payroll. . . . The original SNA blueprint is showing its age after 18 years, despite many improvements along the way. IBM needs to bring its networking technology into the 1990s and prepare for the turn of the century, when networks will blast text, data, and video. . . . But while IBM must satisfy cutting-edge customers with new products for high-speed multi-media communications, it can't alter SNA so radically that existing networks are rendered obsolete.

AGMMs also interacted with the industry and sector groups supervised by the WWOC as well as the Application Solutions LOB, whose general manager was the head of the WWOC. One AGMM explained that "these groups talk in terms of solutions, while the LOB Lab must translate their customer knowledge into technical product specifications. Lab managers tend to work within their established product paradigms, but funding from the WWOC or Application Solutions provides me with an opportunity to influence development priorities."

Within U.S. M&S, AGMMs interacted with certain headquarters and field marketing managers. At U.S. M&S headquarters, there was an M&S director responsible for overseeing the marketing and sales of a set of products or services throughout the United States. In general, these directors' responsibilities aligned with a particular LOB's product line, and they had final approval authority over promotion plans for that line in the United States. These managers were given specific product-line targets annually by the U.S. M&S organization, and were measured on the line's U.S. performance in terms of revenues, units sold, gross profit, and customer satisfaction indices. Similarly, within many of the 8 geographic Areas in U.S. M&S, there were Product Marketing Managers responsible for sales support activities for a given set of products or services, and measured on the Area's sales volume performance with those products or services. The Area Product Marketing Managers reported to the Area Director of Marketing, who was responsible for allocating that Area's sales and marketing resources in line with specific targets established annually with U.S. M&S headquarters and each LOB.

[3]Peter Coy, "IBM Needs a Network, But Not Too New," *Business Week*, April 20, 1992, p. 95.

Beginning in 1990, the assignment of profit-and-loss responsibility in the Areas was being moved downward. Previously only the Area General Managers were accountable for Area P&L performance; now the Area Directors of Marketing also shared that responsibility. In addition, the company planned to vest P&L responsibility with the newly created position of Trading Area General Manager. The Trading Area, depending upon the customer base, might be a city, a region, or an industry sector. IBM established 10 Trading Area GMs in 1990, but planned more than 60 within two years. Depending upon the LOB's business, AGMMs also interacted with Country Managers in international groups. Country managers had responsibilities and metrics similar to those of Area General Managers in U.S. M&S. One executive explained that "our business increasingly crosses borders, both before and after the sale, and that increases coordination requirements in marketing planning and implementation."

Each AGMM had organized his or her unit differently. But by early 1991, each AGMM had a staff of 25–50 people focused on areas such as market research and analysis, product planning with development groups, and marketing support activities of various kinds.

Perspectives on the AGMM Role

The casewriters spoke with various managers at IBM concerning the AGMM role. All managers stressed that the AGMM units functioned differently in different LOBs, and a number emphasized that the new role "helps to get labs to prioritize their work in line with market opportunities, and not only systems imperatives that are driven by technology decisions made a decade or more in the past." One manager offered an example:

> You build the product differently depending upon its main distribution channel. With the direct channel, the goal is a system that adds power and that the large customer and IBM's systems engineers can then fully equip into an integrated system compatible with installed applications. With indirect channels, more costs are support costs of various kinds, and you minimize these costs for IBM and its channel partners by having more support already built into the machine, by allowing for compatibility with a range of third-party applications, and by minimizing the necessary product training costs. The AGMMs help to make visible for the Labs what I call the infrastructure effects: the real costs to IBM of post-development marketing, sales, distribution, support, education and training expenses associated with a product line.

Other managers, however, believed that most AGMMs were "only in a small way engaged with Development to shape the offering: AGMMs may have a voice in the Development process, but they don't have significant development money to allocate in their LOBs. So, they have limited ability to change things in order to reflect channel or other marketing requirements."

A development manager emphasized that "in our business, crucial product development decisions must often be made years before introduction, and the consequences of those decisions linger for years afterwards. Meanwhile, customers—even the most forward looking—are rarely looking beyond a 2–3 year time horizon in assessing their I/S needs; budgeting procedures rarely allow them to think longer term. Also, as compatibility and open-systems requirements increase, it's crucial that IBM have a coordinated plan for making transitions from one product generation to the next. Market research and customer surveys are necessary but limited means for making important early decisions about requirements."

In the field, a number of managers believed the AGMM organizations were a useful vehicle for making specific product or account issues visible. One product marketing manager noted that "I can use the AGMM in this line to get issues escalated for higher-level attention." An account executive noted that, depending upon the relationships established with individuals in an AGMM organization and those individuals' backgrounds, "the AGMM is a good source for executive marketing efforts. Also, their badge connotes 'development' to many customers, and so they are a credible way to brief customers regarding product-line directions."

However, other managers, especially in M&S headquarters and Area marketing positions, believed the AGMMs tended to "meddle in tactics":

> We put mainly former sales managers in AGMM positions, and they've tended to act as inspectors of field marketing plans rather than drivers of development plans. They should focus on product strategy issues, and let the geographies focus on implementation. But they push to get involved in the sales plan for their product lines, promotions, advertising, and key-account activities. The basic attitude seems to be, "what has M&S done for my line lately?"

An industry-group executive emphasized that "worldwide responsibility for product-market selection is a key aspect of the AGMM's role. U.S. revenues are less than 50% of IBM's revenues, and it's increasingly important that we spread limited and interdependent development resources on a worldwide scale." However, some executives, especially in the international groups, noted that most managers in the AGMM units were "Americans who grew up in the U.S. organization. They have few international assignees, so when there's an issue between U.S. and one of the other areas, the United States usually represents the single biggest chunk of that product line's revenues and the AGMM often defaults to the U.S. position."

A corporate executive commented that "the AGMMs face ongoing tradeoffs between optimizing their LOB's position and IBM's overall profits and participation in a solution. But the AGMM is measured on that LOB's performance, and where multiple LOBs overlap with their offerings, I see the AGMMs basically competing with each other for field support rather than developing a common plan." Another executive demurred: "The

AGMM position is still relatively new, but I've already seen some horse-trading across LOB AGMMs. These informal negotiations are very useful." Other managers offered more general observations:

> For 25 years, our product units and their labs have been accustomed to doing things themselves so as to ensure these things actually get done; for over 50 years, our field marketing units have taken annual quota numbers very seriously. Our culture encourages people to feel accountable *and* to want maximum control over their own resources and priorities. Meanwhile, we want to decentralize and empower lower levels while maintaining a coordinated customer interface. The AGMM often takes the heat in the resulting turf and control struggles, because this position gets involved in many activities previously handled by the lab or sales on its own.
>
> * * * * *
>
> The very notion of an "Assistant General Manager of Marketing" is a concession to a transition we're going through from being product- to market-oriented. The AGMM position should be a self-consuming artifact: if others do their jobs properly, that role should wither away.
>
> * * * * *
>
> The nature of the job means that the AGMM is easily perceived as the "outsider" by both camps: to be a Marketing person in Development is to be perceived as opting for resource commitments based on transitory or account-specific evidence; to represent Development to field Marketing is to be perceived as providing "too little/too late" help with urgent account requirements. The key tasks facing each AGMM are a) developing rapport and trust with their LOB managers, and b) deciding where their individual efforts are best used to develop consensus among the groups they deal with. If this is not done, the AGMM will spend all its time fighting fires.

Issues from the AGMM Perspective

Regarding product development decisions, one AGMM noted:

> As I see it, the AGMM position was created to provide marketing input into product requirements. My job is to get the LOB to buy into this, and I use market data as well as established relationships around IBM to help this process along. But I am *not* the requirements Czar; the labs ultimately own the requirements they agree to. In a fast-moving capital-intensive business like ours, no one person should be the sole czar for requirements. My role is to mediate requirements specifications in order to get a better balance among systems imperatives, time-to-market issues, and evolving market needs in priority segments.

Another AGMM commented: "I view my role as deciding what business this LOB should be in. Operationally, that means having ultimate responsibility for market selection decisions. Traditionally, IBM has never met a market it didn't like; my job is to help target development resources toward areas where we have major opportunities and advantages, and then to work with the geographies to establish the requisite market coverage and applications solutions needed to optimize this LOB's presence and profits in those markets."

Regarding interactions across LOBs, an AGMM emphasized that "a LOB ultimately spends money to make money for its product line. Part of effectively 'mediating requirements' means recognizing this reality. Also, overlaps among our offerings are not necessarily bad: it lets the customer choose, and I'd rather see another IBM unit get that sale instead of a competitor."

Concerning interactions with field marketing units, an AGMM said that "I am necessarily a merchandiser for my LOB's line, and that means getting involved with marketing activities in the geographies. I made over 100 customer calls last year: that's keeping in touch with requirements, stoking field attention, and gathering important data for discussions with Development. Equally important, my responsibilities are worldwide in scope so I'm naturally concerned about consistency in our advertising, product positioning, and support activities around the world. However, marketing units in the geographies ultimately own the resources for these activities, and their concerns are at the country or area level." Another AGMM manager noted: "My LOB's line is dependent on software sales and third-party partnerships. So, yes, I try to get involved in the sales plan for the field. It's a challenge to get thousands of people accustomed to measuring opportunities and success in terms of hardware revenues and account control to move in terms of business partnerships and the present value of software leases."

Interactions with U.S. M&S, according to one AGMM, "are probably where the most interesting, and animated, discussions occur":

Many U.S. marketing managers are accustomed to being the biggest spoke on IBM's wheel and to performing their activities without "interference." That was certainly my attitude toward the importance of my geography and "help" from corporate when I worked in U.S. marketing. But the U.S. accounts for less than 40% of my LOB's revenues and it is not the area forecasted to have among the higher rates of growth in IS purchases in the 1990s.

Also, "one person's ceiling is another person's floor": because of physical proximity as well as heritage, U.S. managers often had de facto direct access to development groups. So, my unit tends to represent an additional "roadblock" between them and the labs. For international units, however, the AGMM is a handy gateway for providing and aggregating input into labs' thinking.

Another AGMM commented:

An additional factor is the historical difference between marketing career paths in U.S. versus international areas. In the United States, IBM rotated marketing and sales personnel across branches and among headquarters, product marketing, and sales positions. This rotation had many benefits, but one result is that many of the key players I interact with in U.S. M&S view their job as a 1- to 3-year stopover position. That lack of continuity doesn't help me manage the matrix I'm in; it leaves little time and few budgeting cycles in which to develop knowledge, relationships, and quid-pro-quo interactions.

Internationally, countries like Japan, France or Germany have different languages and customs and are not as big as the United States. So, the hierarchy is flatter and, historically, marketing managers have remained in their positions longer than their counterparts in the U.S. Of course, as we move toward more Trading Areas in the United States and more post-1992 integration in Europe, this contrast in marketing career paths may change.

All AGMMs agreed that the recent changes in sales compensation from product points to general revenue targets, in shifting P&L responsibility to M&S, and the creation of Trading Area General Managers would have a significant impact on AGMM interactions. But they disagreed about the impact on the key tasks facing the individual AGMM in each LOB. One perspective was provided by a 1990 survey of IBM Account Executives and Directors of New Business Marketing. The survey asked these field managers to indicate their views regarding five LOB "platforms" based on three criteria: financial reward, marketing effort, and customer importance. Aggregate results are presented in **Exhibit 5**.

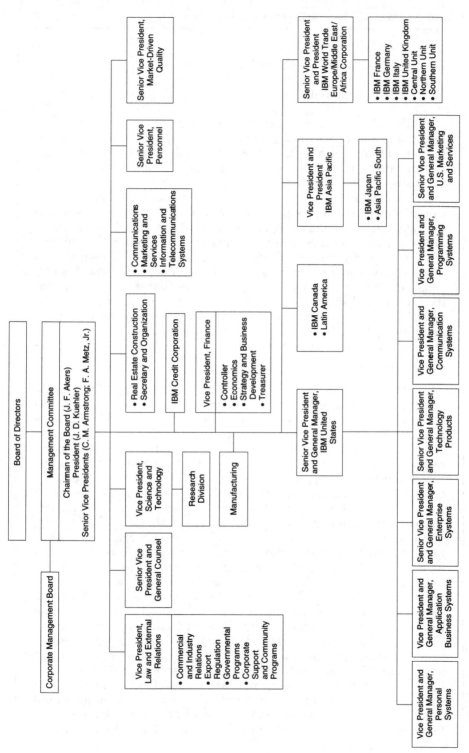

EXHIBIT 1 IBM Corporate Organization (May 1990)

EXHIBIT 2 Memorandum: "Being Market-Driven" (excerpts)

Executive Instruction Number 1 May 15, 1989

Subject: Being Market-Driven

IBM's basic beliefs—respect for individual; service for the customer; and excellence must be a way of life—have never been more important than they are today, as we recommit ourselves to be a market-driven company—the best at satisfying the needs and wants of the customers in the markets we choose to serve.

The customers we serve, and those we hope to serve, require careful integration of products and services into total solutions. These solutions often come from a variety of IBM organizations, business partners, and associates. The teamwork required cannot be achieved without respect for all of the individuals involved—the people who use our products, the business partners and associates who help us create and support total solutions, and every IBMer across the country. To accomplish this, we must be guided by four market-driven principles: make the customer the final arbiter; understand the market; commit to leadership in the markets we choose to serve; execute with excellence across our enterprise.

Responsibilities

Marketing organizations worldwide have the lead in assuring thorough understanding and segmentation of their current and prospective customers. These organizations include the Applications Solutions and Marketing organizations in IBM U.S., their counterparts in geographic units outside the United States, the assistant general managers of marketing within the development lines of business (LOBs), and operating units which have solutions unique to their missions such as services organizations and the IBM Credit Corporation.

The general managers of our geographic units are responsible for formulating industry and functional strategies, and prioritizing and selecting their solution opportunities. They are required to communicate their industry strategies and product and service requirements to the development LOBs, and to submit their top solution opportunities and related requirements to the Worldwide Opportunity Council (WWOC) through their representatives on that council. The WWOC is responsible for prioritizing and selecting worldwide solution opportunities targeted for IBM leadership, assuring the appointment of solution owners and teams, and monitoring progress.

A parallel process will be in place for product leadership and systems requirements since the industry strategies are dependent on them. Identification of these items and establishment of ownership is the responsibility of the development LOBs. Each development LOB will establish its own prioritization taking into account the top solution requirements important to the LOB, as well as systems requirements from other development LOBs. For requirements not included on the WWOC prioritized list sponsors may contact individual LOBs, but such requests do not carry the primary prioritization of the WWOC.

The individual LOB priorities will be negotiated into an overall IBM optimization by the geographic units and the development LOBs. Disagreements must be escalated promptly. The result will be input to the investment cycle in which commitments will be made to pursue leadership in the selected markets. For all solutions, sponsors may go inside or outside the company, but are responsible to assure that the opportunity is thoroughly understood, a solution owner is named, all elements critical to the successful delivery of the complete solution are identified and Customer Value Leadership criteria are established.

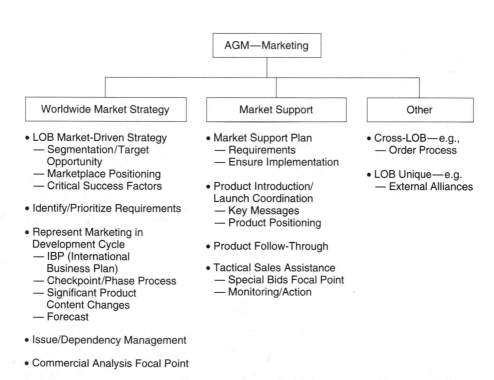

EXHIBIT 3 Outline of AGMM Responsibilities

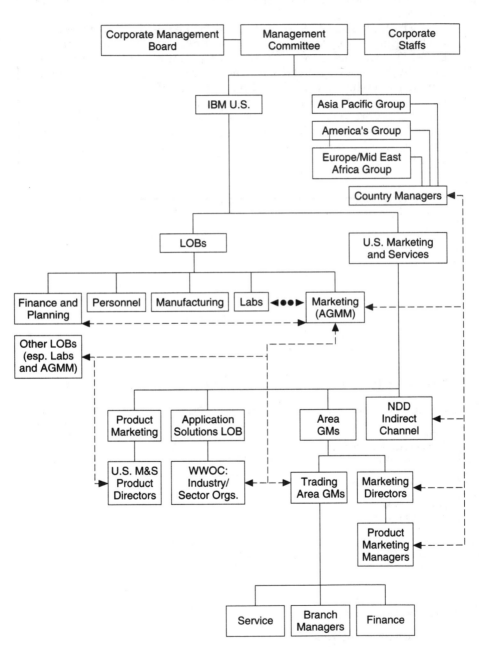

EXHIBIT 4 Overview of AGMM Organizational Interactions

EXHIBIT 5 Survey Questionnaire (summary)

This survey is intended to identify how field IBMers evaluate and prioritize their marketing opportunities regarding five IBM "platforms":

1. Mainframes (S/390)
2. Midrange (AS/400)
3. Intelligent Workstations (PS/2)
4. Systems Application Architecture (SAA)
5. Networking Systems (LANs, WANs, etc.)

Three key marketing motivators evaluated are:

1. Financial Reward:	Will selling this platform significantly impact my earnings?
2. Marketing Effort:	Do I feel confident that I know how to go about marketing this platform?
3. Customer Importance:	How important is this platform to the success of my customer's business?

The following scale was used:

Scale	Financial Reward	How Important Marketing Effort	to Customer's Business
5	Extremely high reward	Straightforward	Can't survive without this
4	Significant reward	Fairly easy	Extremely critical
3	Some reward	Modestly difficult	Some impact on business success
2	Very little reward	Extremely difficult	Little impact on business success
1	Almost no reward	Very, very difficult	"Nice to have"

Ranking of Responses by Category

Financial Reward

MOST rewarding:	Mainframes
2nd	Workstations
3rd	Midrange
4th	Networking
LEAST rewarding	SAA

Marketing Effort Required

MOST confidence:	Mainframes
2nd	Midrange
3rd	Workstations
4th	SAA
LEAST confidence:	Networking

Customer Importance

MOST important:	Networking
2nd	Mainframes
3rd	Workstations
4th	Midrange
LEAST important:	SAA

Case 3

IBM:
Assistant General Manager of Marketing (B)

This case study concerns assistant general managers of marketing units (AGMM) in two IBM Lines of Business (LOB): Enterprise Systems and Application Business Systems (see **Exhibit 1** for an overview of each LOB). The case describes the organization and representative activities within each AGMM unit as of January 1991.

ENTERPRISE SYSTEMS (ES)

Enterprise Systems developed and manufactured IBM's mainframe computer systems as well as associated systems software, storage devices, printers and other peripherals (see **Exhibit 2**). According to industry observers, mainframe hardware and associated products and services accounted for about 48% of IBM's 1990 revenues and about 53% of 1990 gross profits. Competition included companies such as Fujitsu, NEC, Unisys, Hitachi,

This case was prepared by Professor Frank V. Cespedes and Research Associate Laura Goode as the basis for class discussion rather than to illustrate either effective or ineffective handling of an administrative situation.

Amdahl, and Groupe Bull as well as companies that focused on specific product segments such as Tandem and Cray Research. Worldwide growth for mainframe products had slowed to an estimated 4% per annum by 1989, down from consistent double-digit growth rates through the early 1980s.

By 1991, this LOB's major product line was the System/390, including the ES/9000 family of processors which included: 10 air-cooled systems ranging in unit price from $70,000 to $3 million, and 8 more-powerful water-cooled systems priced from $2.5 million to more than $22 million. When this important addition to the mainframe product group was introduced in September 1990, it was IBM's "most comprehensive announcement of products, features, and functions in more than a quarter century . . . New hardware and software functions focus on almost every aspect of enterprisewide computing, extending the customer's ability to interconnect systems of varying types and allowing end users to access data wherever it may reside in an enterprise." An industry journal commented:[1]

> The new role is for the mainframe to become the repository for system management and database management functions while much of the computing is moved down to the departmental and distributed levels. Not all of the components have been delivered, but the scenario has been established.
>
> . . . IBM strove to design a systems architecture that enables (customers) to integrate all types of data and to use common standards for networking and sharing data across an enterprise. Five key attributes for the S/390 emerged from discussions with customers: 1) flexibility to adapt to configuration changes quickly and without shutdowns; 2) enterprisewide security to ensure data and application integrity and to safeguard corporate assets; 3) manageability that enables users to solve problems before they become processing bottlenecks and that automates remote systems control so that users can shift information processing out of data centers; 4) ability to add processing power, I/O (input/output devices) throughput, and storage capacity; and 5) ability to handle innovative new applications such as image processing.

A related development was the introduction in 1990 of a set of software programs called Office Vision, which was part of IBM's Systems Application Architecture (SAA: "an evolving set of strictly defined rules for the connections, or interfaces, between programs, databases, and complete computer systems in the IBM product line"). SAA development, the responsibility of the Programming Systems LOB, reflected an industrywide trend toward so-called "open systems architecture" that (in contrast to traditional proprietary systems architecture) could eventually allow mixing equipment from multiple vendors within the same system. In a departure from previous development efforts, IBM was sharing SAA specifications with outside software companies in an effort to encourage adoption of SAA as an industry standard.

[1]J. Moad, "Can Big Blue Reposition Big Iron?" *Datamation* (February 1, 1991), 54.

The ES LOB included 14 development labs: six for hardware/storage/peripherals development (three in New York State and one each in California, Arizona, and Germany) and eight for software development (seven in various areas of the United States and one in Germany). ES development also involved frequent interaction with six labs (in the United States, the United Kingdom, and other areas around the world) from other LOBs including Programming Systems and Communication Systems. In addition, the ES LOB had 12 manufacturing plants and, in total, about 28,000 employees in 1990.

ES AGMM

Mr. Martin Clague had been the ES AGMM since December 1988. Mr. Clague had been with IBM for 22 years, having previously been a marketing rep, branch manager, product-line planning manager, marketing operations vice president within U.S. M&S where he was in charge of the seven Areas in the East Coast region, as well as marketing and other management positions in IBM international units, including a stint as executive assistant to the president of IBM Europe. He described his current position in the following terms:

> I'm here to provide marketing input into product requirements. In practice, that means mediating systems specifications and market needs. But I do not set specifications with the 14 ES labs; that's beyond my scope. I provide ongoing marketplace information as an input for setting priorities concerning the many, complex, interrelated decisions made by Development managers in this LOB. I am also a liaison between Marketing and Development, and between these groups and the Industry organizations. This third dimension is a growing voice in the product-sales dialogue for this and other LOBs.
>
> Finally, I see myself as a brand manager—someone responsible for consistent, coherent worldwide merchandising of the ES line throughout the geographies. I made about 120 customer calls last year. Those calls are part of the merchandising task, and they provide market and key-account information useful in discussions with Development. Unlike the other LOBs, ES has an AGM of Development. The result is that strategy becomes, by definition, more shared, causing the AGMM to focus more on marketing and merchandising.

Mr. Clague interacted with four groups within IBM. First, he met with AGMMs in other LOBs, especially Programming Systems and Application Solutions. "Those LOBs provide much of the software that makes our hardware useful," he noted. "Also, as IBM moves toward providing compatibility across the line, decisions about application priorities and general platforms coherent with target markets require increased communication across the LOBs. The AGMMs are one conduit for sharing marketplace perceptions and important developments within each LOB." In addition, since the position was created, all AGMMs had met quarterly with Victor Goldberg, IBM vice president, Management Systems and Organization, to discuss common issues.

Second, Mr. Clague interacted with marketing managers in the geographies. He estimated that about 55% of his field time was spent outside the United States—"a percentage in keeping with the amount of ES revenues that come from non-U.S. areas," he noted. Most of these meetings concerned product announcements and introductions, including communications and other marketing programs associated with ES products and services. Mr. Clague explained:

> Especially as the ES line becomes the hub for truly enterprisewide computing systems at customers, our accounts become increasingly global in scope and their purchasing decisions are made with input from multiple customer locations around the world. Hence, our messages on issues such as price/performance features, future product directions/migration paths, and companywide support services must be commensurate around the world. Customers need to be confident that IBM has a unified, coordinated, worldwide product strategy for these systems, and I work to provide this coordination in our geographies.
>
> However, marketing budgets and decisions, including communications, are ultimately owned by the individual geographies, whose focus is Europe, Asia, U.S., etc. So, I have to work to get my unit included in planning and decision-making for advertising and announcements up-front, and not after the fact. Without constant "nudging," the geographies won't necessarily make these decisions for ES with a worldwide message in mind.

Mr. Clague also interacted with account teams. He noted that, in the ES line, "it's not uncommon for an account to purchase a package of equipment valued at $50–$100 million or more. In these deals, customers often demand direct contact with the LOB." Mr. Clague often made such calls, had a staff member serve as LOB representative, or helped to arrange for Development managers to meet with the account. In addition, as part of IBM's Partnership Executive program, in which about 200 large accounts were assigned a senior IBM executive as facilitator for any issues requiring top-management attention, Mr. Clague had responsibilities for nine accounts. He explained that, "as Executive Partner, I sometimes get involved in account planning and specific issues. But my other contacts with account teams are as representative for the LOB. Because I was a salesman for six years, a marketing manager and a branch manager, I'm smart enough to know what I don't know: the history, personalities, and truly important 'fault lines' at an account. Therefore, I don't try to change account strategies; I'm just the executive whose badge says 'product LOB' on it."

Third, Mr. Clague worked with the Industry and Sector organizations in the Applications Solutions LOB. IBM had identified certain target industries for which specific cross-LOB solutions were being developed. Each industry group was measured on market share and revenue performance, across all IBM product lines, for its particular industry. Five of these targeted industries—Manufacturing, Insurance, Banking, Distribution, and Public Sector—were traditionally large buyers of ES products. Mr. Clague noted that "I depend on these groups for requirements input; they talk in terms of solutions and applications across IBM's line, and the LOB must translate this into product specifications. In my opinion, we're not yet good at doing this, partly because the process is still new and partly because product development at ES necessarily works on a much-longer and wider development cycle than most other LOBs."

Fourth, Mr. Clague met with managers in the ES product divisions. Various AGMM managers worked with product division managers to develop two- and five-year plans regarding product introductions and product timing. Mr. Clague described this process as follows: "We take the technologists' product plans and translate it for the staff Marketing units in the geographies in order to influence their priorities and get their input. The product divisions tend to have affordability, systems imperatives, and technical leadership as their priorities, while Marketing is typically concerned with pricing and applications and is much less concerned with any one product line's long-range plans. So, it needs to be an iterative process, and any major disagreements can be escalated up to the LOB General Manager and, if necessary, to the MC."

Reflecting on the role of the AGMM, Mr. Clague commented:

> My unit has product marketing and product planning skills, but we're not developers and don't fund the requirements process in the labs or manufacturing. One of our biggest tasks has been trying to get the product divisions to think in terms of solutions throughout their development cycles. Conversely, in the field, the ES line often aligns with big accounts and very big-ticket purchases; so, customization issues are often uppermost in the minds of the field marketing units seeking to close those sales. One of our biggest tasks in the field is assuring consistency and coherence in our merchandising of the line around the world.
>
> The fact is that we sit in the middle between the LOB's development and manufacturing units and the geographies' marketing and sales units, but we don't "own" many resources on either side. So, information, personal relations, and judicious use of the escalation process become paramount management tools.

ES AGMM Organization: Roles and Responsibilities

Exhibit 2 outlines the ES AGMM organization which, in January 1991, was composed of 52 people responsible for three areas: market/systems strategy development, market support operations, and product introductions. The following pages provide a more detailed description of major roles and responsibilities within each area.

Market/systems Strategy   Ed Robbins had worked as an IBM marketing rep, a product manager for Storage Systems, in headquarters product-line planning functions, and as executive assistant to the general manager of U.S. M&S, before joining the ES AGMM. Mr. Robbins commented: "My key tasks are to publish this LOB's business plan, assure that market requirements are fed into labs throughout the planning process, and consolidate and coordinate individual lab plans—both within ES and with certain key labs in other LOBs." Reporting to Mr. Robbins were program managers for Market Opportunities, Market Requirements, and Market Strategy. These managers were responsible for gathering market information to aid in the strategy evaluation process, analyzing market requirements, and managing market research so as to better segment the market for large information processing capabilities. Also reporting to Mr. Robbins were two managers who, each assigned to an ES product division (Storage Systems and Data Systems), focused on issues more directly related to their respective division's product and business plans.

The business plan listed the products the LOB expected to bring to market during certain time frames. The plan specified product assumptions (including performance characteristics and planned introduction dates), forecasted volume levels, and revenue estimates. Mr. Robbins noted that "this overall ES plan is the result of individual labs' decisions regarding their constraints and investment priorities." This plan was utilized in the annual corporate planning process which consisted of a fall two-year operating plan and spring five-year plan. Mr. Robbins noted that these multiple processes were required to uncover any release-date conflicts, to monitor any differences between planned introductions and actual dates and components, and to manage LOB interdependencies. He described the process associated with the two-year plan as involving four major steps: (1) January: Worldwide Strategy Requirements; this first step was now driven by the Application Solutions LOB, which set certain target industries and solutions that, in turn, each LOB was expected to serve via its product and service components. (2) February–June: Worldwide Product, Marketing, and Service strategies; each LOB developed a two- to five-year plan outlining a budget and implementation schedule for accomplishing the goals determined during step 1. These plans were consolidated by the corporate strategy group and reviewed by the MC. (3) July–October: Business Investment Decisions; the MC made approval decisions regarding the LOB plans as well as resource-allocation decisions in areas such as headcount, capital investments, and LOB performance targets. (4) November–December: Budgeting; the LOB, within the resource parameters established in the previous step, put together a one-year budget with estimates for the following year. Mr. Robbins commented on several issues that tended to surface during the business planning process:

> One issue is dealing with the inevitable adjustments. As mainframe market growth has slowed in the 1980s, the ES LOB has downsized; so

we have large but increasingly finite resources. For example, last year we got to November and were then instructed to adjust downward by 5% the resources available to the LOB. This tends to force the issue of priorities and also generates numerous cross-lab investment, planning, and scheduling decisions.

Because large systems are such an important part of our heritage, installed base, account relations, and compatibility plans, feedback quickly generates a list of requirements that exceeds our resources. Meanwhile, the hardware and software labs have different development cycles (hardware typically much longer than software), but many interdependencies. In addition, each lab tends to prioritize vertically—that is, it focuses attention on maximizing human and capital resources for its own set of activities.

To address this issue, Mr. Robbins was emphasizing that certain "Focus Areas," rather than traditional product platforms, be used as the units of analysis in the planning process. Focus Areas included certain key technologies or applications areas (e.g., transactions processing, networking applications, integration of mainframes and workstations). "We should focus on these areas as priorities in our development process," said Mr. Robbins, "and work with other LOBs to maximize our offering in each area. But this is a big paradigm shift":

> For years, our large systems group has been successful by being technology driven against a changing but discrete set of big-iron competitors. Also, we've long developed and positioned our machines as general-purpose processors, not special-purpose application vehicles. But now our customers face multiple choices in how they will solve their problems, even from within IBM. In some areas, for example, customers can choose between purchasing one S/390 or 100 PS/2s as the processing vehicle. This cross-elasticity means that the labs must increasingly look at what ES products can do uniquely or best, and then use these Focus Areas as a calibration point for driving our priorities and resource tradeoffs.

The primary Development interfaces for Mr. Robbins and his staff were the lab directors and their Product and Planning managers. Each ES lab director was evaluated based on period development costs, keeping to scheduled commitments for product development, and product quality. The lab director's direct reports included several product and planning managers responsible for overseeing the lab's plans, coordinating with the LOB's manufacturing plants, and managing the actual design of product specifications. These managers, Mr. Robbins emphasized, "do the real work of making the machines run":

> We are good at gathering information from our installed base. Each lab has a long list of product requirements—features, add-ons, or system improvements that someone said should be done. But the sum to-

tal is greater than our available resources, and based on customer—rather than market segment—information. Part of my function is to provide an overall framework for making these spending decisions so that they maximize our overall revenues.

The ES line is so large and touches on so many potential applications, however, that this is easier said than done. Also, the development cycle here is probably the longest of any LOB, and so much of what *can* be done today is driven by what *was* done—by past commitments and investments. In reality, we in the AGMM probably have an impact, in any given year, on no more than 5–10% of the development budget in this LOB.

Market Support   Mr. Andrew Hurter, director of Market Support Programs, headed a group of program managers who provided field support for large systems marketing activities, including product technical support, product literature, internal and external education efforts, and account "troubleshooting" activities of various kinds. Mr. Hurter started with IBM in 1962 as a Systems Engineer, and then held several marketing and product management positions, including director of product strategy for the Data Systems and Storage Groups in the ES LOB, before moving to his current position in 1988. All program managers on his staff also had joint experience in IBM's product and marketing units. Mr. Hurter commented:

> Where Ed Robbins' group looks at product content and long-range plans, my group focuses on existing products in the short term: my main job is to optimize the marketplace performance of our line in the current quarter. Our product set tends to generate major purchase decisions that we deal with on an account-by-account basis. I can talk about specific needs with specific people at specific accounts. This type of involvement contrasts with that in most other LOBs.

Mr. Hurter and his staff often worked with account teams regarding a large ES purchase. "When customers make large mainframe acquisitions," Mr. Hurter noted, "they generally conduct very careful needs and resource assessments upfront. So, negotiations about configurations, pricing, delivery, support packages, services, and other matters can get lengthy and complicated. The account teams generally welcome our involvement in that process." These activities also brought Mr. Hurter into frequent contact with branch managers and the Large Systems Product marketing managers in each area. The subject of these meetings was often specific terms and conditions, including price, for a potential big-ticket ES transaction. Mr. Hurter described one mechanism utilized to facilitate these interactions:

> About once a month for the past three years, I have traveled to branch offices with three other managers: a representative from U.S. M&S [or another relevant country] headquarters, IBM's Special Bids group, and

IBM Credit Corporation. All of us are at the director level or above, and therefore can usually deal with specific issues that need to be addressed in order to close a sale. We may deal with a dozen or more account situations in a day, and insist that the account team make its case directly and concisely.

Mr. Hurter noted that his primary concerns at these meetings were "equity and repeatability. As I look at the proposal, I ask myself, 'do I want to make this a standard element in our marketing program?' ES transactions are often customer-specific, but each transaction is highly visible in the IS community and sets a precedent." Mr. Hurter also sought to manage the ES product mix and available inventory in responding to requests. "More than others at those meetings," he noted, "I know what our current product line, manufacturing, scheduling, and service/support situations are. So I can often propose a deal, based on upgrades or a differently configured product/service package, that meets customer requests without establishing an undesired precedent." He commented that "different managers at that meeting naturally have different priorities. The account team, of course, wants to close the sale; Special Bids is concerned about maintaining pricing policies, and the Credit Corporation focuses on the financial terms of different purchase vs. lease options":

> But the important thing is that, in the vast majority of cases, the account team leaves with an answer they can take back to the customer. Also, after a few hundred such situations, our group develops a pretty good "ear" for what's really going on in the marketplace for these products. One clear trend is that, in recent years, customers are making decisions later and later in the acquisitions process. This is a function of competition, the nature of the industry, and the impact of enterprisewide computing on the types of negotiations required. What happens, then, is that customers want delivery of a very complicated system very soon after the deal closes. Often our decisions are made only a few weeks, or even days, before desired shipment. The result is that development and manufacturing at the ES LOB often have to take on more of the risks involved, and I'm there in part to help us structure the risk-assumption in a manageable way.

Mr. Hurter's market support group also brought field information back into the ES LOB. He noted that this activity was largely informal: "We bring a wealth of knowledge back about product requirements and price-point pressures, and I alert both my development and finance brethren here to this information. But we're often looking at different time horizons. My data is rich but account-specific, and most customers are looking only 12–18 months ahead when they discuss I/S requirements. The labs, however, are thinking in 5–7 year timeframes and in terms of requirements that can span a number of customer groups. This makes it difficult to get Development to commit dollars based on this information."

Market Support managers also represented ES outside and inside IBM. Outside IBM, they communicated with the trade press, industry pundits, and (at the request of account teams) customers. Within IBM, they often spoke to Marketing training classes and other groups about the LOB's product directions and opportunities. Mr. Hurter noted: "I emphasize the increasing trend toward utilizing mainframes to manage and control I/S networks; that these large systems are the only way to manage data integrity at the highest level—a bigger issue as corporations increasingly view information as a key resource; that there are many applications that will never move to PCs or other single-user systems; and that, despite what often sounds in the business press like an obituary for large systems, these products remain a very healthy and profitable business for IBM." Finally, Mr. Hurter often met with marketing groups in the United States and other geographies: "I work to assure that ES products are adequately emphasized in their programs, and that the proper customer and field incentives are in place."

Product Introductions   Two groups in the ES AGMM were responsible for announcement and merchandising of ES products: one for CPUs (managed by Mr. Peter Tarrant), and one for peripherals (managed by Mr. William Nelson). "Our announcements are viewed as statements of direction by users, consultants, competitors, and other groups," noted Mr. Tarrant. "In addition, our product transitions are crucial: huge cash flows are at stake when you're moving from one generation of machines to the next, since customers sometimes stop buying your current machines while they decide whether to purchase new technology." The AGMM's involvement began twelve to eighteen months before introduction, and the goal was to ensure that the field was adequately educated about the new products, that product literature and promotional materials were accurate and available at the time of announcement, and that the announcement was coordinated while also appropriately customized for various worldwide markets.

The September 1990 System/390 and ES/9000 processor announcement (the largest in IBM's history in terms of number and revenue value of products) involved over 400 people. Although the announcement centered on the S/390 line produced by the ES LOB, a total of 140 hardware and software products, from 21 labs in 5 LOBs, were included. Mr. Tarrant was appointed as the chairman of the announcement group six months before introduction. In speaking with the casewriters, he utilized a number of charts that helped to outline the scope, timing, and different parties involved in such an announcement (see **Exhibits 3A** and **3B**). Commenting on the process, Mr. Tarrant noted that "our traditional announcements focused solely on product features. But Marty Clague was insistent that we merchandise the System/390 and ES/9000 announcement around platforms, applications, and user situations. This was a big difference for us, and had different implications for different areas within IBM."

Mr. Tarrant first put together the group of professionals from throughout the world who produced the announcement "deliverables" (i.e., the brochures, manuals, and other materials concerning the products and applications). Each geographical marketing organization at IBM (United States, Canada, Latin America, Asia Pacific, and EMEA) produced and funded its own deliverables. But the ES AGMM was a review point, responsible for worldwide consistency and coordination. Those involved in developing the materials included development personnel, product marketing managers, systems engineers, marketing reps, and headquarters marketing personnel, as well as 50 brochure writers from outside firms. The entire group was first educated about the product line by Development, and then cross-geography teams were established to oversee the form and content of the announcement materials. To illustrate the scope of the required effort, Mr. Tarrant pointed to a 28-page, single-spaced document entitled "Announcement Guide" which listed support materials for the S/390 (other guides were available for the other products involved), including a synopsis and intended audience for each document (see **Exhibit 3B** for an excerpt). "The actual documents," noted Mr. Tarrant, "fill a few warehouses and a number of branch offices." Mr. Tarrant also suggested three criteria in evaluating product announcements and introductions:

> First is the scope and quality of the communications about the new products and services. Internally, marketing and sales communications, including training, are crucial. Externally, communications with the media, trade press, consultants, and user groups are fundamental. We've always faced a tension here: between building excitement and understanding for an upcoming product, and managing the life cycles of existing products. The key is as small a gap as possible between announcement and shipment and, within that window, thorough education and motivation of the field.
>
> Second is the quality and relevance of the support materials. We now have many different applications, competitors, and end-user constituencies for different parts of a product line like the S/390. The support materials must go way beyond bits and bytes in order to be relevant.
>
> Third is the extent to which the announcement process itself generates the motivation of managers in the geographies. Compared to other LOBs, ES products are tried and true. There are advantages to this situation, but the disadvantage is that we have to work to get the field's attention in the midst of many new, less-complicated, shorter selling-cycle products from other LOBs. With sales compensation tied to total revenues, big-ticket ES products are often a big help in making volume quotas; but we don't get our proportional share of field time as measured by our share of total IBM revenues.

Commenting more generally on AGMM activities, Mr. Tarrant noted:

> IBM's move toward more decentralization, more P&L responsibility in the field, and more Trading Area General Managers has increased the

amount and variety of market-requirements information coming into the AGMM. In addition, changes in customer demographics, market growth rates, and purchasing patterns often lead to field demands for different product sizes and configurations. These are big, asset-intensive decisions for a product line like ES.

In staffing the AGMM, you need a balance between "short-timers" and "long-termers." On the one hand, rotating 12–18 month assignments in the AGMM for marketing managers keeps our field contacts and information current; on the other hand, our development and announcement processes are lengthy, and it takes time and continuity for an AGMM manager to understand the ES product strategy, develop contacts and trust in the development labs, and master the complexity of product introductions. My staff is about 80% short-timers and 20% long-termers, and I think that's about the right mix.

APPLICATION BUSINESS SYSTEMS (ABS)

The ABS LOB developed and manufactured IBM's mid-range product line, including processors, operating systems software and storage devices for products ranging in unit price from approximately $10,000 to $200,000. According to industry sources, market shares in these product segments (traditionally known as "minicomputers") were as follows:

	1985	1986	1987	1988	1989
IBM	20.8%	17.5%	18.4%	18.25%	29.4%
Digital Equipment	9.5	11.7	15.0	15.5	11.6
Hewlett-Packard	6.3	6.4	5.6	6.2	3.3
Wang	5.2	4.7	4.2	3.8	2.5
Fujitsu	2.6	3.6	3.7	4.1	5.7

One observer noted: "Minicomputers: the reports of their death have been highly exaggerated. True, they have been squeezed from below by the PC and workstation networks and from above by the mighty mainframes. The segment's share of overall industry sales has shrunk to 27% (in 1990) from 34% in 1984. Consequently, this segment has more walking wounded . . . than any other part of the computer industry. [But] IBM has had tremendous success with its new line of AS/400s.[2]

ABS's major product line was the AS/400, introduced in 1988 and (including the sales of peripherals, systems software, and maintenance contracts associated with this product family) the source of about $14 billion in revenues for IBM in 1990. According to industry sources, about 40%–50% of AS/400 installations in 1989–1990 were migrations from IBM's older S/36 and S/38 systems, while a smaller proportion of sales was attributable to

[2]B. R. Schlender, "Who's Ahead In The Computer Wars," *Fortune* (February 12, 1990), 64–65.

customers downsizing from a mainframe system to high-end AS/400 systems. Most remaining sales were either competitive replacements or sales to businesses making their initial purchase of a system. An estimated 60% of the potential market for mid-range, multi-user computer systems was at small and mid-sized companies; the other primary prospects were departments of large companies seeking a specific solution and/or industry-specific application. Many of the latter sales were orders for dozens or even hundreds of machines, and such "multiples" represented about 25% of 1990 AS/400 volume. Major competitors for the AS/400 included Digital Equipment's VAX Systems line, Compaq Computer's recently introduced SystemPRO line, and products by companies such as Altos Computer Systems, NCR, HP and others.

According to a trade-journal survey, AS/400 installations (through mid-1990) included the following industries:

Wholesale/Retail	26%	Banking	4%
Manufacturing	25%	Government	3%
Communication/Utilities	6%	Insurance	3%
Business Services	6%	Education	1%

To reach these segments, ABS relied heavily on external parties. IBM's relationships with these "Business Partners" ranged from joint marketing programs to collaborative development efforts to equity positions. The 1989 Annual Report described the role of these alliances:

> When we choose not to rely entirely on IBM's resources and join with other companies whose strengths complement and extend our own, the result can be access to technology, to software, or to specific markets and distribution channels. Around the world, for example, IBM has relationships with more than 10,000 joint marketers, systems integrators, and Business Partners who reach and support the majority of our AS/400 and PS/2 customers.

Within the ABS LOB (see **Exhibit 4**), there was one development lab and manufacturing site (in Rochester, Minnesota), which in 1990 was the recipient of the Baldrige Quality Award. The ABS LOB Rochester product management organization had their roots in IBM's General Systems Division (GSD), which was established in the 1970s to focus on mid-range systems. One executive commented:

> Throughout the 1970s, GSD was a stepchild unit at IBM that didn't receive as much corporate attention and resources as the big-system Data Processing Division (the predecessor of the ES LOB). One result is that "necessity became the mother of invention": the mid-range lab and manufacturing site has probably been more flexible in crafting industry-specific requirements, working with third parties, and using field information for product-development purposes.

The AS/400 line was utilized for applications that overlapped both larger and smaller systems sold by IBM. One trade journal commented:[3]

> Some I/S organizations are scrapping their S/370 systems and switching to networked AS/400s. The very AS/400 features that were supposed to appeal to the small- to medium-sized user (a relational database that is built into the operating system, a simple networking scheme, the machine's all-around user friendliness, its ability to be operated with a small programming staff) are attracting interest at large shops. . . . The bad news is that some of those sales are to users who might have migrated to (a new mainframe) but who now are detouring to the less expensive AS/400 line. The good news is that some of those customers include DEC users, plug-compatible competitors, and companies that have tried to get by with PC networks. "Sure, it means some lost revenues from companies that probably would have moved to (mainframe) machines," says an industry consultant. "But IBM has to be pleased that the AS/400 may stop inroads into IBM accounts. IBM is pragmatically aware that downsizing is the name of the game over the next decade. Unit prices may be lower, but you place more machines."

At the low end, the Personal Systems LOB introduced in 1990 a new workstation product, the RS/6000, originally targeted for scientific and engineering applications at unit prices ranging from approximately $12,000 to $90,000. The same trade journal noted:[4]

> Months after the announcement, the technical community is still buzzing about the RS/6000's raw workstation performance. Even the introductory model exceeds 27 million instructions per second and boasts impressive floating point performance that competitors (such as Sun and Digital) find difficult to match. These credentials, combined with at least a promise of enterprisewide operability, have IS managers looking beyond IBM's original positioning of the machine as a technical workstation. Now they're looking at the machine's potential for integration into existing corporate networks and as a platform for systems development. . . . Observers see some overlap, particularly with IBM's AS/400 line. The director of marketing at [an IBM reseller] says his company is seeing a lot of interest in the RS/6000 in markets traditionally served by minicomputers such as the AS/400. "In many areas, we're seeing a demand for the machine as a general-purpose business computer running our office automation software. I think it'll be interesting to see how far that goes."

In early 1991, the ABS LOB announced 11 new AS/400s including a high-end machine some 2.5 times faster than the biggest AS/400 previously

[3]David Stamps, "The AS/400's Surprise Role," *Datamation* (May 1, 1989), 49–50.
[4]Bob Francis, "Big Blue's Red Hot Workstation," *Datamation* (October 15, 1990), 28–32.

available and new low-end machines with improved price/performance. Ads introducing the new line commented: "What do you get if your company needs a computer that's bigger, faster, more connectable, easier to grow, easier to manage, and less expensive than the IBM AS/400? The new, bigger, faster, more connectable, easier to grow, easier to manage and less expensive IBM AS/400."

ABS AGMM

Mr. Bob Dies, the ABS AGMM, had joined IBM as a systems engineer in 1969, and then became a marketing rep, marketing manager, branch manager, regional manager, and head of product management in the Data Systems Division in 1984. In 1986, as part of a field reorganization in IBM U.S., Mr. Dies became president of the South-West Marketing Division, responsible for managing field marketing in about one-half of the continental U.S. (the president of the North-East Marketing Division at the time was Mr. Robert LaBant, the General Manager of the ABS LOB since 1989). Mr. Dies became the ABS AGMM soon after the position was formally established in 1988. He described his position in the following terms:

> When I became AGMM, the AS/400 had just been introduced successfully under Bill Grabe's leadership, and so the tasks were expanding past announcement management. We needed to build the business beyond our installed base of S/36 and S/38 users, and this required new marketing input and programs in addition to those associated with an initial product release.
>
> I view my key role as deciding what business this LOB should be in. Operationally, that means getting involved and having ultimate responsibility for market selection decisions. My job is to help target development resources toward areas, defined in terms of application segments, where we have major opportunities and advantages, and then to work with the geographies and partners to establish the requisite solutions, coverage, and skills needed.

Mr. Dies and other ABS executives had established a "Requirements Process" outlining key steps and primary responsibilities at each step (see **Exhibit 5**). Mr. Dies emphasized two aspects of this process: "First, market selection and segmentation are made explicit early in the process, even before systems issues are considered. Traditionally, IBM has *not* been good at market segmentation and we *must* be good at this in ABS, given the nature of our line, its uses, and competition. Second, time-to-market as well as capital are explicit parts of the investment decision. Accelerating development time and reaping first-mover advantages are probably more important throughout the industry, but especially in the many niche application segments that, in the aggregate, constitute our major opportunity in ABS."

In making market selection decisions, Mr. Dies noted that three criteria—

product design issues, market access/coverage issues, and solutions/applications availability—were paramount: "Imagine a three-legged stool consisting of product, coverage, and solutions. In ABS, we must pay more attention than other LOBs to all three legs of the stool. If we can't put in place any one of these three factors for a given segment, that opportunity should not be funded and pursued." To help coordinate design and manufacture of ABS products, Mr. Dies worked with managers in the ABS development organization in Rochester, Minnesota. He noted that:

> IBM has always had lots of customer data, but not much market-segment data. Thus, the labs have sometimes designed an optimal product for the installed base and then told Marketing to "run with it" to all potential users. Now when the lab here has a new idea, my role is to see how market and channel requirements and opportunities do or don't fit with the idea.
>
> Also, channel-productivity issues are important design criteria in our LOB. What makes sense for large systems sold by a dedicated account team is a general-purpose product that IBM systems engineers and the large account's DP staff can then configure for their specific needs. But with industry-oriented resellers as a key channel, the product needs more functions built into it so as to lower the support costs and requirements for IBM and the reseller. In turn, this means that market selection needs to play a greater role in product configuration decisions.

Mr. Dies also explained that development decisions in ABS should recognize what he called "the nature of the revenue food chain in our business":

> There are six sources of revenue in information systems: the hardware; peripherals; maintenance revenues; upgrade revenues; any financing revenues; and revenues from applications software. In ABS, we have a better shot than some other LOBs at capturing more of that total revenue potential. In micro-computers, for instance, many of those revenue components do not exist in quantity or are easily captured by external parties; in mainframes, a whole infrastructure of specialized parties has arisen to capture different portions of that revenue chain. But our proprietary AS line gives us an advantage in capturing after-market revenue in appropriately selected segments.

Once a target market was selected, Mr. Dies worked with both external and internal groups in establishing solutions. Externally, establishing and managing relations with Business Partners who developed and/or marketed AS/400 solutions were crucial: "Probably the most important AGMM activity in this LOB," noted Mr. Dies "is to make the Business Partners effective advocates of our products." Internally, Mr. Dies' interacted with Sector/Industry and Marketing units at IBM. He estimated that these efforts were split "about 50:50 between U.S. and International units," and contrasted the "internal marketing" requirements in each area:

In the U.S., separate organizational units own the industry-oriented sector units and the field sales organizations, and the move toward Trading Area management increases the complexity. In the U.S., I typically first approach the Sector units to get funding for specific solutions, and then work with headquarters marketing groups on merchandising this solution via our sales force. Overseas, one Country Manager owns the sales force and, because most countries lack the scale and size of the U.S., there is usually not a separate sector/solutions organization. As a result, it's a simpler interface for me.

In targeting solutions, Mr. Dies played an active role in the LOB's selection of 50 Application Opportunity Segments. This list was developed by first choosing broad industry groups (e.g., Distribution businesses) as potential opportunities for ABS products, and then adding successive levels of detail (e.g., beverage distribution) for solutions development. Mr. Dies emphasized that the "detail is key in our business. We don't sell 'retail systems'; we sell solutions to food stores, mass merchandisers, boutiques, etc. Similarly, we can't target 'financial services'; we must target discrete segments and applications at commercial banks versus brokerage firms versus community financial institutions, etc. The best solutions add the most value on this basis, and the most effective Business Partners are usually those aligned with specific segments."

Mr. Dies indicated that, of the three components of ABS market selection decisions, "coverage is probably the most difficult to put in place." The need to provide products/solutions both by market niche and geography often required coordination of numerous Business Partner and IBM sales organizations, and each group presented different marketing constraints and opportunities. "I believe our major constraint to growth in this LOB," Mr. Dies noted, "is channel coverage and capabilities":

> Business Partners are increasingly numerous, but it's not easy to find a partner with a good application in the needed geography. Also, as our systems get more powerful, some potential applications outstrip the development or marketing capabilities of many Partners. Conversely, the IBM salesforce sells the entire IBM line and, despite recent moves in this direction, often lacks the level of vertical orientation that we require. In addition, with sales compensation based on total revenues, mid-range systems sold on the basis of specialized applications and co-marketing efforts with external Partners are, from the viewpoint of marketing reps in some branches, not necessarily the biggest revenue generators or most efficient way to make Hundred Percent Club.

Commenting more generally on the AGMM role, Mr. Dies noted:

> Depending upon how the money is counted, the ABS LOB is the second- or third-largest IS business in the world. But IBM's heritage is developing and selling large systems to large accounts—a business

where the sheer consistency of the vendor is important. This need for consistency is still reflected in many of our basic marketing and development policies. The core of the mid-range business, however, is many small segments with diverse requirements. Many of the skills required to meet these requirements, moreover, don't reside in-house, so various external Business Partners become important and they, too, are a diverse bunch. Also, product life cycles in mid-range are shorter than in larger systems, so speed-to-market is important.

A task facing our AGMM unit is meeting these diverse requirements in the context of a larger organization established on the principles of in-house control and worldwide consistency. We spend a lot of time in this LOB trying to be explicit and consistent in our market-selection and development decisions, and then merchandising the line differently in different segments and geographies.

ABS AGMM Organization: Roles and Responsibilities

Exhibit 4 outlines the ABS AGMM organization which, in January 1991, was composed of 26 managers responsible for two major areas: market strategy and market support.

Market Strategy William Zeitler had been with IBM for 20 years in technical marketing, systems engineering, product marketing, and development positions before becoming the ABS director of market strategy in 1989. He noted that "my unit is responsible for the over-all strategy of ABS products in the markets we choose to serve; we think of ourselves as the 'headlights' for the LOB—shedding light on where our products and solutions need to be a bit farther down the road; and we also influence investment levels and priorities." Within Mr. Zeitler's unit, four groups worked on different aspects of market strategy.

The Systems/Strategy Process unit consisted of managers responsible for monitoring mid-range trends, competitive offerings, and the positioning of ABS products. In the past, Mr. Zeitler noted, "competitive analysis at IBM has typically focused on product price/performance comparisons. By contrast, we analyze positioning issues in terms of applications requirements, service and support costs and needs in a segment, and coverage issues; and the role of systems/strategy managers is to make these elements explicit in the LOB's budgeting process."

Market Planning was handled by a staff of Segment Managers, each assigned to a market that ABS had chosen to pursue and provide a solution for. The segment managers, Mr. Zeitler explained, "team-up with product managers in the lab. The lab people drive the product part of our efforts, while the segment managers drive the nonproduct parts—for example, what applications are important, service requirements, and the links between product design and field selling requirements. In effect, the segment managers put requirement and financial gates on development efforts with a particular segment in mind."

Functional Strategies referred to a unit that focused on connections among application requirements, distribution requirements, and service/support strategies.

Business Development consisted of a small group that helped to establish and coordinate alliances with external groups intended to fill any hardware or software gaps in the ABS line. These alliances differed from Business Partners in that the latter were typically utilized for a specific segment's application or coverage requirements, while alliances were typically established to develop a core product requirement (e.g., with Ethernet for network capabilities).

The primary Development interfaces for Mr. Zeitler and his staff were the various Lab Directors and their Product and Planning managers in Rochester, Minnesota. He noted that "I have some relationships there from previous positions, and the GM of this LOB has a marketing background. Also, the Rochester facility is a first-class operation, as evidenced by the recent Baldrige award." He indicated that, when there were differences between Development and AGMM units, they typically concerned how "feature-rich" a product should be:

> Remember that each lab is organized to focus on one or more components—the processor, peripherals, software, etc.—of what is finally a technically complex end-product. Each lab works for years on its chunk of the product, and the natural tendency is to optimize that chunk—to provide the state-of-the-art configuration—within cost and scheduling goals. But the overall result is often an end-product with costs too high to support a competitive market price or too late to capture important first-mover advantages. Our role in the AGMM is to increase the market tension in this process. One way we do this is by having more direct access to information about cost/feature tradeoffs earlier in the product development process.

The ABS AGMM unit had a limited budget that could be used to fund certain development priorities. Mr. Zeitler noted that "our development monies are small compared to the lab's total budget, but these monies can be used to help establish tradeoff priorities." He cited a recent example:

> We in the AGMM believed strongly that a new low-end AS/400 would be an important addition to our line, and we established a price point for such a product. We then informed the relevant product manager in the lab that her group could have $15 million and a certain time frame to spend on this development project. She came back with a figure of $25 million and a longer development schedule, and our response was to indicate that we would take our $15 million to IBM's Asia Pacific Technical Operations group in order to get the work done. Her reaction was, "we'll investigate our assumptions and get back to you." The good news is that this process forces a healthy prioritization

of development time and resources in the LOB; the bad news is that I'm not the most popular person in the Development group.

Another issue between the AGMM market strategy unit and the Labs was often the respective roles of IBM and selected Business Partners in the solutions provided to a segment. Mr. Zeitler's unit conducted ongoing audits and analyses of the financial allocations associated with each selected market and then generated plans proposing optimal deployment of IBM development reosurces in these areas. These data and plans were then discussed at meetings with the labs in which spending levels were negotiated. Mr. Zeitler noted that "these meetings give us an additional understanding of price/features tradeoffs and, conversely, it gives the labs more information about how our products are (and aren't) being utilized. A key here is the depth and currency of market information we bring to the table, and we're helped in this regard by the AGMM Market Support groups."

Market Support Mr. Mark Ryan, director of market support for the ABS AGMM, had worked in a variety of marketing positions at IBM as well as one year as executive assistant to the CEO. He noted that, "a combination of field and headquarters experience is essential in this position. The field experience and contacts are crucial, and understanding how things do and don't get done at headquarters is very useful." Mr. Ryan's group handled three sets of activities: Market Operations, Application Programs, and Special Offerings.

Within Market Operations, one group focused on product announcements and introductions. This included ensuring that proper product and application education was in place (both for IBM field units and Business Partners), that the content of the product literature was accurate and accessible, that the literature was distributed in a timely manner, that the necessary promotions were developed, and that the trade press and industry consultants were adequately informed. Mr. Ryan noted that "while the field units actually implement product introductions, our group coordinates it and that's a year-round process. Especially in this line of business, an announcement is now much more than details about the box; it involves explaining and coordinating the package of applications, services, channels, and other factors that accompany the hardware." During and after introduction, an Industry Marketing manager in the AGMM was the liaison with industry groups in various IBM units concerning the product line.

A Marketing Programs manager was responsible for much of the product positioning analyses associated with the ABS line as well as educating field units and Business Partners about the line. Mr. Ryan emphasized that "about 75% of our volume in this LOB is touched by a Business Partner. It's essential that they understand the intended uses of a product and how to sell relevant applications to target segments." A Marketing Support manager oversaw meetings of the LOB's Customer Advisory Council and Business Partner Advisory Council. At these meetings, ABS managers provided information about product developments and solicited feedback from key customers and Business Partners. Mr. Ryan noted that the information exchanged at such meetings was usually very technical, and these meetings had been run by the Development lab. But the AGMM took over responsibility for these councils in 1989.

Unique to the ABS AGMM unit was a telemarketing operation that called all installed ABS customers within three months of installation in order to check on customer satisfaction, identify any problems, and consider whether an account was a candidate for migration from an S/36 or S/38 (in 1990 there were approximately 450,000 such systems installed worldwide to more than 230,000 customers) or ancillary sales of an AS/400. This unit had been established in 1988, and provided this information to ABS development groups and market research in the AGMM itself. In 1990, the ABS AGMM began selling this information to other LOBs and field marketing units. Mr. Ryan noted that, "initially we simply gave this information to U.S. M&S and other marketing units, and their attitude seemed to be, 'you are the LOB and we're Marketing, so stay out of our business.' But now that they pay for the information, and have seen its value as a source of leads and other marketing activities, they have more of a sense of ownership and are more supportive of this AGMM activity."

Application Programs managers handled different activities associated with establishing solutions for ABS products. A Business Partner Development manager handled contracts, requirements, and funding issues that arose between ABS and potential Business Partners identified by the AGMM's industry marketing manager. In these partnerships, IBM typically loaned Business Partners capital to finance the porting of an existing application to ABS equipment. In return, IBM received a percentage of the Business Partner's sales of that application for three to five years. Mr. Ryan noted that "we assume much of the financial risk and provide lots of marketing presence and support. The Business Partner's risk is the investment in time and other resources required to develop the application. A Business Partner may decline to work with us for any of a number of reasons: they don't have the necessary personnel or other resources, they're happy with their current status, or a given Business Partner is a 'platform bigot' whose skills are tied to a different operating system. In the aggregate, however, we've found our program to be very attractive and successful, and we decline more potential Business Partners than we accept." A Business Partners Programs manager was responsible for keeping established Business Partners informed about any features, functions or relevant applications for the ABS line. In addition, an AGMM manager ran the LOB's Migration Support Lab, which consisted of technical personnel who assisted installed S/36 and S/38 users in migrating to the AS/400 line. This lab also located and disseminated tools that IBM and its Partners had developed to manage the necessary translations of programming code and other matters.

Special Offerings and Key Account Support managers helped to structure large, multiple-unit deals for the ABS line. Mr. Ryan also became involved in such activities, and noted that "our group represents the LOB to the customer, and within limits we can commit required development/customization resources."

A Merchandising manager was responsible for managing the image of ABS products, both internally and externally. This included numerous presentations within IBM about ABS products and goals as well as external merchandising activities with the trade press and other groups. Finally, a manager of International Assignees had been recently appointed to handle relations with international units, including any Business Partner or development issues that a given country or region might present.

Mr. Ryan also chaired quarterly, all-day meetings of the AS/400 Executive Steering Committee, which consisted of managers from the ABS LOB and mid-range product managers from the geographies. The agenda for a recent such meeting covered the following topics: discussion of sales performance of recent low-end product introduction and recommendations; proposal for new client-server capabilities to high-end product; presentations from various Industry Group managers; discussion of AS/400 vs. RS/6000 positioning issues; review of announcement plans for new AS/400 product by major geographical area. Mr. Ryan commented: "The ABS LOB is a $14 billion business. But it currently represents less than 10% of IBM's assets and a business opportunity—small and mid-sized commercial customers—that is relatively fragmented and diverse by our traditional standards. We must work to keep our internal marketing units knowledgeable and motivated to sell our line, and we must also recognize that our major business opportunity is growing faster in other countries than in the United States."

CONCLUSION

In separate meetings with the casewriters in early 1991, both Mr. Clague and Mr. Dies emphasized that the AGMM role was still evolving and that, during the past three years, their individual activities as AGMMs had involved a fair amount of "learning by doing." Asked to provide advice or guidelines to any future AGMMs, each stressed the particular circumstances that characterized different LOBs and they identified the following as some of the key issues that the manager of an AGMM organization must consider:

- In a given LOB, how should one define the basic role of the AGMM unit in relation to other groups—at that LOB as well as in various corporate and field units—that perform similar and complementary activities?
- What is the best allocation of available AGMM time and resources among the various groups (e.g., LOB Development groups, field marketing units, industry organizations, other LOBs, and external parties including customers and partners) that the AGMM potentially deals with? How can the appropriate allocation be encouraged via structures, systems or process within the AGMM organization?
- How can the AGMM build the necessary connections, trust and (in the words

of one manager) "leverage" required to manage the interactions and negotiations with other important groups at IBM?

- Finally, within a given AGMM organization, what mix of background experience, skills, and temperament should guide staffing decisions? How do these criteria fit with traditional and emerging marketing and management career paths at IBM?

EXHIBIT 1 IBM Lines of Business (LOBs): Overview

Enterprise Systems, responsible for IBM's mainframe products and associated software, storage systems, printers, and other peripheral equipment. "Customers today are calling upon ES products to handle increasingly complex tasks such as managing global networks consisting of thousands of terminals, rapid processing of millions of transactions, and manipulating very large data bases. These systems provide IBM's greatest information-handling capabilities."

Application Business Systems, responsible for IBM's mid-range processors and related software and operating systems, including the AS/400, S/36, and S/38 minicomputers. This LOB also developed storage devices for IBM's mid-range and Personal System/2 products. "Midrange systems represent a substantial opportunity for growth for IBM . . . Many of the midrange systems sold each year are bought by large companies for use as departmental systems or as part of distributed configurations. However, about two-thirds of these systems are purchased by small- and intermediate-sized businesses. Their data processing requirements are growing dramatically—as much as 2.5 times faster than those of large enterprises."

Personal Systems, responsible for IBM's desktop systems, including the Personal System/2, the high-performance RT workstation, and their operating systems software and supplies. "The potential of the desktop market will grow further as the performance, capacity and ease of use of personal systems and workstations continue to improve . . . The RT systems, IBM's Reduced Instruction Set Computer (RISC) technology workstation, can perform complex information processing tasks that normally require much larger computers. It can be used for manufacturing tasks and for engineering/scientific applications, as well as for a variety of business and administrative applications, including accounting, financial analysis and data base management."

Programming Systems, 27 labs responsible for development of data management software, programming languages, and application development software, as well as the development and implementation of Systems Application Architecture (SAA). "SAA development efforts are concentrated on three basic customer requirements. First, users want a uniform view of applications across multiple systems. Second, application program interfaces—including tools, languages and services—should be consistent in all environments. Finally, standards should be consistent to facilitate the exchange of applications across different systems. Under SAA, applications written for one computer can be shifted without difficulty to a different system and run efficiently."

Communication Systems, responsible for communications products including controllers, modems, connectivity and network management software, Systems Network Architecture (which provides rules and codes that enable users to establish and manage information networks), and internal telecommunications for IBM U.S. "Customers must be able to manage and distribute information through all levels of their business in a timely, reliable and cost-efficient manner. Ensuring that customers have the tools to do this is the mission of the Communication Systems LOB . . . Success in the rapidly growing telecommunications market rests on increased connectivity, including linking IBM equipment to that of other vendors."

Technology Products supplied other LOBs' development and manufacturing sites with semiconductors, circuit packaging, and other components for use in the company's product line.

Application Solutions, embedded within the U.S. Marketing & Services organization, was created to "unite application development, systems integration, professional services, and market development activities, and also to focus on furthering IBM's ties with companies that develop, market, and install IBM products. . . . Application Solutions' first priority is to understand the customer's business thoroughly and then devise a solution. That solution could come from IBM's broad range of information-handling products, or could be a unique system that combines IBM's offerings with those of other companies . . . Industry marketing units and the market development organizations within Application Solutions work with enterprises to identify new opportunities for applying information technology."

Note: All quoted comments from 1988 IBM Annual Report.

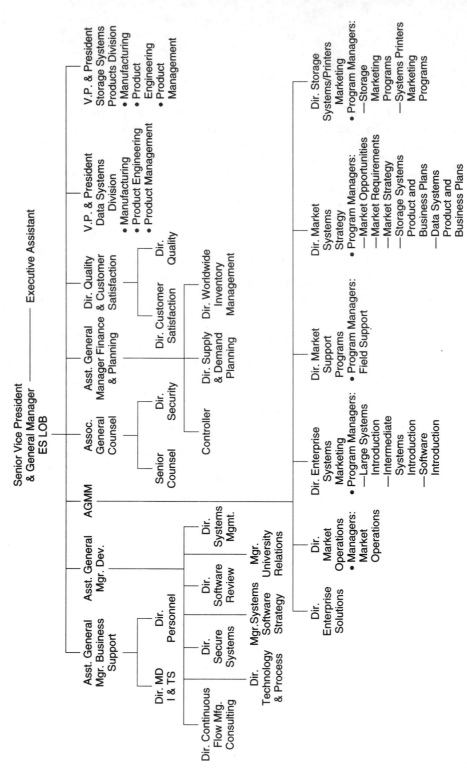

EXHIBIT 2 Enterprise Systems: Organization Chart

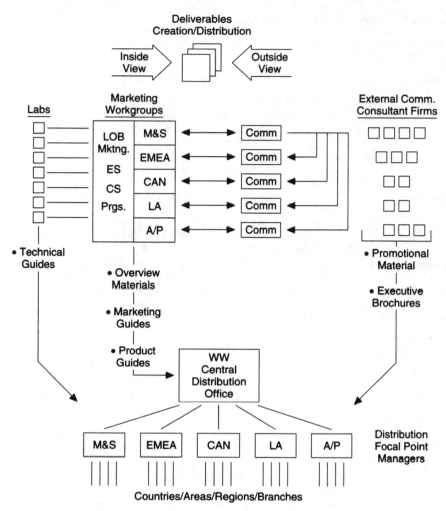

EXHIBIT 3A   Enterprise Systems: Product Announcements

EXHIBIT 3B   S/390 Announcement Guide (Excerpts)

This guide provides a listing of promotional and technical support materials for the System/390 announcement.

Category	Title/Description/Audience
Presentation Guide	System/390 Executive Overview: This presentation provides a very high-level overview of the S/390 announcement, and relates the announcement content the customer's business concerns. It is intended for the CEO and CIO executive levels.
Presentation Guide	System/390 Systems Excellence: Provides a comprehensive overview of the S/390 products from a systems perspective. Intended for IS executives and DP managers.
Reference Guide	Enterprise Systems Architecture: The purpose of this guide is to give a quick reference and comparison of the functions, features and benefits of the MVS, VM, and VES software platforms as they relate to ES Architecture S/390. The audience is IS executives, DP management, and DP staff.
Presentation Guide	ES/9000 Competitive Considerations: Reviews the competitive considerations for the ES/9000 lines and positions the customer value and systems leadership of the line. The audience is IBM marketing representatives and systems engineers.
Reference Guide	Services Offerings: This is a guide to all IBM Services sales promotion brochures, specification sheets and flyers. It is designed to assist the field in ordering appropriate literature for sales calls. The audience is IBM marketing reps.
Brochure	Financing Your ES/9000 Enterprise Solution: This brochure introduces IBM credit support for the ES/9000 product line. The advantages of financing with ICC are outlined along with the range and diversity of ICC offerings. The audience is CFO, IS executives, and DP management.
Storyboard	SAA Language Access Query Interface Storyboard: This package allows you to demonstrate some of the key features and functions of the SAA Interface. The package includes a demo and script. Available through electronic media. Audience is IS and DP management.
Presentation Guide	Technical Computing Perspectives: The ES/9000 with optional Vector Facility represents a significant ability to fulfill processing needs of technical end users. This publication outlines the use of computer servers, file servers, workstations, and mixed-vendor networks for scientific and technical computing, and summarizes available software support. Audience is DP management and technical end users.
Brochure	IBM System/390—Extending the Reach of Your TPF System: Discusses how currently installed TPF users, through the implementation of System 390, will realize an increased payback in terms of capacity, availability, and price/performance. The specific industry segments mentioned include airlines, financial firms, and retail distribution systems. Applications referenced include reservations, credit authorization, bank tellers, switch, query, and police dispatch. The audience is IS executives.

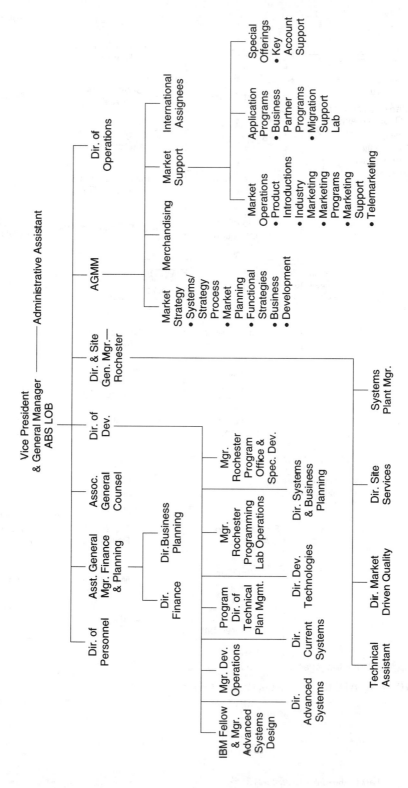

EXHIBIT 4 Application Business Systems: Organization Chart

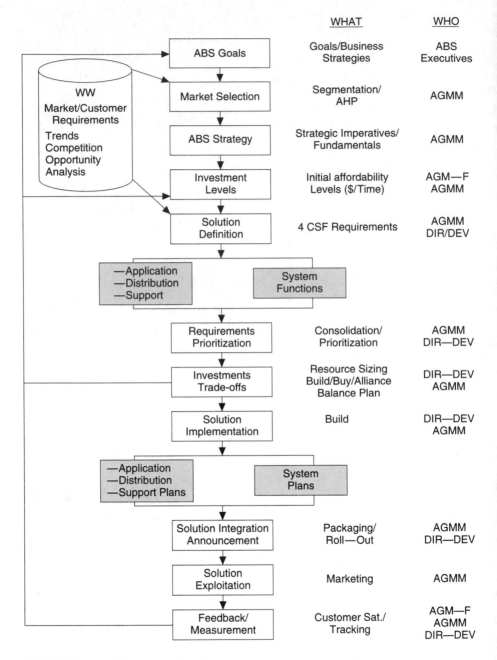

	WHAT	WHO
ABS Goals	Goals/Business Strategies	ABS Executives
Market Selection	Segmentation/ AHP	AGMM
ABS Strategy	Strategic Imperatives/ Fundamentals	AGMM
Investment Levels	Initial affordability Levels ($/Time)	AGM—F AGMM
Solution Definition	4 CSF Requirements	AGMM DIR/DEV
—Application —Distribution —Support / System Functions		
Requirements Prioritization	Consolidation/ Prioritization	AGMM DIR—DEV
Investments Trade-offs	Resource Sizing Build/Buy/Alliance Balance Plan	DIR—DEV AGMM
Solution Implementation	Build	DIR—DEV AGMM
—Application —Distribution —Support Plans / System Plans		
Solution Integration Announcement	Packaging/ Roll—Out	AGMM DIR—DEV
Solution Exploitation	Marketing	AGMM
Feedback/ Measurement	Customer Sat./ Tracking	AGM—F AGMM DIR—DEV

WW
Market/Customer Requirements
Trends
Competition
Opportunity
Analysis

▨ Solution Management Related

EXHIBIT 5 ABS Requirements Process Overview

EXHIBIT 6   Representative Calendars (Fall 1990)

M. Clague:

Day 1:   8:45–10:00   ES Quality Meeting: Marketing,
                      Manufacturing
        10:00–11:30   ES Segmentation Meeting: AGMM Proposal
        11:30–1:00   Worldwide Opportunity Council: New
                      Solutions
         1:30–2:30   Hold for Management Committee
         2:30–3:30   Prep for Customer Call
         4:00–5:00   Customer Call (large commercial bank)

Day 2:   8:30–10:30   U.S. Strategy Integration: AGMMs
        10:30–12:30   Transactions Processing Review
         1:00–2:00   User Group Requirements: Development
         2:30–3:30   Petroleum Industry Review
         4:00–5:30   LASER Branch Managers Meeting: Present ES
                      Directions
         5:30–7:00   Spring Planning Cycle Organizational Meeting

Day 3:   8:30–12:00   General Managers Meeting: Present Quality
                      Report
        12:15–1:15   Interview: *Business Week*
         2:00–   Travel to Amsterdam/Prep for Customer Call

Day 4: 10:00–12:00   Customer Call (large airline)
         1:30–3:00   Q&A Session With IBM Europe Staff: ES
                      Directions
         3:00–4:30   Meetings with ES Product Directors
         5:00–   Travel to Copenhagen/Prep for Customer
                      Call

Day 5:   8:00–9:30   Hold for Conference Call: Announcement
                      Strategy
        10:00–11:00   Meet with Account Team
        11:00–12:00   Customer Call (large commercial bank)
         1:00–2:00   Meet with Account Team
         2:00–3:00   Customer Call (large insurance company)
         4:00–   Travel to New York City

B. Dies:

Day 1:   8:30–10:00   Channel Scenarios Meeting
        10:00–11:30   Solutions Development Meeting
        11:30–1:00   Monthly Measurements
         1:30–2:30   Business Partners Strategy
         2:30–5:00   ABS AGMM Staff Meeting

Day 2: 8:00–9:00   Prep for Customer Call
        9:00–10:00   Customer Call (large commercial bank)
        10:00–12:00 General Managers Meeting: Present ABS LOB
                     Fall Plan
        1:00–2:00   Hold for Management Committee Meeting
        2:00–3:00   Baldrige Communication Plan
        3:00–   Travel to Atlanta
        8:00–   Dinner with Area Manager

Day 3: 8:30–11:30   Meetings with Area Management: ABS
                     Strategy,Product Plans, Financial Model
        11:30–12:30 1990 Sales Plan Meeting via Teleconference
        1:00–5:00   Regional Kickoff Meeting: Present ABS
                     Directions
        7:00–   Travel to New York City

Day 4: 8:00–9:00   AS/400 Software Meeting: AGMM, Labs,
                     Channel Management
        9:00–11:00   ABS/U.S. Industry Requirements and
                     Programs: Overview
        11:00–12:00 SAA Briefing
        11:00–12:00 SAA Briefing
        12:00–1:00   Lunch with another AGMM
        1:00–2:30   S/36 and S/38 Migration Update
        2:30–4:30   Business Partners Meeting
        4:30–6:00   Review for Worldwide Opportunity Council
                     Meeting

Day 5: 8:30–10:00   Worldwide Opportunity Council Meeting:
                     Present Request
        10:45–1:00   ABS 1991 Revenue Outlook Meeting: ABS
                     Management
        1:00–2:30   Market Selection Meeting
        2:30–4:00   Customer Call (large distributor)

PART II

Consumer Goods Markets

Coordinating Sales and Marketing in Consumer Goods Firms

An executive describes a common situation at consumer goods firms:

> Our marketing managers operate at a national level and with specific product orientations. They're not as familiar with regional or account differences.
>
> Meanwhile, Sales is driven by specific accounts, volume shipments, and trade deals. It's my observation that Marketing and Sales managers do talk to each other, but typically when it's clear that they won't hit their numbers. Then, interaction increases significantly.

A sales manager at this firm describes product managers as "ivory-tower headquarters theorists, unaware of field realities." A product manager describes salespeople as "primarily interested in the deepest deal that moves the most product, regardless of the impact on profitability." Meanwhile, service personnel (in this case, delivery and in-store merchandising personnel) complain that their activities are constantly "disrupted by the *ad hoc* arrangements that increasingly characterize Marketing-Sales interactions in a marketplace where trade customers are more powerful and demanding."

Many firms have recognized that success in the current consumer marketing environment requires better coordination between brand "pull" and

Frank V. Cespedes, *Journal of Consumer Marketing*, Vol. 10, No. 2 (1993), pp. 37–55, © MCB University Press, 0736–3761.

sales "push" programs (Kopp and Greyser, 1987), with consequent impacts on the activities of brand managers (Quelch et al., 1992). But little research has been devoted to identifying dimensions of required coordination between these groups, market developments that affect their interactions, or how managers can usefully evaluate organizational changes aimed at improving performance of their joint activities.

This study (see Appendix) found that the factors affecting marketing-sales coordination requirements in consumer goods firms go way beyond the oft-documented fact of increased spending on trade promotions, and that companies are responding to these requirements with a variety of organizational initiatives. This article first discusses factors that make better brand-sales integration a prerequisite for effective marketing practice in many consumer goods categories. Next, the strengths and vulnerabilities of current initiatives in this area are considered. Then, the article outlines implications for managers interested in improving linkages between these groups.

CHANGING COORDINATION REQUIREMENTS

In most consumer goods firms, product marketing and field sales have historically been managed as separate but complementary activities, with the emphasis on brand development efforts targeted at consumers. The primary goal has been to establish product positioning and differentiation compelling enough to "pull" consumers toward a preferred brand. In turn, this consumer preference becomes a key element in the salesforce's negotiations with the trade for shelf-space and promotional support. Although this view of marketing-sales relations is often attributed to the institution of brand-management organizations, it had long been characteristic of major consumer goods manufacturers. In 1910 an executive at the Shredded Wheat Company emphasized: "If the advertising department is what it should be, the salesmen will be merely distributors. It is their job to keep in touch with the trade. They don't need to sell goods. The goods are already sold . . . The advertising manager should evolve, originate and formulate the selling arguments that are to be used by the sales organization" (De-Weese, 1910). As Strasser (1989) also documents, "In most companies, sales management developed separately from advertising, and the relations between the managers of sales and advertising departments were often troublesome matters of company politics."

This model of interaction assumes a sequential process in which product management's marketing plans are executed by field sales personnel at wholesalers and retailers. In this alignment, brand management becomes the central "hub of the wheel" or a group of "little general managers"—to use common metaphors for describing product management's traditional role in consumer marketing. The following 1991 job description, from a major U.S. packaged-goods firm, illustrates traditional responsibilities:

The Product Manager is the primary force behind all programs affecting the Brand. The Product Manager assumes broad strategic responsibilities and serves as the company expert in all matters pertaining to the Brand. The Product Manager is responsible for initiating and leading business development programs, executing and controlling the marketing plan, coordinating all department and staff resources, developing strong working relationships with the ad agency, and training/developing the Brand group.

In contrast to Product Marketing's "broad strategic responsibilities" at headquarters, Field Sales in various geographic locations has the role of implementation or "managing distribution"—to use a common means of construing sales management's traditional role in consumer marketing. The same packaged-goods firm outlines the responsibilities of sales management as follows:

1. Track volume and share trends for key brands in assigned market area and at specific retail accounts.
2. Develop sales presentations for retail buyers/merchandisers, including business reviews.
3. Evaluate field sales performance with regard to:
   • obtaining new item distribution;
   • selling merchandising support;
   • achieving optimal shelf-positioning.

With these roles and responsibilities, coordination of these groups is important. But such "coordination" typically involved training, sales planning, and promotion scheduling efforts aimed at ensuring that the field "doers" in fact do what the marketing strategists have planned. What factors are affecting this delineation of marketing vs. sales tasks and so changing coordination requirements between these groups? Managers interviewed for this study indicated that the relevant factors include important changes in what is being bought by the trade customers of consumer goods firms (nature of the product offering), the marketplace in which manufacturers' goods are sold (market fragmentation), how they are sold (supply chain management requirements), and under what product life cycle conditions they are sold (see **Figure 1**).

In the aggregate, these developments require alterations in conventional distinctions between marketing strategy and sales implementation, and—within traditional citadels of brand marketing—make the salesforce a crucial crossroad in organizing and implementing marketing efforts.

Nature of the Product Offering

In the traditional alignment of marketing-sales responsibilities, the "product" is synonymous with the "brand." The manufacturer sells this product *to* the consumer *through* the trade. But more concentrated trade channels have altered exchange terms in many product categories, requiring manufacturers to tailor their product programs to individual retailer needs

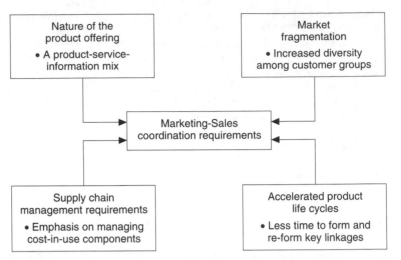

FIGURE 1 Factors Affecting Marketing-Sales Coordination Requirements

and local market conditions. One result is that what successful manufacturers increasingly offer to their trade customers is a product-service-information mix composed of the brand(s), service support, and ongoing information exchange about product movement, shelf-management, and other selling conditions.

A salient example is the buyer-seller relationships established in the past few years between P&G and certain retail chains. Via on-site account teams and on-line links between its factories and the retailers' stores, P&G has established customized ordering systems and automatic replenishment programs in a number of product categories. This has benefits for both retailer and manufacturer. For the retailers involved, warehouse and backroom inventories can be reduced substantially (from a typical 30 days' worth of detergent, for instance, to as little as two days). Further, faster turns of smaller amounts of inventory often allow the retailer to reorder and generate sales before payment to the manufacturer is due, thus generating cash flows without additional working capital allocations to finance the inventory—a significant buying criterion at many highly leveraged retail organizations. For the manufacturer, such arrangements mean more predictable shipments (with consequent improvements in order accuracy and delivery scheduling), some reduction in promotional dealing (improving production scheduling), and more shelf-space and merchandising support.

In these arrangements, the manufacturer provides brands but also customized delivery, installation, ongoing information about shelf and merchandising support programs, and other aspects of what (in many industrial product categories) is often called "systems integration." Consumer goods firms rarely use such terms in describing their marketing efforts. But customizing package size, delivery terms, promotions, and perhaps advertising, for an important account or class-of-trade is a form of systems integration increasingly prevalent in consumer marketing. From the trade customer's point of view, these services are growing portions of the value added by a given supplier. From the supplier's point of view, marketing-sales coordination becomes more important as its trade programs involve a product-service-information mix that must reflect increasingly segmented opportunities.

Market Fragmentation

Consumer heterogeneity may always have been latent in so-called "mass markets." But due to data-processing and communications technologies, the search costs associated with locating these differences are now lower and, in many mature consumer product categories, this information is worth more to marketers than in previous decades.

In recent years, the installation of point-of-sale systems capable of scanning Universal Product Code (UPC) symbols has dramatically increased the quantity, quality and timeliness of information available. This information can be used to prepare reports and analyses by product (UPC-level detail allows breakdown by category, brand or brand size), market (chain, store or class-of-trade), merchandising activity (e.g., impact of display, ads, extent of local distribution), time (of year or day—important information in many seasonal and impulse items), and other measures such as price point versus competing products. This type of information has, in turn, uncovered many differences in buying behavior by region, consumer group, class-of-trade and account. Among other factors, "local" and "micro-marketing" efforts are a response to this information, as companies seek to get closer to consumer and trade customers via efficient customization of their marketing programs. From a strategic viewpoint, it is important to notice that such data are available to all members of the distribution channel and (via syndicated services) to all firms within a product or retail category. Hence, intelligent use of such information has become a competitive necessity, further accelerating the proliferation of market segments.

For product managers, this means a significant change from their traditional perspective, which typically focused on a product at a national level and on developing consumer influence via mass marketing vehicles such as network television advertising. Emerging efforts often mean delivering communications and purchase incentives to targeted trade and consumer groups on a regional, store or even household basis. For sales managers, these programs often mean more complexities and responsibilities in their customer interactions, e.g., new account management requirements, the need to coordinate multiple sales and service personnel who call on different locations of the same account, and more responsibility for allocating effectively the promotions and other trade-oriented expenditures that now comprise the largest component of marketing expenses at most consumer goods firms.

It is difficult to respond to diverse markets on a centralized basis from headquarters. The local sales organization is often better informed about retail and channel requirements (as well as their willingness to pay for or support a given program) than headquarters marketing personnel can be. This increased diversity ultimately means the realignment of the traditional sales role to include important marketing responsibilities both before and after the sale to trade entities. As a senior executive at one manufacturer emphasized, "To perform its job, our salesforce currently uses marketing input but increasingly needs marketing skills. On the other side, marketing managers currently vie for salesforce support in the execution of their brand programs but increasingly need the local sales unit's input in the development of programs. They are organizationally separate but systemically interdependent as the weight and frequency of their joint decisions increase."

Supply Chain Management

Managers were also concerned with the impact of supply chain activities on their marketing and sales programs. A key issue repeatedly cited by managers is a change, spurred by dissemination of direct-product-profitability (DPP) measures and just-in-time (JIT) inventory philosophies, in traditional purchasing criteria at many retailers and wholesalers.

DPP calculations have alerted firms to various product acquisition costs beyond selling price, including paperwork and other costs associated with expediting orders, product evaluations, and correcting mistakes in shipments. Suppliers with low prices or deep promotions but poor order-fulfillment systems finally entail higher acquisition costs for trade buyers. Similarly, JIT programs have increased the salience of product possession costs, including financing, storage, inspection, check-in and other handling costs associated with a brand at a class-of-trade. For many consumer products, possession costs are substantial and can equal or exceed acquisition costs. According to estimates by Andersen Consulting, grocery products took an average of 84 days to move from factory to retail shelf in 1991; food manufacturers' storage and distribution costs ran approximately 10 percent of sales, while their trade customers spent 3–5 percent of sales on the same functions. Further, one study (Buzzel et al., 1990) has estimated that the forward buying motivated by trade promotions inflated inventories and so increased possession costs in food distribution channels by 2 percent of retail sales, or nearly $3 billion, by 1990.

Supply chain initiatives seek to lower these costs by optimizing product and information flows between the manufacturer and relevant wholesale and retail entities. For the manufacturer, implementation of this concept affects marketing-sales interactions in at least two ways. First, supply chain management is inherently a multifunctional activity, affecting each element of the marketing mix. Size, packaging and other elements of product policy, for example, are increasingly influenced by logistics costs, in turn requiring closer coordination between brand groups and the sales and service groups who typically manage actual flow of product from the factory to the shelf. Quaker Oats Company now includes supply chain efficiencies (in addition to annual sales and/or operating profit performance) as a bonus criterion for nearly 400 managers. More generally, supply chain activities (and, equally important, the increased transparency of these activities to trade customers) make it necessary that both sales and marketing personnel possess skills that make them aware of and proficient in the systemwide implications of heretofore functionally driven decisions such as trade promotions, line extensions in a new size, or packaging changes for a brand item.

Second, sales tasks change as supply chain investments seek to move the trade selling proposition from current transaction/price to longer-term operating value/cost-in-use. This increases required marketing-sales interactions. At the firms studied, product managers typically had the product-profitability data, knowledge of planned product introductions, and other information necessary to customize profitably terms-and-conditions with customers; sales and service personnel had the local knowledge necessary to know what specific accounts do and do not add value in each area of supply chain activity. As an example of the coordination dimensions involved, consider some of the handling, delivery, merchandising and pricing differences across retail formats in one product category. A manager made the distinctions in **Table 1** for a laundry product sold to multiple classes-of-trade.

The senior sales executive for this product emphasized that "Responding to these differences changes the role of a consumer-goods salesforce. Whereas in the past we were often simply the dispatchers of increasingly big and complex trade promotions, we now must understand the particular reseller's economics and operations, act as business managers, and optimize our firm's participation in sensible store marketing programs."

Product Life Cycles

Shorter product life cycles also affect marketing-sales coordination requirements. During the 1980s in food distribution, for example, new store size increased 47 percent (from an average of 27,200 square feet in 1981 to 40,000 in 1989), while the number of new products introduced by manufacturers increased by nearly 800 percent from about 1,000 in 1981 to more than 9,000 in 1989 (Gorman Publishing, 1990). One study (McLaughlin and Rao, 1991) found that, by the late 1980s, buyers at supermarket chains were listening to about 12 new-product presentations weekly and rejecting about two-thirds of new products presented. Further, nearly 50 percent of those surveyed had a policy of deleting one (or more) items for each new item accepted. As one marketing manager stated: "Shelf-space is now the Khyber Pass in our industry [and] there is less time available for a new product to demonstrate demand . . . buyers increasingly evaluate vendors' programs in terms of the impact, not only on that product's sales, but its impact on the category, any private labels within the category, and often related categories jostling for that shelf-

TABLE 1 Supply Chain Requirements across Trade Segments: Laundry Products Example

Trade Segment	Handling	Delivery	Merchandising	Pricing
Club stores	Pallets/shoppable cases with sales-ready fixtures	Direct to store in regularly scheduled/large order deliveries	Full pallet displays	Lowest price per use/oz. on all shipments; c. 5% margins
Drugstores	Small cases	Frequent, small order deliveries	Small displays; six-month lead time necessary for features	HABA = core business with high mark-ups; our product = traffic builder
Convenience stores	Small cases/on-shelf	To/via wholesaler warehouses	Driven by wholesaler's particular push program	Often a function of store location
Discount/mass merchandisers	Pallets that move well in high-storage system	Drop ship on JIT delivery schedules	Features often involve all brands at same time	Low margins on feature items; variety of everyday margins
Conventional grocery stores	Pallets that move well through system	Regional distribution centers	Display-oriented	Depending on chain and region, a variety of all above

space. And all of this can now be done on a local market, and even store-by-store, basis."

Shorter product life cycles affect marketing-sales relations in two ways. First, while not all new products are introduced to all channels, most new products do require wide distribution across classes-of-trade. Thus, as one executive explained, "Marketing provides broad product, promotion and merchandising concepts. But the field must now adapt Marketing programs appropriately and salespeople [in dealing with trade buyers] must become category experts. This differs from traditional industry sales practice, which emphasized personal relationships at the store level . . . and increases the required information flows between our brand and sales units." Second, shorter product life cycles also mean that these managers have less time to exchange, and assimilate, this information. Hence, even as the other factors discussed here increase required coordination between marketing and sales units in consumer goods firms, accelerated product life cycles tend to decrease the time available for utilizing available coordination mechanisms. This has put pressure on traditional marketing-sales linkages in many firms and stimulated new organizational initiatives.

REORGANIZING FOR BETTER MARKETING-SALES COORDINATION

At the companies studied, major initiatives fell into three categories (see **Figure 2**): an emphasis on headquarters *structural* devices, such as revamped liaison units; changes in field marketing *systems*, such as multifunctional account management teams; and alterations in broader management *processes*, including career paths and training programs. This categorization is neither exhaustive nor mutually exclusive. Most firms were utilizing a variety of linkage mechanisms among (and, in addition to) those discussed here. As **Figure 2** suggests, moreover, these elements are interdependent: new headquarters structures without supporting field implementation systems, or new account-management systems without the human resources capable of working across organizational boundaries, have limited impact. But the mechanisms dis-

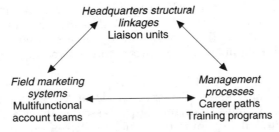

FIGURE 2 Organizational Changes to Improve Marketing-Sales Coordination

cussed here were the most widely used and, at different companies, each often represented the "platform" upon which management hoped to build complementary initiatives for improving marketing-sales integration. What follows is an evaluation of the benefits and key issues associated with each linkage device.

Liaison Units

Many consumer goods firms have long had headquarters sales planning units as a funnel for marketing-sales interactions. But as integration requirements have expanded, some firms have reorganized these groups into broader category sales management (CSM) or trade marketing (TM) units. The change is often more than semantic, as explained by one executive:

> Sales Planning had a tactical focus on helping individual brands get to market via development of sales attention. Input into brand planning was negligible. CSM units focus on the entire category and work directly with product, finance, and manufacturing as well as sales managers. This position reflects the fact that our trade customers think in terms of categories, not just individual brands. It also reflects a recognition that strategic thinking is not the exclusive province of brand management; field units must be the source of ideas as well as execution.

One benefit of establishing such units is that they clearly signal the importance of marketing-sales collaboration in companies where these activities have long resided in separate departments, each with its own measurement systems, career paths and operating procedures. Usually staffed by sales as well as product personnel, these units also help to shape product plans and promotions with field realities in mind. They provide a specific decision-making mechanism in an environment where important trade-offs and market-relevant information increasingly reside at the interface between product and sales groups, rather than within each area. At one firm, the trade marketing unit holds two-day quarterly meetings with regional sales managers and brand personnel who, in successive one-hour sessions, present upcoming product and promotional plans. At one such meeting, field feedback included the following topics:

> This plan isn't relevant to food wholesalers, who are important in my region. We need to take into account the following aspects of their operations . . . My experience with last year's couponing event indicates . . . . After all I've heard today, I'm afraid we're overloading promotional events in that quarter, and dissipating their impact in the field.

These units can also make dispersed trade and regional requirements salient earlier, and higher, in planning processes. Managers often stressed the analogy with quality initiatives: such units, as one executive commented, help to "make visible issues that cut across product and sales groups, just as quality circles helped to build our awareness of the cross-functional requirements of total quality management." In a similar vein, one CSM explained that, at marketing planning sessions, "My role is to constantly remind brand management that we sell to consumers through different classes-of-trade, and these channel requirements affect all elements of our marketing mix. It's better to deal with these requirements proactively in brand strategies, rather than reactively in the form of more trade deals."

Management issues associated with these liaison units involve the costs, role and credibility of this linkage mechanism. These units typically represent another management layer with attendant costs in salaries, support systems and overhead. As a result, such units require a certain critical mass in the product portfolio and customer base to be economically viable, and so tend to appear in larger companies where the additional management layer is, in itself, a mixed blessing for marketing decision making.

At some companies, moreover, these units were perceived by product and sales managers as interlopers rather than integrators. This may be inherent in the role of such units, which must balance consistent product strategies with customized channel requirements—or, as one liaison manager commented, "If either Marketing or Sales is entirely happy with us, something's wrong. We must guard against clever marketing programs that can't be sold to the trade and against volume-driven sales requests that aren't profitable." In practice, therefore, these units tend to be the focus of many contentious negotiations. In my interviews, for example, it is significant that brand managers consistently referred to trade marketing personnel as "salespeople," while sales executives at the same firms referred to them as "brand planners."

To develop the necessary credibility and organizational influence, these units require managers with current knowledge of changing product and field realities. This presents a staffing challenge. Experienced brand and sales managers are often reluctant to take a position which has no direct line authority over either group. And, to keep knowledge of marketing and sales conditions current, these units typically rotate personnel every 1–3 years, which means that some portion of the unit is always perceived as "learning what their job is." The head of one trade marketing unit commented:

> On the one hand, we need frequent rotation to keep our field contacts and information current; on the other hand, it takes time and continuity to understand the various product strategies, develop contacts and trust in the brand groups, and master the complexities of the marketing planning process. Staffing this unit is a difficult balancing act.

But unless this difficult balance is achieved, these units are often viewed as gatekeepers who (as one brand manager complained) "generate meetings but provide no specific expertise to the field or product marketing."

Multifunctional Account Teams

Another development, at the companies studied, was the establishment of account teams composed of individuals from marketing, sales, and often manufacturing, finance and logistics functions. Motivating these new alignments was the ability of powerful, multilocation accounts to demand from vendors product-service packages tailored to their operating characteristics and, conversely, the inability of manufacturers' traditional account management systems to deal with these requirements. In the 1980s, new retail formats prospered on the basis of specialized distribution systems between suppliers' factories and the retailers' outlets. "Category Killers" which were relatively small firms in 1980 (e.g., Home Depot, Circuit City) had, by the end of the decade, the buyer power to demand specialized systems. In grocery categories, the top 100 retail chains accounted for 15 percent of total sales in 1975 and 80 percent by 1990. In faster-growing trade segments, the concentration trend was even more emphatic: among discount stores, the top three chains accounted for 67 percent of total industry sales in 1990, and the top ten for 85 percent; among warehouse club stores, the top three accounted for over 70 percent of sales in 1990, and the top ten for 95 percent (*Management Horizons,* 1990).

Multifunctional teams differ from most traditional account-management programs in two ways. First, the buyer-seller exchange places a premium on effective supply chain management, and the team's primary responsibilities often involve reducing acquisition, delivery and possession costs for buyer and seller. A sales executive noted: "Much of what Sales can do in the store and with trade buyers is determined by what happens farther back in each company's supply chain. Shelf space, share and profits are contingent on our ability to minimize variability along the supply chain for a class-of-trade."

Second, because of this emphasis, account management requires the alignment of multiple areas of expertise at both buyer and seller. **Figure 3** presents a partial organization chart for one such team in 1991. Customer personnel who worked directly with this team included the corporate controller, three regional directors of store operations, three merchandising di-

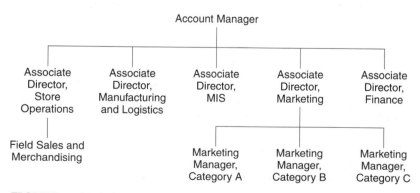

FIGURE 3   Multifunctional Account Team

rectors, the VP of merchandise support systems, a director of transportation, a manager of accounts payable, and buyers in different product categories. Account managers in such situations are not necessarily from sales, because key activities involve integration of service, finance, and/or logistics functions at buyer and seller.

One benefit of such arrangements is their impact on information flows between marketing and sales. At the firms studied, brand-management systems had, over decades, established deeply engrained priorities in companies' data gathering, analysis and dissemination. As one executive explained, "In this system, class-of-trade information was not part of the main data loop and sales information was much less important than brand information." This system evolved during a time when smaller independent retailers and wholesalers comprised the bulk of accounts sold and serviced by the salesforce. By the 1980s, the trade landscape had changed, but information systems at many of these firms processed market data according to established priorities. One result was often a lack of information about growing channels and, in the field, difficulties in allocating resources effectively.

Another benefit is the impact on business planning. Salespeople at major accounts are often first in the organization to recognize emerging market problems and opportunities. But, in most consumer goods firms, sales departments often lack the means, and incentives, to respond with more than tactical (and, usually, price-sensitive) programs. A major reason is that, with traditional account-management systems, sales efforts have been fragmented among different areas, hampering the vendor's ability to track and manage the costs and benefits of multiple product and service programs at important accounts. One firm established multifunctional teams in place of many traditional selling assignments because, as an executive explained, "We had different ordering, shipping and billing procedures with the same customer. So, our sales managers really spent most of their time rectifying variances, not developing programs that optimized our shelf space and store support. Because of this fragmentation, the golden rule in account planning was, "stack it high and price it low." We sold, and if that created problems for other functions like manufacturing or logistics, so be it."

Important issues concerning multifunctional teams involve account selection criteria, the impact on organizational decision making and accountability, and personnel challenges. This approach generates many company-specific investments for the manufacturer. Yet, as one executive commented:

Which customers don't become multifunctional partners? That's a tough issue. Product managers looking at positive results at account X want to extend the procedures to account Y; meanwhile account Y wants the customized service that account X is getting. And if we don't give that service, one of our competitors will. Also, many of the marketing-sales linkages required to implement the concept are specific to a class-of-trade. I'm not sure individual trade customers incur the same switching costs we do.

While these arrangements may spur integration at the account level, moreover, wider functional reporting relationships usually remain intact. Hence, when important decisions must be made, the lines of authority are often unclear and this can inhibit a timely response. At one firm, a dozen signatures (including two executive vice presidents') were required to approve team initiatives with accounts. Further, account-team funding was usually allocated by product group as a proportion of how much of that product was bought by a particular account. For those marketing groups providing the bulk of funding, this procedure inevitably raises concerns and complaints about "who works for whom" when account-team goals and specific product goals do not coincide.

Finally, these account management systems raise a variety of human resource challenges. Personnel from marketing and other areas often resist what they perceive as a "selling" assignment, and the basic role of the team requires unique skills from its members. After experience with this approach, one firm circulated a report outlining staffing criteria for multifunctional account teams. The report noted that the criteria "expand beyond those traditionally used [because of] the structural and cultural changes we are undertaking with major customers," and included the following:

> Technically competent in their disciplines; has the trust and confidence of senior management, peers and subordinates in their discipline; able to communicate effectively up, down and laterally in both the customer and our internal organizations; knows how to "work the system" to create the capacity required to execute; has a track record and appropriate management style; works effectively in a team; has good project management skills; able to develop, coach, and counsel; manages against "principles" versus "rules."

This combination of skills—functional expertise, cross-functional knowledge, customer-contact abilities, "teamwork" skills, and a good track record in terms of traditional evaluation criteria—is not easy to find in most companies, and takes time (and organizational changes) to develop.

Career Paths and Training Programs

For decades at many consumer goods firms, career paths for successful marketing and sales personnel had the characteristics outlined in **Figure 4**. Brand assistants were typically recruited from MBA programs while new sales reps were usually recruited directly from college or military service. In each area, career time horizons and promotion policies differed. A human resource executive at one firm explained that, historically, 80 percent of new sales hires were expected to be "career hires" (i.e., salespeople throughout their tenure with the firm) and 20 percent were "developmental hires" (potential managers within and perhaps beyond the sales function), while nearly all brand hires were treated as "developmental hires" within an up-or-out promotion philosophy that involved frequent rotation among product groups. By contrast, successful salespeople stayed much longer in a territory because promotion within sales did not entail "switching" accounts in the same manner that the mobile brand manager switched product marketing assignments.

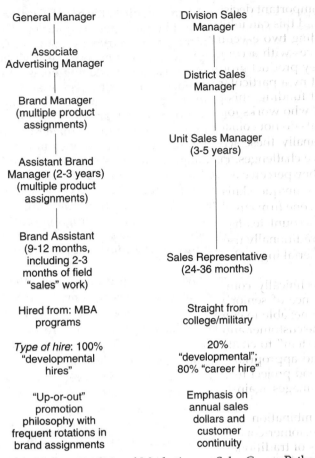

General Manager	Division Sales Manager
Associate Advertising Manager	
	District Sales Manager
Brand Manager (multiple product assignments)	
	Unit Sales Manager (3-5 years)
Assistant Brand Manager (2-3 years) (multiple product assignments)	
Brand Assistant (9-12 months, including 2-3 months of field "sales" work)	Sales Representative (24-36 months)
Hired from: MBA programs	Straight from college/military
Type of hire: 100% "developmental hires"	20% "developmental"; 80% "career hire"
"Up-or-out" promotion philosophy with frequent rotations in brand assignments	Emphasis on annual sales dollars and customer continuity

FIGURE 4   Traditional Marketing vs. Sales Career Paths

People with different training and experience must nonetheless work on joint activities—for example, the allocation of promotional monies to different sales groups. But as one marketing executive described this process, "the sales force was essentially a 'black box' from the viewpoint of brand personnel. Most had little idea how the sales force operates. For instance, I didn't know how different sales positions were compensated and evaluated. We missed many opportunities and probably wasted lots of money." This process had other costs as well. A senior sales executive commented:

> As a district manager, I often resented negotiating with brand people younger and less experienced than I. They were essentially "reinventing the wheel" each year, and your region usually got what it wanted. But you felt like a second-class citizen in the company when these decisions were officially made by someone who really didn't know as much about in-store dynamics as you did.

To address this situation, some firms have altered career tracks to provide assignments in both sales and marketing. Others have expanded the length and type of field sales exposure required for new brand personnel. In addition, new positions focus middle managers on joint marketing-sales activities. One company established zone marketing manager (ZMM) positions, staffed primarily by people with brand experience. ZMMs have two roles. One is developing and administering marketing goals and budgets which, in a departure from past practice, differ by region and class-of-trade. The other is coordination with headquarters marketing groups, especially for product introductions. Brand planning and R&D remain centralized, but ZMMs provide the major means for a brand manager to "sell" the field on a new initiative. Conversely, ZMMs negotiate with brand groups for types and levels of media spending, promotions, and sales incentives. Other firms have moved experienced brand personnel into field market analyst positions. The goal is to place in major market areas a person who can augment marketing skills with knowledge of local trade and consumer behavior, and so work with product managers to develop programs customized to a trading area. An executive noted: "As the trade changes, the field will have more control over expenditures and must understand the marketing ROI implications."

Training programs have also been revised. This often involves formal joint training of both marketing and sales personnel during their initial years with the firm, or joint management development programs for more senior managers. Other companies have opted for less formal, on-the-job initiatives. For some, changes in marketing information systems are opportunities for joint training. At one packaged-goods firm, a shift to scanner data as the basis for many market research reports involved brand personnel visiting sales offices to explain the nature of the data, its uses, and the kinds of numbers that marketing personnel expected to monitor closely. "In turn," the head of Market Research explained, "brand groups were educated by salespeople concerning how trade buyers do and don't use this data, caveats concerning Marketing's intended analyses, and actions that could help to improve marketing effectiveness in certain regions and accounts."

One benefit of having worked "both sides" is increased awareness of the other unit's operating conditions, constraints, and contributions. Managers with both marketing and sales experience are more likely to develop programs with an awareness of the reciprocal requirements. Such assignments also help to build what one observer calls the "thick informal networks one finds wherever multiple leadership initiatives work in harmony . . . Too often these networks are highly fragmented: a tight network exists inside the marketing group and inside R&D but not across the two departments" (Kotter, 1990). This is traditionally true of marketing and sales departments at most consumer goods firms. With training initiatives, moreover, these assignments can also develop what one executive called "system savvy." According to this executive, "Most managers are 'good citizens' who want to do what is right for the firm, not just their area. But they're often unaware of the impact of their decisions on other parts of an interdependent business system. Our joint training programs and career rotation aim at disseminating this system savvy."

However, the management issues raised by these initiatives are formidable. Joint training programs usually entailed additional training beyond the still-required functional training in product management tasks and selling skills. As well as incremental expenses, therefore, more people are spending more time in training and less on "core" activities; and this is seen as a significant opportunity cost in a cost-conscious environment where many firms are not adding marketing or sales personnel. Unless supported by other processes, moreover, such training is likely to have little long-term impact. One manager explains that "After each joint training seminar, people always leave enthused. But back on the job, numbers must be met in each area and the enthusiasts still encounter functional stovepipes."

Similarly, the career paths discussed here require multiple-year time horizons from both the organization and the individuals involved. Also required is the willingness to assume the inherent career risks in a situation where most senior managers have risen to their positions by acquiring within-function expertise. A brand manager noted that, "I had an offer to move into a mid-level sales position, but my boss discouraged me. He said it would not help me get more responsibility with the bigger company brands. I think he was honest with me: a friend did go into Sales and, when he came back, was treated as an interesting oddity." Conversely, cross-functional movement often raises perceived equity issues. A sales executive explained that, "Product managers who come to Sales are usually younger people slated for more responsibility in Marketing. They're expected to be adequate during their Sales stint. But salespeople perceive a double standard, where average-performing marketing personnel get favored over outstanding salespeople for promotions to Corporate. This creates morale issues that many district managers resent."

For these reasons, these training and career path initiatives were limited to a small minority of marketing and sales managers, who often encountered substantial obstacles precisely because most careers in their organizations were managed according to a different paradigm.

MANAGERIAL IMPLICATIONS

Because their brand franchises, competitive positions, and point-of-sale requirements differ, the types of coordination mechanisms adopted by firms in this sample varied. Specific organizational recommendations, moreover, depend on a firm's strategic goals. But certain themes emerge from this discussion as well as diagnostic questions useful for managers seeking to improve marketing-sales interactions in their companies.

The Importance of Boundary Roles

The formal liaison units discussed here were often viewed ambivalently by the marketing and sales groups they dealt with. But they were being created or expanded at most firms studied because, when managed effectively, they play a valuable boundary-spanning role in companies. Without a dedicated unit, informal methods of managing marketing-sales coordination are often too time-consuming, treated as a "secondary priority" by each group, or are ineffective because attempts by marketing or sales personnel to alter the other's plans are viewed as infringements on another's domain. Especially in an environment where time-to-market and segmented trade programs are more important than in the past, these units provide a means for capturing and accelerating learning about important interface activities and for combining one group's product-consumer perspectives with another's channel-account perspectives.

Key diagnostic questions about this coordinating mechanism include:

- Who are the managers selected for such units and do they possess the organizational credibility and interpersonal skills required?

These units typically have little direct authority and so are highly dependent on the personal stature and influence of the individuals involved. As one liaison manager commented: "We don't 'own' resources on either side. So, information, personal relations, and judicious use of top management become our paramount management tools."

- What responsibilities are lodged with these units, and what decisions remain with individual marketing and sales groups?

These units necessarily encroach on decisions that were the responsibility of marketing or sales. The established balance-of-power is disrupted, with resulting conflicts. These arguments can help to "right the balance" between marketing and sales. But these turf battles take time, slow decision making, and can subvert the initial goal behind establishing the unit: quicker responsiveness to diverse market conditions. The head of one trade marketing unit commented: "A few months after this unit began, it became apparent that we needed a better job description. So, with important Marketing and Sales executives, we outlined those areas where my unit has either the final say, veto power, or recommendation responsibilities. This narrowed our scope, and not everything happens the way I want it to happen. But it's also improved our ability to implement what is in our domain."

- How does the unit actually operate: as forum for the exchange and resolution of perspectives or as proxy for customer contact?

These units are conduits for marketing and sales managers needing complementary information, and also circuit breakers whose implicit role is to prevent marketing groups from overwhelming sales with uncoordinated programs. In this research, every liaison unit emphasized that its role was, in part, to "shield the field" from the aggregate volume of product literature, promotional programs, and informational requests developed by product managers. But the danger is that, over time, these units unwittingly become another barrier between marketing and sales—primarily a circuit breaker rather than a logistically efficient conduit. Top management's role is to monitor this process and ensure that such units are not used by either marketing or sales as a proxy for actual feedback from consumers and trade customers.

The Role of Research and Information Systems

Market factors have increased the interdependencies of marketing and sales in consumer goods firms. In different ways, each initiative discussed here seeks to improve the two-way information flows now required. In many firms, however, a reexamination of formal research activities is also required. (For a more detailed discussion of the impact of traditional research and information management processes on sales-marketing coordination, see Cespedes, 1993.) Key questions include:

- To what extent is the firm's formal market research relevant to the multiple sales and marketing groups now responsible for development and implementation of programs?

In theory, the market research function should aid in developing a common information base for marketing and sales. But in practice this was not the case at most firms examined. One reason, as an executive at a research firm explained, is that "in most companies, 'market research' really means 'marketing research.' The research function views product marketing as its client because research funds usually come from the marketing budget. By contrast, research in consumer goods firms has had relatively little contact with Sales' issues." Just how limited this contact can be is suggested by the allocation of the market research budget at one large firm as recently as 1990: the company spent nearly $40 million on consumer research, but allocated only four people (and less than $1 million in research funds) to studies of its top 200 trade accounts—the buyers and channels for over 80 percent of the firm's sales.

- Does a joint marketing-sales database exist?

In some firms, a key role for market research has become the development and maintenance of a joint marketing-sales database. Research managers work with brand personnel to maintain cost data and other elements of the system, and with sales personnel to develop appropriate reports and other tools that encourage field use of the system. "Information previously fragmented in the hands of headquarters and sales offices," a manager noted, "is coming together. Interaction between Marketing and Sales via this system has made each group clearer about profit opportunities, and this has altered our product offerings, pricing, and sales focus."

- Do MIS and measurement systems help, or hinder, information flows between marketing and sales?

At the firms studied, trade spending was typically captured via three incompatible information systems lodged in brand, sales and logistics units, and could only be aggregated at the national level across product groups. For these firms, specifying promotional paybacks by class-of-trade or account was often impossible or required time frames far in excess of the relevant selling cycles. Meanwhile, channel and competitive activities increasingly require the integration of such data. Further, while new market data are proliferating, reward systems often hinder use of such data. One firm provided its salesforce with account-specific information based on scanner data, but found little use for the information. An executive commented: "Sales' traditional metrics here are tied to volume as measured by warehouse withdrawals. Hence, reps kept asking for the equivalent numbers in withdrawal terms since those numbers were still discussed in their performance evaluations."

The Value of Functional Clarity

A final theme emerging from this research may appear paradoxical: it concerns the value of differentiating functional roles in order to improve performance of joint activities. As the discussion of career path and training initiatives indicates, marketing-sales coordination is aided by the development of personal networks and generalist, cross-functional skills among managers. But it also required that a firm develop repeatable processes for interactions between specialists. Hence, there is intangible but real value in articulating what one executive calls the "clarity of purpose required for effective implementation: organizational clarity about what each unit contributes uniquely to overall business performance."

At some companies, this involved the development and discussion of frameworks designed to distinguish roles and responsibilities. **Figure 5** provides an example from a packaged-goods firm, where four increasingly interdependent organizational units—Product Development, Product Management, Sales and Product Supply—are distinguished along certain dimensions: the major joint activities for which their coordination is necessary; each unit's key contributions to customer satisfaction; the primary external focus of each unit (trade customer or end consumer); and elements of the marketing mix over which the unit has decision-making authority.

In this example, Product Management and Sales must coordinate pricing, promotion and merchandising programs, but each retains decision-making authority over different aspects of these programs with trade customers or consumers. Product Management is responsible for advertising, promotion, packaging and pricing decisions for consumers; Sales is responsible for distribution, merchandising, shelving and promotional programs at trade customers. Likewise, Sales and Product Supply (logistical units) must coordinate service programs in different classes-of-trade. Sales makes decisions about distribution and merchandising activities within the quality and cost parameters established by Product Supply. A senior executive at this firm explains: "Sales and Marketing have more cross-functional requirements but less time to execute. A chart like this doesn't 'solve' conflicts. But it has helped to expedite decision making, while underlying where accountability for joint activities ultimately resides."

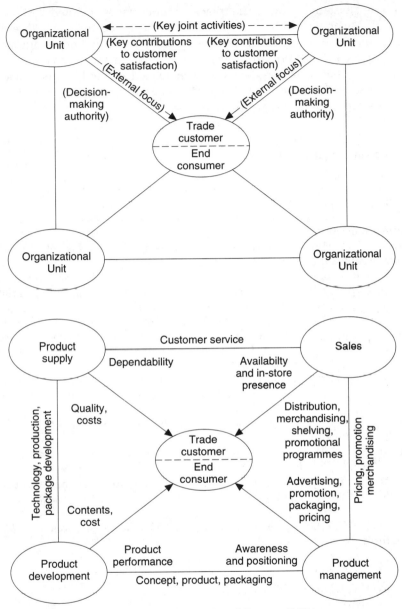

FIGURE 5 Joint Activities and Functional Responsibilities

The example can also help to emphasize another aspect of marketing-sales coordination. While developments make better integration of these units a prerequisite for effective marketing at consumer goods firms, there is also a continuing need to maintain dedicated expertise in each area. Hence, the goal should not be to eradicate differences between the groups or, as in recent years, to preach that "everybody is responsible for customer satisfaction." In a fast-changing marketplace, as one manager noted, "Marketing and Sales hear with different ears, and both perspectives are necessary." Rather, the issue is how to link efficiently and effectively knowledge and action located in different areas and "traditions" in most consumer goods firms. In evaluating the organizational changes discussed in this article, and their potential applicability to their own sales and marketing efforts, managers should keep this distinction in mind.

NOTES AND REFERENCES

BUZZELL, R. D., QUELCH, J. A. and SALMON, W. J. (1990), "The Costly Bargain of Trade Promotion," *Harvard Business Review,* Vol. 68, pp. 141–149.

CESPEDES, F. V. (1993), "Market Research and Marketing Dialects," *Marketing Research,* Vol. 5, pp. 26–34.

DEWEESE, T. A. (1910), "The Advertising Manager," *Printers' Ink,* 14 July, p. 141, quoted in Strasser, S. (1989).

Gorman Publishing Company (1990), *Prepared Foods: New Products Annual,* New York, NY, p. 159. In this study, a new product was defined as including variations in flavors, colors or varieties but excluding new sizes, packages or "simple improvements." Thus, the number cited here is substantially less than the number of new stock-keeping units added during this period, each of which is often treated as a "new product" by trade buyers because each requires a separate order number, scanning code, and, in many cases, price.

KOPP, R. J. and GREYSER, S. A. (1987), "Packaged Goods Marketing: Pull Companies Look to Improved Push," *Journal of Consumer Marketing,* Vol. 4, pp. 13–22.

KOTTER, J. P. (1990), *A Force for Change,* Free Press, New York, NY, p. 92.

Management Horizons (1990), "Retailing 2000: The New Dimensions," Price Waterhouse, Dublin, OH.

McCLAUGHLIN, E. W. and RAO, V. R. (1991), *Decision Criteria for New Product Acceptance: The Role of Trade Buyers,* Quorum Books, Westport, CT, pp. 59–61.

QUELCH, J. A., FARRIS, P. W. and OLVER, J. (1992), "The Product Management Audit: Design and Survey Findings," *Journal of Product & Brand Management,* Vol. 1, pp. 45–58.

STRASSER, S. (1989), *Satisfaction Guaranteed: The Making of the American Mass Market,* Pantheon, New York, NY.

APPENDIX: RESEARCH METHODOLOGY

The study consisted of 75 personal interviews at six consumer goods manufacturers as well as interviews with two research suppliers to these firms. At participating companies, the focus was on business units with 1991 sales ranging from less than $100 million to more than $2 billion, representing a cross-section of product categories within consumer goods: food products (3), paper products (1), household products (1), and personal care (1).

All six companies sell their products to retail and wholesale customers in at least three of the following classes-of-trade: supermarkets, convenience stores, mass merchandisers, drug stores, department stores, club stores. All employ in-house salesforces, and four also utilize independent broker organizations, to represent their product lines to the trade.

At each company, interviews were conducted with both marketing and sales managers, management in other functional areas, and (when present in a firm) with formal marketing-sales liaison managers. Other data included internal company documents supplied by interviewees, personal observation while attending company meetings, and customer calls with salespeople. In addition, a number of detailed case studies about specific marketing-sales coordination issues were developed.

Interviewees' job responsibilities were as follows:

Sales management	23
Marketing management	21
Market research	9
Marketing-sales liaison	7
Other	15
	75

Other category includes interviews with corporate managers, general managers of business units, and managers in other functional areas such as MIS, human resources, and logistics.

Interviews averaged 90 minutes in length and were unstructured, but interviewees received in advance a copy of the research questions being investigated. Thus, most interviews focused on one or more of the following questions (depending upon the position of the interviewee): (1) What are the major issues facing your area in interactions with sales/product marketing? (2) What internal or external factors determine the relative importance of coordination with this group, the tasks that must be coordinated, and the kinds of conflicts or opportunities that arise? (3) What mechanisms exist in your firm for managing these joint tasks, and what is your perception of their strengths and weaknesses? (4) In practice, how do things most often "get done" at the marketing-sales interface, i.e., what are the informal as well as formal means for managing sales/marketing interactions for joint tasks?

Case 4

Pepsi-Cola
Fountain Beverage Division:
Marketing Organization

In November 1986, Mr. John Cranor, president of Pepsi-Cola's Fountain Beverage Division (FBD), was considering reorganizing the division's marketing efforts. Although FBD had been growing rapidly, Mr. Cranor believed the fountain business differed in several ways from the bottle-and-can business that dominated Pepsi's operations and which was organized along brand-management lines.

FBD was responsible for sales of soft drink syrup to fountain outlets—i.e., any location where a consumer purchased a soft drink not in a bottle or can. Industry conventional wisdom and some preliminary analysis established these categories of outlets: quick serve restaurants (QSRs),[1] sit-down restaurants, cup-vending machines, convenience stores, institutional feeders,[2] movie theaters, sports arenas, hotels, and cafeterias. These categories

---

This case was prepared by Professor Frank V. Cespedes and Research Associate Jon E. King as the basis for class discussion rather than to illustrate either effective or ineffective handling of an administrative situation.

[1]"Quick serve" in the food service industry was equivalent to the widely recognized term, "fast food."

[2]Also called manual feeders or contract feeders, these were service companies which operated food services on the premises of their customers such as universities or corporations.

varied in size, volume, market, range and number of beverages carried, and in other ways. At issue was whether these differences affected Pepsi's success in each class of outlets, and consequently should be focused on in order to allocate marketing resources most effectively. Should FBD's marketing be organized by channel (rather than brand); and, if so, what would this mean for the division's structure and for the skills required to operate within a new organization of marketing activities?

PEPSI-COLA

The Pepsi-Cola Company was founded in 1902 in North Carolina by Mr. Caleb Bradham, a pharmacist who developed the soft drink after several years of experimentation at his pharmacy soda fountain. By 1910 he had franchised 280 independent bottlers in 24 states to make and sell syrup and bottled Pepsi-Cola. Sugar price fluctuations after World War I bankrupted the company in 1923 and, after another attempt, the Pepsi-Cola Company was declared bankrupt a second time in 1931. The dominant competitor in the industry was the Coca-Cola Company; although founded under similar circumstances in 1886, Coca-Cola was a $40 million company in 1931, selling one of the most advertised and profitable products in the country.

Throughout this period, Coke and Pepsi bottling franchises were sold in perpetuity: the franchisee had exclusive and permanent rights to bottle and sell the cola in a geographical area. Only a bottler's "gross negligence" could invalidate this contract, but the franchise could be resold. Although the franchised bottler was prohibited from selling any other cola, other flavors of soft drinks were permitted. However, while Pepsi's franchises included rights to all sales (bottle or fountain) Coke franchised only bottling rights, and sold fountain syrup through distributors. Coca-Cola's focus had long been on the fountain market; in fact, its first bottling franchise was sold for only $1 because it was not expected to thrive. In contrast, Pepsi, beginning in the 1930s, focused on retail outlets. As one manager noted:

> Bottlers have large investments in plant, machinery, inventory, transportation equipment, and a field force that services accounts, opens new accounts, places ads, coolers, vending machines and other items in the place of purchase, and sees to it that customer inventory is maintained appropriately. Historically, the bottlers were even more important to Pepsi than Coke, because in Pepsi's system they have responsibility for distribution to fountain operations in addition to managing the bottling operation itself.

Loft, Inc., a chain of 200 candy stores with soda fountains, bought the bankrupt Pepsi-Cola Company in 1931. Loft had been a Coca-Cola account, and its president felt that Loft could reduce cola costs 40% with Pepsi. In 1933, in the midst of the Great Depression, a Loft candy salesman recommended selling 12-ounce Pepsi bottles at the same retail price as Coca-Cola's 6-ounce bottles. Sales suddenly jumped in an economy-minded marketplace, and the company started an aggressive campaign of signing up more bottlers. By 1937, the company was running 5 concentrate[3] plants, and 313 bottlers operated across the country. By 1941, Pepsi had enfranchised 469 bottlers and began to offer loans to bottlers to make capital investments.

However, trouble hit Pepsi again after World War II, and again due to sugar prices. Attempts to raise retail prices crippled sales. In 1949, Pepsi hired from Coca-Cola a new president, Mr. Alfred Steele, who focused on several policies: emphasis on quality control and product research, training programs, and a commitment to "partnership" with the Pepsi bottlers. Mr. Steele commented that, "Our job was not to sell the bottler something in the hope that he could sell it, but rather our true forte was to help him to move more goods at a profit." He told the bottlers, "You can save your way to bankruptcy or spend your way to prosperity." Marketing programs were developed area by area, concentrating on the cola battlegrounds one at a time.

Mr. Steele also repositioned the product; it was reformulated as a lighter, less caloric soft drink. Mr. Steele's wife, actress Joan Crawford, became the glamorous ideal of the Pepsi drinker. Instead of pursuing Coca-Cola's customers with a lower price, Pepsi now aimed the theme of "light refreshment" at young, middle class American women and the home market. This demanded focusing on grocery stores rather than fountains. One observer commented:

> Efforts were increased in the fountain area in the 1950s, but Coca-Cola had always been very strong there. Long before Pepsi, Coca-Cola had been installing equipment with its logo in soda fountains and luncheonettes all over the country. That equipment came with contractual obligations that the distributor put only Coca-Cola in it. First-mover advantage was very real in that channel. Less so in retail groceries where many different brands competed for limited shelf space. Here, a better deal offered by a more flexible Pepsi could result in more prominent retail display, of great importance for a low-ticket impulse item.

Pepsi's image in the 1960s shifted with the "Pepsi Generation" campaign, but the same marketing style remained. Mr. Alan Pottasch, in charge of Pepsi's advertising in that era, commented, "We stopped talking about the product and started talking about the user, and that is a major difference. What you drank said something about who you were. We painted an image of our consumer as active, vital, and young at heart."

By 1975, Pepsi had drawn ahead of Coke in grocery store sales, but Coca-Cola led in the overall market through its position in fountain ac-

---

[3]Pepsi-Cola sold beverage concentrate to bottlers, who added carbon dioxide, sweetener, and water to make beverages and beverage syrup.

counts, including large fast food chains such as McDonald's. Fountain and vending accounted for two-thirds of Coca-Cola's revenues at the time.

Advertising increasingly became the battleground for the "cola wars," but Coca-Cola began to cut prices selectively in critical geographical areas. By 1980, approximately 50% of nationwide wholesale grocery sales of Coke and Pepsi were discounted, and the average cost of Coke was slightly lower. Operating margins for both companies dropped from the mid-1970s to the mid-1980s.

The 1980s also saw efforts by both companies to exert greater control over their franchised bottlers, especially those with substandard performance. This included encouraging franchise buy-outs and even direct purchase. By 1986, Pepsi owned 32% of its bottler franchises, responsible for 40% of its retail volume. The other bottlers were split about evenly between multibottler conglomerates (owned by companies such as General Bottlers, General Cinema and RKO) and independent single franchisees.

PEPSICO, INC.

Pepsi-Cola had begun to expand its product line in 1963 with the introduction of Diet Pepsi. By 1986 the company sold a range of colas and other carbonated soft drinks (CSDs) with and without sugar, caffeine, and fruit juice, in over a hundred countries. In 1965, Pepsi had started to diversify by merging with Frito Lay, Inc., a snackfood manufacturer, and later added restaurant chains including Pizza Hut, Taco Bell, and Kentucky Fried Chicken.

PepsiCo, Inc. had net sales of $9.3 billion in 1986, separated among soft drinks (39%), snack foods (32%) and restaurants (29%). (See **Exhibit 1** for financial data.) Eighty-one percent of Pepsi's $3.6 billion soft drink business was domestic, representing approximately $12 billion in domestic retail sales (31% of the U.S. market). Pepsi's CSD 5-year growth rate was 6.5% annually: 30% faster than the industry; the flagship Pepsi-Cola brand was the best selling brand of any kind in supermarkets. The PepsiCo Annual Report noted, "Americans consume more soft drinks than water—about 42 gallons a year for every man, woman and child. More soft drinks [are consumed] than milk, wine, juice, tea and liquor combined."

The domestic market for soft drinks was split into 3 major channels: retail (primarily grocery) stores (62%), can-vending machines (13%) and fountain (25%). Pepsi's business was divided among those three channels at approximately 55%, 30% and 15% respectively. The company's strategy for growth in the soft drink industry was enumerated in its Annual Report:

1. Emphasize brand Pepsi.
2. Build a strong portfolio of brands.
3. Increase fountain syrup and vending sales.
4. Leverage the company-owned bottling system.
5. Focus on high-potential, underdeveloped international markets.

At the end of 1986, PepsiCo was divided into two major groups: beverages (Pepsi-Cola Company) and foods (Frito-Lay and restaurant chains). Pepsi-Cola Company was divided into 3 operating groups: Pepsi-Cola Company (U.S. soft drink operations), Pepsi-Cola International (international soft drink operations), and PepsiCo Wines and Spirits. The U.S. soft drink operations were further divided into three divisions: Pepsi-Cola Bottling Group (PBG) was responsible for all company-owned bottling franchises, Pepsi-Cola Bottle & Can (B&C) marketed all nonfountain soft drinks to franchised bottlers, and Pepsi-Cola Fountain Beverage Division (FBD) marketed syrup to fountain outlets. (See **Exhibit 2** for organizational chart.) PBG managed each of its owned bottling franchises separately, but manufacturing managers reported to headquarters manufacturing as well as to franchise management.

Colas dominated the U.S. CSD market with 69% of retail sales; lemon-lime was 11.3%, juice-added (various flavors) 5.3%, "pepper-type" 4.6%, root beer 2.7%, orange 1.5%, and all others 5.6%. Estimated 1986 market shares for each of Pepsi's CSDs are shown below.

Pepsi-Cola	18.6
Diet Pepsi	4.4
Mountain Dew (lemon-lime)	3.0
Pepsi Free (no caffeine, regular and diet)	2.0
Slice (10% fruit juice in several flavors)	1.5
Diet Slice	1.0
Others	0.1

Fountain Beverage Operations

Pepsi-Cola sold concentrate to its bottlers; bottlers then mixed concentrate with water and sweetener to make syrup. Syrup was either sold directly to fountain accounts, or was combined with carbonated water for bottling.[4] FBD marketed fountain syrup but the local bottlers manufactured it, delivered it, and then either collected revenues from retailers on a cash-on-delivery basis and forwarded the appropriate portion of these revenues to FBD or, if the account was a "charge" customer, ensured that the account paid FBD directly. At the fountain itself, syrup canisters were attached to a dispenser and pressurized with carbon dioxide tanks. The dispenser had a fixed number of nozzles (usually 4 or 5); each nozzle could dispense one flavor. Few outlets served both Coke and Pepsi for several reasons. First, many retailers considered cola a commodity; second, since dispenser nozzles were limited, offering two colas would limit alternative flavors; and third, neither manufacturer was likely to provide superior market support for an outlet which also promoted the competing cola.

Coca-Cola generally did not sell concentrate to bottlers: instead, it sold the presweetened syrup, thus retaining the sweetener margin (which

---

[4]For the purposes of this case study, "bottling" will refer to both bottling and canning.

in Pepsi's case was split between the bottler and the sweetener supplier). Coke also used distributors to deliver syrup, and paid them about 25¢ per gallon. These factors gave Coke an estimated 80¢-per-gallon margin over the price Pepsi could retain, since much of the difference went to the local Pepsi bottler who produced and distributed the syrup to outlets. A Pepsi manager pointed out that there were, however, advantages to Pepsi's situation:

> A good Pepsi bottler can bury the competition: Coke's third- and fourth-party distributors and service people are hard to coordinate. Coke also charges big premiums to local accounts, yet has no field sales force; they can't cover all those accounts as well as our bottlers can.
>
> Developing new fountain business requires capital and staff that the bottler doesn't have, and won't consider at the margin Coke offers. It requires delivery vehicles, drivers, sales reps, trained service mechanics, and production facilities; few bottlers will do that for the 25¢ per gallon that Coke pays its distributors. So Coke has started to buy out their distributors.

Mr. William Hober, FBD's sales vice-president, added:

> Coke has, however, national standards and a consistent product line since their distributors are hired on that basis. In contrast, our bottlers may carry only brand Pepsi and few or none of our other flavors; they may even carry a competing flavor instead of ours in the lemon-lime or orange category. Unfortunately, if we were to try to get a different bottler in the area to carry Slice, our main bottler would get upset, endangering our primary business.

FOUNTAIN BEVERAGE DIVISION (FBD)

FBD was established in 1978 to market Pepsi brands to large national quick serve restaurant (QSR) chains, the biggest customers of fountain syrup. This group included companies such as McDonald's, Burger King, and Wendy's. Initially, FBD was comprised of only 5 headquarters personnel. One FBD manager noted:

> Supermarkets and vending machines require of the established bottler less service or capital and produce terrific returns. For example, vending machines are simple to run, provide depreciation cash flow, investment tax credit, and lots of business. Bottle & can business generally provides an 80% gross margin for the bottler. Fountain, in contrast, involves a variety of customer-owned dispensers demanding of the bottler higher maintenance, training, and quality control measures, and requiring integration with the customer's personnel and operations. Delivery routes add complications to the bottler's existing system, and he has a lot to learn to make his operations in this area efficient, because fountain has been virtually ignored for so long.

We have to point out to bottlers the advantage of adding fountain as a complement to their existing business: fountain represents a quarter of the entire CSD beverage market, a huge market for incremental volume increase. We also have to educate bottlers that the ROI in fountain can be as high or higher than in bottle-and-can, *if* the initial investment is made.

Pepsi had 10% of the fountain market in 1978, and Coca-Cola carried most of the rest. Mr. Cranor's predecessor at FBD (and current president of Pepsi USA), Mr. Ronald Tidmore, pointed out to Pepsi-Cola top management that the $2 per gallon margin Coke reaped from its 20 million concentrate gallons of fountain business equaled an extra $40 million that Coke could invest back into fierce bottle & can competition. He asserted, "If we're going to stop Coke from subsidizing grocery sales from profits made in fountain, we have to develop our own fountain business. This means building up our fountain field force." In the late 1970s, a sales force was gradually established by temporarily assigning personnel from other Pepsi-Cola divisions to FBD.

Early on, bottlers remained disinterested in fountain because of the low volume: the 250 million retail gallons nationally in 1978 was not enough to draw attention, compared to Pepsi's 2 billion retail gallon bottle & can business. FBD's mission became to sign up new fountain accounts in order to boost volume. FBD contracted with bottlers to split sales responsibility between large and small accounts: the line was drawn such that FBD retained sales management of any account with two or more outlets in two or more bottlers' territories. FBD would approach the headquarters of such accounts to arrange a contract (including setting a price). FBD also established a special national accounts sales force to manage the 14 largest Pepsi fountain accounts. (See **Exhibit 3** for a chart of sales responsibilities.) Just before moving into the presidency of Pepsi-Cola USA, Mr. Tidmore arranged to double the number of district sales managers (account reps) in FBD in 1986 to a total of 83.

Current Position and Organization

By 1986, FBD had increased its market share to 29% of the $10 billion retail fountain market, and some bottlers had set up their own fountain sales forces for local accounts. That year, FBD sold $210 million in concentrate to bottlers who in turn sold $472 million in syrup to fountain outlets; this represented $25 million profit after tax to Pepsi-Cola. Revenues had increased 12% over 1985, volume 8% market share 1.4 points, and profit 21%. (See **Exhibit 4**.)

In 1986, 69% of Pepsi's fountain volume was national business, the rest locally sold accounts managed by the bottlers. However, only 35% of operating profit was attributable to national business. Mr. David Weinberg, FBD's vice-president for New Business Development, noted, "Selling to national accounts is not as proportionately profitable as selling to smaller accounts because it is more competitive. It demands marketing services, co-op advertising, and low prices. But it does provide high volume and credibility, it gets consumers sampling, and it is highly visible to smaller accounts."

Mr. Cranor had joined FBD in early 1986. He had been with PepsiCo for ten years, mostly in Frito-Lay. Mr. William Hober, VP of Sales for Fountain, was also new in his job, but had been in field sales at Pepsi-Cola for 25 years. Mr. John Swanhaus had been FBD's VP of Marketing for 2 years, and had been at Pepsi-Cola for 10 years in Bottle & Can and Wines & Spirits. Top managers at FBD usually stayed in the division for 2–3 years before moving to another division.

The unit was staffed by 300 people in sales, marketing, finance and control, and systems operations (see **Exhibit 5**). Brand marketing involved 16 people; another 4 people were dedicated to regional marketing. Sales was divided into 4 geographic divisions plus National Accounts. National Accounts headquarters personnel included a 4-person new business development group and 10 account managers for managing sales to the 14 largest customers' headquarters (not outlets). Each field sales division had 3 or 4 regions, 2 division development managers (DDMs) and 3 National Account sales managers (NASMs). NASMs were responsible for National Account outlets in their areas; DDMs acted as consultants to the bottlers. Each sales region was divided into 5–7 districts run by district sales managers (DSMs: account reps). This geographic organization had been in place since FBD acquired a sales force.

SALES

In 1986, the FBD field sales force had added 40 new positions; one manager pointed out that this level of expansion was unheard of at Pepsi because of its "lean" operating style. This expansion raised the number of district managers to 83, each with a discretionary budget of $250 thousand for motivating the 1–10 bottlers in his or her district toward fountain accounts. Specific uses included local advertising and merchandising incentives, and sometimes capital investment. Mr. Hober characterized this amount of cash as "not a lot," but more was available at the divisional sales managers' discretion.

DSMs were 26–30 years old and were paid a base salary of $45 thousand; bonuses ranged from $3–8 thousand. This compensation was considered very competitive. Entry level salespeople had 3–5 years of experience in consumer packaged goods sales, or 5–7 years in advertising/promotions. New DSMs received 4 weeks of formal training in their first year, as well as up to 4 weeks on the job training with the regional sales manager, other DSMs, NASMs and development managers. Each DSM reported in detail on every bottler in the district three times a year, including evaluations of outfitting (i.e., appropriate production and distribution equipment), commitment, and the area's fountain market.

The DSM was responsible for every bottler in that district, as well as all accounts not established as National Accounts (the 150 largest) or bottler-managed (local). FBD field sales reps made about two-thirds of their calls on bottlers and one-third on retail fountain accounts; before Mr. Hober took over sales in 1986, much less of the rep's time was spent on the bottler. Mr. Hober had considered and rejected the option of splitting the sales force in two (bottler/retailer):

> A function-oriented division concentrates on analysis and loses local market sensitivity: managers start caring about what "bottlers" think rather than what "the bottler in Baton Rouge" thinks. Success in this business comes from negotiating, developing relationships, nurturing accounts, and dealing with problems one by one. A rep can't fully serve a bottler unless he or she knows the local fountain market *better* than the bottler.
>
> Since our reps are responsible for bottlers and accounts, they can keep on top of all the important details about the area's market. The DSM who works in Baton Rouge knows what the bottler faces in Baton Rouge, and when he sells a new account he has something tangible to offer the bottler in return for the bottler's commitment of time and money to the fountain market.

Mr. Swanhaus added, "Account problems tend to take place on the local, not national level, so we want people where they're needed." Mr. Swanhaus had originated a field marketing program at Bottle & Can when he was VP of marketing operations there. The theory was that national programs were often too unwieldy to solve local problems. He established a similar organization at FBD by placing 12 managers in charge of programs tailored to their geographical areas (in addition to the 16 managers in brand development at FBD headquarters). Mr. Hober liked the idea and was interested in taking Mr. Swanhaus' organizational strategy even further by moving more of the available finances for development and promotion into the districts, and placing NASMs and DDMs into the regions (they were currently at the divisional level). This combination would move toward putting profit & loss responsibility at the regional manager level.

Bottlers

One division sales manager pointed out:

> Before we started getting involved with bottler operations, most bottlers didn't know if their few fountain accounts were profitable or not. Analysis found they typically were, or could be with more effort. But if the bottler is not interested and committed, nothing happens. The division development manager will do an "infrastructure study" which entails separating fountain accounts and operations into a subunit of the bottler's organization. Then we can study volume and

profitability, making recommendations where necessary, and offering cash flow subsidies to get the fountain business going. The idea is to get the bottler to understand the fountain market in terms of investment economics and focus resources on fountain business. There are three necessary steps: establish an operating unit dedicated to fountain accounts, add fountain complements such as cups, other equipment, and routes; and then quadruple sales.

Infrastructure studies took 8 weeks and had the objective of developing a strategy for growing fountain business 15% annually. Pepsi FBD offered bottlers financial incentives for making required asset investments, which varied depending upon the size of the bottler's market area and the aggressiveness of the bottler's business plan. Fountain dispensing equipment constituted the bulk of the incremental asset requirements, and this ranged in price from $800 to $3,200 per unit (depending upon the type of fountain equipment appropriate for a given retail outlet) with an average of about $1,500 per unit. The plan would present a defined goal, and included evaluation of pricing, merchandising, staffing, control, delivery operations, fixed costs, contribution, and ROI for the bottler's market. Comparisons were made with historical performance, market potential, local B&C results, national fountain results, and committed bottlers in similar markets. Where time permitted, analysis was made of specific accounts in the area. In general, an entire business plan was developed for the bottler's fountain operations.

Bottlers were dealt with individually, even if they were owned by Pepsi Bottling Group. One division sales manager commented, "Bottlers are "rugged individualists" and very tough negotiators: they never want us to think we're doing enough for them."

Customers

One FBD manager noted:

In our business, it always takes at least two sales to make one: we must sell to the outlet and also convince the bottler to make the changes required to keep selling and servicing that account. If the customer is a decentralized chain, moreover, each outlet must often be sold individually even if chain headquarters has established a contract with us.

Mr. Hober commented, "It takes price competition to get new accounts, but it takes a service record to renew an account. However, the most important thing in selling is account knowledge, or 'system savvy.'" Mr. Cranor's objective for FBD was to attain the leading market share in fountain business by 1994; a New Business Development unit (NBD) was created in June 1986. Before that, new customers had been secondary to increasing volume in existing outlets because of route economics: it was cheaper and simpler to ship more product to an existing route stop than to add another location. NBD was set up to deal with large, complex accounts which required time and depth to understand and sell. The group was given complete flexibility on where to focus, but was not intended to manage an account once it was established: National Account Managers would become more and more involved as the sale progressed, and assume account responsibility after the original sale. NBD was also not intended to become directly involved with local accounts.

Ms. Burden noted that bottlers were being more strongly encouraged to establish their own sales forces for fountain business:

> FBD's focus has been so far on large accounts because those are legally defined as Pepsi's customers. However, we now want to get the bottlers more involved because our bottler service system has more potential than Coke's distributors, who are essentially delivery people. The bottler is important regardless of account ownership: if we want to capitalize on our advantage, the bottler must feel ownership of the fountain business.

Mr. Cranor had commissioned a study of "buyer values" (i.e., the issues most important to fountain syrup buyers). The study confirmed many perceptions, but also established some differences in needs and preferences among retailers in various categories. Across categories, the five most important issues in general were (in order of decreasing importance) price/economic incentives, equipment and service, account management, product quality, and marketing support (the report broke these issues into numerous details). Mr. Cranor commented, "We were somewhat surprised to find that equipment and service advantages are almost as important as spending and allowance support in the selection of a soft drink supplier. This finding further encouraged our efforts to build our bottler service support into a leadership advantage." (See **Exhibit 6** for an outline of the report's findings.)

MARKETING

FBD had the highest growth rate of any part of PepsiCo; however, fountain industry growth was slowing. For example, QSR growth was expected to be down to 2% from the 7.7% rate of the past few years. Mr. Cranor was concerned with how to maintain a high growth level as the remaining (non-Pepsi) market shrunk, and as Coca-Cola increased its attention to the threat FBD posed. He established three strategies for 1987: first, retain and grow national accounts; second, grow local business rapidly; and third, focus resources for maximum impact. Ms. Burden commented:

> FBD has grown for many years without any organized channel analysis; this is a very action-oriented company and fountain is not Pepsi's

traditional business. But by 1985 all the biggest customers were covered, and those that were still Coke customers were committed for some time. Now growth must come from two areas: building current accounts in size, and bringing in smaller national and local customers.

FBD needed little focus at first because the market was so untouched. But now Coke is becoming more aware and consequently tougher to compete with, and only 10% of the market is sold by anyone other than Coke and Pepsi. For example, only one of the top 25 restaurant chains serves a third competitor, and that's because the beverage company owns the chain. So to get new accounts now we have to go head to head with Coke, and we want to pick the best way to do that.

FBD had traditionally stressed to fountain customers that soft drinks were traffic builders for their stores and offered advertising support, point-of-sale promotions, and other services which would help increase store traffic. Mr. Cranor noted that brand marketing at FBD was dwarfed by Bottle & Can (which spent $130 million in 1986 on advertising alone), and had therefore traditionally supported B&C's focus on the consumer:

> We therefore studied each market and its soft drink consumers in order to develop a brand portfolio for each region, trying to convince fountain customers that our brands would enhance their images. Many of these vendors weren't interested.

Mr. Weinberg added:

> Many fountain customers don't take soft drinks seriously as a marketing tool. Many believe their soft drink business is "captive" in the sense that their customers aren't going to walk in or out of the establishment because of the beverage selection. Consequently, brand isn't as important as service and support (technical, sales, and marketing), and image isn't as important as understanding the fountain customer's business.

Frustration with this situation had in part motivated Mr. Cranor to consider an emphasis on channel marketing, rather than brand marketing, at FBD. He suspected that image enhancement would be important in some fountain channels but not in others, and marketing effectiveness might be improved by focusing on these differences. However, Mr. Cranor also noted some potential difficulties in reorienting FBD's marketing activities:

> It's hard to legitimize a sales-oriented division in a brand-oriented company. It goes against the grain here to dwell on channel processes. But many fountain customers are indifferent to brand advertising expenditures. In fact, I suspect FBD could simply stop spending money on advertising because the people down the hall at Pepsi Bottle & Can spend so much on consumer ads and promotions.

In this business, volume is volume: what's the difference if the fountain outlet sells Pepsi or Slice? What's important is that Pepsi products are at the fountain and that competitors' brands are not. But we're now in only 70,000 out of a total of 220,000 chain fountain outlets, and we clearly can't go after 150,000 new outlets at once. We should focus on a few major segments, and there are several criteria we can use to focus: size, growth, our historical success with a fountain channel, and the nature of our competitive advantage.

Channels

During the winter of 1985–86, FBD unexpectedly achieved success with convenience stores because of an idea called "Dual Cola." 7-11 convenience stores started offering a choice between Coke and Pepsi, and other stores imitated the practice. Pepsi encouraged the trend in an effort to gain share in many chains. Although there were many successes, it became clear to sales managers that different sales strategies were effective in different channels. Mr. Swanhaus noted, "When our QSR tactics were extended to other restaurants, they met with little enthusiasm. Convenience stores run a very different kind of business from their point of view, and they did not respond well to being talked to as if they were QSRs. They wanted features we hadn't yet thought about, such as joint can/fountain programs, since they sell both."
Ms. Burden added,

Unfortunately there is not much information available in the fountain industry on volume and behavior patterns. We have long seen differences among quick serve restaurants, theaters, and convenience stores. But in the past, someone would have an idea, assign someone else to analyze it, and work from there ad hoc. Now we must develop tighter analysis, parallel points of comparison, and a marketing framework.

During the summer of 1986, nine channel categories (listed on page 1 and **Exhibit 7**) were established. Mr. Weinberg commented on the process:

Understanding different channels means understanding different criteria. We broke outlets down into categories based on overall similarities and differences in buying criteria. This separation was necessarily somewhat arbitrary for the sake of making clean lines and not too many subclassifications. It's not been based on any sophisticated template or checklist: there are many opportunities out there, so we are still opportunistic.

Mr. Cranor commented,

Other manufacturers may have QSRs and convenience stores isolated, but that's all. We can also target low-competition, high-margin channels that the others are ignoring. The demand is to understand the channel, its mechanisms, consumers, and history, and develop a strategy, test it, and roll it out fast. I want to know how the buyer makes decisions, what's important, and how soft-drinks can help him achieve his goals.

For example, hotels do 10 million gallons of syrup business each year; what can FBD do for hotels that Coke can't? Hotels want simple operations, and Pepsi's bottlers can serve all the restaurants, bars, banquet halls and can vending machines, while Coke has various bottlers and distributors driving in and out. That's the kind of competitive advantage we need to exploit. Sit-down restaurants also seem to respond to one-stop service: they will likely buy from the supplier who delivers everything they need without complication. Even supermarkets are now starting to serve fountain drinks at deli counters.

Marketing collected available estimates of volume in each channel as well as collective judgments about potential economic returns for FBD and its bottlers in each channel (see **Exhibit 7**). QSRs were the largest channel, accounting for over half the total volume. The largest QSR, McDonald's (a Coca-Cola customer), made up 23% of the QSR segment, or 8% of total national business. QSRs had also led growth trends, closely followed by convenience stores. Although FBD had contracts with Burger King and had been very effective in the QSR channel, national volume had declined in five of the other eight channels in the past four years.

Channel profitability for FBD was based primarily on the level of marketing spending required to support accounts in a channel; QSRs and other restaurants provided only adequate returns compared to other categories. Cup vending accounts required little support from FBD, but heavy equipment investments made these accounts prohibitive to bottlers and older technology made them inconvenient (to bottlers and consumers) compared to can vending. Many cup vending accounts were actually operations run by institutional feeders. Sports arenas demanded huge promotional spending, and in fact were only considered national business so that both Pepsi and the bottler could share the expenses.

Ms. Burden also prepared a listing of the top 25 fountain accounts in the nation as well as a matrix comparing channel growth and market size with Pepsi's share of that channel (**Exhibit 8**).

Conclusion

Mr. Cranor reviewed FBD's current position and data about fountain channels with the following questions in mind. Should FBD focus its marketing activities on channel distinctions and, if so, how and according to what criteria and priorities? What restructuring within FBD would be required to put any new programs in place, and what were the implications of any changes for current marketing managers, the sales force, bottlers, and the place of FBD within PepsiCo? Finally, if marketing were reoriented to focus on channels, how should any changes best proceed for a smooth transition and maximum effectiveness?

EXHIBIT 1 **Pepsi-Cola Fountain Beverage Division: Marketing Organization**

Selected Financial Data: PepsiCo, Inc.($ in millions)

	1986	1985	1984
Net Sales			
Soft drinks	$3,588.4	$2,725.1	$2,565.0
Snack foods	3,018.4	2,847.1	2,709.2
Restaurants	2,684.0	2,081.2	1,833.4
Total continuing operations	$9,290.8	$7,653.4	$7,107.6
Foreign portion	$1,225.8	$951.9	$963.9
Operating Profits			
Soft drinks	$348.6	$283.4	$86.6
Snack foods	342.8	392.5	393.9
Restaurants	210.1	198.1	183.8
Corporate expenses, net	(221.2)	(202.4)	(213.5)
Income from continuing operations before income taxes	$680.3	$671.6	$450.8
Foreign portion	$64.7	$70.0	$(139.9)
Capital Spending			
Soft drinks	$193.9	$160.7	$83.6
Snack foods	298.6	286.3	188.9
Restaurants	384.6	331.0	252.5
Corporate	9.2	7.9	30.8
Total continuing operations	$886.3	$785.9	$555.8
Foreign portion	$81.4	$67.3	$36.4
Identifiable Assets			
Soft drinks	$2,617.7	$1,318.6	$1,038.9
Snack foods	1,603.8	1,487.1	1,254.5
Restaurants	2,659.5	1,326.7	1,020.7
Corporate	1,147.6	1,760.5	1,277.0
Total continuing operations	$8,028.6	$5,892.9	$4,591.1
Foreign portion	$2,275.0	$1,054.3	$687.5
Statistics and Ratios			
Return on average shareholders' equity	23.5%	22.8%	15.1%
Return on net sales	4.9	5.5	3.9
Total debt to total capital employed	47.5	34.4	26.5
Employees	214,000	150,000	150,000

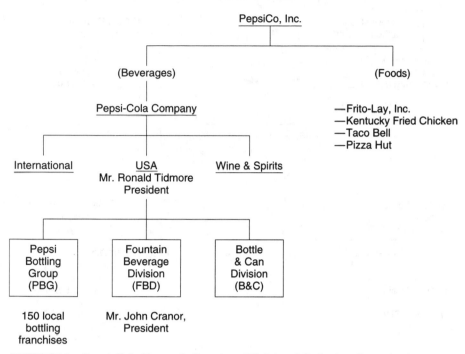

Corporate Organization

PepsiCo, Inc.

(Beverages)

(Foods)

Pepsi-Cola Company

—Frito-Lay, Inc.
—Kentucky Fried Chicken
—Taco Bell
—Pizza Hut

International

USA
Mr. Ronald Tidmore
President

Wine & Spirits

Pepsi
Bottling
Group
(PBG)

Fountain
Beverage
Division
(FBD)

Bottle
& Can
Division
(B&C)

150 local
bottling
franchises

Mr. John Cranor,
President

EXHIBIT 2   Pepsi-Cola Fountain Beverage Division: Marketing Organization

Product Flow Chart

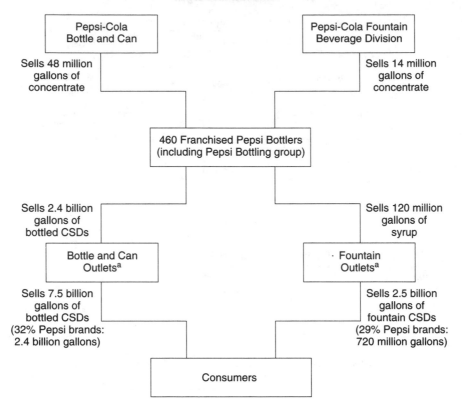

aSome outlets, such as convenience stores, sold both fountain and bottled beverages.

EXHIBIT 3   Pepsi-Cola Fountain Beverage Division: Marketing Organization

EXHIBIT 4   Pepsi-Cola Fountain Beverage Division: Marketing Organization

FBD Syrup Gallonage Sold to Fountain Accounts (millions)

	1986		1987 Goal	
	Volume	*Increase over 1985*	*Volume*	*Increase over 1986*
National Business[a]	65.8 gal.	5.6%	69.7 gal.	6.0%
Local Business	29.5	14.0	34.0	15.0
Total	95.3 gal.	8.1%	103.7 gal.	8.8%
National S.O.M	28.9 share points	0.4 share points		
Local S.O.M	29.4	3.4		
Total S.O.M	29.1	1.4		

[a]Any account with two or more outlets in each of two or more bottlers' territories.

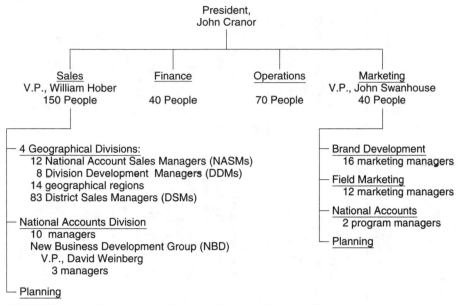

FBD Organization

President, John Cranor

| Sales V.P., William Hober 150 People | Finance 40 People | Operations 70 People | Marketing V.P., John Swanhouse 40 People |

- 4 Geographical Divisions:
  - 12 National Account Sales Managers (NASMs)
  - 8 Division Development Managers (DDMs)
  - 14 geographical regions
  - 83 District Sales Managers (DSMs)
- National Accounts Division
  - 10 managers
  - New Business Development Group (NBD)
    - V.P., David Weinberg
    - 3 managers
- Planning

- Brand Development
  - 16 marketing managers
- Field Marketing
  - 12 marketing managers
- National Accounts
  - 2 program managers
- Planning

EXHIBIT 5   Pepsi-Cola Fountain Beverage Division: Marketing Organization

EXHIBIT 6   **Pepsi-Cola Fountain Beverage Division: Marketing Organization**

Customer Values by Category (Check mark indicates "very important")

Buyer Values	Cafeterias	Contract Feeders	Hotels	Convenience Stores	Theaters	Chain Restaurants
Customized, Individualized Marketing Programs	✓	✓	✓	✓	✓	✓
Marketing Programs that are Appropriate to Our Segment	✓	✓	✓	✓	✓	
Joint Vending and Food Service Programs		✓	✓	✓		
Market Share/Customer Reference	✓	✓		✓		
Proven Industry Leadership and Expertise		✓		✓	✓	
Proven Profitability of Selling Soft Drinks	✓	✓	✓	✓	✓	✓
Billing and Rebate Flexibility to Ease Use of Marketing Support	✓		✓			
Innovations to Improve Our Operating Efficiency/ Capacity	✓	✓	✓	✓	✓	✓
Guaranteed High Service Levels	✓	✓	✓	✓	✓	✓

EXHIBIT 6 (*continued*) **Comparing Images of Pepsi and Coke: The Customer's Viewpoint**

PEPSI

Most Frequent

Aggressive

Unorganized
A Regional Company
Marketing Oriented
Quality Company

Frequent

Less Frequent

Entrepreneurial	Great Marketing Company
Solid	The Avis Role
Competitive	Stronger Sales Organization
Operational & Service Oriented	Going through the Motions
Better Commercials	Better Attuned to Corporate Relationships
Turnover	Ethical
Spotty Service	Reactionary
Lagging in Marketing Programs	Systemically Flexible
Quality	Followers
Wrapped Up in Themselves	Daring
Retail-Oriented	Upstart
Midwestern	High Energy
	Ready-Aim-Fire
	More Interested in the Business
	More Able & Willing to Work with You

COKE

Most Frequent

Conservative
Marketing Oriented
Professional
Quality Company
The Cadillac

Frequent

Arrogant

Established
Autocratic
Aggressive
Innovative

Less Frequent

Relying on Past Reputation	More Personnel Resources
Domineering	Better Structure & Organization
Promotional	More Marketing Support
Game Player	More Capable People
Docile	Motherhood
Insensitive	More Adaptable
Inflexible	Not Adaptable
Leaders	Traditional
The "Big Blue" of Soft Drinks	Stable
Nonfinancial	Consistent
Diversification to the Max	"Coke Is It"
Stodgy	The Big Company
Resting on Laurels	Vacillating
Not as Aggressive	Wrapped Up in Themselves
Bureaucratic	Popular
Renewed	National

EXHIBIT 7   Pepsi-Cola Fountain Beverage Division: Marketing Organization

FBD Performance by Channel

Channel	1986 National Volume	1986 % of National Volume	1986 Pepsi National Share	1986 Non-Pepsi National Volume	1982–86 National Volume Growth Rate	1982–86 Pepsi Volume Growth Rate	Economic Returns Pepsi/Bottler	1986 Local Volume[a]
Quick Service Restaurant	118 MM gals.	51.9%	37.7%	73.5 MM gals.	7.7%	16.1%	Marginal/Good	6 MM gals.
Sit-down Restaurant	29	12.7	7.4	26.9	1.2	1.2	Marginal/Good	34
Cup Vending	25	11.0	23.5	19.1	0.7	(1.0)	Good/Negative	19
Convenience Stores	22	9.9	37.8	13.7	7.4	6.8	Good/Good	1
Institutional Feeders	10	4.5	12.6	8.6	1.2	(1.7)	Good/Good	5
Theaters	8	3.7	13.0	6.9	2.3	(1.1)	Good/Good	1
Sports Arenas	7	3.0	11.7	6.2	4.5	(13.5)	Negative/Negative	2
Hotels	5	2.0	12.2	4.4	(3.6)	2.7	Good/Good	4
Cafeterias	3	1.4	4.0	2.9	3.5	(7.1)	Good/Good	3
Totals	227 MM gals. 100%		28.5%	162.2 MM gals.	5.0%	10.6%		75 MM gals.

[a]Volume available to local, bottler-managed accounts.

Fountain Beverage Account Prospects

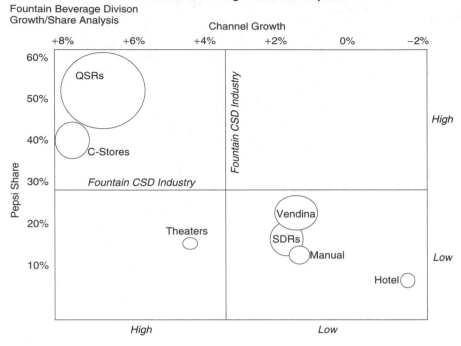

Fountain Beverage Divison
Growth/Share Analysis

Top Restaurant Chains

Chain	1985 Revenues (millions)	Outlets	Cola Served
Mcdonald's	$11,000.9	8,901	Coca-Cola
Burger King	4,290.0	4,534	Pepsi-Cola
Kentucky Fried Chicken	3,368.0	7,106	Pepsi-Cola
Wendy's	2,664.0	3,442	Coca-Cola
Pizza Hut	2,580.8	4,845	Pepsi-Cola
Hardee's	1,890.0	2,562	Coca-Cola
Dairy Queen	1,572.0	4,805	Coca-Cola/Pepsi-Cola
Domino's Pizza	1,084.0	2,891	Coca-Cola
Taco Bell	1,065.0	2,328	Pepsi-Cola
Denny's	1,043.2	1,121	Coca-Cola
Big Boy	946.0	810	Coca-Cola
Red Lobster	869.4	386	Coca-Cola
Arby's	811.0	1,550	Royal Crown
Long John Silver's	667.0	1,369	Coca-Cola
Church's Fried Chicken	639.9	1,549	Coca-Cola
Ponderosa	639.1	637	Coca-Cola
Jack-In-The-Box	597.0	800	Coca-Cola
Dunkin Donuts	476.7	1,447	Pepsi-Cola
Shoney's	570.0	497	Coca-Cola
Sizzler	500.0	475	Coca-Cola
Baskin-Robbins	484.1	3,217	Coca-Cola
Roy Rogers	471.8	543	Coca-Cola
Friendly	471.4	750	Coca-Cola
Western Sizzlin'	436.0	574	Coca-Cola
Bonanza	421.0	552	Coca-Cola/Pepsi-Cola

EXHIBIT 8   Pepsi-Cola Fountain Beverage Division, Marketing Organization

Case 5

Packaged Products Company: Handy-Pak Introduction

In April 1991, Ted Balian (senior product manager for New Business Development), Karen Maslin (director of Research and Analysis; R&A), and others at the Snack Foods Division (SFD) of Packaged Products Company (PPCo) were considering the upcoming roll-out of Handy-Pak, a new line of peanuts in distinctive packaging. Handy-Pak's packaging was intended to differentiate the product and expand the market for nuts products by appealing to consumers' desires for convenient, resealable, fresh snacking nuts. PPCo's nuts products were sold through its direct sales force into convenience stores, drugstores, and mass merchandisers and through independent broker organizations into grocery stores. Each sales channel represented different opportunities and constraints for the development and execution of marketing programs.

This case was prepared by Professor Frank V. Cespedes and Research Associate Laura Goode as the basis for class discussion rather than to illustrate either effective or ineffective handling of an administrative situation. The corporate names, as well as certain company and industry data, have been disguised.

Copyright © 1992 by the President and Fellows of Harvard College. Harvard Business School case 9–593–057. Rev. June 7, 1994.

COMPANY BACKGROUND

Established through the merger and acquisition of a number of independent packaged-goods producers, PPCo marketed a range of products through four operating divisions: Paper Products, Health and Beauty Care, Laundry Products, and Snack Foods. Each division was treated as a relatively autonomous unit with its own production, sales, product management, market research, purchasing, personnel, and finance functions (see **Exhibit 1**). SFD, headquartered in Columbus, Ohio, and with 1990 sales of more than $1 billion, manufactured and sold candies, gum, and other confections as well as crackers and nuts. The latter product group was the division's largest source of sales volume and traditionally sold strongest in the fourth quarter.

SFD products were sold through grocery/supermarkets, drugstores, mass merchandisers (i.e., a discount or general merchandise outlet such as KMart or Wal-Mart), and convenience stores (i.e., outlets in gas stations as well as chains such as Southland or Cumberland Farms). Other channels included vending machines, food service businesses, and military installations. Many SFD marketing decisions were influenced by channel characteristics. One manager explained:

> Prominent point-of-sale programs are important for most SFD products. But the type of display varies across product category and trade channel. In convenience stores, for example, consumers often eat our products shortly after purchase, and (within limits) price point is irrelevant. In faster-growing channels like gas station mini-marts, space is limited and being at the counter is crucial. It's different in grocery stores or mass merchandisers where aisle placement and detailed plan-o-gramming within the aisle are important.

In turn, SFD product managers were increasingly urged to develop and design products, merchandising programs, and promotions with these channel differences in mind.

Industrywide, larger supermarkets (more than $2 million in annual sales per store) represented over 60% of total package nut dollar volume in 1990, followed by drugstores (15%), mass merchandisers (10%), convenience stores (10%), and small independent grocery stores (less than 5%). Within each class-of-trade, however, there were large variations in sales performance. All dry-grocery items, for example, accounted for about 20% of mass merchandiser sales in 1990, but the amount varied significantly from one chain to the next. Similarly, while snack foods accounted for an estimated 1.5% of supermarket sales volume, a Snack Food Association study indicated they generated more than 7% of store profits and that consumption of different snack food categories varied by region (see **Exhibit 2**).

For SFD nuts products, supermarkets were sold and serviced by 50 broker organizations, and other trade channels by the SFD sales force. For other SFD products, supermarkets, drugstores, and mass merchandisers were sold and serviced by the SFD sales force; convenience stores, smaller independents, newsstands, and other "down-the-street" outlets were the responsibility of independent candy/tobacco jobbers. The extent of trade promotions varied significantly by product category, and marketing managers believed that this had implications for the "share of mind" that sales channels gave to each product group.

In the past three years, SFD had introduced new ad campaigns and products in each of its major categories. An executive noted that "new products can increase our sales, shelf space, and brand equity, while responding to some basics in our business: our products are predominantly impulse items that should be in many different forms and anywhere the urge strikes—food stores, gas stations, train stations. Anywhere."

SFD Nuts Marketing Organization

Reporting to Carol Bellamy (vice president of marketing) were marketing units for nuts, confections, crackers, and New Business Development. Nuts marketing consisted of product managers in four groups.

Peanuts, SFD's largest source of nuts volume, were sold in three types (oil roasted, dry roasted, and honey roasted) in a variety of can and jar sizes. SFD held a major share position in this category.

Mixed and tree nuts were also leading brands in their categories. This product group included cashews, walnuts, almonds, pistachios, and sunflower nuts, offered in oil-, dry-, and honey-roasted varieties. Compared to peanuts, mixed and tree nuts had higher price points, both for SFD and the trade.

Cello/Single Serve included all single-serve (1 and 2 oz. sizes) and snacking-size (larger than 2 oz.) cellophane-bagged products as well as baking/cooking nuts of several types.

The New Business Development group identified opportunities and introduced new products across the categories in which SFD competed. In most cases, ongoing product management responsibilities were turned over to a marketing group about one year after introduction. (Handy Pak was an example of a New Business project that, if successful, would eventually be moved into the peanuts marketing group.)

Each product manager had P&L responsibility for assigned brands as well as other responsibilities outlined in the following position description:

> The Product Manager is the primary force behind all programs and recommendations affecting the brand. The Product Manager assumes broad strategic responsibilities and serves as the company expert in all matters pertaining to the brand. The Product Manager is responsible for initiating and leading business development programs, executing and controlling the marketing plan, coordinating all department/staff resources, developing strong working relationships with the ad agency, and training/developing the Brand group.

Reporting to product managers were associate and assistant managers who worked on brand projects in areas such as advertising, promotions, packaging, or R&D. Product managers generally were MBAs having 5+ years with SFD or previous brand experience at other firms.

New assistant product managers spent six weeks in a field sales office, and a few product managers had some additional sales experience (generally with firms other than PPCo). One product manager noted: "My key measures are brand profit contribution, market share, and dollar volume. These measures cut across other functions' metrics. Sales, for example, is measured primarily on unit volume shipments, and I try to educate the sales force about brand profitability so they can understand why I act as I do." Another product manager (who had been a brand manager with another firm before joining PPCo) noted, "At my previous firm, I had an offer to move into a mid-level sales position, but my boss discouraged me. He said it would not help me get more responsibility with the bigger company brands, and set me behind my peers in brand management who would be assuming more responsibility while I spent time in the field. I think he was honest with me: one brand manager at that firm did go into Sales, and when he came back to corporate was treated as an interesting oddity." A marketing manager commented: "In Brand, it is always your goal to spend more time in the field; after all, you want to increase the field's attention to your products. But other responsibilities typically crowd out the time planned for field interaction." A human resources manager noted: "Our marketing managers operate at a national level and with specific brand orientations. They're not as familiar with regional or account differences. Meanwhile, Sales is driven by specific accounts, volume shipments, and specific trade deals. It's my observation that Marketing and Sales *do* talk to each other, but typically when it's clear that they won't hit their numbers. Then, interaction increases significantly."

In the nuts category (see **Exhibit 3**), SFD competed with other national brands such as Franklin Nuts and Hawk Snacks (like SFD, both divisions of large multiproduct consumer-goods corporations) as well as numerous private label and small regional brands. The national brands had list prices 10%–20% higher than private label products, while regional brands varied across price points. Annually, nuts were purchased by more than 35% of U.S. households (representing over 50% of the population), with the typical household buying 3–4 pounds. Peanuts in cans and jars accounted for the large majority of purchases, followed by mixed nuts and cashews. In surveys, consumers listed nut type as their most important purchase criterion followed by price, brand, and container size. Nut users were evenly distributed among males and females, with 30% less than 35 years old and 70% more than 35.

During the 1980s, snack food sales, driven by many new "light" low-calorie lines and convenient microwave product forms (e.g., popcorn), grew by more than 7% annually and in 1990 represented a $29 billion market at retail. But a trade journal noted that "the nut category has had little to brag about":

The growth that followed the launch of honey roast varieties has been followed by a prolonged slump. Annual sales increases throughout the last half of the 1980s averaged less than 2%. Category growth last year came from the mixed nuts and baking nuts segments. . . . Consumers use nuts as snack food, but the category lacks top-of-mind awareness and is considered more expensive and less convenient than chips or popcorn. . . . The importance of a quick turnaround in the space-conscious supermarket world was articulated by a buyer from a Midwestern wholesaler: "If something doesn't happen soon, we may start paring lines down." [Another] stated: "If nuts are merchandised properly, people will buy them. I don't think the category is dead . . . but it must be innovative."[1]

According to the Snack Food Association, nut sales in 1990 were down 1% in sales volume and 4% in poundage from 1989. "Despite the high level of new product introductions," an industry report noted, "it appears that the economy encouraged consumers to switch to lower-priced snacks. With the 1991 economy still in a recession/weak-growth mode, we look for comparable volume performance."

SFD Sales Organization

The SFD sales function was organized geographically, with regional sales directors (RSDs) reporting to the vice president of Sales. RSDs managed both the SFD sales force and broker sales channels and were responsible for attaining the region's distribution, merchandising, and sales goals within approved budgetary guidelines. These goals were assigned during the annual marketing planning process in which objectives, by brand, were established by the marketing organization and then sent to Sales for allocation among territories. Sales compensation involved a salary plus a bonus tied primarily to attainment of sales volume goals.

Reporting to RSDs were national accounts managers (NAMs) and division sales managers (DSMs) as well as administrative personnel. National accounts—customers with a central buying, merchandising and/or policy group but with stores or warehouses in several major markets—accounted for about a quarter of SFD sales. NAMs were responsible for attaining volume and merchandising objectives by building permanent distribution of designated products throughout the various locations and managing promotion dollar accruals for their accounts. NAMs worked with senior headquarters managers at accounts, conducted formal business reviews, and were responsible for coordinating the sales and merchandising activities of both SFD and broker salespeople that called on an account's various locations.

Division sales managers were responsible for direct and broker sales efforts and attainment of assigned sales objectives. DSMs developed and managed forecasts and sales programs (including merchandising programs)

[1] Michael Sansolo, "Snack Foods," *Progressive Grocer* (July 1990).

and conducted performance reviews of SFD salespeople and broker organizations in their territories.

Reporting to DSMs were key account managers (KAMs) and district managers (DMs) for broker and direct sales channels. Key accounts were trade customers with multiple stores or warehouses and central buying. KAMs were responsible for attaining volume and dollar objectives, building permanent distribution of designated products, securing and maintaining merchandising standards, and managing promotional activities at assigned accounts. Promotion priorities included attaining off-shelf displays, feature pricing, and retail advertising support.

Broker DMs were responsible for planning and evaluating broker programs in their districts while ensuring profitable attainment of assigned sales objectives. Food brokers represented on commission (which, industrywide, averaged 3% of sales) 5 to 60 different principals, usually manufacturers of branded products. For principals, brokers meant lower selling expenses than a direct sales effort. A 1990 Food Marketing Institute study found that introducing a new item cost, on average, about $4.82 per SKU per store via direct sales channels versus $1.08 per SKU via brokers. In addition to sell-in efforts, broker reps generally provided merchandising assistance by arranging shelves, rotating stock, and checking shelf tags while also setting up displays, feature ads, and other point-of-sale promotions for their principals.

Food brokerage was historically a fragmented business with many new entrants and exits as employees left brokers and took principals with them. In recent years, however, consolidation among brokers had increased. One industry executive noted that "many brokers have gone out of business because stores are increasingly owned by chains that buy direct or are affiliated with large wholesalers. And the fewer brokers there are in an area, the more potential conflicts arise between brands." Another noted that "brokers represent more products than a single manufacturer typically does, so they can provide breadth of coverage in a market area and often spend more time in any one store than a direct sales rep, developing stronger relationships with account personnel." The head of a food broker commented: "The business has really changed over the past 10 years. Both manufacturers and retailers are asking us to perform more activities for more new products, and the information requirements have increased dramatically. We're finding that, especially in grocery channels, marketing programs are being developed for individual accounts and different groups of stores within a chain, based on income, ethnic or other characteristics of their patronage."

Direct DMs had the same responsibilities as broker DMs, but worked with 10 to 15 SFD sales representatives and retail specialists. Salespeople were assigned a number of direct buying accounts, and were expected to make at least 6 calls daily, with performance evaluated in terms of sales volume, distribution levels, and attainment of assigned merchandising and promotion goals. Depending upon the account, salespeople interacted with different levels of account personnel for a variety of selling, administrative, service, and other issues. Their merchandising activities included implementing approved plans and plan-o-grams, securing additional product facings, and correcting out-of-stock conditions. Most SFD sales reps worked out of their homes, but met as a district group for quarterly sales meetings.

Retail Specialists were part-time personnel who had flexible hours but assigned territories and routes. Their duties included erecting and maintaining display materials, regularly inspecting and rotating products, and obtaining the best facings for SFD products on racks, shelves, and other in-store merchandising vehicles. The RS position was created in 1990 to off-load from salespeople some of these merchandising tasks.

The Sales Planning function was responsible for the design and coordination of all promotions and sales force incentive programs. Robert Carpenter, director of sales planning, noted that "this means our mission is to plan the work and then work the plan":

> We review local programs developed by Sales and provide direction to ensure these programs accord with Brand strategies. We also seek to ensure that volume and contribution goals are achieved in all classes of trade. Sales Planning thus wears "all the hats," depending on a program's requirements. We are a liaison between Marketing, Sales, Distribution, and Manufacturing. In part, this means translating other functions' requirements into effective field communications.

Reporting to Carpenter were planning managers for each SFD product group, each with other managers (aligned by brands) reporting to them. Group managers stayed in Sales Planning for a number of years, while others typically came from field sales positions for a two-year assignment. Managing promotions required negotiating the types and amounts of the trade deals with the relevant brand groups and RSDs; the product manager had the final say as to how and where these marketing monies would be spent. Carpenter commented:

> It takes a certain type of individual to work well in Sales Planning. He or she must understand a number of different product lines, and it helps to have special knowledge of certain areas like brokers, wholesalers, and various classes-of-trade. At the same time, the person must be detail oriented and possess excellent communication skills. Increasingly, computer usage is a bigger part of the job. Finally, Sales Planning inevitably involves much negotiating across functions and you never please everybody. Moreover, when things are going well, neither Sales nor Marketing pays much attention to you.

Sales Planning reported to the vice president of Sales Operations, Neil Exter, who also managed Logistics and Customer Service (order entry including electronic data interfaces with a number of retail, wholesale, and broker accounts). Exter noted:

From my perspective, there are certain basic facts about our business. Down-stream, most retail buyers handle 50 to 80 SFD items and we ship to these accounts with widely varying delivery schedules. Up-stream, we buy tons of agricultural commodities, and volume drives purchasing discounts as well as manufacturing, order-entry, and distribution efficiencies. Hence, we have profit responsibility in Marketing and primarily volume responsibility in Sales, and both are fundamental. If either Marketing or Sales is entirely happy, something's wrong. We must guard against clever marketing programs that can't be sold and volume-driven sales requests that aren't profitable.

Merchandising Requirements

Developing broad merchandising strategies was product management's responsibility; program design was handled primarily by Sales Planning and in-store implementation by the field sales force and broker reps. An SFD executive noted that "store interest in our products is high because of the strong marketing support that results in high consumer take-away. But in our categories, the brands merchandised most effectively enjoy the greatest sales. To sell at their best, our products need to be displayed in more than one location and in a variety of display types."

In SFD merchandising programs, the following activities were important. *Shelf arrangement:* SFD strove to position its brands either next to or above competing items in each category. *Special displays:* location early in the traffic pattern of a store was a key factor in display effectiveness. In supermarkets, end-of-aisle and areas in or next to high traffic aisles were prime locations for displays such as free-standing racks, counter racks, prepacks (shipping containers designed for use as free-standing floor units), and shelf extenders or j-hooks (small racks or hooks attached to a shelf, usually to display items outside their regular sections). *Secondary displays:* displaying two or more related items (e.g., soda and peanuts) in a single tie-in display. *Point-of-sale-material:* signs placed on the shelf or on special displays.

Plan-o-Grams[2] were the primary vehicle utilized by salespeople and retail buyers to manage the placement of selected products on a display. To help consumers quickly locate specific brands and pack sizes, SFD recommended that products be grouped into separate categories and, within each category, shelf space be based on each product's sales contribution by class-of-trade. In most classes-of-trade, SFD competed for shelf and display space with other nuts vendors as well as marketers of snacks, soft drinks, and other items. An industry observer noted, "During the past decade, the definition of 'snack' has broadened considerably and hundreds of new items have been introduced. Shelf space is now at a premium throughout the industry and, unless you're going to bid-up slotting fees and other monies, it's

---

[2] A plan-o-gram is a schematic diagram of a rack, shelf, section, or department in a retail store, indicating the shelf position and facings (i.e., number of packages of an item across the front row) for each product.

specific information that will or won't get you more space." Studies indicated that, compared to many other products typically displayed in supermarkets, nuts generated better consumer sales response to in-store feature displays and snack nut sales were maximized in sections of 40 to 50 linear feet of shelf space. Salespeople were urged to emphasize these facts to retail buyers.

By 1991, the number of SKUs in the average supermarket was approaching 18,000. According to one study,[3] buyers at supermarket chains listened to about 12 new-product presentations weekly, each lasting about 20 minutes during the one morning of the week typically allocated to vendor presentations. The study found that, on average, buyers turned down about two-thirds of new products presented, and that nearly 50% of those surveyed had a policy of deleting one or more items for each new item accepted. At chains, headquarters buyers usually had authority to authorize initial distribution, discontinue an item, set retail price, and determine an item's general store location, shelf position, number of facings, and display support (if any). At wholesalers, authority for these activities was more decentralized to field managers or independent owner-operators affiliated with a wholesaler.

RESEARCH AND ANALYSIS

Until 1989, a Marketing Services department reported to the vice president of Marketing at SFD and provided research for product management. In 1989, Karen Maslin was hired from another consumer goods firm to head this department, which became more closely aligned with SFD's MIS. group and with responsibilities expanded to include forecasting and promotion evaluation in addition to consumer analysis studies. In 1990, Sales as well as Marketing assumed a portion of research expenses, and in 1991 the group's name was changed to Research & Analysis.

For SFD product managers, R&A provided analyses of data from syndicated research services; customized research (typically initiated by a request from a brand manager) concerning product testing, copy testing, consumer tracking studies, market assessments, focus groups, or positioning studies; and ongoing research to monitor brand performance, market developments, and competitive threats or opportunities. Each product group had its own research budget and negotiated annually with R&A.

Several managers referred to R&A as "the Switzerland of the organization: neutral territory and a free-standing conduit of information among Marketing, Sales, R&D, Manufacturing, and Finance." Maslin commented:

> From my experience at other firms, I was aware of the barriers that tend to arise between Marketing and Sales, and I had opinions about what Research can and cannot do to bridge these differences. I also be-

[3] "New Item Special Report," *Progressive Grocer* (November 1987).

lieve that, for all practical purposes, it's impossible to over-communicate in most companies.

I try to hire people who can act as "deep generalists": knowledgeable businesspeople with technical research capabilities, rather than technical specialists in a given research methodology. My feeling is that Research rarely finds or develops unique information; our major value-added is packaging and disseminating the learning among different functional audiences. We look at who would most benefit from certain kinds of information, who can add to it, and how to make the data a catalyst for constructive interaction among the different groups that build and sustain our products in the marketplace.

In describing R&A's role, three factors were emphasized: the impact of scanning data, the need for more fact-based selling efforts, and initiatives in shelf management.

Impact of Scanning Data Until the mid-1980s, the primary source of information about package-goods product movement was warehouse withdrawal data and field audits of selected retail stores, both provided by industry research firms. The former service tracked product movement from warehouses to retail outlets but not actual sales from retailer to consumer. The latter service involved audits of selected supermarkets and other outlets by field representatives who counted current inventory and noted changes since the previous audit. In both cases, only selected retailers participated in the service, and the time between actual product movement and receipt of such data by retailers and manufacturers was typically 2 to 3 months.

During the 1980s, the diffusion of Universal Product Codes (UPCs) and automated retail scanner systems changed the information available. Scanners gathered sales data at UPC levels of detail (which generally correlated with SKUs). Stores provided this raw data to research firms in return for the processed data, a local market area report, and credits toward specialized studies. In turn, these syndicated research services sold the processed data to manufacturers and other interested parties. Scanner systems allowed weekly collection of data about product movement, pricing, and selling conditions (e.g., relevant promotions and advertising) by store in any combination of 26 market areas in the United States. By 1990, a majority of grocery stores had scanners, and other classes-of-trade were installing scanners rapidly.

In 1989 R&A began shifting from warehouse withdrawal to scanner data. Maslin commented:

Retailers use this data to make stocking and merchandising decisions, but our sales programs were speaking a different language than the retail buyer. Internally, moreover, scanning data became the foundation for an information flow that created a need for a common language between Marketing and Sales. For example, when retail buyers have detailed data about product movement in their particular markets and stores, national brand data are less persuasive.

Field use of scanning data was pilot-tested in one SFD region. R&A managers then met with field salespeople in a feedback session. "In general," Maslin noted, "they welcomed the additional data, especially local market data. But its use required training and ways of making the data more easily comprehensible to salespeople. Their common theme was, 'help me translate this data into actionable business implications.'" Another manager noted: "Sales' metrics are tied to volume and volume was traditionally measured by warehouse withdrawals. Hence, many reps were initially confused by the change, didn't understand its implications for marketing efforts, and kept asking for the equivalent numbers in warehouse withdrawal terms."

R&A also established means for generating Account Reviews (see below), upgrading equipment in sales offices, providing training by region on system usage, and disseminating scanning data to SFD brokers. In addition, the information also led SFD executives to investigate new measurement and evaluation systems for marketing and sales managers.

Fact-based selling was a term used to describe initiatives aimed at improving the amount and types of information utilized by salespeople. A sales executive noted:

> Marketing provides broad product, promotion, and merchandising concepts. But with more local data available to the trade, the field must customize Marketing programs appropriately. Also, the trade is moving faster than many manufacturers in this regard. The more aggressive chains are hiring MBAs for headquarters buying positions, raising salaries, giving them category responsibility, and having P&L metrics drive their bonus compensation which, in some chains, is 30% of a buyer's total compensation.
>
> Our salespeople must also become category experts. They must understand the stores' marketing programs and how best to optimize our participation in those programs. This differs from traditional industry sales practice which emphasized personal relationships at the store level, a focus on individual products (vs. category movement), and a constant flow of trade deals.

To address these issues, R&A was providing more research services to Sales. One service was the development of Account Reviews, which analyzed specific category issues at a trade account and provided recommendations. An R&A manager who had worked with salespeople on developing and presenting a number of reviews commented:

> The requests are typically initiated by an account manager or DM who sees a major opportunity or threat at a trade customer. My role is to consolidate data from internal and external sources and provide a customized profile of the account and our role in the category. Then, with salespeople, we prepare competitive analyses, category overviews, and recommendations down to plan-o-gram and stocking levels.
>
> Sales' role is to understand how the buyer perceives our products

and the category. Also, the audience for these reviews is usually a number of buyers, the account's VP of Operations (who gets more involved in the trade's stocking decisions as awareness of product handling costs increases), and other executives. When Sales has cultivated a good account relationship, it's also created a climate in which people will truly listen to our data, appreciate the level of detail, and act on strategic recommendations.

Another initiative concerned trade promotion analyses. Paul Gilbert, an R&A manager, had joined PPCo in 1988. He explained:

> When I got here, trade spending was increasing but documented via 3 incompatible IS systems that could only aggregate this data at the national level across product groups. This did not foster real evaluation and accountability for promotion spending. I worked with software vendors on designing a simpler means of gathering this information and integrating it with internal shipment, account review, and regional sales data as well as with external scanner data that can tell us what specific promotions mean for product movement, forward buying, and sales over multiple time periods.

A third initiative focused on providing computerized applications that made data retrieval and analyses easier for individual salespeople. The goal was to move many of the studies described above from headquarters to field sales offices.

A fourth initiative involved the development of field positions staffed by people with previous brand management experience. The goal was to place in major market areas a person who would develop in-depth knowledge of local trade and consumer behavior while working with R&A, Sales Planning, and individual product managers at headquarters to develop sales and marketing programs customized to that trading area. An executive commented:

> The information explosion has changed buying procedures at many retailers and left many package-goods salespeople feeling out-gunned. Buyers increasingly evaluate vendors' programs in terms of the impact, not only on that product's sales, but its impact on the category, any private-labels within the category, and perhaps related categories jostling for that shelf space in a crowded supermarket. And all of this can now be done on a local-market, and even store-by-store, basis.

Shelf Management   Field shelf management procedures traditionally consisted of generating a plan-o-gram that accorded with PPCo merchandising guidelines in a product category. However, local store conditions affecting product turn rates, consumer pull, and profitability were not used to customize the shelf set to an account or class-of-trade. As part of Account Reviews, R&A managers began utilizing new software that allowed incorporation of such data.

R&A had also been involved in a change in shelf management policies. SFD had stocked all its nuts products (including baking nuts) in all package types together in a store's snack aisle. As one manager explained, "The idea was to demonstrate our collective brand strength in one core location. Also, the notion was that baking nuts were more of a planned purchase, so consumers buying baking nuts might also buy adjoining snack nuts." This strategy drove SFD nuts merchandising (and sales force training) throughout the 1980s. With the introduction of a new line of baking nuts, however, this approach was questioned. Some managers believed SFD was losing sales to competing lines in the baking aisle. R&A conducted studies which indicated that by moving SFD baking nuts into the baking aisle, sales of both baking and snack nuts increased. Hence, SFD and broker sales reps were being urged to do this as opportunities arose (e.g., additional store locations, new product introductions, or annual resets at current accounts).

Commenting on these various initiatives, Maslin noted:

> Most of these activities involve consolidating data traditionally gathered in different functional areas and then disseminating it in forms appropriate to each area. Marketing and Sales, for instance, have mutual interests but different information needs and orientations. Brand managers want detailed data; they're trained to use such data for strategic planning and as tools in seeking more resources during budgeting sessions.
>
> By contrast, Sales has historically not utilized substantial data in their account activities, and they're somewhat overwhelmed by the growing volume of data. The field's attitude often is, "wind me up and let me execute": ideally, they want to be handed a presentation ready to be used. Format and a few key points are important to them. Also, at smaller retail outlets, the selling process is very different from the KAM or NAM who sets up a formal presentation to a large grocery chain's buyers. In mom-and-pop outlets, SFD and broker reps must sell quickly to store managers as they're walking through the store handling inventory or writing up invoices.
>
> I don't see R&A as an information bridge or substitute for traditional marketing and sales efforts. Rather, we're more a conduit for increasingly necessary marketing/sales exchange.

HANDY-PAK

In early 1990, Ted Balian, as product manager for New Business Development, began researching packaging options for SFD peanuts. His objectives were to explore consumer responses to overall packaging trends (especially as related to environmental concerns) and to various packaging prototypes he had developed, including a vacuum pack. With Karen Maslin, he conducted focus-group research and noted, "We soon discovered that while consumers recognize and acknowledge environmentally friendly packaging, convenience still wins out over other considerations and the vacuum pack generated very favorable responses in terms of freshness and convenience."

Based on these focus-group reactions, Balian sought funds to conduct additional research and pursue the opportunity. The core product concept was to place SFD peanuts in a brick-shaped, resealable, vacuum pack (similar to the coffee "brick packs" introduced by various vendors in recent years). Balian noted that "the closed vacuum package represents to consumers some of the same benefits as current cans and jars do [i.e., stability, stackability, good product integrity]. When the package is opened, however, it becomes a resealable bag and more portable than a can or jar." He also emphasized the importance of speed-to-market since the vacuum pack technology was commonly available and competitive activity in the category was increasing.

In March 1990, Balian received approval and a budget, and by April had assembled a project team with representatives from R&A, Operations, Manufacturing, Finance, and Sales Planning. During the next eight months, the team investigated consumer attitudes toward the product concept and contents. **Exhibit 4** summarizes this research, which included a home use test, positioning research, and a simulated test market (chosen over a conventional in-market test in order to preserve confidentiality and save time). Quality Assurance also conducted physical distribution tests by shipping pallets of Handy-Pak by truck across the country; it found that the vacuum pack held its integrity at all altitudes and suffered less shipping damage than peanuts in cans or jars. Meanwhile, R&A tested ad copy for the best means of communicating product and packaging attributes. "Consumers' only experience with nuts presently is either eating them in single-serve packages or out of a can, jar, or serving bowl at home," noted Maslin. "Handy-Pak offers a convenience that must be demonstrated. Consumers suggested showing the package being opened, tossed, consumed away from home, resealed, or flattened after use." Ads were then developed around these themes (see **Exhibit 5**).

By late 1990, SFD was ready to integrate Handy-Pak into the 1991 marketing planning process. SFD's annual national sales meeting was scheduled for January 1991. Also scheduled for introduction at this meeting were two other nuts products as well as a number of line extensions and major new items from the confections and crackers product groups. As a result, while all products would be announced at the January meeting and sell-in at retail would begin thereafter, Handy-Pak was scheduled for shipments to stores in June 1991.

These multiple product introductions also resulted in the following market-introduction plan for Handy-Pak. National TV advertising would begin in late September of 1991, accompanied by $.50 FSI coupons. Cable Direct (a direct mail vehicle with higher redemption rates than traditional media) would distribute $.40 coupons in November. Specially priced 60-

count prepack shipping cartons, with attached $.50 Instant Redeemable coupons, were scheduled for October and November delivery to participating retailers, while in-store couponing would be conducted in January of 1992.

Product Introduction

Handy-Pak was introduced in 3 SKUs (unsalted, lightly salted, and regularly salted peanuts) in 11-ounce, brick-shaped vacuum packages (12 to a case), and list-priced at $2.59/package (about 8% more per pound than national brands in 12-ounce jars). At the SFD sales meeting in January 1991, Ted Balian emphasized that, for the trade, Handy-Pak offered several advantages:

> A package of Handy-Pak is 8% lighter but 25% smaller than a 12 oz. can; and a pallet contains 45 more cases and 540 more packages [46%] than a pallet of 12 oz. peanuts in cans or jars. Due to its rectangular shape, Handy-Pak packs out 100% more product than cans or jars in only 29% more linear inches. This means greater efficiency for the retailer in terms of lower warehousing and freight costs and better utilization of shelf space. With fast turns and higher margins, that means more direct product profit. Also, Handy-Pak's convenience and portability may move more nuts consumption toward the summer months when outdoor activities are most prevalent. This would greatly enhance the category.

Balian also noted that, as a new category concept, Handy-Pak would require careful attention to shelf location and merchandising. The priority for shelf placement was to position Handy-Pak on the store's snack nut shelf directly below the pegboard cello section and above nuts in cans and jars (see **Exhibit 6**). If SFD baking nuts were currently in the snack nut section, they should be moved to the baking aisle and replaced with Handy-Pak.

To support this merchandising strategy, the development team had created a special shelf rack system that held 14 packages. Designed for easy assembly and long life, the shelf rack could be used to create a Handy-Pak section in the nut aisle. Intended primarily for high-volume grocery accounts, the 14-inch deep racks were fastened to shelves and spring-loaded to keep the brick packages organized, neat, and front-facing. Balian commented:

> The Handy-Pak line should be viewed as a "business system" as well as a new product line. It's important to control and protect the product in its trip to consumers through innovative displays and high-quality, high-tech shelf racks. These efforts are intended to maximize the visual impact and to reduce the in-store labor needed to keep displays and shelves arranged, faced, and fronted. It can also provide a platform for future product introductions.

Conclusion

At the national sales meeting, the Handy-Pak announcement was greeted positively by SFD and broker sales representatives. In the weeks following, the product development team traveled to different regions and heard the following reports from the field:

> Marketing has introduced many new products this year. Handy-Pak will have to wait its turn while the sell-in for those products continues to build. Besides, with advertising and coupons for Handy-Pak not appearing until the fall, it's tough to convince retailers about consumer pull support at this point.

> * * * * *

> Moving baking nuts from the snack aisle to the baking aisle means dealing with additional trade buyers where our sales force doesn't have established relationships. Also, most baking nuts are sold in groceries where we distribute via brokers. The brokers' strength is their ability to sell at headquarters, not the ability to execute merchandising details; and many brokers already represent products in both aisles. So, they're concerned about replacing another principal's product if they move our baking nuts.

> * * * * *

> The Handy-Pak product *is* unique, and that's good and bad news. Some salespeople say that if a product looks strange, it must be a hard sell. They also want to see results from "a real test market, and not lab studies" before talking with retail buyers. Others say that some buyers will stock Handy-Pak, but at the expense of shelf space allocated to nuts in cans and jars, and both direct and broker reps are reluctant to do that.

> * * * * *

> The shelf-rack organizing system is clever, but there are a wide variety of shelves out there and it doesn't always fit easily. Also, it takes substantial incremental effort to sell-in and install the system, especially for broker reps.

By early April 1991, Ted Balian was concerned about the quantity and quality of effort being devoted to the Handy-Pak sell-in. Placement levels were running below projected distribution goals, and some major grocery, drug, convenience, and mass-merchandiser chains were uncommitted concerning their stocking and shelving plans for the new product line. In a meeting with Karen Maslin and others on the development team, he noted that "all indications are that we have a product that can substantially increase our brand franchise in higher-growth directions. But we need high distribution levels to do this and, in the current retail climate, essentially have one chance to do it right. I'm willing to argue for resources in support of any alteration in our marketing and sales programs that also supports the product strategy. This might mean changes in pricing, promotional plans, sales support, or sales incentives. What should we do at this point to strengthen the marketing plan and field effort for Handy-Pak?"

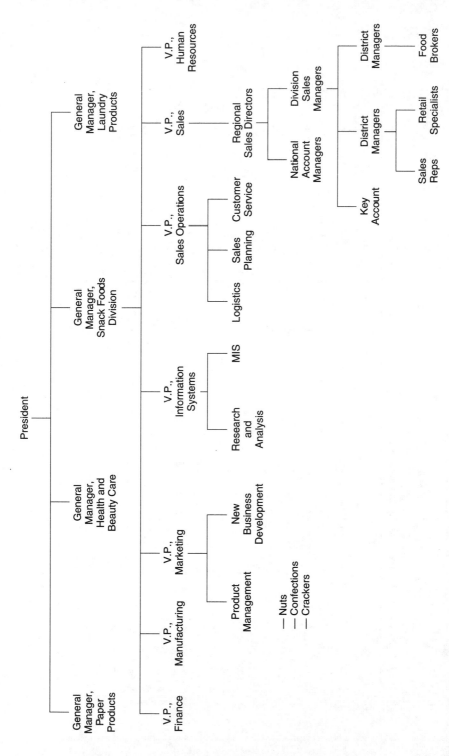

EXHIBIT 1 Packaged Products Company: Organization Chart

EXHIBIT 2 Regional Markets by Snack Categories

Snacks	Pacific	Mountain	West North Central	West South Central	East North Central	East South Central	South Atlantic	Mid-Atlantic	New England	Total U.S.
Potato chips	27.6%	32.5%	34.8%	30.2%	34.2%	36.2%	32.7%	31.4%	33.7%	32.2%
Tortilla chips	28.1	26.4	22.5	27.7	18.2	18.4	15.6	11.9	12.2	20.0
Corn chips	5.3	6.4	4.9	9.3	4.9	6.5	5.0	3.3	3.9	5.4
RTE popcorn	1.8	2.5	2.6	1.4	2.6	1.6	2.2	3.1	4.6	2.4
Microwave popcorn	5.7	4.7	5.7	5.6	6.6	7.9	8.5	6.4	8.0	6.6
Unpop. popcorn	5.6	5.7	6.6	4.5	5.8	4.4	4.2	3.5	4.9	5.0
Extruded snacks	4.5	5.0	5.8	6.2	5.2	6.0	6.3	4.8	4.5	5.4
Pretzels	3.6	3.7	4.5	2.9	9.0	4.3	7.1	17.6	6.3	7.2
Snack nuts	11.5	9.1	8.4	7.0	8.8	8.8	12.0	13.6	16.2	10.6
Meat snacks	1.8	1.5	1.3	0.8	1.2	0.8	1.8	1.8	2.0	1.5
Pork rinds	1.0	0.7	0.5	1.2	0.6	1.4	1.4	0.3	0.2	0.8
Party mix	1.1	0.9	1.1	1.1	1.2	1.0	1.4	1.0	1.4	1.1
Potato sticks	0.3	-	0.4	0.4	0.5	1.4	0.5	0.5	1.1	0.5
Onion rings	0.1175175	-	0.2	0.3	0.2	0.4	0.2	0.1	0.2	0.2
Variety packs	2.0	0.9	0.7	1.4	1.0	0.9	1.1	0.7	0.8	1.1
	100.0%	100.0%	100.0%	100.0%	100.0%	100.0%	100.0%	100.0%	100.0%	100.0%

EXHIBIT 2 (continued)

Per Capita Snack Consumption by Region (pounds per person)

Potato chips	5.04	6.90	7.60	5.61	6.30	6.54	5.31	5.16	9.01	5.96
Tortilla chips	5.14	5.61	4.92	5.14	3.35	3.32	2.54	1.95	3.56	3.70
Corn chips	0.97	1.35	1.07	1.72	0.91	1.18	0.82	0.55	1.03	1.00
RTE popcorn	0.32	0.53	0.58	0.26	0.48	0.29	0.36	0.51	1.23	0.45
Microwave popcorn	1.03	0.99	1.24	1.04	1.21	1.42	1.38	1.04	2.12	1.22
Unpop. popcorn	1.02	1.22	1.44	0.84	1.07	0.99	0.69	0.58	1.32	0.94
Extruded snacks	0.82	1.05	1.27	1.15	0.97	1.08	1.02	0.78	1.21	0.99
Pretzels	0.65	0.78	0.99	0.53	1.67	0.78	1.15	2.89	1.67	1.34
Snack nuts	2.10	1.94	1.83	1.31	1.62	1.58	1.95	2.24	4.04	1.96
Meat snacks	0.34	0.33	0.29	0.14	0.22	0.14	0.30	0.29	0.53	0.27
Pork rinds	0.19	0.15	0.11	0.22	0.10	0.25	0.22	0.05	0.06	0.15
Party mix	0.19	0.19	0.24	0.20	0.21	0.20	0.23	0.16	0.39	0.21
Potato sticks	0.05	0.06	0.09	0.07	0.10	0.07	0.08	0.08	0.28	0.09
Onion rings	0.02	0.02	0.04	0.06	0.03	0.06	0.03	0.02	0.04	0.03
Variety packs	0.37	0.19	0.15	0.26	0.19	0.16	0.18	0.11	0.22	0.21
Total (lbs. per person)	18.25	21.31	21.86	18.55	18.43	18.06	16.26	16.41	26.71	18.52
Population (millions)	36.008	13.380	18.525	28.043	41.849	14.784	42.330	29.168	12.192	246.279

Source: Snack Food Association.

EXHIBIT 3 Nut Category Overview

	Dollar Market Share			Distribution			
	1988	*1989*	*1990*	*Grocery*	*Conv.*	*Drug*	*Mass Merchandise*
Packaged Products	25.5%	23.0%	25.1%	98%	80%	76%	98%
Franklin Nuts	19.2	19.1	16.5	52	35	65	75
Hawk Snacks	15.7	18.0	17.5	66	11	25	20
Private Label	14.3	14.4	14.7	80	3	15	10
Other	25.3	25.5	26.2	—	—	—	—

Note: 1) Share figures are across all classes-of-trade, while firms' market shares and distribution (% of stores stocking a company's nut line) differ in each class-of-trade. 2) "Other" category includes regional and local firms in the product category.

Nut Sales Trends by Product Segment and Class-of-Trade

	Grocery	Convenience	Drug	Mass Merchandiser
Under 2 oz.				
1988	8.5%	25.2%	9.2%	
1989	8.1	27.2%	8.6	(Negligible)
1990	7.9	26.2	8.3	
Cello Baking				
1988	29.1		7.5	3.2%
1989	29.1	(Negligible)	7.9	4.3
1990	30.3		7.7	3.8
Cello Snacking				
1988	10.5	60.0	6.6	10.7
1989	11.0	65.8	7.5	11.6
1990	10.7	71.4	8.4	13.4
Cans and Jars				
1988	51.9	14.8	76.7	86.1
1989	51.8	7.3	76.0	84.1
1990	51.1	2.4	75.6	82.8
Total $ Volume ($ millions)				
1988	$1,110	$88	$159	$113
1989	1,112	94	174	131
1990	1,114	96	176	126

To be read: "Of the $1.114 billion of nuts sold in grocery stores in 1990, 7.9% were under 2 oz. packages, 30.3% were cello baking nuts," etc.

Share of Salty Snacks

	1980	1990
Nuts	27.4%	13.6%
Potato chips	48.1	45.5
Corn/tortilla chips	21.1	25.6
Popcorn	3.4	15.3

Source: Snack Food Magazine.

EXHIBIT 4   Handy-Pak: Consumer Research

HOME USE TEST/FOLLOW-UP FOCUS GROUPS

Objectives: Test the Handy-Pak (HP) concept against actual product usage and against HP in a can; determine which nut types were favored and consumer purchase intent after use.

Test design: Consumers were first exposed to a picture and concept statement and their reactions were recorded; consumers then used prototype HP product in their homes; surveys were then conducted to gather quantitative data; some consumers were then invited to post-use focus groups.

Major Findings:

- Very positive consumer reactions; HP snack bag seen as: convenient, safe for kids, fresh, portable, easily opened and reclosable.
- All three peanut types (salted, unsalted, and lightly salted dry-roasted) tested in HP packaging were favored over the can product, even when the nuts themselves were exactly the same.
- In follow-up focus groups, consumers talked about out-of-home usage occasions (car, beach, camping), stating they had used HP in new ways that cans and jars did not serve.
- 85% expressed positive purchase intent (vs. norm of 70% for test of this type), with 43% stating they "Definitely would buy" (vs. norm of 30%).

SIMULATED TEST MARKET

Objectives: Test the concept in different ways to measure attitude changes based on weight/price/volume perceptions; verify Home Use Test results.

Test Design: Consumers in 14 cities used 11 and 12 oz. versions of the product at home for 2 weeks (all products were packed in HP packaging, but with different labels to reflect their weight and volume); then data was gathered concerning consumer attitudes; this data was used as input to a computer model (which simulates different levels of marketing support and competitive conditions) in order to project levels of volume/cannibalization.

Major Findings:

Consumer Perceptions (% agreeing with each statement):

	HP 12 oz.	HP 11 oz.
As good/better than expected	95%	91%
Definitely would buy	52	56
Definitely/Probably would buy	90	91
Better value than current product	43	41
Could not name anything they disliked about Handy-Pak	71	70

CONCEPTOR II POSITIONING TEST

Objectives: Determine what are the most important aspects of Handy-Pak to consumers, and how they should be prioritized in advertising, packaging, and promotional materials; five positioning statements were tested: Fresh, The All-Family Snack, Unique, New/High Tech, Convenient/Contemporary.

Test Design: In 10 cities, consumers were asked to rank various product benefits and attributes described in each positioning statement; using a statistical process, the data was reordered to provide an optimal positioning statement, taking parts from all five stand-alone positions.

Major Findings:

- Tests for consumer perceptions of product uniqueness (a measure of consumer curiosity that leads to trial) indicated scores above norms:

Product is extremely different:	24 (Norm = 5)
Product is extremely/very different:	61 (Norm = 20)
Excellent/Good Value for the money:	76 (Norm = 65)

- Optimal positioning has the following major elements: (a) Portable/Convenient; (b) Reclosable; (c) 3 salt levels (salted, lightly salted, unsalted). Other benefits include "airtight," "fresh," and "price/value."

Graphics Test

Objectives: Determine which of four graphic designs generated most brand recall and positive reaction, and whether a "smooth" or "bumpy" package better communicates the graphics and overall product benefits.

Test Design: HP packages were photographically inserted into a series of photographs of typical retail nuts sections. Consumers then took a simulated shopping trip through a photographic "store"; they were asked to buy items in different categories, and none knew nuts were the subject of the test. Using a computerized "joystick," consumer moves up and down aisles, zooming in and out to closely examine products, while computer monitors which products were examined and for how long. A questionnaire was then filled out, asking for consumer reactions and purchase plans in each category.

Major Findings:

- Consumers scored "bumpy" packages higher than "smooth": bumps were seen as indication of vacuum-packing and freshness. "Vacuum-packed" and "Easy to Carry" were the package elements that caused positive purchase intent.
- 81% agreed that HP would be "easy to take out of the house and on trips."

Try Handy Pak Snack Nuts
Peanuts In The New Vacuum-Packed Bag

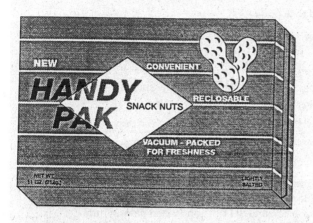

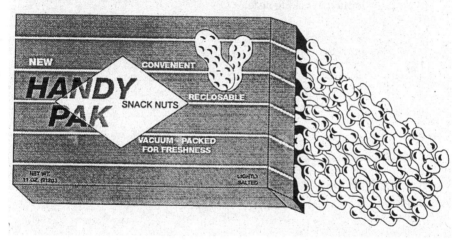

EXHIBIT 5 Sample Ad

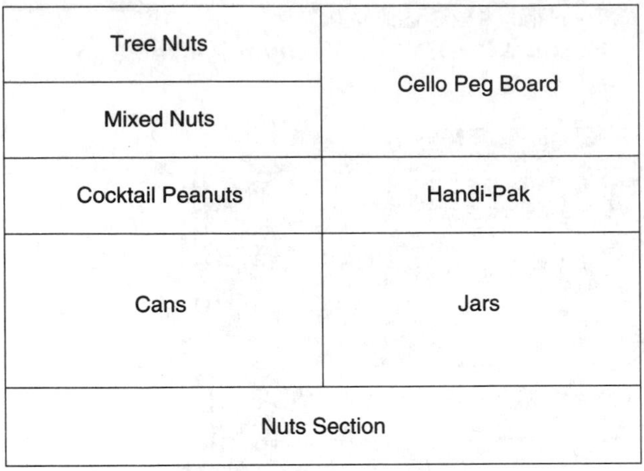

Tree Nuts	Cello Peg Board
Mixed Nuts	
Cocktail Peanuts	Handi-Pak
Cans	Jars
Nuts Section	

EXHIBIT 6 Handy-Pak Merchandising
Recommendations: Primary Location (when baking nuts
are located in baking aisle)

Case **6**

MEM Company, Inc.: English Leather

In May 1992, Gay Mayer, president of MEM Company, a producer of toiletries, was considering alterations in the firm's marketing programs, including a redeployment of field sales efforts and changes in sales compensation policies. Any changes, moreover, would be made in the context of strategic decisions concerning English Leather, the firm's major product line.

COMPANY AND INDUSTRY BACKGROUND

MEM was founded in Vienna, Austria, in 1883 by Mark Edward Mayer (whose initials became the company name) to manufacture soaps and women's perfume. (Gay Mayer, who joined MEM in 1964 after graduating from college, was the fourth generation of Mayers to head the firm.) MEM moved to the United States in 1933, and emphasis on men's fragrances began a few years later when a department store mistakenly displayed MEM

This case was prepared by Professor Frank V. Cespedes and Research Associate Laura Goode as the basis for class discussion rather than to illustrate either effective or ineffective handling of an administrative situation. Certain data have been disguised.

Copyright © 1992 by the President and Fellows of Harvard College. Harvard Business School case 9–593–035. Rev. July 7, 1994.

cologne for women in the men's department where it rapidly sold out. The company soon redesigned the package, made slight formula changes, and launched the product as "Russian Leather." In 1950 the name was changed to "English Leather" in response to Cold War concerns and a retail buyer's desire to merchandise the product with high-quality English clothing.

Sales of English Leather cologne grew gradually until the 1960s when a national advertising campaign was launched using the slogan, "All my men wear English Leather or they wear nothing at all." Headquarters were established in Northvale, New Jersey, in 1965, and the company went public in 1966. During the next two decades MEM acquired other lines, including the Tom Fields "Tinkerbell" line of children's toiletries, the Love's Baby Soft line of teenage girl's fragrances, Heaven Sent women's fragrances, Aristocrat Leather Products (wallets and accessories), and licensing rights to Acqua di Selva and Members Only (premium-priced imported men's toiletries marketed by a subsidiary primarily through department and men's specialty stores). In addition, the English Leather brand was expanded to include aftershave lotions, face savers (shave creams and lotions), body guards (soaps and deodorants), and headliners (moustache wax). In 1991, 85% of company sales (**Exhibit 1**) were in the United States, 12% in Canada and the United Kingdom, and 3% export sales to other countries.

Like most firms in the industry, MEM did not develop fragrances. They were supplied by about 30 international firms where chemists combined as many as 50 raw materials for a fragrance formula. Typically, MEM would specify a price range and target consumer group and invite fragrance developers to submit samples, which were evaluated on a range of attitudinal dimensions. Certain fragrances were then tested in selected markets. However, as one executive noted:

> This research is usually inconclusive, and other factors besides the fragrance itself affect success in this product category. Consumers associate themselves with a brand image that is personality/lifestyle-driven and highly aspirational—that is, it reflects not who they are but who they would like to be. And, you communicate that image via consistency in pricing, advertising, promotion, and the physical appearance of the product.

Compounding and packaging of toiletries products were handled in the Northvale plant. The breadth of the product line, the frequent need for short production runs, seasonality of sales, and the labor-intensive packaging process (especially for gift sets) limited manufacturing efficiencies. Mayer noted:

> Most manufacturing space is devoted to hundreds of individual components of plastic, wood, paper and glass packages and containers. Yet, new products and line extensions are important. Fragrances, while hard to establish in the marketplace, can be very profitable once established. Also, a broad product line helps to utilize fixed manufac-

turing capacity. In addition, the aging of an established brand's image is a normal occurrence in this category, and you attract younger users via new products and positionings.

Toiletry sales were traditionally concentrated around the Christmas, Father's Day, and graduation gift-giving periods, with nearly half of retail sales in November and December. MEM (where over 80% of sales typically occurred from July through December) commonly held a cash surplus during the first half of each year, but had to borrow during the second half to finance trade dating programs. Under such programs, the retail trade did not pay invoices on midyear orders for Christmas shipments until year-end, although a sliding discount scale for prepayment was offered. In August 1990, in the middle of preparations for the Christmas season, MEM's lead bank, facing problems in its real estate portfolio, notified MEM that its line of credit was not being renewed and that all debt had to be paid down by year-end. Michael Kazimir (senior vice president, Finance) was hired in November 1990 to help manage the crisis. He noted:

> The scramble to line up the more than $20 million needed to finance inventory and Christmas receivables took six months and over $600,000 in extra legal fees and bank charges. We secured interim financing, were able to get suppliers to take extended payment on overdue invoices, and in 1991 established longer-term financing and an excellent working relationship with two major banks. By January 1992, all the short-term borrowings were paid off. But the crisis motivated us to look at the entire business and consider which brands and programs fit with the changing nature of the industry and our longer-term strategy.

Men's Toiletries Market

Aftershaves and colognes are fragrances blended with varying quantities of other materials, principally water and alcohol. Once packaged, both remain chemically stable until, applied to the skin, evaporation releases the fragrance. Definitive data on men's toiletries use were sparse (partly because substantial male use of products targeted at women was believed to occur). Traditionally, women were believed to make 65%–70% of men's fragrance purchases. But research also indicated that 75% of men surveyed purchased one or more aftershave or cologne items in the course of a year. Dual-career households and time constraints were believed to support a trend toward more male self-purchase. A 1990 study found that men 18 to 49 years of age spent 30 to 45 minutes daily on personal grooming, with 80% using an aftershave or cologne and 33% using both. Cologne use was most prevalent among men 18 to 24 (73%) and decreased proportionately with age to about 50% among men 40 and older. By contrast, aftershave use was highest among men 40 to 49 (65%) and lowest among 18- to 24-year-olds (40%). **Exhibit 2** provides additional data concerning brands and purchasing behavior.

Most observers described men's toiletries as a three-tier market. The upper tier (c. 30% of the market) included prestige brands, many with "designer" labels, such as Polo or Halston, featured in department and specialty stores with prices of $20 or more per SKU (approximately $15+ per ounce). In this segment, cost of goods sold was about 20% and gross margins about 40%, although margins had been declining due to the increased use of gift-with-purchase and purchase-with-purchase promotions.[1] Promotional funds typically accounted for 15% of sales, and suppliers also paid for the cosmetician behind the counter in store fragrance departments.

The second tier (approximately 40% to 50% of annual fragrance sales) was the mid-priced mass market where most MEM products competed. These products were distributed through independent and chain drugstores (about 60% of segment sales volume in 1991), mass merchandisers (24%), and food stores (16%). Mid-priced brands generally sold for less than $20 per SKU (between $1 and $10 per ounce), and with proportionally higher cost of goods sold than prestige brands. Some observers distinguished among three types of mid-priced fragrances: new brands (such as Santa Fe or Aspen); "contemporary" brands (such as Stetson, Chaps, and Jovan Musk); and "traditional" brands (such as English Leather, Brut, Old Spice, and British Sterling).

The third tier was low-priced, functional brands, such as Skin Bracer, Aqua Velva, and Brut 33. These brands sold for less than $5 per SKU ($.75–$1.00 per ounce) through drug, mass merchandiser, food, and discount stores and were believed to have their highest usage among lower- and middle-income men 45 years of age and older.

In 1991 the best-selling brands were Old Spice (10% of men's fragrance dollar sales), Stetson (8.5%), Skin Bracer (5%), Brut 33 (4%), and English Leather (3.8%). Dozens of other brands had shares of 1%–3%. Old Spice, Skin Bracer, and Brut each had substantial food-store distribution in addition to drug and mass merchandiser channels. MEM executives had for years received inquiries from food chains about carrying a limited selection of MEM's faster-moving items, but believed that substantial food-store distribution would damage the brand's positioning with the trade and consumers in its current channels.

Women's toiletries were a $3.5 billion market at retail in 1991, while men's toiletries were $1.3 billion at retail ($760 million in factory sales). During the 1980s, however, men's fragrance sales had grown faster than women's. New men's fragrances were common, but less than a third were still on the market three years after introduction. One industry observer noted: "Cracking the mass men's fragrance market is difficult; only Jovan, Chaps, and Stetson have really made it in this area since the 1960s when English Leather, Brut, and others came in. The rest are now in scent heaven.

---

[1] These promotions offered consumers either a free item of the purchased product, or another item at a discounted price, as incentives to purchase the promoted item at the "regular" list price.

In the prestige market, Polo, Obsession, and others entered successfully in the 1980s, but there were also many casualties."

Citrus, tobacco, and leather scents once dominated as the basis for men's fragrances, but during the 1980s newer scents used essences formerly limited to women's brands (e.g., florals, fruits, and orientals). Similarly, while men's fragrances were traditionally positioned and advertised as sexy and/or classic (with imagery tied to the brand name or scent), more diverse images had been emphasized by newer brands such as Eternity for Men ("mind and mood") or Jovan White Musk ("for the grown-up, more sensitive sexual animal"). But as one observer noted, "The fastest-growing brand in the '80s was Drakkar Noir [introduced in 1985]; and its boxing-match ads, 'feel the power' slogan, and 'power piece' gift-set promotions indicate that macho imagery is still relevant in the category."

Mayer believed three developments had significant implications. One was the blurring distinction between stores carrying prestige brands and those carrying mass market brands. This was due in part to the increasing practice of "diverting" in which distributors, buying products on promotion, acquired brands meant for upscale stores but sold these products to mass-market retailers at discounts of 25% or more off list price. One industry newsletter observed that, in department stores, "there has been a tremendous increase in price promotions. [And] the fact that department stores are reducing sales staffs while increasing promotions puts [manufacturers of prestige brands] in dangerous territory." In response, some prestige brands had broadened distribution to mass-market channels, while recent introductions in the mass-market category had higher price points as well as packaging and imagery evocative of department store brands.

Another development was the acquisition by large consumer products companies of men's fragrance brands and firms. In 1987, Nestle acquired Chaps as well as Cosmair and its Drakkar Noir, Polo, and Armani brands; in 1989, Unilever purchased Faberge and its Brut brand; in 1990, Procter & Gamble acquired Old Spice from Shulton; Colgate acquired Mennen Company in 1991; Benckiser (a large German consumer goods firm) acquired Quintessence's Jovan Musk and Aspen brands in 1991 and Coty's Stetson brand in 1992. An observer noted:

> Branded fragrances are attractive because of the longevity of their franchise and the high cost of launching new products—often a multiple of first-year sales volume in a category where few new products last more than two years. Companies also buy a brand or company for its distribution. An established sales presence in a given channel makes it easier to add new products, and consolidation among retailers has increased.

One result of the acquisitions had been changes in advertising and promotional spending for men's fragrances (**Exhibit 3**). The top 10 advertised brands spent an estimated $98 million in 1991 versus $42 million in

1989, increasing their share of category media spending from 43% to 67%. In 1991, P&G, in an attempt to reposition Old Spice for younger users, introduced new packaging and display vehicles, spent over $19 million in advertising, and another $10 million in "scent samples" as part of magazine inserts. In early 1992,[2] P&G's chairman stated:

> Why does a soap and detergent company venture into the world of fashion and glamour? This is our kind of business and getting more so every day. . . . [P&G's strength] is mass marketing quality products to the young consumer. Therefore, Noxell Cover Girl was a great way to start. A year later, we decided to tackle the male market with Old Spice. We found that 66% of men aged 25 to 34 considered Old Spice a fragrance for older men. In less than a year, Old Spice has a new marketing program, a new hydrogel product for younger men's sensitive skin, and new advertising to attract younger male users.
>
> There will always be a significant prestige segment of the market. We are not much of a player in that market, especially in the United States. [But] the top three companies in sales today are all global mass marketers of consumer products (Nestlé, Unilever, P&G) and all are very R&D/product-driven in their corporate strategies. . . . This will accelerate the pace of innovation and raise consumer expectations for meaningful performance from cosmetics.

The third development involved distribution channels. In 1985, 30% of cosmetic and fragrance sales occurred at department store counters. By 1991, the figure was 21% with the difference attributable to increases in drug, food, discount, and mass-merchandiser channels where self-service was more common than cosmetician-supplied advice about fragrances. Within the drugstore channel, chain stores grew from 14,000 to 18,500 outlets during the 1980s while independents decreased from 37,000 to 34,500. In 1991, about 75% of men's fragrance dollar sales in the drugstore channel went through chains. The chains were sophisticated in their use of scanner data and inventory systems and also more powerful in pricing and delivery negotiations. A number of chains required that fragrance firms supply products on guaranteed-sales terms (i.e., items not sold by a given date could be returned to the supplier). In practice, this resulted in numerous markdowns and promotions. Gay Mayer observed:

> Guaranteed-sales contracts further complicate a seasonal business, especially for multiproduct gift packs. Handling costs are about 15% of the sales volume of returned items and can destroy the margins inherent in most chain sales where 60-day, on-counter promotions are now common [i.e., the retailer agrees to carry a manufacturer's product, place it on the counter in a display unit, and return any unsold product after 60 days].

[2] *Drug and Cosmetics Industry Magazine,* February 1992, pp. 49–51.

These pressures were especially intense during the past two years, when the economy was soft. But even when the economy improves, our business will be more demanding than ever. Orders will flow later and with shorter lead times for delivery. "Partnership," the new buzz-word in the industry, is real—although for the most part driven by the account. In addition, our competitors have gotten bigger. Our opportunity and challenge is to react fast and smart.

ORGANIZATION

MEM employed about 400 people, organized as indicated in **Exhibit 4**. Corporate headquarters and the main manufacturing facility were adjacent buildings. At headquarters, there were no private offices and, until 1987, no partitions between office spaces. Mayer and other executives sat at desks next to each other in the main office area. One executive commented:

> Gay has always said that he wants a $100 million business that operates like a $5 million company. He emphasizes simplicity of operations, frequent and open communications (especially verbal), and minimal rules and paperwork. When there's a customer request or other urgent issue, there are few "proper" channels. Most often, I simply turn to Gay or other relevant managers sitting near me and ask for advice, assistance or approval.

Mayer noted that "flexibility is one of our major assets," and he cited two recent examples. In 1991, Kmart required that fragrance suppliers provide special displays that conformed to Kmart specifications. "When Steve Feigenbaum [VP of Sales] learned about this, he spoke with Judy Domanski [VP of Marketing] the same day. Judy had the required format designed and delivered, and we were able to increase our shelf space at that account long before other, bigger firms responded," said Mayer. More recently, MEM had negotiated an exclusive arrangement with Wal-Mart for an off-season promotion at a deeply discounted price but with a no-returns condition. "We moved 80,000 items of previously unsold inventory," noted Mayer, "and the key is that when Sales comes across such opportunities, Marketing, Manufacturing, and Finance are quickly brought into the loop. We assess the costs and benefits and, if it's attractive, execute." Kazimir added: "Flexibility, speed, and discipline are important. The key is to focus our limited resources most effectively."

Marketing Organization

Until 1986, one person oversaw marketing and sales activities at MEM. In 1986, marketing and sales were separated, and a VP of Marketing was hired from a large consumer goods firm. An executive recalled:

Like other entrepreneurial fragrance firms, we had few formal planning or budgeting procedures, and the new head of marketing established needed controls and processes in a changing business. But he also brought the habits of a larger, slower, staff-rich corporation with him. Some believed his penchant for formal presentations and "more research" impeded interaction between headquarters and the field.

In 1991, this person left MEM (for a position at a large consumer goods firm), and Judy Domanski was promoted from brand manager for women's products to VP of Marketing. She had joined MEM 10 years earlier (after some years with Helena Rubinstein, Inc.) and had sales as well as marketing experience. The company manual noted that "the Marketing Department is the product and idea-initiating arm of the company, responsible for all phases of the product including the product form, the packaging, promotion, price, and profitability. Marketing interfaces with virtually all departments in the company, but most closely with Sales, in bringing products to market."

Reporting to Domanski were product marketing directors for Men's Products (Stephen Brodeck) and Women's Products (Rosemary McCarthy)—both hired in 1991 from other firms in the industry—as well as a manager for Creative Services (Lissette Pasarin, who directed freelance work for packaging and promotions). Product management was responsible for the marketing plans, advertising direction, and promotional and merchandising programs for assigned brands, and evaluated chiefly on sales and profitability performance.

Men's products included the original English Leather fragrance, English Leather Lime (introduced in 1966 in cool-looking frosted bottles), Timberline (a woodsy scent introduced in 1968 in brown packaging with a wilderness panorama), Wind Drift (introduced in 1970 with citrus scents and distinctive cork caps), Musk by English Leather (an amber scent introduced in 1973 to appeal to a younger audience for use primarily on weekends and special occasions), and Spiced (introduced in 1984 to compete with the market leader, Old Spice). Each brand was offered in product forms such as soaps, deodorants, shave creams, and all-purpose lotions. But aftershaves and colognes accounted for about 70% of "open stock" sales (i.e., sales of individual items rather than gift set combinations) of MEM men's products.

Also within men's products was FATHOM cologne, introduced in 1990 and targeted at 18- to 24-year-old men. With substantial advertising and promotional support, FATHOM achieved distribution in more than 80% of MEM's accounts, and 1990 sales exceeded $7 million. But 1991 sales declined to less than $3 million. Some managers attributed this to a bad economy in which fragrance sales in general were flat; others believed FATHOM was one among many new fragrances that prove unsuccessful after initial sell-in efforts. In early 1992, management decided not to allocate additional advertising funds to the product.

Women's products included Heaven Sent (a floral powdery scent developed by Madame Helena Rubinstein in 1937 and acquired by MEM in 1982), Heaven Sent Musk (a line extension introduced in 1986), Love's Baby Soft (a floral scent which was the leading teen fragrance in the United States), Love's Gentle Musk, Love's Soft Jasmin, Love's Rain Scent, and Love's Fresh Lemon. The Love's brands were originally developed in the early 1970s, acquired by MEM in 1986, and extended to include cosmetics and accessories as well as fragrances. Rosemary McCarthy noted, "Other firms are entering the teenage girl's market at a brisker pace, and I want to defend our franchise with increased advertising and promotions that will make the line a bit more hip and trendy for the teen market." By contrast, sales of the Heaven Sent line had been declining for several years; in 1991 it was the focus of a repositioning program which involved new packaging, more gift packs, increased promotional spending, and new advertising that featured "a soft romantic image and return to traditional values."

Margins varied widely by product form, generally being highest for individual open-stock cologne items and lowest on deodorants and shave creams. Gift sets were priced as the sum of the prices of their component items. But incremental packaging and labor costs, as well as any accompanying promotions, made gift sets low-margin items. However, gift sets were an important vehicle for stimulating trial and attracting new users.

Tom Fields, Ltd., was a subsidiary that sold Tinkerbell, the leading line of toiletries for girls ages two to twelve. In 1992, MEM planned to extend promotional and advertising activity with customers that featured Tinkerbell products on a year-round basis and to introduce a new licensed line for Christmas '92 which would be featured on television and sold via toy stores. Aristocrat Leather Products was also a separate subsidiary, acquired in 1984 to sell English Leather brand wallets and accessories. After losing money, Aristocrat was downsized in 1989 and in 1991, and the English Leather trademark for small leather products was licensed to a third party. In 1992, MEM continued to have some commitments but had essentially exited this business.

Sales Organization

MEM products were sold in about 21,000 retail outlets, responsible for at least 80% of U.S. men's fragrance sales. All shipments were made direct to stores or to the regional warehouses of retail chains. Wholesalers were not significantly involved in MEM's distribution. Until 1960, MEM products had been distributed primarily through department and men's specialty stores. During that decade, MEM was among the first of the "department store brands" to expand distribution to drugstores and mass-merchandise chains, such as Sears and J.C. Penney. (**Exhibit 5** indicates sales by class-of-trade for selected MEM products.)

Until 1965, MEM relied exclusively on independent manufacturers' reps (MRs) to sell its products to retailers. The first MEM salespeople were former MRs for MEM or salespeople hired from competing firms. Mayer recalled:

> Most had years of sales experience in the industry, and therefore little sales training was required. Moreover, they had established relationships with store buyers and were often given a blank order sheet by the buyer and told to fill in the items and amounts appropriate for that store. When I became president [in 1972], I certainly didn't want to upset those relationships. I emphasized to our salespeople that they should run their territories as if it were their own business; we would support their efforts with products, promotions, and advertising, and also try to minimize the paperwork.

As the sales force grew, MEM appointed a VP of Sales and Marketing, a national sales manager, and eventually division and region managers. In 1991, MEM had 55 sales representatives, seven region managers, and three division managers reporting to the national sales manager (Neil Van Eerden), who reported to Steve Feigenbaum, vice president of Sales. Feigenbaum had initially been an MR selling MEM products, then sales manager for the Tom Fields and Aristocrat Leather subsidiaries, and was national sales manager for MEM when his predecessor, who was VP of Sales for nearly two decades, retired in 1991.

The sales force was organized into geographical territories and all sales reps worked out of their homes. They were responsible for the full line of MEM's men's and women's products at assigned accounts, although MEM did not impose quotas by product line or total sales quotas by territory. Average salesperson compensation was $35,000 and involved about 70% salary and 30% commission. Competitors typically did not offer as high a commission component of total compensation but, unlike MEM, they reimbursed expenses. One executive noted: "Our sales force turnover has been much lower than the industry norm, and many salespeople have been with us for years. They're experienced and must also be versatile in order to sell in several classes of trade which differ in their merchandising objectives and practices." Some sales reps had Key Account responsibilities with smaller regional chains, but most of their activities were with independents and the outlets of regional and national chains across different classes-of-trade.

Regional managers (RMs) supervised five to nine sales reps and were expected to spend a minimum of three days per quarter with each salesperson. Each RM also had a number of Key Accounts, which ranged from regional to national in scope, as well as 40 to 50 smaller "down-the-street" accounts. Division managers accompanied RMs on appropriate Key Account sales calls and worked with sales reps as time permitted. Division managers also had assigned accounts, and special customized projects with larger chains would typically be managed at this level.

Other sales positions included a regional manager (who sold to military customers and managed the Kmart account) and an administrative manager of Sales & Marketing Services (responsible for call-report forms, sales materials, co-op advertising funds, and other sales support matters). MEM also continued to utilize manufacturers' reps in two territories: the Dakotas (due to the relatively low number of accounts in a large geographical area) and New York City (where the MR had a 40-year relationship with MEM).

Sales reps filed weekly call reports indicating orders by product line and promotions by account. In turn, salespeople received from headquarters a semiannual Sales Analysis report (current versus prior years' sales volume by product line by account), a semiannual Chain Report sent to salespeople having chain headquarters in their territory (volume by product line for each store, intended for use in identifying underperforming stores in discussions with the chain buyer), and an Open Order Report (weekly listing of all existing orders scheduled for shipment in a territory). Accounts were classified by sales revenue potential, and call frequency was expected to vary accordingly. In general, major accounts (more than $7,500 in potential annual sales volume of MEM products) were to be seen every 30 to 45 days; accounts generating $3,500 to $7,500, every 60 days; accounts generating $1,000 to $3,500, every 90 days; and accounts with less than $1,000 in annual sales potential two to three times yearly. Several thousand accounts bought in quantities too small to justify a sales call and were serviced via mail orders. Conversely, a few large customers classified as National Accounts were handled from headquarters. These included retailers such as Kmart, Sears, and J.C. Penney. MEM's field sales reps still regularly contacted individual stores of such accounts to write orders, merchandise the products, conduct inventory checks, and perform shelf services.

Sales Tasks

MEM salespeople called on all classes-of-trade in their territories. The key contacts in each major trade class were as follows.

In *department stores,* toiletries buyers were responsible for placing orders, selecting the proper mix of merchandise, and managing inventory levels. In larger department stores, buying was a full-time position; in smaller stores, the buyer might also spend some time behind the counter. Buyers were very busy, and an appointment and presentation (covering current vs. prior-year sales, specific promotion and merchandising plans, and any co-op ad plans) were generally required. A MEM manager noted: "Buyers want to know 'what's new' and how it fits with their particular need or desired store image. So, it's important for our salespeople to know whether the account is a fashion or price store, their customer demographics, what services they provide, and their merchandising policies." Merchandise managers (who typically reported to individual store management, not headquarters buyers) were responsible for developing volume for one or more store departments and for approving any orders or promotions involving their assigned areas. A MEM sales manager noted, "To develop full store potential, you must be on easy speaking terms with this individual. English Leather products often fit very well in other departments such as men's clothing or in special gift areas, and any such tie-ins are typically the merchandising manager's call. So, even if the buyer offers to handle dealings with this person, we encourage our salespeople to present their ideas personally."

The advertising manager handled co-op advertising. Most department stores had basic ad formats designed to create a particular image, and thus manufacturers' requests for special attention were often denied. However, a persuasive rationale and good relationships with ad managers often gained special ad space for a manufacturer. The display manager was responsible for all in-store and window displays. One MEM executive noted that "in all classes of trade, we repeatedly find that the more displays and facings you get, the more product you move." Store sales clerks and cosmeticians kept the stock clean and displayed, took periodic inventories (usually monthly) for the buyer, and often suggested the amounts to be reordered. MEM salespeople were urged to call on store sales clerks before seeing the buyer in order to learn about current events at the point of sale. Finally, the store manager, while often difficult to see, typically had final approval over significant buying, merchandising, or advertising plans.

Mass merchandisers generally had both a self-service Health & Beauty Care Department (HBC) and a separate cosmetics area (which might be company-owned or leased by a supplier or third-party firm) with glass cases and full- or part-time sales personnel. MEM's objective was to have its men's products in both areas, with shelf space greater than or at least comparable to its competitors in the category. A sales manager commented:

> Some mass merchandisers purchase primarily at headquarters, while others purchase on an individual basis. Larger mass merchandisers have their own particular rules, and buying is generally handled at headquarters. The role at store level is basically to follow the rules established between MEM and that chain's headquarters and to maintain the inventory and shelf merchandising plan. But at mass merchandisers sold on an individual store basis, the store merchandise manager runs the show. On every call, you must show that you are keeping merchandise in stock, out front, and clear of junk. You must let store merchandise managers know what you have done for them lately, and specific dollar sales objectives versus the same period last year are key to getting the shelf space and position desired.
>
> In most mass merchandisers, there's also a department manager (reporting to the store merchandise manager) who doubles as a sales clerk in HBC or cosmetics. This person keeps things tidy and pulls stock from the back room. Any orders they sign must usually be approved by the merchandise manager. But rapport with the department manager provides better access to store inventory figures which, in a good relationship, will be ready for you when you call.

Independent drugstores had decreased in numbers but Gay Mayer noted that "this channel still represents an important outlet which moves product, maintains our quality image, and usually stocks a broad assortment of our goods." For many years, MEM's sales force was among the largest of any fragrance firm, calling on accounts more often than its competitors. Especially in independent drugstores, MEM had achieved better distribution penetration than most of its competitors. At independents, the druggist owning the store or (in franchised outlets) the store manager had final authority for fragrance buying, merchandising, promotion, and advertising decisions. Some larger independents also had cosmeticians, and their recommendations carried weight. A salesperson commented:

> Occasionally you'll make a drugstore call without interruption; when you do, rejoice! Generally the owner or store manager will be called away several times during your sales call, and you must use that time with sales clerks, training them in basic product information and how to merchandise any new items as well as checking up on competition. Often an enthusiastic sales clerk or cosmetician will create point-of-purchase displays and counter setups once you point out how they can key them to the season, a holiday, or a local event.
>
> In most independents, the druggist is a professional pharmacist, not a merchandising expert. So, any help in putting up displays, establishing promotions, or otherwise merchandising the line to build volume is most welcome. Years of such help leads to a situation where the druggist leaves ordering and merchandising across our line up to the salesperson.

Chain drugstores had in recent years increased their scope of operations both geographically and in terms of number and diversity of items stocked. The purchase process at chains focused on headquarters where the buyer for fragrances and other beauty aids was responsible for placing orders. A MEM executive observed, "Chain buyers are primarily interested in turnover. But they're also responsible for inventory control and interested in keeping handling, shipping and storage costs down. Hence, coordinating deals and arrival of product with the chain's ad, merchandising, and promotional schedule is very important. Such coordination means that many other chain personnel are also important to the MEM salesperson." The chain merchandise (or sales promotion) manager was responsible for developing volume in a category, and usually worked closely with the appropriate buyer. Merchandise managers typically worked out a calendar as much as a year in advance to cover promotions, sales drives, or other events. "Because of this lead time," one manager noted, "we're often in the midst of next year's Christmas sell-in before results from last year are available. This makes sales forecasting difficult and generally requires ongoing alterations in marketing plans during the year as prior year's results *do* become available." Merchandise managers also had direct access to store personnel and could call meetings or issue sales bulletins concerning specific items or promotions.

The advertising manager designed and scheduled the chain's ads, generally for newspapers on a weekly or more frequent basis. Chains typically ran "omnibus ads," ranging from a third to a full page and covering a number of items in a category (see **Exhibit 6** for an example). For co-op ads in support of special promotions, however, MEM sought placement outside the omnibus ad. At larger chains, a district (or division) manager was responsible for a group of stores and needed to be kept informed about any agreements established with chain headquarters. DMs also often had influence over advertising and merchandising plans for their stores. Feigenbaum explained:

> Developing maximum volume from drug chains calls for activity at several levels. The basic promotional sale is always made at headquarters, where several people must be convinced: the buyer, who writes the order; the merchandise manager, whose efforts move the merchandise; the display manager, whose windows and display help create demand; and the ad manager, who must be convinced to give us proper space outside the regular omnibus ad.
>
> But momentum picks up sharply when you also sell the idea to each district manager. And the final push is to develop the full cooperation of every store manager and cosmetician. Most promotions are intended for the store Toiletries Department—an area suitable for displays and with clerks that can push merchandise. But MEM products must also receive their share of shelf space in the high-traffic, self-service locations where more and more items are displayed. Any failure of cooperation at the store level must be remedied by alerting the chain's district manager or, if necessary, the merchandise manager at headquarters.
>
> Over the years, we have found that chain drug people are simply too busy to buy anything but a promotion that involves minimum effort on their part. This requires careful planning among our own Sales and Marketing people since even a great idea, presented without attention to in-store execution, will fail and hurt us the next time we call on chain headquarters.

Marketing-Sales Interactions

There were several ways in which MEM attempted to coordinate its marketing and selling activities. For over a decade, the firm had held monthly meetings of a Marketing Committee composed of Gay Mayer, the VP of Marketing, product management, and the vice presidents of Finance, Sales, and Operations. An executive commented:

> Marketing Committee meetings generally are informal discussions of where we stand with a given account, program, or new product. The topics range from detailed packaging and display issues to broader product or promotion plans and the implications for purchasing, manufacturing, and finance. These meetings generate timely feedback and

help in anticipating interfunctional requirements. But as our former head of Marketing often noted, these meetings also get many nonmarketing personnel involved in brand decisions, and other functions often have as much of a vote as Marketing.

Marketing managers also presented their programs at the annual National Sales Meeting and at quarterly meetings with regional and division managers. A product manager noted, "My priorities are up-to-date feedback about field events and getting the sales force to devote maximum effort during the major seasonal sell-ins, especially Christmas and Father's Day." The product manager continued:

Because our salespeople carry men's, women's, and children's products, they tend to cherrypick depending upon their relationship with the buyer, the account's purchasing history, or their personal "feel" for which products or promotions will catch on. Also, the tendency in Sales is the same as at other firms where I've worked: despite Marketing's research and efforts to convey the brand strategy at sales meetings, each rep's current perception of a product or program is often determined by what the buyer on their last call said.

Marketing managers and other executives also made sales calls, especially to larger accounts. Mayer noted: "I spend about 20% of my time making over 100 customer visits annually and am on the phone daily with salespeople at all levels of the organization. The calls let a buyer or merchandise manager at an account know that the president of MEM is behind a given program, and that can make a difference in the level of support we receive. I also want our salespeople to know that their CEO acknowledges the importance of field-level activities and can clean and stock the shelves." A product manager commented:

Talking with key buyers and salespeople is invaluable, and I wish I could do more of this. Given the lead times involved for gift packs and other events in a seasonal business, getting feedback and buy-in early is important. But I can't be in the field all the time, or important product management work doesn't get done.

Also, our salespeople call on hundreds of accounts across trade channels and are very busy during the selling seasons. Despite efforts to get their feedback early, there's still a certain amount of post-hoc "editorializing" about Marketing programs—after the programs have been designed and there's little we can do to change them. Last year, for example, Marketing designed a major display program around a special laminated shelf marker. We were ready to go into production when I happened to notice that in certain big drug chains the space where we planned to put the marker was used for bar coding strips tied into the store's inventory control system. We wasted time, and almost wasted a lot of money, because field input didn't arrive earlier in the process.

Another factor was the working relationship between Steve Feigenbaum (VP of Sales) and Judy Domanski (VP of Marketing). "We both became vice presidents in 1991," noted Feigenbaum, "and have worked together at MEM for 10 years. Our offices are adjacent and we speak daily." Domanski added:

> Steve and I have seen the business change dramatically and realize that we must work together in developing customized programs for our key customers. When we became VPs, Gay emphasized the need for very open and regular communications in order to move faster and smarter than the giant companies against whom we compete every day.

ENGLISH LEATHER

Sales of the English Leather line (EL) grew steadily from the mid-1960s, reaching a peak of about $30 million in 1984. An executive commented that during those years,

> English Leather was the hottest product in the market. Its association with English clothing in department stores connoted quality, and expansion into mass-market outlets made this quality image available to more people. Its advertising was also timely. Ads featured assertive, bold, confident, and liberated women explaining what they expected their men to wear. This coincided with a change in American culture that allowed women to exercise more control over such issues, and English Leather became the fragrance that embodied this attitude.

In the 1980s, the brand's sales declined, as did its share in important channels:

Unit Market Share in Drugstores

	1982	1985	1988	1990
English Leather	9.1%	7.5%	5.5%	4.3%
Brut	6.6	6.1	4.5	4.1
Brut 33	4.0	3.8	2.9	2.9
Old Spice	14.3	10.7	8.4	7.1
British Sterling	3.9	3.5	3.2	2.5
Stetson	4.3	6.6	7.5	7.9

Executives attributed the sales decline to several factors. First, many new products were introduced during this period. "Where the evoked set for EL users was three to five other brands," one manager noted, "there were over 25 brands competing for attention and shelf space by the late 80s.

And as designer and traditional department store brands entered the mass market, English Leather's position at the high end of the mid-range segment was threatened." Second, in recent years advertising expenditures for the brand were cut: in 1989 an across-the-board decrease in marketing expenditures was instituted in response to falling sales, increased cost of goods sold, and financial pressures; in 1990, much of the available money for ads and promotions was devoted to the launch of FATHOM; and in 1991 the repackaging of Heaven Sent and support for the growing Love's Baby Soft line were the focus of marketing expenditures.

Selected Competitive Advertising Expenditures ($ in millions)

	1978	1983	1988	1991
English Leather	$3.95	$3.6	$4.0	$1.0
Old Spice	5.50	6.6	6.4	15.0
Brut	1.48	1.4	2.7	12.5
Stetson	–	4.2	7.3	7.5

Third, some believed packaging and pricing (see **Exhibit 7**) were potential problems. A marketing manager commented: "EL sells at four ounces for the same price as competing brands in one- to two-ounce bottles. But on the shelf all the boxes look the same size. MEM could have increased prices without significant adverse reactions from consumers, and used that money to fund additional advertising. Instead, sales declined and the brand's cost structure eroded." Finally, as another manager explained, "In a category where trendy is important, it's difficult for older brands. Among other things, the popularity of fragrance types changes." In 1990, 17% of EL sales were cologne, 21% aftershave, 13% body guards, 2% face savers and headliners, and 46% via gift sets of cologne, aftershave, and body guards.

In 1991, Stephen Brodeck became marketing director for men's products. His major task was to assess EL's position, identify any opportunities for increasing sales and profits, and make strategic recommendations for the brand. He initiated research to determine consumers' perceptions of English Leather and to develop user profiles. As part of this effort, a research firm conducted focus-group sessions with three groups (men 18 to 24, 25 to 34, and 35 to 49) as well as surveys of 300 male users of competing products, 100 EL users, and 100 women who buy colognes/aftershaves for men (see **Exhibit 8** for selected findings). Brodeck commented:

> We learned that men 18 to 24 years old have the greatest involvement and usage rate in the category: they're aware of newer brands and form more distinct impressions and brand images. Men 25 to 34 are interested but not as involved as younger men; they're more apt to choose brands they like, rather than their wife's or girlfriend's favorite brand; and they like location themes, especially western/open-space themes. Men 35 and older are the least involved in the category and of-

ten continue to use a brand that was trendy when they were in high school or college; they're attracted to themes emphasizing user's sophistication and urbanity.

English Leather use skews toward older middle-income males that exhibit many traditional "middle America" family characteristics: they see themselves and the brand as reliable, friendly, and possessing a certain amount of sophistication. No significant geographic or ethnic differences emerged, and our heavy user is as likely to use "traditional" brands such as Old Spice or Brut as he is to use "contemporary" brands such as Stetson.

After analyzing the research, Brodeck recommended a marketing plan intended to restage and revitalize the EL brand. The primary target would be men 35 to 49, with a secondary target being men in the 25 to 34 age group. "Older men are more likely to be current EL users," noted Brodeck, "and so more susceptible to usage-frequency advertising, while men 25 to 34 will also be affected by this advertising. It will require significantly more expenditures to raise awareness and use of EL among men 18 to 24." In its ads and positioning, EL would be presented as a "classic" brand for "confident men"—an image, Brodeck believed, compatible with other data indicating a renewed emphasis in the 1990s on "traditional" values and family/community involvement. This positioning would include imagery featuring contemporary, active male-female relationships. No special ad execution would be aimed at women, since data indicated similar impressions of EL among males and females and because male self-purchase in the category was believed to be increasing. However, ads would run in women's magazines prior to Christmas, the category's peak gift sales period. "The key," noted Brodeck, "is to execute ads so that the emphasis is on 'classic,' rather than 'old-fashioned,' and on emotions with which our target consumers identify." He estimated that, in the current environment, a meaningful TV ad campaign would require $8 million to $10 million in annual expenditures. But financial constraints made a $4 million to $5 million budget necessary. Hence, he recommended spending the majority of available EL media funds on print advertising (in magazines such as *People, Women's Day, Road & Track,* and *Sports Illustrated*), supplemented by radio ads. "These are media where our share-of-voice can be much higher, where our target audience can be reached, and where we can afford to have a presence throughout the year."

The plan also called for consolidating the brand's major lines (Original EL, Musk, and Spiced) in a redesigned package with a different box color and smaller 3.4- and 1.7-ounce bottles. "The redesign would have an etched label intended to communicate modernity and elegance," Brodeck commented, "and umbrella packaging can improve shelf impact while obtaining greater efficiencies in media spending. Smaller bottles also help to create a quality image for fragrances, while increasing the use-up rate. Right now, we may have *too* strong a price/value relationship in a category where this is not necessarily seen as positive." Repackaging and new-bottle costs for the EL line were estimated at $350,000 for designs, molds, and other start-up production expenses.

Brodeck also noted that "the sales force has done a good job in maintaining the gift-set business. But gift-set margins have declined in recent years while EL open-stock sales have fallen. We need to sell more open-stock product, and the proposed merchandising plan emphasizes this. We would target key accounts with custom gift-set programs [e.g., special sets and display pieces], but also open-stock displays aimed at generating more year-round use."

Reflecting on the EL line, Brodeck commented: "The brand has some real strengths and equity. Longer-term, we need a new brand, or a flanker brand, for the 18 to 34 age group. But I think it would be a mistake to abandon or harvest English Leather, or alienate the brand's current users, in an attempt to capture a younger user group."

Conclusion

In considering the proposal to restage English Leather, Mayer heard from various executives. Some argued that any revitalization program should focus on the 18- to 24-year-old segment. "Younger men represent current volume and future sales in this business," argued one manager. "They use more product per person, are easier to influence because their fragrance preferences are still evolving, and they don't currently have a strong image of English Leather so the brand can start there with a relatively clean slate. The growing brands focus on younger men; and men 35 and older often buy *because* younger men wear the fragrance." Other managers doubted that any revitalization of EL could be accomplished without substantial TV advertising, and some believed that the sales force had simply grown "too comfortable selling gift sets on promotion."

Some managers believed that the money proposed for EL would be better spent on developing a new brand. One executive commented:

FATHOM wasn't successful, but the basic strategy made sense. We need two major men's brands in order to utilize factory capacity, increase our shelf facings and impact in the stores, and enhance our space and negotiating leverage in co-op ad placements. English Leather seems firmly tied to gift sets, and another brand should be developed to generate sales for other occasions. As for the EL sales decline, I think we have a better shot at expanding distribution into food stores, rather than repositioning the brand in our current channels.

Many recent acquisitions in the industry occurred because the acquirer was primarily interested in the higher-volume deodorant business, not the fragrance business. This could generate opportunities for us to purchase an "orphan brand" from a larger firm. Cash from food-store volume, and cash for the EL revitalization program, might be better spent on such a purchase.

Finally, some executives argued that the costs of restaging EL would dominate MEM's marketing expenditures for two to three years, draining resources from the Love's line and its growing teenage market as well as the Tinkerbell and Heaven Sent lines. "Together, women's products and Tinkerbell now account for almost twice the sales of English Leather, and they've been growing. It's not clear whether English Leather still has legs after four decades, and we shouldn't abandon or harvest these other brands."

While considering what to do about English Leather, Mayer was also considering proposed changes in the firm's field sales programs. One proposal concerned sales compensation. MEM salespeople were currently paid a base salary and commissions on orders booked at assigned accounts; expenses were not reimbursed. Some managers wanted to alter the plan to conform to standard industry practice: an increase in the starting base salary to that of other toiletries companies (about $35,000), with expenses reimbursed and a bonus tied to quota attainment at accounts. One manager commented:

> Under this revised plan, total compensation would likely remain about the same, but it would more accurately reflect field realities. As chains move toward headquarters buying, our field reps are less able to influence sales volume in their territories where they call on individual stores in the retail chain.
>
> With our current plan, salespeople probably spend disproportionate time calling on the smaller independent stores—where they can still make a sale and book a commission. And with salespeople paying for travel and other expenses, some aren't making expenditures that can build our presence in accounts. The proposed new system can motivate our reps to cover their territories more fully, and we at headquarters can also have more control over how they spend their time and what products they sell.

Other managers argued that "our best salespeople have been in their territories for years and know their accounts better than anyone at headquarters can. They allocate their time to maximize sales per effort and expense expended, and that's as it should be."

Another proposal called for the creation of part-time merchandising positions in the sales force. As currently proposed, field merchandisers would report to regional managers, work approximately 16 hours a week at an hourly rate and be responsible for ensuring adequate stock levels, appropriate displays, and other shelf-management tasks at retail sites. A manager commented:

> There is a clear industry trend toward the part-time merchandiser position. More field tasks *are* in-store merchandising tasks, and we don't need highly-paid salespeople to perform these tasks. Also, some of our salespeople complain about the changing nature of the job: they like to sell, not stock shelves. The fully burdened cost of a salesperson

can pay for three or four part-time merchandisers, and at many accounts that would be a better allocation of our limited resources.

Some managers believed that merchandisers should be deployed geographically, and others believed that they should be assigned to specific accounts. There was also disagreement about whether or not merchandisers should be authorized to write orders or to focus solely on stocking, shelving, and display activities. However, other managers wondered whether a part-time merchandiser program was viable for MEM. "It's not easy to separate sales and service tasks in this business," said one manager, "and our position in stores depends on fast response and targeted programs. Will a succession of part-time people help or hurt the execution of that sales strategy?"

Finally, some executives believed that, especially in the larger accounts, field marketing requirements increasingly differed among the trade classes through which MEM sold its men's and women's products. They argued that the current geographical deployment of salespeople should be changed to create more channel specialists that would focus on a given trade class. "Our major retail channels are blurring in terms of the fragrance brands they carry," said one manager. "But they differ in terms of selling and merchandising requirements, and the bigger accounts are now powerful enough to demand customized programs. If we can handle these programs more effectively for selected trade channels, that could be a big counterweight to the increased ad expenditures in the category."

Due to the lead-times involved in developing new ad, packaging, and merchandising programs, decisions concerning English Leather would have to be made soon; and Mayer wanted any changes in sales programs to be compatible with decisions concerning the firm's flagship brand.

EXHIBIT 1   MEM Company: Financial Information ($000)

	1987	1988	1989	1990	1991
Sales by product line:					
English Leather and other					
men's products	$36,011	$35,056	$32,203	$31,875	$21,076
Women's products	15,240	15,928	17,937	18,333	17,174
Tinkerbell	12,463	14,635	19,686	18,892	19,015
Wallets and accessories	7,419	5,264	4,484	2,235	684
	71,133	70,883	74,310	71,335	57,949
Costs and expenses:					
Cost of sales	33,752	35,615	40,122	35,827	29,601
Selling and shipping	24,683	27,491	26,023	27,086	20,665
General and administrative	6,757	6,611	6.729	6,704	6,038
Restructuring charge[a]	—	—	1,900	—	200
	65,192	69,717	74,774	69,616	56,504
Other expenses:					
Interest expense	868	1,169	1,796	1,560	1,125
Royalty payments	1,063	728	581	161	23
Financing expense	—	—	—	608	224
Provision (benefit) for income taxes	1,858	(292)	(1,297)	(41)	29
Net income (loss):	2,151	(439)	(1,559)	(479)	44
Per share:	.81	(.16)	(.59)	(.19)	.02

[a]Restructuring charges in 1989 and 1991 attributable to revaluations and downsizing of assets of Aristocrat Leather Product subsidiary.
Source: Company annual reports.

EXHIBIT 2   Aftershaves and Colognes: Brand Awareness and Purchasing Behavior

How did you happen to first try your favorite brand of aftershave/cologne?

Received as gift	43%
Recommended by friend/relative/spouse	17
Smelled at store and liked scent	14
Smelled on someone else	8
Advertising	6
Received a sample	4
Recommended by salesclerk	2
Other/don't know	10

Which of the following brands are you familiar with?

	Unaided Awareness	Total Awareness
Old Spice	55%	86%
Brut 33	43	84
Aqua Velva	35	76
English Leather	30	80
Polo	25	58
Avon	19	56
Aramis	18	42
Stetson	18	55
Skin Bracer	13	57
British Sterling	12	58

EXHIBIT 2   *(continued)*

	Unaided Awareness	Total Awareness
Jovan for Men	11	50
Obsession for Men	8	35
Others	1–8	5–30

Which of the following brands do you currently have on hand?

Brand	Total	18–24 Years	25–34 Years	35–39 Years	40–49 Years
Old Spice	28%	17%	27%	36%	34%
Brut 33	29	17	22	23	21
English Leather	17	14	18	19	18
Polo	16	24	17	10	12
Stetson	12	14	14	15	7
Avon	11	6	10	16	14
Aqua Velva	10	7	8	11	15
Aramis	10	6	12	11	10
Drakkar Noir	8	18	7	6	2
British Sterling	8	4	8	11	8
Jovan for Men	8	4	11	7	5
Obsession for Men	7	8	7	7	5

How long have you been using your favorite brand of cologne/aftershave?

Less than 1 year	16%
1–2 years	17
More than 2 years	62
Don't know	5

Which one of these aftershave/colognes is your favorite brand?

Favorite Brand	Total	18–24 Years	25–34 Years	35–39 Years	40–49 Years
Old Spice	15%	8%	13%	17%	22%
Polo	7	12	9	3	4
Brut 33	7	5	6	9	8
Stetson	6	9	6	8	2
English Leather	5	4	3	6	8
Aramis	4	2	5	6	6
Obsession for Men	4	9	2	3	3
Drakkar Noir	4	10	4	0	1
Aqua Velva	4	3	4	0	6
Jovan for Men	3	1	4	2	4
Halston	2	3	3	2	1
British Sterling	2	1	1	4	3

How important is each of the following factors in using a cologne/aftershave?

	Very Important	Somewhat Important	Not Too Important	Not at All Important	Don't Know	Total
Others like the way it smells on me	54%	32%	9%	4%	1%	100%
Price	22	43	23	11	1	100

EXHIBIT 2 *(continued)*

	Very Important	Somewhat Important	Not Too Important	Not at All Important	Don't Know	Total
Available in a wide variety of outlets	23	37	25	13	2	100
Nonallergenic	35	21	23	17	4	100
Well-known brand	16	34	30	18	2	100

How influential are the following activities on your brand purchase decision?

	Strong Influence 10, 9, 8	No Influence 7, 6, 5, 4	Influence 3, 2, 1	Don't Know	Total	Mean Rating
Free samples via mail	43%	35%	21%	1%	100%	6.4
Two-for-one special	42	37	20	1	100	6.4
Special trial size	36	40	23	1	100	6.0
Free gift with purchase	34	38	27	1	100	5.7
Advertising	24	49	26	1	100	5.5
Cash rebate/coupon	20	36	43	1	100	4.5

If you switched brands in the past year, why did you switch?

	Aftershave	Cologne
Fragrance	45%	51%
Wanted change	39	44
Skin care	13	2
Lifestyle/attitude	4	3

EXHIBIT 3 Media Spending: Men's Fragrances and Toiletries (Spending by Media Type)

	1990		1989	
	$ Millions	*% Total*	*$ Millions*	*% Total*
Magazines	34.1	29.3	39.0	32.5
Network TV	37.5	32.2	40.9	34.1
Spot TV	31.7	27.2	29.4	24.5
Syndicated TV	6.7	5.7	4.4	3.7
Cable TV	4.0	3.4	3.1	2.6
Total TV	79.9	68.5	77.8	64.9
Network radio	1.0	0.9	0.4	0.3
Sunday magazines	1.3	1.1	2.7	2.3
Total media[a]	116.6[b]	100.0	119.9	100.0

[a]Comparable estimates for 1991: Total media spending of $98 million invested in magazines (31%), network TV (34%), spot TV (23%), syndicated TV (5%), cable TV (5%), radio (2%), and Sunday magazines (1%).

[b]Brut advertising not reported in 1990.

EXHIBIT 3   *(continued)*

Spending by Quarter

	1990		1989	
	$ Millions	*% of Total*	*$ Millions*	*% of Total*
First Quarter	11.6	9.9	11.9	9.9
Second Quarter	33.3	28.5	30.1	25.1
Third Quarter	13.7	11.7	15.3	12.8
Fourth Quarter	58.0	49.8	62.6	52.2
	116.6	99.9	119.9	100.0

[a]Comparable estimates for 1991: 13% in First Quarter; 25% in Second Quarter; 19% in Third Quarter; and 43% in Fourth Quarter.

Top Ten Men's Fragrance and Toiletries Advertisers[a]

	1990 (000)	1989 (000)
1. Old Spice	$10,214.2	$4,502.6
2. Stetson	7,628.5	8,778.0
3. California for Men	7,497.2	5,156.4
4. Preferred Stock	6,584.9	—
5. New West	6,246.3	962.3
6. Obsession	6,105.1	4,984.6
7. Eternity	5,168.5	2,219.5
8. Drakkar Noir	4,394.6	4,829.4
9. Afta	3,496.1	4,597.1
10. Tuscany	3,888.1	5,024.3
Total Top Ten	$61,223.5	$41,954.2

[a]Comparable estimates for top-10 spending brands in 1991: Old Spice ($19.2); Stetson ($7.0); Preferred Stock ($6.9); Egoiste ($6.8); Skin Bracer ($5.8); Obsession ($5.4); Calvin Klein ($4.9); Brut ($4.0); California for Men ($3.1); Polo ($2.9); for a total of $66 million (67% of category media spending).

Spending by Brand over a Nine-Year Period: Men's Fragrances (millions of dollars)

	1981	1982	1983	1984	1985	1986		1987	1988	1989
Brand										
Stetson (Coty)	$3.9	$4.6	$4.1	$5.7	$6.4	$5.8		$6.6	$7.5	$8.9
Obsession Men (Min)	—	—	—	—	—	—	NEW	6.5+	4.5	5.0
Hero (Match)	—	—	—	—	—	—		NEW	5.0	5.1
Tuscany (Lauder)	—	—	—	—	—	—		2.6	3.6	5.0
Drakkar (Cosmair)	—	—	—	—	1.1	2.0		4.0	6.7	4.8
Polo (Warner/L'Oreal)	0.4	0.4	1.3	2.2	2.3	4.7		3.1	4.0	4.8
Skin Bracer Afta	—	—	2.7	3.7	4.3	3.9		4.3	3.6	4.5
Old Spice (Shulton)	5.4	7.8	6.6	10.2	7.5	6.2		5.0	6.5	4.5
Iron (Coty)	–	–	–	–	—	—	NEW	5.3	5.8	4.5

EXHIBIT 3 *(continued)*

	1981	1982	1983	1984	1985	1986	1987		1988	1989
Brut (All)										
(Match)	1.3	2.6	1.3	1.8	4.7	3.7	4.1		2.6	4.4
Farenheit (Dior)	—	—	—	—	—	—	—		NEW	3.8
English Leather										
(MEM)	3.6	3.2	3.6	4.1	4.8	3.3	3.6		4.0	3.7
That Man (Revlon)	—	—	—	—	—	—	—		NEW	3.5
Skin Bracer										
(Mennen)	2.8	3.5	5.6	5.5	5.6	6.6	6.5		4.5	3.3
Aramis (Lauder)	2.8	3.5	2.6	5.0	6.6	3.8	3.1		3.5	2.9
Claiborne Men	—	—	—	—	—	—	—		NEW	2.8
Passion for Men										
(Uni)	—	—	—	—	—	—	—		NEW	2.7
Aqua Velva										
(Beecham)	2.1	3.3	3.5	4.7	4.2	1.1	4.0		4.4	2.7
Santa Fe (Shul)	—	—	—	—	—	—	—	NEW	3.7	2.6
Jovan Musk Men	1.2	0.5	1.1	0.6	2.5	1.1	0.2		2.4	2.5
Jazz (YSL)	—	—	—	—	—	—	—	NEW	0.5	2.3
Chaps (L'Oreal)	3.5	3.5	4.0	3.5	3.5	3.4	2.4		2.5	2.1
Aspen (Quint)	—	—	—	—	—	—	—		NEW	1.9
British Sterling	0.2	0.7	1.0	1.0	1.8	1.1	1.0		0.7	1.1
New West										
(Lauder)	—	—	—	—	—	—	—	NEW	0.8	1.0
Halston (Revlon)	0.6	0.9	0.7	0.2	1.5	0.7	0.8		0.5	0.6
Calvin Klein										
(Unilever)	—	—	—	—	1.0	3.8	1.6		1.5	0.8
Canoe (Dana)	0.8	0.5	0.4	0.7	0.5	0.6	0.5		0.8	0.8

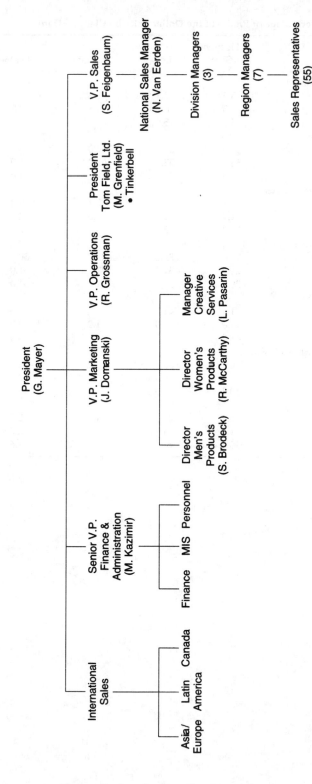

EXHIBIT 4 MEM Company: Organization Chart

EXHIBIT 5   Percentage of Product Line Dollar Sales by Class-of-Trade

	Heaven Sent	Loves	Fathom	English Leather	Other
Department Stores					
1991	5.5%	7.1%	1.2%	4.1%	1.3%
1990	5.3	6.2	6.3	4.5	5.0
1989	5.2	5.6	-	4.8	9.0
Chain Drugstores					
1991	57.0	53.0	47.0	46.0	43.0
1990	56.0	53.0	65.0	43.0	46.0
1989	51.0	53.0	-	41.0	42.0
Independent Drugstores					
1991	2.5	1.5	2.4	2.4	3.5
1990	2.7	1.8	3.0	2.5	3.2
1989	3.0	2.3	-	2.8	2.9
Mass Merchandisers					
1991	27.0	32.0	32.0	30.0	22.0
1990	26.0	31.0	21.0	31.0	20.0
1989	28.0	29.0	-	31.0	24.0
Armed Forces Stores					
1991	1.1	<1	2.5	3.6	2.5
1990	<1.0	1.0	1.2	3.9	4.0
1989	<1.0	1.1	–	5.3	7.8
Specialty/Gift Stores					
1991	4.9	5.9	12.2	11.1	17.7
1990	7.8	6.4	4.4	12.5	16.5
1989	10.2	8.6	-	13.7	14.4
International Export					
1991	1.9	<1	1.4	2.7	10.0
1990	1.5	<1	<1	2.7	4.8
1989	10.2	<1	-	1.6	3.3

Source: Company records.

EXHIBIT 6 Example of Retail Omnibus Advertisement

EXHIBIT 7 Sample 1991 Prices for Men's Fragrances

	Size	Retail Price	Retail Price/oz.
Preferred Stock	1.7 oz.	$17.55	$10.32
Stetson	3.5 oz.	16.00	4.57
Chaps	1.8 oz.	15.00	8.33
British Sterling	2 oz.	14.95	7.48
California for Men	2 oz.	14.49	7.25
Aspen	2 oz.	12.99	6.50
Santa Fe	1.7 oz.	12.00	7.06
Hero	1.7 oz.	11.50	6.76
English Leather	4 oz.	11.50	2.88
Chaz	2.2 oz.	11.25	5.11
Jovan Musk	4 oz.	10.99	2.75
Coty Musk	4 oz.	10.50	2.63
Iron	1.7 oz.	10.49	6.17
Canoe	2 oz.	10.00	5.00
Brut	1.5 oz.	9.00	6.00
Old Spice	4.25 oz.	5.80	1.36

EXHIBIT 8 English Leather: Research Findings

	18–24 yrs.	25–34 yrs.	35–49 yrs.	Total
Market Size:				
No. of males in United States (1991; in millions	13.44	22.13	24.71	60.28
% who use EL or competing aftershave/cologne brands	35.4%	30.2%	30.0%	31.3%
Net users (in millions)	4.76	6.68	7.41	18.85
Percentage of total	25.2%	35.4%	39.3%	100.0%
Brands on Hand				
English Leather	29%	30%	40%	33%
Brut	32	27	34	31
Drakkar Noir	68	41	21	43
Jovan	13	20	23	19
Old Spice	32	36	47	38
Polo	51	39	21	37
Stetson	17	13	27	19

Usage Frequency (% of those with brand on-hand):

	Daily or More			1–6/Week			
	18–24	*25–34*	*35–49*	*18–24*	*25–34*	*35–49*	*Never*
English Leather	10%	17%	30%	33%	41%	60%	12%
Brut	15	42	35	57	65	75	8
Drakkar Noir	46	28	43	88	87	95	0
Jovan	16	35	35	39	65	62	7
Old Spice	22	15	42	44	55	73	11
Polo	20	19	33	58	67	76	1
Stetson	24	31	30	71	62	75	5

EXHIBIT 8 *(continued)*

Purchase Influence (% of those with brand on-hand):

	Purchased by User	Asked Someone Else to Purchase	Received as Gift
English Leather	39%	20%	41%
Brut	54	19	37
Drakkar Noir	65	12	23
Jovan	52	13	35
Old Spice	47	20	33
Polo	51	15	34
Stetson	56	11	33

English Leather Package Evaluation:

	Random Users	El Users	Women
Label is easy to read	71%	77%	57%
Cap is easy to handle	61	71	57
Wooden cap is attractive	43	64	37
Package is masculine	35	52	46
Liquid is attractive color	31	46	32
"All my men" slogan is appealing	25	44	29
Box is attractive	22	35	25
Package has modern look	21	36	25

Brand Perceptions (% of users of each brand):

	English Leather			Drakkar Noir	Old Spice	Brut	Stetson	Jovan
	18–24	25–34	35–49					
Is a classic brand	27%	38%	44%	35%	53%	30%	21%	29%
Is a modern brand	20	27	27	82	33	33	36	41
Department store brand	20	24	26	25	24	26	14	21
Has fragrance that women like	14	20	29	66	30	20	35	32
For everyday use	12	16	25	36	32	20	23	23
Contemporary scent	11	20	19	47	27	23	18	27
Is exciting	5	12	13	56	20	14	26	26
Is exotic	3	8	9	48	14	16	16	19
Is too expensive	5	8	8	21	5	7	12	7

User Perceptions (% of all male users of aftershave/colognes):

	English Leather	Drakkar Noir	Old Spice	Brut	Stetson	Jovan
Likes to hike	51%	38%	60%	48%	64%	39%
Rides horses	50	45	44	49	57	36
Goes hunting	50	22	53	47	45	23
Goes to museums	49	63	51	36	46	50
Drinks beer	49	46	59	67	50	32

EXHIBIT 8   *(continued)*

	English Leather	Drakkar Noir	Old Spice	Brut	Stetson	Jovan
Goes to church	48	48	53	38	41	32
Goes to singles bars	46	72	49	51	58	60
Reads novels	45	47	43	42	43	53
Mows the lawn	39	22	50	51	33	24
Downhill skier	30	53	39	39	39	44
Goes to rock concerts	29	53	31	33	42	39

PART III

Services Markets

Once More:
How Do You
Improve
Customer Service?

The business community is presently flooded with articles, books, speeches, and workshops stressing the importance of "keeping close to the customer" as a means of achieving competitive advantage and market leadership. However, while customer service has become a dominant topic, experts repeatedly find that good service is more the exception than the rule. Is it an issue of attitudes, culture, and the lack of a "service obsession" at companies, or are other factors more relevant? What is "customer service" in a given situation, and how can managers diagnose internal activities that help or hinder external responsiveness?

One reason customer service workshops have not brought marked improvement is that they usually preach to the converted. Most managers realize that service is important, but often core organizational issues impede good service. Emphasizing "service culture" may momentarily galvanize the firm, but it ultimately will not help if management preaches service without addressing organizational factors.

A decade ago, *In Search of Excellence* (Peters & Waterman, 1982) focused attention on the components of service, providing examples of companies and individuals that exhibited qualities of superior customer service. However, in many ways service now occupies the status of "motivation" as defined by Frederic Herzberg (1968) in his classic article, "One More Time:

Frank V. Cespedes, in *Business Horizons*, Vol. 35, No. 2 (March–April 1992). Published by Indiana Graduate School of Business.

How Do You Motivate Employees?" Anxious for quick answers to a complex issue, many managers enthusiastically greet new quick fixes. Friendliness, responsiveness, and zeal become the fundamental attitudes associated with good service. Unfortunately, these attitudes are analogous to what Herzberg called hygiene factors—necessary but insufficient catalysts for obtaining the behavior and results desired.

WHAT IS CUSTOMER SERVICE?

Many companies define customer service as product delivery and repair. As a result, they tend to focus on delivery time, order fill rates, and billing-error minimization to determine "good" or "bad" service.

However, other factors also help determine the value of a purchase to a prospective buyer. The most obvious of these involves the product's price/performance characteristics, quality ratings as determined by the industry or respected outside rating agencies (Underwriters Laboratories in electrical equipment or *Consumer Reports* for many consumer durables), and the specifications of the product relative to the purchaser's particular requirements. But various prepurchase and postpurchase elements that add value to the item also must be seen as components of customer service. These nonproduct components include any information and ordering costs, in-bound logistical costs, operation and maintenance costs, and in many cases, disposal or trade-up costs.

Having understood that customer service should encompass broader product and nonproduct components of customer satisfaction, two ideas must be kept in mind when evaluating service efforts and goals.

First we examine value-in-use. This idea is that "the product is what the product does" (Corey, 1983); the product is the total package of benefits customers receive when they buy it. This includes the functional utility of the goods; any technical assistance in applications development provided before the sale; training or repair services provided after the sale; assurances of timely delivery through the supplier's distribution network; and any brand-name or reputation benefits that help the buyer promote its product or services to customers. Benefits might also include the buyer-seller relationship itself. Particularly in industrial markets, interpersonal relationships developed among people in buying and selling organizations have intangible but real value. Conversely, the package of benefits in some situations might not include personal contact because it is more efficient to reorder or conduct other aspects of the transaction via automated, on-line systems.

The point here is that customer service should include more than product-related functions or employee "friendliness." "Service" must encompass an entire range of possibilities by which a vendor can contribute to the customer's business operations. The ultimate economic justification for providing such services is to shift purchase criteria away from sheer price toward other value elements that help differentiate a vendor in its market.

For example, consider marketing developments in the health-care industry. Since 1983, when the government changed its reimbursement procedures for Medicare patients, hospitals have encountered intense cost pressures, making them more sensitive to price. One result of this new price sensitivity was the formation of more (and more powerful) group purchasing organizations (GPOs) in which a number of hospitals made volume purchases in return for substantial price discounts. Because of the volume they represented, these GPOs were typically designated "major" or "national" accounts by most suppliers. However, as one sales director noted, "Our national account program was really a national discount program, eroding our margins and often our contacts with end users at hospitals."

Nevertheless, in recent years some suppliers have altered their marketing strategies to redefine "customer service" and deliver a value to GPOs extending beyond price. For example, some drug companies now "bundle" products—offering discounts on sole-source items when purchased along with multisource products. Such services benefit hospitals by substantially lowering transaction costs in frequently purchased product categories. These services also enable vendors to better position their off-patent products. Additionally, bundling enables vendors to negotiate multiyear contracts with GPOs across product lines, further reducing costs while increasing the vendors' "share of mind" at end-user levels. Other suppliers have developed inventory management programs, which have grown in perceived value as more hospitals adopt just-in-time inventory policies. Still others give client hospitals data on the total costs of patient care in a given diagnostic category and explain how product acquisition, training, and disposal procedures affect these costs. Furthermore, some suppliers now recognize their field sales force is part of the product they sell. End-user preference for many health-care products is built on the individual sales representative's detailing and follow-up activities, as well as on the technical strength of the vendor's product.

For example, Becton-Dickinson negotiates corporate contracts with GPOs, but focuses its field sales efforts on the hospital "bench people"—lab technicians and doctors who actually use the products, care intensely about the quality and reliability of what they use, and complain loudly to hospital administrators if they do not get the product they want. As one Becton-Dickinson manager notes, "In recent years, I've seen a number of instances where purchasing wanted to standardize acquisition around a less expensive product, but the labs complained and insisted on our product." The common theme in these examples is that the suppliers provided and promoted services affecting the value-in-use of their products.

In consumer packaged goods, the concentration of retail trade, availability of point-of-sale data, and direct product profit information make such services crucial in maintaining retailers' shelf space. In many industrial-product markets, "strategic partnerships"— and a company's position as preferred supplier—often depend on the vendor's ability to manage customer service in the broader sense. More generally, the evolving nature of production makes it increasingly difficult to distinguish between "manufacturing" and "service" businesses. As Gershuny and Miles (1983) have shown, the standard criteria used to distinguish between these two sectors are so problematic that calculating economic activity on this basis requires making many subjective or arbitrary choices. Moreover, firms' product offerings to customers now typically consist of tightly interrelated mixtures of tangible goods, real-time services, and ongoing information exchange (Norman & Ramirez, 1989), which in turn require an integrated view of production, marketing, and customer service.

One advantage of approaching service from this broader perspective is that it enables the company to develop value-based pricing policies reflecting the costs and benefits of the total product offering. In addition, this often enables the firm to differentiate a product or service traditionally viewed as a "commodity." For example, L. E. Muran sells stationery, pencils, and other office supplies in a market made even more competitive in recent years by the entry of high-volume, low-priced "office superstores." In response to this heightened competition, Muran and individual corporate clients jointly produce a catalog of regularly ordered items and then distribute the catalog to each of the client's secretaries. The secretaries check off what they need, and the Muran sales representative picks up the orders daily. Muran then delivers individual orders to each customer location within 48 hours and also delivers regular "usage by department" reports to customer headquarters. The director of worldwide purchasing at one such customer site notes, "We used to buy stationery, allocate space for a stockroom, and maintain four people and a supervisor to run it. Now we order all these supplies from Muran and call it our 'stockless stationery' policy."

Having understood the broader concepts of service, it becomes apparent that customer service means different things to different customers. Many companies struggle with customer service because they treat "service" as a constant quality between buyer and seller—a discrete set of characteristics buyers are "looking for"—rather than as a variable across market settings. As a result, companies often spend much time and money developing customer satisfaction indices that serve only as exercises in pseudospecificity and mock quantification. These indices typically average different characteristics into a single set of factors that at best satisfy few individual customer purchasing and service criteria. Additionally, when efforts are made to avoid averaging, these indices become mere checklists of characteristics that are oblivious to many trade-offs between services offered and relative costs.

Critical elements of service typically vary by type of customer, as well as different phases of the order cycle and account relationship with an individual customer. For example, applications engineering or other technical services may loom particularly important for companies having few R&D or in-house service organizations. However, they are valued less by large companies with extensive R&D and in-house service personnel, where there is higher value placed on ordering ease and prompt delivery.

Several years ago, General Electric conducted an extensive audit of service factors in its industrial business units. Its findings are applicable to companies that similarly sell a variety of products in diverse markets. GE managers distinguished between what they called "flow goods" (standardized products usually ordered from stock and sold through distributors) and "project business" (semicustomized orders with substantial engineering content, typically involving various products assembled as a system by different GE business units). GE's results indicated marked differences in the service expectations of customers across the "flow goods" and "project business" order cycles (see **Figure 1**).

	Pre-Order	Order-to-Shipment	Post-Shipment
"Flow" Business	• Accurate, timely quotations • Knowledgeable sales force	• On-time, complete, accurate shipments • Accurate, timely order tracking/status reports	• Timely, responsive complaint resolution • Quality, timely in-warranty and out-of-warranty service
"Project" Business	• Accessibility and responsiveness of personnel • Quality, timely application support • Product availability information	• Flexibility to react to customer changes to the order • Experienced project managers • Ownership/authority for multi-product department orders	• Competent installation support • Accurate, timely billing • Effective spare parts support

Source: "General Electric: Customer Service" (Harvard Business School Case No. 588-059).

FIGURE 1   Critical Elements of Customer Service: Typically Vary by Phase of the Order Cycle and by Type of Business

Accurate and timely quotations, and field sales representatives knowledgeable in current pricing and delivery terms-and-conditions, are particularly important when generating "flow business" orders. These products are often sold by distributors as part of a larger package of goods (most not manufactured by GE); thus accurate and timely quotations are key to both end-users and intermediaries. In contrast, "project" business lead times and selling cycles are longer. Technical staffs' accessibility and responsiveness to customers' often ill-defined and evolving specifications are primary service components.

In the order-to-shipment phase, punctual and accurate shipments, as well as shipment tracking reports, are valued "flow" business services. Whereas the products are often relatively inexpensive and standardized, their availability is usually crucial to throughput at the customer's manufacturing plant. Consequently, reliable order shipments and tracking are especially valued. Efficient, standardized, and predictable procedures are important elements of distribution for these products. However, in "project" businesses, more uncertainty inherently lies in the order-to-shipment phases. Thus, "project business" customers value a supplier's flexibility and willingness to react to changes in the order. Standardized terms and conditions can actually become impediments to the execution of required services for these businesses. Due to this fluctuating environment, experienced project or account managers are the most important and valued promoters of customer relations.

Quick response to complaints and warranty claims are key components of after-sale service for "flow" goods customers. In fact, providing out-of-warranty service for these products often serves to distinguish one vendor from the next in "flow" product categories. As a result, a close working relationship with distributors is often an important prerequisite for good service in this type of business. However, "project" business post-shipment service involves a different range of supplier-customer activities, including installation, training, and the maintenance of spare parts for these semicustomized "system sales."

These differences must be recognized and managed, for they influence the relevant time period used in measuring service levels and costs as well as the amount and type of services inherent in achieving customer satisfaction in each type of business. For example, FileNet, a leader in the growing image processing industry, places service emphasis on applications development, system configuration, customer training, installation, and post-sale maintenance and repair. It offers two distinct service contracts that provide different maintenance and repair responsiveness, based upon the customer's relative sensitivity to downtime and the availability of in-house programmers able to assist in applications development.

Many other companies are simultaneously involved in "flow" and "project" transactions with customers. Rather than use homogeneous measures of customer satisfaction, these companies must develop a portfolio of service strategies. In addition, these differences influence the degree and type of internal coordination required to provide effective service.

CUSTOMER SERVICE AND INTERNAL MARKETING

Customer service, as defined here, is inherently a multifunctional activity. This can be illustrated by considering the typical order cycle in most industrial businesses (see **Figure 2**). Within the selling company, as the order

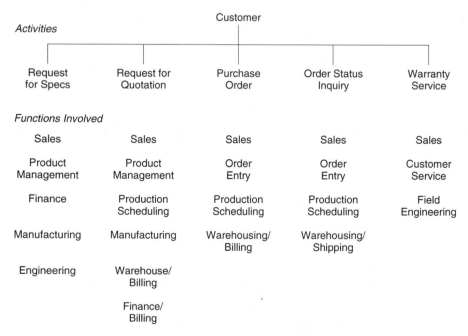

FIGURE 2 Customer Service Involves Most Functions in an Organization

moves from the customer's request for specifications and quotation to the purchase order and after-sale warranty service, the progress of an order typically involves numerous functions.

Two aspects of the order cycle are particularly noteworthy. First, field sales is typically involved in nearly all activities. Therefore, any service initiatives not recognizing field sales' role (and the implications of service changes for sales training, compensation, or performance evaluation) are likely to be short-lived or actively subverted by the company's primary customer-contact personnel. Second, though typically held responsible by the customer for any order processing problems, salespeople (or other front-line customer-contact personnel) usually have little direct authority or expertise concerning the many other areas involved in filling the order. Those most directly responsible for managing customer encounters face a series of internal marketing tasks to develop and maintain appropriate service levels. They must often persuade personnel in other functions, each of which has its own particular standard operating procedures, to help customize the order and attendant services for a particular customer.

One reason service problems persist at many companies, despite management's repeated chanting of the "keep close to the customer" mantra, is that those within the firm active in selling, marketing, manufacturing, and financing typically have different incentives and thus view "the customer" differently. For example, sales personnel often welcome, and argue for, product-line extensions or customized "solutions" in an effort to cover different market segments and accounts with a variety of product configurations. However, what may seem only a minor modification to a salesperson often entails a major operating change in manufacturing, service, or product management. Product-line extensions may require new processes, employee training, different production equipment or service expertise, and "disrupting" established (and seemingly "proven") operating procedures in all areas.

Similarly, marketers usually do not need to be convinced about the importance of service; they often argue for substantial investments in "same-day service," flexible terms and conditions, or no-fault/money-back service guarantees, all in an effort to "increase our share"—a typically salient goal of the marketing function in most firms. Meanwhile, finance people often evaluate a proposed investment of product design, capacity, and service in terms of quantifiable IRR, NPV, or short-term cash-flow implications. And accounting affects the inputs of these calculations by allocating service overheads in ways that both sales and marketing (as well as individual product managers) often consider "wrong" or "arbitrary" (Anderson, 1981; Barwise et al., 1989).

In each instance, the sources of potential conflict are clear. People in different areas of a firm typically have distinctive skills, resources, and short-term objectives. But external responsiveness requires internal coordination across these areas, placing customer service squarely in the middle of the crossfire between necessary cooperation and potential conflict. Moreover, this situation is further complicated because product-related elements receive the bulk of managerial time and attention, even though nonproduct elements of customer value are often crucial. Consider, for example, the following areas fundamental to completing tasks in any complex and time-constrained organization.

Management Responsibility

In many companies, the product elements of customer service have focused management responsibility in the form of product or brand managers, but the various nonproduct elements do not. If good service can be likened to a performance (Shostack, 1985), consider that in movie-making there is one person who is responsible for "continuity"—making sure the scenery in one take is congruent with the scenery for next day's filming of the same scene.

However, in most business organizations, the different activities required to develop and process an order typically have no one function or manager responsible for overseeing all the required activities. The closest thing to an order overseer in many companies is the formal customer-service staff, which usually plays a reactive role to customer complaints and has little actual authority to expedite or alter the flow of an order. The result, as one manager describes it, is the "Florence Nightingale brigade: customer-service staff trying to patch up and soothe a customer wounded in an internal war neither of them started."

In the computer industry, nearly every major vendor has recently stressed some form of "systems integration" provision to accommodate large clients and influential data processing buyers, who have increasing needs for smooth network communications around the world. But many of these same vendors sell and service this offering through hardware, software, and peripherals organizations that are heritages of a previous stage of competition. The result is often uncoordinated service, for separate components arrive at different times and in different quantities. Another result, as one irate computer customer recently commented, is a "pass-the-buck situation, where several product divisions are involved but nobody has control over the complete system."

Plans and Budgets

Management responsibility usually means developing formal business strategies and plans, complete with budgets and financial tracking of activities. Again, companies often have management controls in place for product-related elements, but nonproduct elements are managed on a more ad hoc basis, often without any planning process, financial controls, or method for making inevitable trade-offs among different customer groups. Indeed, the emphasis during the past decade on "service culture" has motivated many companies to consciously eschew plans and budgets for service activities. "We want our service people to be action-oriented zealots for the customer," is the tone of reasoning here, "and not fettered by plans or budgets that put them in a short-term or bean-counting frame of mind."

But often the unintended result of these good intentions is that service initiatives tend to be driven by the most pressing needs at the time. The ongoing procedures of the firm do not reflect the continuing importance of service, resulting in a reactive, intermittent approach, characterized by periodic programs aimed at service "excellence." In many instances, these programs actually damage the firm's service reputation: they raise customer expectations but do not deliver consistent levels of service quality, and the customer tends to focus on "lapses" from the promised threshold.

These programs can also damage management morale. At one large U.S. corporation, for example, the CEO had grown concerned about customer complaints, so a well respected senior vice president was appointed to head a task force to fix service problems. However, the vice president soon found that "customer service [is] not a new issue [here]. The Corporate Marketing files quickly coughed up numerous internal and outside reports on service dating back over 20 years. In fact, customer service has traditionally been the most studied, least engaged issue in [this] company, and even the recent top management attention [is] perceived by middle managers as just another fad."

How does the firm prevent service from becoming a fad? Because service components are typically dispersed throughout a company, planning and budgeting become important means for service realization. These seemingly "bureaucratic" and "action-inhibiting" mechanisms also make factors perceived as intangible (and therefore "unimportant") more tangible to busy and resource-constrained functional areas.

Measurements and Evaluations

One reason service programs are difficult to sustain is that few managerial measures actually relate customer support expenses to profit-and-loss criteria. The cost accounting systems in most companies are set up to allocate costs by product volumes; they in turn drive the salient financial and performance measurements at the firm (Kaplan, 1984). Marketing managers can track activities by brand; marketing research staff can measure product sales by region, channel, or competitor; and manufacturing managers can track variances by product category. However, even as customer service receives more rhetorical emphasis, customer data are usually absent, leaving most managers with little knowledge of account profitability. Moreover, as one observer notes, when companies do track customer support expenses, rather than product-related profitability, they usually measure it in terms of sales volume or gross margin with no allocation of SG&A costs or assets (Myer, 1989).

Further, this responsibility is often vested in the sales organization staff. Their compensation is generally tied to revenue goals, giving them every incentive to endorse any service program, regardless of its profitability impact. This situation has been exacerbated in recent years as sales-automation efforts, implemented at great cost and with great attention to user-friendly technology, have tended to "freeze" in place obsolete accounting systems that generate little actionable data about customer-maintenance costs. The frequent result is what one manager calls "the service boomerang: based on our accounting measures, we charge toward providing certain "value-added" services to customers; but then charge right back when the actual ROA is disappointing."

Culture-building activities may be resoundingly successful, and everyone may well realize that "service is important." However, in the absence of specific measures (and the presence of continuing pressures to make quarterly earnings), service expenditures become "discretionary"—allocated when budgets allow and dropped when cost pressures increase. This is analogous to the typical cycle of advertising expenditures in many firms: the level of spending is actually the result rather than the cause of historical sales volumes. That is, firms tend to cut advertising spending when sales are flat or when cost pressures are most intense. But one can argue that at this juncture, advertising and service are most important.

Accountability

This is the scarcest resource in any complex organization, its dearth being particularly apparent in the area of customer service. In an effort to manage the multifunctional efforts required to provide good service, companies increasingly define service as the responsibility of all employees. But in any large organization, "everybody's business" tends in practice to be "nobody's business." This unintentionally exacerbates the "lack-of-accountability" syndrome plaguing service efforts at many firms. At GE, for example, one of the first steps taken by corporate managers charged with improving service was simply to locate the people in each GE business unit primarily responsible for customer service. "We were surprised by what we didn't find," noted one executive. "There was no one person responsible for these matters in the businesses, and so no champion to raise awareness of the issues involved."

This situation can be debilitating in terms of actual service provided because, as another manager describes it, "customer service is inherently an optics issue: it has to remain visible and a central part of someone's agenda. Otherwise, things don't happen, or they consistently happen after the fact." In most Western companies, de facto responsibility for service resides with the sales and marketing function: when dissatisfied, customers typically complain to the field salesperson, and different marketing managers are involved at nearly all points of the typical order cycle described in **Figure 2**. Indeed, most definitions of marketing in our business school textbooks cite customer service as central to marketing activities. When pressed for a description of their fundamental role in the organization, most marketing practitioners also cite "customer service," or its fraternal twin, "serving customer needs."

By contrast, responsibility for service is a less specialized function in most Japanese firms, where engineering and manufacturing managers pursue more continuous contact with customers after the product is bought. When a Japanese company learns a customer is dissatisfied with the design of its product, it is not uncommon for the company to dispatch the design engineer, who then determines if the problem is significant enough to warrant redesign. By contrast, customer complaints in Western companies are handled much farther downstream in sales and marketing, and then brought upstream through manufacturing and product development.

Many factors account for these differences, including the now well-known differences in employment policies, manufacturing policies, and historical emphases on quality control (Aoki, 1988; Mahon and Dyck, 1982). But despite statements to the contrary by some Western observers, service is not "everybody's business" in the Japanese firm. The engineer (or manufacturing manager or product-development leader) is often held personally accountable for customer reaction. When customer service is an issue, the task facing Japanese managers is the same as for their Western counterparts: to expand and maintain their colleagues' understanding of customer needs, priorities, and preferences. It is the worst of both worlds, however, to remove product design and delivery from production and field sales—where palpable knowledge of customers and products ultimately resides—and then turn around and declare that customer satisfaction is "everybody's business."

MANAGING CUSTOMER RETENTION

Given the issues outlined here, it should not be surprising that good service seems more often the exception than the rule. Improving service can start by helping management be clear about both the product and nonproduct components of customer value in the business, and then by paying attention to structures and systems that aid in the coordination of service components dispersed in the company.

In many businesses, realigning internal activities to provide better service is ultimately justified by competitive pressures. However, in the short run, this holds true only if management understands the economic value of customer retention and the factors that build and extend the buyer-seller relationship.

This has always been a salient feature of high-fixed-cost service businesses, where up-front costs of property, plant, and equipment can only be justified if the customer "stays with us" beyond the initial transaction. As a result, banks, credit card companies, airlines, and other such businesses were among the first to stress customer retention and "relationship marketing" programs of different sorts (Reichheld and Sasser, 1990).

This imperative is also increasingly true of traditional manufacturing businesses. In these firms, new production technologies and big buyers' needs mean that suppliers must sell a system of tangible goods and intangible services, the cost of which requires customer retention over time to be economically justified for the supplier.

The marketing dynamics of customer retention at cable television companies can help illustrate issues relevant to a variety of other product-market environments. Given the cost structure of a cable franchise, the variable costs of serving an installed customer are minimal. Ideally, such customers become "annuities," as they remain part of the subscriber base and generate monthly fee revenues. In this respect, the economic value of a cable customer is the discounted value of a series of payments associated with that customer over a relevant time period. Conversely, customers become profitable to a cable franchise only after they have stayed on the system for some time. For example, one franchise found that a "basic cable" customer had to remain a subscriber for at least six months before the franchise recouped its costs of installing and servicing that customer. Including the amortized costs of plant construction, a basic customer had to be a subscriber for eleven months before it returned a profit for the firm. As a result, "churn" (people disconnecting the cable service for some reason) has always been a prime concern, and cable-TV firms have developed a variety of marketing programs aimed at understanding churn and minimizing its potentially devastating effects on supplier profitability.

One method of understanding customer retention is to distinguish between two types of disconnects in the customer base: those related to the product (customers dissatisfied with the franchise's particular program offerings or the quality of its transmission service) and those related to the nonproduct elements of customer value (customers dissatisfied with any of the particular transaction services or customer-support aspects of the cable franchise). In addition, there are two time periods during which the cable company can influence the behavior of customers: before and after installation of the product (see **Figure 3**).

In quadrant I of **Figure 3**, account selection and sales management policies are the primary marketing tools for managing customer retention. The goals are to attract customers whose product preferences are in line with the supplier's current product offerings and to establish sales systems that encourage a focus on such customers. In the cable business, for example, management can take some relatively simple actions at this juncture of the buyer-seller relationship: implementing marketing programs that educate potential customers about specific program offerings so that their expectations are in line with reality, or structuring sales incentives that discourage salespeople from selling pay-TV packages that customers later cancel.

In quadrant II, the supplier's evolving product policy becomes the primary marketing lever for customer retention. Many cable franchises have found that programming changes in line with the changing demographics of a franchise area are key to preserving the subscriber base. Similarly, post-installation follow-up by the sales representative (or service personnel) can help lower the amount of churn during the first months af-

	Pre-Installation	Post-Installation
Product	I	II
• Quality	Account Selection • Market Segmentation • Customer Education	Product Policy • Product Improvements • New Products
• Price-Performance	Sales Management • Training and Deployment • Sales Incentives	Communications Policy • Follow-Up • Complaint Resolution
Non-Product	III	IV
• Transaction Services	Order-Entry Procedures Inventory Management	Account Management • Team Selling Efforts • Sales/Service Coordination • Solutions Orientation
• Customer Support	Delivery Performance Technical Assistance/ Applications Development	• Responsiveness: — Customer Database — Internal Information Systems

FIGURE 3 Marketing Dynamics of Customer Retention

ter installation—an especially critical period for customer retention. Sending direct mail, using other vehicles aimed at explaining the purchased service in greater detail, or providing a phone number to call if there are any problems would also be helpful.

In quadrant III, the company's pre-installation transaction services and customer-support procedures should be the focus of marketing attention. Here, easy and reliable order-entry procedures, delivery performance, technical assistance (installation), and administrative procedures (contract terms and conditions) are the basis for customer satisfaction. In the cable business, joint work between the cable vendor and apartment-complex managers (or other important intermediaries between the supplier and end-user) has often been the key to better performance along these dimensions of customer value. In other businesses, cooperation between the supplier and distributors, strategic alliances, and development of sophisticated information systems to expedite transactions are often critical at this juncture.

Finally, in quadrant IV, the selling company's long-term value as a supplier is the key determinant of customer retention. For marketing, this generally means paying attention to policies and programs aimed at continually improving the supplier's ability in two areas: 1) gathering and exchanging information useful in developing solutions to the customer's evolving requirements, and 2) maintaining the internal systems that are a prerequisite for external responsiveness. In the cable business, this means developing and maintaining a customer database that helps the supplier track usage patterns and continually develop appropriate programming packages and promotions. In many other businesses, however, the task is more complex, requiring changes in both the supplier's sales programs and internal costing systems. In selling, many changes in the business environment are forcing vendors to adopt account-management programs that seek to improve coordination across geographically and organizationally dispersed selling units (Cespedes, Doyle, and Freedman, 1989).

But the absence of customer-level data in most companies' cost accounting systems is a major impediment. Here, activity-based cost analyses are useful because many important service costs vary, not with short-term changes in output (as assumed by most established systems), but with changes over a period of years in the design, mix, and range of a company's products, customers, and channels of distribution (Cooper, 1988). This is an accounting issue that directly affects the account manager's ability to gauge the value of customer retention and so argue internally for required resources. And it indirectly affects top management's willingness and ability to be profitably oriented toward responsiveness and service.

The framework in **Figure 3** is only a first look at customer retention dynamics, but it can help operationalize what "keeping close to customers" entails. By breaking down this worthy but ephemeral advice into manageable segments of the buyer-seller relationship, marketing, sales, and service managers can focus their limited time, attention, and resources on areas and actions likely to provide the best returns on customer investments.

How do you improve customer service? In large part, you improve it by managing the paradox inherent in a market orientation: external responsiveness (the ultimate test of marketing efforts in any firm) requires internal coordination and more attention to the organizational issues outlined in this article. These are structures and systems that customers rarely see or explicitly care about, but they ultimately elicit customer praise or customer complaints.

REFERENCES

PAUL F. ANDERSON, "Marketing Investment Analysis," in J. Sheth, ed., *Research in Marketing,* Vol. 4 (Greenwich, CT: JAI Press, 1981), pp. 1–37.

MASAHIKO AOKI, *Information, Incentives, and Bargaining in the Japanese Economy* (Cambridge: Cambridge University Press, 1988).

PATRICK BARWISE, PAUL R. MARSH, and ROBIN WENSLEY, "Must Finance and Strategy Clash?" *Harvard Business Review,* September–October 1989, pp. 85–90.

FRANK V. CESPEDES, STEPHEN X. DOYLE, and ROBERT J. FREEDMAN, "Teamwork for Today's Selling," *Harvard Business Review,* March–April 1989, pp. 44–59.

ROBIN COOPER, "The Rise of Activity-Based Costing," parts 1–4, *Journal of Cost Management,* Summer 1988, pp. 45–54; Fall 1988, pp. 41–48; Winter 1989, pp. 34–46; Spring 1989, pp. 38–49.

E. RAYMOND COREY, *Industrial Marketing: Cases and Concepts* (Englewood Cliffs, NJ: Prentice-Hall, 1983).

JONATHAN GERSHUNY and IAN MILES, *The New Service Economy: The Transformation of Employment in Industrial Societies* (London: Frances Pinter, 1983).

FREDERIC HERZBERG, "One More Time: How Do You Motivate Employees?" *Harvard Business Review,* January–February 1968, pp. 35–50.

ROBERT S. KAPLAN, "The Evolution of Management Accounting," *Accounting Review,* July 1984, pp. 404–407.

WILLIAM A. MAHON and RICHARD E. DYCK, "Japanese Quality Systems from a Marketing Viewpoint," *Industrial Management & Data Systems,* September–October 1982, pp. 8–14.

RANDY MYER, "Suppliers—Manage Your Customers," *Harvard Business Review,* November–December 1989, pp. 160–168.

RICHARD NORMAN and RAFAEL RAMIREZ, "A Theory of the Offering: Toward a Neo-Industrial Business Strategy," in Charles C. Snow, ed., *Strategy, Organization Design, and Human Resource Management* (Greenwich, CT: JAI Press, 1989), pp. 111–128.

THOMAS J. PETERS and ROBERT H. WATERMAN, *In Search of Excellence* (New York: Harper & Row, 1982).

FREDERICK REICHHELD and W. EARL SASSER, JR., "Zero Defections: Quality Comes To Services," *Harvard Business Review,* September–October 1990, pp. 105–113.

G. LYNN SHOSTACK, "Planning the Service Encounter," in John A. Czepiel, Michael R. Soloman, and Carol F. Surprenant, eds., *The Service Encounter* (Lexington, MA: D.C. Heath, 1985), pp. 243–253.

Case 7

MCI Vision (A)

In early April 1991, Mr. Steven Zecola, vice president of marketing in MCI Communications' eastern division, was considering what actions to take concerning divisional marketing efforts for MCI Vision, a long-distance service designed for small- and medium-sized businesses. Vision had been introduced in July 1990, and 1990 results had surpassed goals. But 1991 first-quarter results indicated that Vision sales were running 50% below target levels.

Mr. Zecola was considering options ranging from revised pricing policies to new customer and salesforce promotions. Simultaneously, corporate product management at MCI was in the process of developing plans to revitalize Vision sales. As well as a pressing short-term decision, Mr. Zecola believed the Vision situation illustrated issues concerning changing competition in the telecommunications business and new marketing and sales requirements for new types of products being introduced by MCI.

This case was prepared by Professor Frank V. Cespedes and Research Associate Laura Goode as the basis for class discussion rather than to illustrate either effective or ineffective handling of an administrative situation. Certain company data, while useful for discussion purposes, have been disguised.

COMPANY AND INDUSTRY BACKGROUND

MCI was the second largest U.S. provider of long-distance telecommunications services, with 1990 revenues of $7.7 billion (**Exhibit 1**). MCI offered a variety of voice, data, and messaging services including global communications, telex, electronic mail, customized facsimile, and advanced network management services. The company's mission statement noted that "MCI's objective is leadership in the global telecommunications industry," and strategic priorities included growing faster than the industry, competing in all significant long-distance markets, expanding MCI's global presence, and "aggressively driving cost efficiencies through automation, rigorous expense control, [and] organizational efficiencies."

MCI was founded in 1968 and, for over two decades, had waged legal and regulatory as well as marketing battles with AT&T and others, requiring (as one executive explained) "high leverage and frequent brushes with bankruptcy, a willingness to repeatedly alter plans in the face of new threats and opportunities, and low tolerance for systems and wallflowers." One result, many observers believed, was a distinct organizational environment. Throughout the 1980s, the average age of employees was less than 31 and, while MCI had grown to 24,000 employees by 1991, attrition rates had exceeded 30% in some years. William McGowan, MCI's chairman since 1968, had repeatedly emphasized that "The greatest handicap [in running a company] is that organizations hate to change. You're always at risk for getting chains of committees, manuals, procedures." The 1990 annual report noted that "MCI has succeeded in this fast-changing industry because we put a premium on attracting and developing resourceful, independent, creative people who know how to drive and manage change. . . . We ensure that our people have the work environment to think for themselves and maximize their contributions." One trade journal (*Computerworld*, 8/21/89) stated that "MCI's culture encourages frequent and open communication among all employees . . . the corporate culture of fast action and no bureaucracy borders on anarchy, according to some observers." In comments to the casewriters, MCI managers described the company atmosphere in the following terms:

> There aren't many formal processes or defined career paths here. During my seven years with the company, I've worked in marketing, sales, MIS, finance, and now international operations, and I had offers from legal and engineering. Cross-functional mobility is encouraged, especially for marketing people who, in a high fixed-cost service operation, must work with many groups in developing products, setting prices, and other activities.

*   *   *   *   *

> What I both love and hate about MCI is that everybody thinks everything is their job. The positive aspect is that people want to be part of a crisis, not run away from it; and we're able to do things

quickly and responsively in the marketplace. The negative aspect is the redundancy and long hours that often result from this "all-hands-on-deck" approach.

* * * * *

I had worked for GE and then McKinsey and, when I got to MCI, it was a week before anyone explained to me how to get an office, payroll number, and other basics, and another week before I realized this place is really a vast sorority and fraternity network that operates on move-or-be-moved principles. Our managers are young and must have a high tolerance for frustration, but they're given good compensation and significant responsibilities for their age and experience. Also, we often have a chance to define those responsibilities and make a real impact on the company and market.

Company Developments

In the 1980s, MCI's revenues grew at a 26% compounded rate as the firm gained market share from about 1% to over 12% by 1990 (see **Exhibit 2**). Until the mid-1980s, the company focused largely on the residential market where the divestiture of the Bell System allowed all U.S. customers to choose among long-distance companies on an equal access basis. MCI concentrated much of its marketing and other resources on winning and keeping customers in this $20 billion segment where calls were typically made off-peak when there is ample network capacity. The company also decentralized into seven largely autonomous domestic divisions in order to align with the regional phone companies that provided local exchange connections for customers. Beginning in the mid-1980s, MCI began efforts to attract more large corporate customers (i.e., greater than $50,000/month in long-distance business), a segment where, in 1985, AT&T had an estimated 95% share. Corporate customers were typically located in major urban areas (where MCI had installed new fiber-optic capacity), and their traffic ran primarily during business hours (when rates were highest). The company established a National Accounts Program in 1986 and, by 1991, had an estimated 12% share of the large business/government segment and (according to FCC estimates) a 17% share of the top 250 users of long-distance telecommunications services.

Throughout this period, MCI also expanded its product line and, with more than $7 billion of capital investments, expanded and upgraded its network. One result was improved service (via, by the end of 1991, a completely digital network) and operating efficiencies. In 1984, for example, MCI spent about $1,000 per new mile of circuitry; in 1990, new capacity made the incremental costs of adding customers very low. One executive noted that "we used to spend a dollar to get back a dollar in revenue. Now, it costs us about $.40. So, although MCI's rates have fallen more than 40% since 1984, our costs have dropped faster, thanks to automation." Another result was the development of software-defined network management services that combined many of the advantages of private networks with the efficiencies of the shared public network. Vnet was MCI's flagship offering in this so-called "virtual private network" category, and was targeted at large corporate accounts that sought a variety of network management, accounting, billing and pricing features without the special equipment and setup fees required by a private network. A third result was the increased ability, via its new network operating systems, to offer customized billing and other services (previously only available to large telecom users) to the General Business segment (GB), which was composed of seven million small and mid-sized companies with $500–$50,000/month in long-distance usage. Vision was MCI's initial such offering to this segment which, in 1990, represented an estimated $19 billion market.

To help position the firm for the 1990s, MCI undertook in 1990 a major acquisition and reorganization. In April 1990 MCI acquired for $1.25 billion Telecom USA, the fourth largest U.S. long-distance carrier with a 1.4% market share and over $700 million in revenues. Telecom had grown at nearly 30% per annum since its founding in 1984 by targeting primarily small and medium-sized businesses with competitive prices and several innovative products such as special calling cards that allowed customers to set up conference calls from any touch-tone telephone. Telecom also had 3,000 miles of high-quality, fiber-optic cable in the Midwest and Southeast, and half of this capacity linked communities where MCI had no such cables.

In November 1990, MCI reorganized from seven geographic regions to a structure aligned by customer segments (**Exhibit 3**). Business customers were to be managed by four regional divisions (primarily responsible for sales and other field marketing activities), with support from a headquarters business marketing unit (primarily responsible for product development and product management). Residential customers, previously the responsibility of each geographic region, were now managed via a headquarters consumer markets unit responsible for nationwide advertising, telemarketing, customer service and other activities in this segment. In addition, a network services unit addressed the network requirements of both markets. (The company's international operations were unaffected by the reorganization.) An internal memo explained:

> Today MCI operates in two very different businesses. We compete in the consumer business for residential customers. Essentially, this is a mass merchandising business, with customers sold and serviced centrally. Equally important, but very different, are MCI's marketing efforts aimed at commercial customers [which] range in size and complexity from large national accounts to small independent businesses. The common denominator is that these customers, for the most part, are sold and serviced on a face-to-face basis.
>
> The separation of our two major market thrusts will enable us to be a more responsive, effective competitor and allow us to address common organizational and marketing tasks: 1) We can further centralize consumer business, resulting in improved efficiencies and ability to

compete for the mass market, and 2) We can continue the process of decentralization of our commercial marketing efforts. Fewer, leaner division structures place more responsibility and autonomy at the local branch level, close to the market and close to the customer.

Corporate Product Marketing

Within the Business Markets unit, the Corporate Product Marketing organization was divided into three categories: Large Accounts (>$50,000/month), General Business (< $50,000/month), and a Government Systems unit.

In the Large Accounts unit, there were product management groups for: 1) Inbound Products (800 and 900 services); 2) Vnet (an outbound virtual-network service sold by MCI's National Accounts and Major Accounts sales groups to large corporate customers); 3) Network Management Services that provided customers with the ability to monitor, analyze, reconfigure, and control their MCI voice and data services; 4) Data Services (a group of high-speed data and private-line applications); and 5) Integrated Billing Services which managed the billing procedures for other MCI products. Billing and invoicing modifications were generally the most complex product changes for network engineers and, due to MCI's investments in software, considered by management a source of potential competitive advantage.

In the General Business unit, there were product management groups for: 1) Dial 1 (long-distance voice service); 2) PRISM/PRISM PLUS (a volume-discounted package of outbound domestic and international long-distance services targeted at GB accounts with monthly billings under $50); 3) Corporate Account Service (CAS) and CAS PLUS (special discounts and reporting features for GB accounts with >$2,500/month in billings); 4) Operator Services (domestic and international services such as collect calls, third-party charging, person-to-person calls, and calling assistance); 5) Messaging Services (various products including electronic mail, facsimile, and telex services); 6) Vision (see below); and 7) MCI Preferred (the newest GB product, introduced in March 1991 and targeted at accounts with $50–$1,500/month in billings; like MCI Vision, Preferred provided voice, data, fax, calling card, and international services in one package, with a consolidated invoice and combined volume discount).

Individual product managers were measured primarily in terms of revenues, although the president of the Business Markets unit had profit-and-loss responsibility. Product development was a joint function of the product marketing groups (based in Washington, D.C.) and the development group (based in Richardson, Texas) which managed product specifications including the software and associated information systems. At MCI, product development had traditionally been "opportunistic and fast," in the words of one executive. In 1988, for example, Mr. McGowan noticed a surge in ads for fax machines in the *New York Times* and decided MCI should create the first customized fax network which, by 1991, generated substantial revenues for the firm. Product pricing was the joint responsibility of corporate Product Marketing, Business Analysis (a unit within Finance), and Development; the former two groups first generated a joint proposal for a new product or enhancement and then submitted it to Development, which estimated costs for each feature. Commenting on their interaction, a Large Accounts product manager noted:

> I compete with other product managers for shared Development resources. So, much of my time is spent with Business Analysis rationalizing my list of needs and trying to place my list higher on Development's list of priorities. A key company asset is the shared network, and that means Development must look at the interrelationships implicated by each product introduction or modification. The complexity of this increases as software-based services become a bigger part of the products MCI offers.
>
> My perception is that, in practice, Development looks at one chunk of products at a time. A few years ago, Vnet got most Development resources; then Residential service was a priority; integration of Telecom USA products is a current priority. As a product manager, it's great when you get the attention and frustrating when you don't; in the latter situation, you try to solicit more input and support from divisional managers concerning needed features.

A General Business product manager commented:

> I sell my initiatives based on the incremental revenue opportunities in this segment: GB represents a big opportunity, *if* we get to market first with innovative services that leverage our network capabilities. Historically, however, MCI has focused Development attention on residential and then corporate markets, and some still perceive GB as a smaller "third-class" priority in comparison to those mass-market and large-volume segments.

A Development manager explained:

> Once Product Marketing defines the product need, we assess the product requirements and costs by talking to other functional groups. We then send these features and costs back to Product Marketing and, if they're satisfied, establish a program management team consisting of individuals from Development, Product Marketing, Finance, Network Operations, Engineering, Legal, and International (if relevant). This team then actually creates the product.
>
> MCI has few guidelines for program management. The good news is that we have talented, energetic people who cross internal boundaries to get things done. As a result, we've introduced more than 50 products in the past few years. The bad news is that the company is sometimes prey to the "hot project" syndrome, and the rest of the business ticks on while people focus on this project. Also, there are

few overall coordinating mechanisms and product overlap becomes more likely as we expand our offerings.

Commenting on product plans, Mr. McGowan noted that "You have to be big enough to be recognized as a candidate for anybody's communication needs and to afford the systems, services, support and personnel. Some number, around 25% of the market or more, has got to be within your capability for you to be considered a full-service carrier. We're going to introduce new services as fast as we can. We're going to provide multiple services to multiple market segments, from residential to the most sophisticated multinational [firm]."

Industry Developments

In 1991, AT&T, MCI, and Sprint held about 90% of the long-distance market. About 400 firms accounted for the remainder; most were resellers that purchased services at bulk rates from the major carriers, and competed regionally for small business customers. Three developments were expected to impact industry competition during the coming decade.

First, after double-digit growth rates throughout most of the 1980s, estimates of domestic long-distance growth were about 5% annually for the 1990s. International growth was expected to be higher.

Second, pricing pressures and marketing expenditures in many segments were expected to continue increasing. In 1989, the FCC granted AT&T "Tariff 12" permission to offer large accounts volume discounts (often, 10–30%) under 18–36 month contracts. Competitors, including MCI, responded by offering similar contracts. By 1991, the majority of large corporate accounts were believed to have signed such contracts. Hence, less large-account business was "up for bid," in the words of one executive. In the residential segment, advertising and promotional expenditures had increased dramatically in recent years. In 1990, AT&T was estimated to have doubled its ad spending to nearly $600 million, while MCI and Sprint each increased their ad spending from about $50 to $75 million. In contrast to earlier years, much of AT&T's advertising was aimed at taking customers away from other carriers rather than increasing usage and primary demand. Ad spending also reflected a need among carriers to introduce and explain a greater variety of services, rather than what industry observers called the POTS products ("plain-old-telephone-service") of past years. Similarly, each carrier had increased its number of field salespeople and telemarketers. One analyst noted that, in recent years "the various players have been employing only one of the four Ps in the market share war— price. [But] the industry is now exercising the other three Ps: product, promotion and place (distribution channels)."

Third, technological trends affected both product development plans and selling requirements in the industry. In 1990, data communications was a faster-growing percentage of commercial long-distance usage than voice communications. Technology was also making more common enhanced and combined services such as computer transmissions, electronic mail, videotext, teleconferencing, and voice mail; and software-defined networks made it more feasible to "down-market" such services to smaller customers as well as high-volume corporate accounts. Similarly, an increasingly important source of product differentiation was the billing options provided to customers. Often these were enhancements to existing products (e.g., additional management reports); but new billing formats had also become the basis for new products. In turn, these developments were expected to alter cost structures and strategic trends in the industry. According to one analyst:

> [In the past] there was little differentiation of products and services across the network; hence, the facilities base overwhelmed all else in the investment process. Barriers to entry were the scale of facilities. Note that in this topology it was relatively easy to cream-skim lucrative business markets. [But] software and marketing expenses are beginning to outweigh facility expense. The "down-marketing" of services to the lower end broadens the market for applications. The barriers to entry move up to relative scales of software and sales expense. Brand-name recognition and product differentiation will be important factors.

MCI'S EASTERN DIVISION

As part of the November 1990 reorganization, the four divisions reporting through the Business Markets unit were structured identically (**Exhibit 3**) and measured primarily in terms of contribution (i.e., net revenue minus expenses). The eastern division, created from a combination of the Northeast and Mid-Atlantic divisions, covered 13 states and Washington, D.C. It was the largest revenue producer among the four divisions, with about 2,500 employees generating more than $1.5 billion in 1990, and included about 60% of Fortune-1000 headquarters. Its president was Mr. Jonathan Crane who, since joining MCI in 1983, had been an account executive in the Northeast division, the vice president of MCI's corporate National Accounts Program, and most recently the president of the Southeast division. One of Mr. Crane's first actions was to reduce divisional staff by about 75 positions, add about 100 people in field sales and support, and give more decision-making responsibility to branch operations. He noted that, "For 20 years MCI necessarily focused on areas such as building a network, hiring a salesforce, making billing work, and getting product out. Now we must use these established strengths in an environment where price competition is less feasible. Service, support, and applications-oriented sales and marketing will increasingly be the basis of competition."

In 1990, Large Account customers accounted for more than 30% of eastern division revenues, General Business customers sold via the field salesforce for more than 40%, and General Business customers sold via tele-marketing for less than 20%. 1991 divisional plans called for a 10% revenue increase, with the growth driven primarily by GB segments.

Eastern Division Marketing Organization

Mr. Zecola was made the division's vice president of marketing in January 1991. He had been with MCI for eight years in areas including Regulatory Affairs, Business Analysis, National Accounts, and Alternate Channels Marketing. The marketing department was responsible for: 1) achieving budget and revenue plans for Silver segment (<$500/month in telecom billings) which, for 1991, was $290 million; and 2) providing support to the field sales organization in achieving Large Account and GB revenue plans. Reporting to Mr. Zecola (see **Exhibit 4**) were the following functions.

Commercial Telemarketing was responsible for achieving Silver segment goals. It sold primarily outbound products such as PRISM, Vision, 800 services, and Preferred via three telemarketing centers. Target accounts were classified as Silver or Gold ($500–$2,500/month in billings). Average monthly billings were $1,400. Telemarketing reps were compensated via a base salary and commissions tied to customers' line usage. Two types of sales were tracked and rewarded: services to new accounts and new services to current accounts. Historically at MCI, telemarketing was an entry-level sales position and successful telemarketing reps became field sales representatives. During his first months in the division, Mr. Zecola had focused on improving customer acquisition in the telemarketing operation. By April, performance had improved significantly and was exceeding plan.

Commercial Customer Service provided free 800 access to small businesses to answer questions regarding MCI's services and to resolve service problems. Mr. Zecola placed a high emphasis on improving the customer responsiveness of this unit, and drove rapid improvements in average speed of answer and correspondence turnaround. Separately, this unit also assigned Customer Service Engineers (CSEs) to accounts generating at least $3,000/month, and provided 800-number assistance to smaller accounts. CSEs reported to branch managers and had dotted-line reporting relationships with marketing.

Technical Services provided technical sales support for larger customers involved in complex installations or voice-and-data enhancements.

Sales Operations was created in late 1990 and included sales-reporting (installations, disconnects, and backlogs by product and segment), recognition tracking and reporting (for sales reps and CSEs), and sales compensation administration.

Planning and Analysis identified new business opportunities and helped to coordinate various sales and marketing programs.

Training was responsible for sales training which, in 1991, was being revised (see following).

Alternate Channel Marketing was responsible for negotiating co-marketing agreements to sell MCI services with other organizations such as Rolm (the equipment vendor) and the National Association of Securities Dealers. The group also pursued Sales Agent programs with authorized third parties to sell MCI services on commissions based on sales volume over a stipulated time period. Agents included office equipment vendors, telecommunications consultants, financial planners, and others.

Product marketing was responsible for coordinating product plans with the corporate marketing units, developing strategies for their assigned products, intrastate pricing, competitive analysis, and field sales support. One product manager explained:

> Product development and interstate pricing are corporate marketing responsibilities. We are supposed to take the product and price as a given and then get field support and execution. But we do have some input and, if Corporate won't make changes we perceive as necessary or fund a division-specific promotion, I can make my case with divisional Planning & Analysis, Steve Zecola, and perhaps Jonathan Crane for divisional money. There's no formalized process. I must convince the right people it's the right thing to do.
>
> Also, corporate marketing assigns products to either the GB or Large Account category, but division product managers' responsibilities cut across these segments. GB and Large Accounts do have different technical and purchasing needs, but there are many exceptions to this rule. In practice, the translation of product plans into customer applications, the combination of products for an account, and attempts to position potentially overlapping products occur at the division level.

MCI placed its products into one of four categories: Commercial Outbound, Inbound, Network Services, and Data/Private Line. Each category had a division product manager and assistant product managers who were measured on revenue contribution.

Commercial Outbound included products (Dial 1, PRISM Plus, CAS/CAS Plus, MCI Card, Fax, Vision, and Preferred) that generated about 50% of divisional revenues, with the older Dial 1 and PRISM products as the largest contributors. Dial 1 was traditional WATS service, and PRISM a long-distance service based on the actual distance of each call, targeted at accounts generating less than $50/month. Preferred was targeted at accounts generating $50–$1,500/month, and Vision at accounts of $1,500–$50,000/month. Ms. Terri Ford, senior manager for Outbound products, noted that "Dial 1 and PRISM are now commodities with little feature differentiation from competing offers. Our field salesforce is comfortable selling them. But Preferred and Vision must be marketed on the basis of their application and enhanced-service benefits."

Commercial Inbound included 800 and 900 inbound services. Ms. Fran Snyder, senior manager for Inbound, noted that these services "are not commodities and imply big switching costs to customers," in contrast to Outbound products where customer switching costs were generally lower:

> For example, a credit card company has its 800 number printed on each card. You must demonstrate significant new applications or features to get them to switch. For new 800 and 900 sales, moreover, you're often dealing with a company's marketing managers in addition to telecom and/or finance people, the selling cycle is longer, and knowing the customer's business in some detail is more important to sales effectiveness. Corporate marketing places Inbound products in the Large Accounts unit, so its messages to the field and incentive programs are typically geared to Large Accounts. But more than 60% of our divisional Inbound revenues come from GB accounts.

To encourage more attention to Inbound products, Ms. Snyder often implemented division promotions and sales incentives, beyond those offered by corporate marketing. Since these incentives were paid from sales branch budgets, the approval of marketing and sales managers was necessary.

Network Services was managed by Mr. Ian Dix whose primary product responsibility was Vnet. Mr. Dix spent two to three days a week making presentations with the division's Major Account and National Account reps, providing sales training on product features, or meeting with installed accounts to gather information then sent to corporate marketing. Vnet was traditionally targeted at large accounts with billings of more than $50,000 a month. However, Mr. Dix noted that "in the past three years, probably 80% of national and major accounts in the division have signed multiyear agreements. Short-term, that revenue is untouchable: either I already have it or can't get it. So, I have geared my 1991 plan to focus more on GB accounts and the field salesforce that sells to those accounts, because that's where the potential business is. However, Vnet is more complex and applications driven than most GB sales efforts."

Data Products included private networks and high-speed data services that generated about 5% of the division's 1990 revenues. Mr. Richard Santoro, senior manager for Data, explained that "Data has been a second-class citizen at MCI: the sales cycle is long-term, technically complex, applications-oriented, involves both Telecom and MIS managers, and AT&T has been embedded at most accounts. So, our salespeople have not typically devoted much time to these products. But data communications are now growing faster than voice, are especially important for the many multinational accounts headquartered in the Eastern division, and our enhanced network and service capabilities give us more technical capability here."

Also part of the Product Marketing unit was Field Communications, which distributed and coordinated information from corporate and divisional product managers to field sales. Each piece of information was assigned a status code: "Hotline" (time-sensitive information such as pricing or rate changes, sent to each branch within four hours); "Direct Line" (important but not time-sensitive information, distributed every two weeks); "FYI" (distributed at division managers' discretion); and "Heads Up" (information about general industry developments or upcoming events, distributed via monthly mailings). Ms. Meg Reilly, manager of divisional field communications, noted that "Part of my job is to protect the field from information overload. Every product group is vying for field attention, and sends most announcements to me with Hotline status. But while I send all information to everyone in the field, I can override a priority status and often downgrade it to FYI or Heads Up." A key vehicle for internal communications was MCI Mail, an electronic mail service which connected every employee and generated more than 400,000 messages daily throughout the company. Managers emphasized that this system had become "a way of life" for every MCI employee, who typically checked his or her file daily and could send a message to anyone (including the chairman) at any time. One manager commented: "With MCI Mail, everybody gets information and knows who to call about an issue; they simply look at who sent the memo."

Eastern Division Sales Organization

The division's sales organization had 34 branches, each headed by a branch manager who reported to the division director of sales. Starting in 1990, the National Account salespeople had a separate structure and reported directly to corporate headquarters. There were 1,800 salespeople in the eastern division, and 100 National Account managers.

Branch managers were paid a salary and incentive compensation tied to two factors: 60% of the incentive depended upon Net Revenue Increase (NRI) and 40% on New Growth Revenue (NGR). NRI had recently been instituted to focus attention on customer retention and usage levels; NGR had previously been the sole component of branch incentives, and was calculated by multiplying the branch sales headcount by the quota assigned to each sales rep level. One branch manager explained: "If a branch starts the year at $20 million in usage revenues, it must be at, say, $24 million by year end. It's not that difficult to gain 20% in business from new accounts, but now we must also be sure not to lose business from existing customers."

Reporting to each branch manager were two to five sales managers, each of whom had four to eight salespeople as direct reports. Most salespeople were assigned geographic territories, but some were responsible for Major Accounts. Sales managers were assigned monthly quotas based on sales headcount in each of three categories: 1) Account Executive 1 (AE1s) called on businesses with billings of $500–$2,500/month; this was the entry-level field sales position, and was staffed by people in their early to mid-20s with about two years' previous sales experience (either with another firm or in MCI telemarketing); 2) Account Executive 2 (AE2s) called on businesses with billings of $2,500–$30,000/month; AE2s were typically

AE1s with one to two years of successful performance; 3) Major Account reps called on businesses with billings of $30,000–$400,000/month (i.e., up to National Account status); about half of Major Account reps were outside hires and half were AE2s with two to three years of successful performance.

All salespeople were paid a salary plus commission. Newly hired AE1s had a six-month bridge compensation period in which they were paid base salary as well as incentive pay, thus allowing new AE1s to learn new job responsibilities without placing their compensation "at risk." Two types of revenue were tracked for all rep levels: New Revenue was business produced from a new account during its first year of usage, and commissions were established at a flat rate but uncapped; Growth Revenue was additional business generated from an existing account due to an intentional sales effort, and an accelerated commission rate structure provided for higher levels of incentive pay as higher levels of Growth Revenue were achieved. AE2s and Major Account reps were also paid incentives for Retention Revenue. This referred to the billings MCI received monthly from the account. AE2s and Major Account reps were responsible for ensuring that Retention Revenue was equal to or above the prior month's.

While incentive earnings opportunities were uncapped, at target the average AE1 had total compensation of $34,000, about one-third of which was incentive compensation; the average AE2 had total compensation of $45,000, about one-half of which was incentive compensation (with 20% of the incentive tied to Retention Revenue); and the average Major Account rep had total compensation of $68,000, about one-half of which was incentive compensation (with 30% of the incentive tied to Retention Revenue). In 1990, 28% of the division's salespeople achieved assigned quota targets and the turnover rate among salespeople was 35%.

Also reporting to each branch was a Customer Support Manager who managed branch CSEs, who were organized in three levels comparable to those of the salesforce. All CSEs were responsible for post-sale support, including managing the installation process via placing and tracking the order and coordinating with internal MCI operations and any external equipment vendors involved in an installation. Other post-sales support activities included conducting account reviews and dealing with any reporting or billing issues that might arise. CSE1s and CSE2s were each assigned 30–50 accounts; Major Account CSEs had an average of 10, and were typically involved in account planning as well as post-sales activities.

CSEs also sold add-on features and additional customer sites for MCI services at established accounts, and received revenue credit (along with the assigned salesperson) for such sales. CSE compensation was primarily base salary, but as of 1990 they were also paid bonuses for new sales and about 10% of CSE compensation was tied to selling activities. Ms. Mary Fitzgerald, customer support manager for the Boston branch, noted that CSEs were vital to customer retention and new revenue growth since they were typically involved with accounts on a weekly basis and with multiple departments: "When we started getting paid on retention and growing the base, we were simply acknowledging and rewarding what had been going on all along. Yet, it wasn't always perceived that way. CSEs are technical people and many don't like to think of themselves as selling, even though that's what they're doing. Conversely, some reps worry about account control; they have an attitude that says, 'no one can do this at my account as well as I can.' But now that branch managers are paid on NRI, the CSE role in sales activities is receiving more attention." New CSEs received one week of training with new salespeople. Ongoing training also involved joint Sales/CSE programs. About 50% of CSEs had previous sales experience and the annual turnover rate was less than 10%.

In the industry, according to one magazine, "MCI's salespeople have earned a reputation as tigers, which they need to be." In recent years, moreover, MCI had recruited numerous salespeople and sales managers from leading computer, business equipment, and other firms. One branch manager, previously with IBM and Raytheon Data Systems, noted that "the youth, vitality, and aggressiveness in the field are a delight, and absolutely necessary when you have about a 15% share in a consolidating business. But MCI is now the dominant vendor in many accounts, and a focus on customer retention and net revenue increase is a change-of-pace for many in the field." A Major Account manager commented: "AT&T is definitely more aggressive lately. They're cutting more special deals and changing prices, things they were very rigid about in the past. Also, their traditional attitude was to focus on the biggest users. But now they're putting in more people at the Major Account level and, to a lesser extent, at GB accounts as well. But we still are more flexible in responding to customers, have an advantage in billing and many other 'soft cost' areas, and in my opinion still out-hustle the competition."

Product Marketing-Field Sales Coordination Issues

As MCI introduced many new products, salespeople often had to deal with new accounts, decision makers, and purchase criteria. At the same time, product managers often "competed" for salesforce attention via sales incentives, contests, customer promotions, field communications, and other means. Mr. Zecola noted that "we have a relatively lean marketing department compared to the size of the salesforce, and now a broad product line with diverse sales support needs. The issue is how best to provide this support while also doing the ongoing product management tasks." To help address this situation, the eastern division had instituted a new sales training program and a new product-sales liaison position.

Ms. Leslie Lampe, divisional Senior Manager for Training, explained:

Our sales training was not providing reps with the skills increasingly necessary for sales success. The training emphasized products at the expense of sales skills, there was no sequential skills development for AE1s and AE2s, and did not prepare reps for applications selling, by which I mean understanding a customer's business well enough to uncover meaningful applications. Newer software-based products have features whose value is perceived through the installation of critical applications, and customers sold on these applications have more "staying power" than if sold on price alone.

In 1991, the division's sales training program (funded from the Marketing department's budget) was revised to emphasize applications training. In part, this meant providing information and training exercises designed to highlight typical communications flows (and potential MCI product applications) within functional areas such as sales and marketing, finance, and others. Salespeople were also trained in "probing questions" designed to uncover potential applications in each area (see **Exhibit 5**). Field Communications began providing salespeople with monthly "application briefs" that focused on divisional success stories where the MCI salesperson or account team's efforts involved a nonprice value-based sale to a high-level nontelecom decision maker and where the MCI service(s) sold required cross-departmental coordination at the customer and by the salespeople involved. A New Hire Mentor Program teamed new hires with experienced salespeople for their first six months in the field, while sales management training was revised to provide coaching tools and other skills focused on personnel development. Finally, a new industry marketing program focused on certain industries in the region (e.g., Hotel/Hospitality and Financial Services) where specialized applications were important.

In mid-1990, the eastern division also established in certain branches a field marketing specialist position (FMS). The initial goal was to provide a field marketing generalist position to assist salespeople with product questions and cross-selling strategies, while also developing a cadre of managers with both marketing and sales experience. The first FMSs were mid-level salespeople with strong track records and field credibility, and the anticipated career path was from FMS to a product manager and/or branch manager position. However, due to Vision support requirements, FMSs soon focused efforts on this product, providing important technical and applications support during the product introduction. One salesperson noted:

> The FMS position is great. It helps me make sense of a broad line and, when I make an important customer presentation, I can focus on the products I'm comfortable with and have the FMS present the more specialized products. I often learn more from listening to the FMS talk to a customer than from a formal product training session. Also, because the FMS has field sales experience, they're accessible and I know many of them personally.

Based on this feedback (and funding requirements), management in August 1990 changed the FMS from a generalist position to one focused on specific products. In 1990, there were twelve FMS positions and the key products were Vision, 800 and Private Line services.

Beginning in 1991, FMSs reported directly to branch managers with dotted-lines to appropriate division product managers (who, with the branch manager, had input into FMS hiring decisions). FMS compensation (a combination of salary and incentive pay) was based on the branch's sales performance in the FMS's assigned products. Deciding whether to hire an FMS was made the branch manager's prerogative. One branch manager noted that "my branch quota remains the same if I hire an FMS, so the decision is based largely on whether I believe an FMS will help generate more revenue than an additional salesperson would. We have five FMSs in this region, and what's evolving is that each has a product-group specialty which we share among the participating branches. My FMS probably spends 90% of her time on branch-specific activities and 10% as the product specialist for other branches." Another commented that "having the field pay for a resource like the FMS has a long history at MCI where cash constraints, decentralization, and monthly quotas taught field managers not to expect centralized supports or subsidies. Also, paying for the FMS drives accountability and forces branch managers to look closely at how the resource is used and whether it contributes to NRI goals."

While the FMS position continued to receive favorable feedback, some marketing managers were concerned that, with branch funding and a product specialty emphasis, the FMS "will become another tactical, short-term position. Branch managers won't allocate money for products requiring longer-term FMS support activities, and some will use the position as a slot to place field reps who are not meeting quota." Others believed the position created another level between marketing and the field, and that inter-product competition for sales attention would now take place at the FMS level.

VISION

By mid-1989, many MCI managers were concerned about the company's position in the GB market. Declining margins in the residential and Large Account segments made GB more important, while smaller regional carriers and recent AT&T efforts had caused MCI's share in GB to decline. In addition, as one corporate product manager noted, "Our development priorities and monies had been going to our Vnet virtual network service for a few years, and (like other carriers) we had no product designed specifically for GB accounts who (unlike corporate customers) have not traditionally viewed telecom services as a strategic investment."

Having identified this gap, debate then ensued about how to address it. Some managers argued for bringing Vnet down-market by repackaging and repricing the product for smaller-volume users. In addition to rapid development time, they cited the advantages of keeping growing GB accounts on the same product as their usage increased. The other option was to develop a new product, based on the Vnet platform but with features and pricing structures customized for GB market needs. By late 1989, the latter option had been chosen for a number of reasons. It was determined that current Vnet software could not easily handle the additional volume of transactions, invoices and reports that GB customers would require. In addition, as one corporate marketing manager involved in the Vision development process explained:

> MCI had worked hard to establish Vnet as a high-end product for large corporate accounts, and we didn't want to dilute that positioning. Conversely, by 1989, Vnet had many features not needed by GB customers, and we wanted a simple product that could be sold in two or three sales calls without all the analyses that a Vnet sale to a large account requires. We also needed a very different billing approach. Vnet accounts have in-house telecom staffs that can analyze telecom usage. But GB accounts don't, and our market research had determined that simple, visible management controls such as call detail reports would be key features in a GB-oriented product. We also needed to establish an identity for MCI in the GB segment and a stand-alone product that the salesforce selling into GB customers could rally around.

Development of Vision took nine months from establishment of a project team to product introduction. In late 1989, corporate management set an announcement date of June 1990 in order to coincide with a national sales meeting. In addition, as one corporate marketing manager noted, "The key with Vision was getting to market quickly: it would be a unique offering in this segment and, for various reasons, we felt AT&T and Sprint could not easily duplicate the product. So we wanted to keep it a competitive secret and maximize the first-mover advantages inherent in an applications-driven product." As a result, most divisional product managers learned about specific Vision features at the time of introduction.

When introduced, Vision offered customers a variety of features and management reports (**Exhibit 6**). Vision pricing was set at a simple flat rate per minute domestically, and with a single invoice that aggregated into a volume discount usage across an account's locations. Initially targeted at GB customers spending between $500 and $50,000 per month, Vision altered MCI's product portfolio as indicated in **Exhibit 7.**

Introduction and 1990 Results

In June 1990, Vision was introduced to 300 branch managers and sales managers at the national sales meeting in Washington, D.C. Several senior executives addressed the group about Vision, emphasizing its many unique features, the opportunity it represented among small-business customers who spent more than $500/month, and its status as MCI's flagship offering in the GB segment, designed to replace PRISM as the product of choice and focus of sales attention at qualified GB accounts. A Hotline message describing the product release and associated customer benefits was also sent that evening to all branches, and a TV ad campaign (with the theme, "Big-business long distance for your business") was begun. In addition, a number of customer promotions were included as part of the introduction, including one free month of service, a credit of up to $1,000 to customers that signed up by August 31, and MCI's assumption of any PIC costs (i.e., fees paid by users to local Bell operating companies for changing carriers), as well as a sales bonus for Vision installations through August 31, 1990.

The field's response was generally immediate and positive. In the eastern division, a number of significant Vision sales were made the day after the product announcement. One sales manager noted that "Our people were hungry for a good GB-oriented product, and we could all see that Vision had many features that competing products didn't have." Mr. Santoro, who in 1990 helped to establish the division's new FMS position, explained:

> Vision was the perfect product to roll out with the FMS program. The salesperson's key task is finding the right customer application for Vision functionality. This means the rep must talk to more than just the Telecom manager and often deal with issues that go beyond telecommunications. It became crucial to have someone in the branch who knew the product in detail and could help develop application selling skills. Vision and our FMS program were developed independently, but the timing coincided perfectly. So, by late July of 1990, we had put together a Vision presentation that makes most rock concerts look boring and, over the next six weeks, our new FMSs took that show on the road to every branch office.

A division marketing manager noted that, "When Vision was introduced, everything else was put on hold for weeks because we didn't have any real advance notice yet realized fast movement was essential. Every product manager was assigned to work on the project exclusively for the first month, and we established and implemented a training program which included the history of its product development, product features, and detailed application training." In addition, Ms. Sharon Lovit was appointed divisional product manager for Vision and, in addition to customer calls, conducted numerous "roundtable" sessions in branch offices where she discussed potential applications and rep feedback concerning customer responses.

By year-end 1990, companywide sales of Vision had exceeded plan. A Vision Customer Satisfaction survey, conducted in December 1990 by The Gallup Organization, found high levels of satisfaction across all types of installed customer groups (see **Exhibit 8** for survey excerpts).

For 1991, corporate marketing established an aggressive $425 million sales goal for Vision, making this product's performance the key determinant of the corporate GB unit's 1991 plan. It was anticipated that half of this goal would be generated by customer migrations from PRISM and half from new Vision acquisitions. For the eastern division, the 1991 Vision plan called for $150 million in sales, making it a key component of the division's GB goals and the Commercial Outbound marketing unit's revenue plan.

1991

During the first quarter of 1991, companywide sales of Vision were down 20% from fourth-quarter 1990 sales and, in terms of usage, Vision minute growth had stabilized at about 650,000 per week. Equally important was the fact that dedicated Vision locations (i.e., customer locations where circuits were installed for Vision service, rather than "switched" on to the network) were running about 30% below plan; dedicated locations typically represented "anchors" that spurred multilocation penetration of accounts. Rather than migrating customers "up-service," moreover, sales statistics indicated that PRISM 1 installations were being sold at nearly twice the rate of Vision dedicated services. At current trends, Vision generated about $1 million/day in revenues but represented about 8% of 1991 MCI revenues (versus a planned 17%) and would fall short of target. Further, AT&T and Sprint were expected to introduce competing products within the coming months.

Eastern division sales reflected companywide results. In late March, Terri Ford (division marketing manager for Outbound services) sent a memo to Mr. Zecola and corporate product marketing managers outlining issues and recommendations. Among the reasons cited for Vision's stalled sales growth was competitive activity in the GB segment and MCI's response. In early 1991, AT&T launched a large ad campaign to promote its Pro Wats product for small-business customers. This product was the feature equivalent of MCI's PRISM product (regular outbound domestic and international long-distance service based on the size of the business and its calling patterns). But AT&T revised its pricing to duplicate the Vision discount structure and initial free month of service for new customers, and also offered reduced international prices on Pro Wats service. In response, MCI during the first quarter of 1991 increased its advertising and promotions for PRISM (including reduced international fees on this product) and substantially cut advertising for Vision.

In February 1991, moreover, MCI had introduced a new product (MCI Preferred) which offered flat per-minute rates, volume and time-of-day discounts, and features such as calling cards, voice messaging and conference calling. Preferred was based on technology and software made possible by MCI's acquisition of U.S. Telecom, and was targeted at Telecom's traditional customer base: GB customers spending $50–$1,500/month on long-distance services. Preferred lacked many report and other capabilities of Vision, but its introduction revised Vision's target segment upwards to GB customers generating $1,500/month or more. Preferred was introduced with an extensive ad campaign, a $1,000 credit to customers who signed up for Preferred by April 1, and extensive product training and attention in field branch offices.

Ms. Ford noted that at the beginning of the year, "We told the field to concentrate on Vision, but then offered and advertised promotions on PRISM and international services." She also noted that the increased promotional activity among all vendors had "encouraged customers to switch back and forth between carriers to take advantage of first-free-month offers. Many existing customers feel that we (and other carriers) only reward new customers, and there is no incentive for loyalty."

Ms. Ford's recommendations included more precise identification of accounts whose business characteristics fit Vision's service features, customer promotions such as a free month for "dedicated" Vision installations as well as rebates tied to time-on-service duration, and sales promotions intended to reward reps and CSEs for sales of specific Vision features. However, she emphasized that any Vision promotions should "facilitate revenue acquisition and maintenance but *not* position MCI as a discount company having a "fire sale" for Vision.

In reviewing these recommendations, Mr. Zecola considered several questions: were Vision's first-quarter results fundamentally a reflection of product/feature issues, competitive activity, or marketing/sales programs? Did the division's sales organization have the required skills and support to be effective with this product? What roles should the division and/or corporate marketing organizations play in a plan to revitalize Vision sales performance? And what would be the impact of any Vision promotions on other products sold by the salesforce, on Mr. Zecola's ability to achieve his Silver segment goals, and on precedents established for the introduction and management of other feature-rich products like Vision?

While considering these issues, Mr. Zecola received an MCI-Mail message from Mr. Crane: "I want to set up a meeting soon with you and others to discuss how we can improve division performance in the GB segment. I would like the output of that meeting to be a GB Action Plan and, as input, would like you to consider what longer-term marketing and sales actions are needed to consolidate our position with GB customers."

EXHIBIT 1 MCI Communications Corporation: Selected Financial Information for Years Ended December 31 (in millions, except per common share amounts)

	1990	1989	1988	1987	1986
Summary of operations					
Revenue	$7,680	6,471	$5,137	$3,939	$3,592
Total operating expenses	(7,060)	(5,489)	(4,553)	(3,704)	(4,036)
Income (loss) from operations	620	982	584	235	(444)
Net interest expense	(192)	(205)	(198)	(169)	(124)
Income (loss) before					
extraordinary item	299	603	356	78	(481)
Net income (loss)	299	558	346	64	(498)
Earnings (loss) applicable to					
common shareholders	270	529	334	64	(498)
Earnings (loss) per common share:					
Income (loss) before					
extraordinary item	1.06	2.26	1.27	.27	(1.75)
Loss on early debt retirements		(.17)	(.04)	(.05)	(.06)
Net income (loss)	1.06	2.09	1.23	.22	(1.81)
Cash dividends per common share	.10	—	—	—	—
Balance sheet					
Gross investment in					
communications system	$8,708	$7,345	$6,577	$5,686	$5,284
Annual investment in					
communications system	1,283	1,052	896	619	1,074
Total assets	8,249	6,484	5,954	5,380	5,258
Long-term debt	3,147	2,241	2,677	2,663	2,676
Stockholders' equity	2,340	1,995	1,359	1,279	1,212

EXHIBIT 2 The U.S. Long-Distance Industry

Long-Distance Revenues[a] (billions of dollars)

	1985	1986	1987	1988	1989	1990
AT&T	27.5	32.3	35.2	35.4	34.6	35.0
MCI	2.5	3.6	3.9	4.9	6.2	6.7[b]
US Sprint	1.2	2.9	3.3	3.2	5.8	6.0
Others	1.3	2.9	3.3	3.2	5.8	6.0
Total	32.5	41.4	45.2	56.9	50.9	52.1

Long-Distance Market Shares[a] (percent of total)

	1985	1986	1987	1988	1989	1990
AT&T	84.6	78.1	77.9	75.5	68.0	67.2
MCI	7.6	8.7	8.6	10.4	12.2	12.9[b]
US Sprint	3.6	6.2	6.2	7.2	8.4	8.4
Others	4.1	7.0	7.3	6.9	11.4	11.5
Total	100.0	100.0	100.0	100.0	100.0	100.0

EXHIBIT 2   *(continued)*

Average Rate per Switched Access Minute ($ per minute)

	1984	1985	1986	1987	1988	1989	1990	84–90 CAGR
AT&T	.279	.276	.260	.227	.211	.191	.176	−7.4%
Other carriers	.159	.173	.191	.154	.151	.172	.170	1.2%
% of AT&T rate	56.9%	62.9	73.4	67.9	71.3	90.0	96.7	—
Total	.259	.255	.244	.206	.192	.184	.174	−6.4%

1989 Long-Distance Marketplace, by Industry Segment

Industry Segment	Industry Revenues ($ Billions)	Estimated 1989–1995 CAGR	Market Share			
			AT&T	MCI	Sprint	Other
Basic long distance	$24.4	10%	65%	16%	11%	8%
International	6.7	20	80	12	8	0
Private line	5.6	15	87	8	4	0
800	5.0	15	87	8	4	1
WATS	4.1	9	70	15	10	5
Payphone	2.0	10	80	8	7	5
Data	1.0	22	89	7	3	1
900	1.0	30	88	2	4	6
Other	1.5	N/A	N/A	N/A	N/A	N/A
Total	50.9	N/A	68	12	8	12

[a]Excludes local exchange carriers.

[b]Excludes Telecom USA.

Source: North American Telecommunications Association, Annual Report 1990.

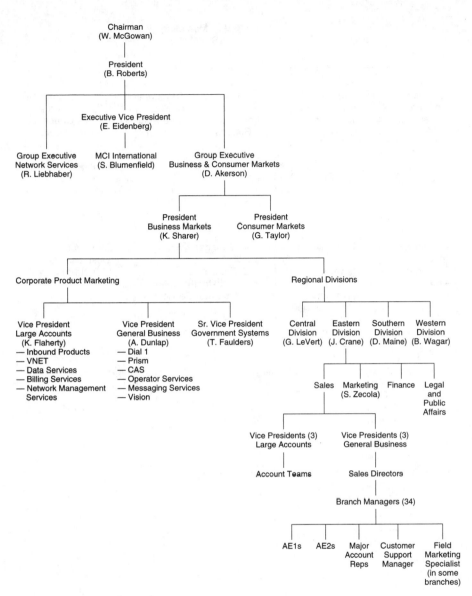

EXHIBIT 3 MCI Organization (November 1990)

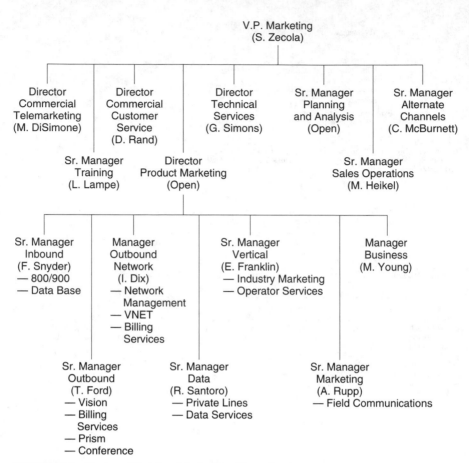

EXHIBIT 4   Eastern Division Marketing Organization

EXHIBIT 5   Applications Selling: "Probing Questions" (Examples)

"Probing Questions" puts pertinent departmental information into a handy list of questions to ask your contact in each functional area. Use these questions and sample product applications when you meet with your contact in:

Sales and Marketing

How are you using telecommunications to shorten the sales cycle?
(MCI Fax, MCI Mail, 800 Service, FX)

How do you disseminate leads throughout your organization?
(MCI Fax, MCI Mail)

Have you used telecommunications reports to see specifically what types of customer and/or geographic areas are utilizing your services?
(Call detail reports, detailed invoices)

How are you monitoring your telemarketers' call activities?
(ID and accounting codes, range privileges)

Would reducing telecom sales-related expenses give you more discretionary income for your budget?
(Call volume discounts, WATS, MCI Mail, other MCI services)

Operations

How are customer orders initiated within your company?
(MCI Fax, MCI Mail, 800 Service)

Are you using telecom services to expedite the order process?
(MCI Fax from customers, data links for inventory control)

Does your fulfillment process require communicating with distant suppliers?
(MCI Fax, MCI Mail, data links, 800 service, Accounting and ID codes)

MIS

(Note that the voice/data mix is now 60/40, but the data market is expected to double within 5 years and grow to 50/50)

Have you considered how telecommunications links can ease your connections to distant company sites for analyzing programs, accessing software tools, testing, debugging, and distributing documentation?
(MCI data services, network management services, MCI Fax, MCI Mail)

Would the ability to customize calling privileges for employees and locations enable you to reduce expenses?
(Range privileges, accounting and ID codes, detailed invoices)

Finance

How much time do you spend validating and tracking long-distance expenses?
(Management summaries, call detail reports, detailed invoices)

How do you forecast and manage ongoing telecommunications expenses?
(MCI Fax, MCI Mail, management reports, billing options, ID codes)

How often do you communicate with outside database services for credit authorization, electronic funds transfer, or other financial transactions?
(MCI data services)

EXHIBIT 6   MCI Vision

Features	Benefits	Applications
Flat rate	Provide simple, easy-to-follow pricing structure	Allows company to forecast expenditures and control costs
Consolidate invoice access methods	Combines traffic and access methods from all locations, for optimum telecom savings	Communications between headquarters, division sales forces, distributors, plants, customers, etc.
Accounting codes	Allows customers to allocate costs	Trace projects and administer project chargebacks
Universal calling range privileges	Allows customers to restrict calling privileges at the location and/or user levels	Reduce costs and improve productivity
Vision card	With an 800 access, it allows calls from any domestic location while contributing to total usage for volume discounts	Personnel travelling between offices and customer locations
Call detail (paper/mag type)	Offers complete summary of activity by personal ID code or accounting code	Manage multiple projects, departments, locations, and organizations
Personal ID codes	Provides verifiable security and cost-allocation capabilities by location or individual	Controls telephone abuse, particularly in remote locations
Six-second billing	Provides additional savings with accurate call pricing	Compete internationally while reducing costs
Remote exchange	Provides customers with a "local number" presence in one place, while handling the calls at a distant site	Market new services and expand client base
Instant ringdown	Eliminates expensive point-to-point private-line charges	Credit card verification

Spending Level

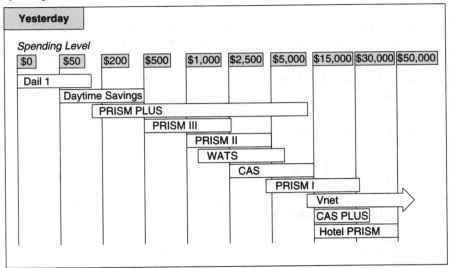

Spending Level

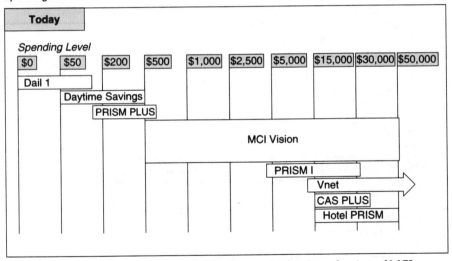

EXHIBIT 7 MCI Product Positioning: Before and After Introduction of MCI Vision

EXHIBIT 8   Vision Customer Satisfaction Survey (Excerpts)

Methodology   Gallup interviewers contacted by telephone a random sample of Vision customers during December 1990. A total of 807 interviews were conducted. Sample characteristics were:

Male: 56% (n=452)   Female: 44% (n= 355)
Division: Eastern (33%), Southern (37%), Central (13%), Western (17%)

Which of the following best describes your role in choosing MCI Vision?

Sole decision maker: 42%
One of the primary decision makers: 32%
Played a major role in researching and recommending MCI Vision, but the final decision was approved by someone else: 26%

What were the primary reasons why your company became an MCI Vision customer?

Response	1st Response	All Responses
Low rates	50%	70%
Type of billings reports	8	14
Sales representative	7	12
Previous experience with MCI	6	8
Good service	5	12
Dissatisfied with previous carrier	4	5
Features/specific services	2	6
Recommended by someone else	2	3
Accounting codes	1	3
Security codes	1	1
Consolidation	1	3
Other	10	23

Overall, how satisfied would you say your company is with MCI Vision?

Very Satisfied:	52%
Somewhat Satisfied:	35
Somewhat Dissatisfied	6
Very Dissatisfied:	1
Don't Know:	6

With regard to your expectations for the product, would you say it has:

Met all of your expectations:	34%
Met most of your expectations:	45
Met some of your expectations:	8
Met only a few of your expectations:	3
Not met your expectations:	1
Don't know:	8

MCI Vision customers have a wide variety of product service options to choose from. Please tell me whether you currently utilize the following:

MCI Vision Calling Card	73%	Remote Exchange	5%
Accounting Codes	39	Custom Calling	5
Personal ID Codes	26	10-Digit Restriction	5
Universal Calling	14	Call Detail Information	
Instant Ringdown	8	on Magnetic Tape	3

For each service option, how satisfied are you with this aspect of MCI Vision?

MCI Vision Service Option	Very Satisfied	Somewhat Satisfied	Somewhat Disatisfied	Very Dissatisfied	Don't Know
Accounting codes (3.53)	58%	29%	4%	2%	7%
Universal calling range privileges (3.55)	53	31	3	1	12
Call detail information on magnetic tape (3.67)	46	23	0	0	27
Personal ID codes (3.62)	60	26	3	0	10
10-digit restrict (3.53)	60	29	5	2	13
Instant ringdown (3.73)	66	32	0	0	2
Remote exchange (3.68)	66	32	0	0	2
Custom calling range privileges (3.49)	58	32	5	3	3
Calling card (3.36)	41	29	8	2	21
Combined volume discounts (3.39)	40	32	4	2	20
Flat rate pricing (3.43)	37	36	3	1	23
International calls (3.43)	27	20	2	2	47
One consolidated monthly billing invoice (3.61)	65	17	5	3	10

[Numbers in parentheses refer to mean ratings. Scale: 1 = very dissatisfied; 2 = somewhat dissatisfied; 3 = somewhat satisfied; 4 = very satisfied]

How important is each service option as part of your total Vision package?

MCI Vision Service Option	Among the Most Important	Important	Not That Important	Not at All Important
Accounting codes (3.37)	47%	41%	8%	1%
Personal ID codes (3.33)	44	43	8	2
10-digit restrict (3.15)	29	55	10	2
Call detail information on magnetic tape (3.08)	27	50	12	4
Custom calling range privileges (2.95)	18	58	18	3
Remote exchange (2.93)	20	54	22	2
Instant ringdown (2.90)	23	39	27	3
Calling card (2.88)	23	47	23	6
Universal calling range privileges (2.82)	18	46	27	5

[Numbers in parentheses refer to mean ratings. Scale : 1 = not at all important; 2 = not that important; 3 = an important service; 4 = among the most important services]

How responsive has MCI support staff (excludes salespeople) been to your questions, comments, or complaints with regard to MCI Vision?

Very responsive	63%
Somewhat responsive	21
Not very responsive	5 [Mean = 3.59]
Not at all responsive	2
Don't know	9

Case 8

American Mobile Satellite Corporation

In April 1992 Brian Pemberton, president of American Mobile Satellite Corporation (AMSC), was considering AMSC's product line and marketing programs. AMSC was preparing to launch satellites that would provide wireless mobile communications throughout the United States, Puerto Rico, Virgin Islands, and 200 miles of coastal waters. Mr. Pemberton commented:

> AMSC initially focused on gaining regulatory approval. We're now in construction mode: raising capital, lining up the technology, and developing the system required to offer mobile communication services. Simultaneously, we must ramp-up marketing efforts to acquire customers, establish distribution channels, and define the product line and its applications. It's a bit like building a boat while you're in full sail, but the nature of the business opportunity requires this.

This case was prepared by Professor Frank V. Cespedes and Research Associate Laura Goode as a basis for class discussion rather than to illustrate either effective or ineffective handling of an administrative situation.

Among the issues requiring decisions were the nature of distribution channels for AMSC services and the potential role of high-speed data capabilities in AMSC's product line.

INDUSTRY BACKGROUND

The first commercial satellite, Early Bird, began service in 1965, providing voice, data and video communications between fixed points on land. In the 1970s, NASA developed means for satellite communications at sea and between fixed and mobile land transmitters. In response to growing demand for mobile communications in the 1980s, the Federal Communications Commission (FCC) created one license for mobile satellite service in the U.S. market and asked interested parties to apply. In 1988, eight applicants joined to form AMSC and, in May 1989, were granted the FCC license. These companies included: McCaw Cellular Communications (29.4% ownership of AMSC), the largest U.S. operator of cellular phone systems; Hughes Communications (29.4%), manufacturer of communications satellites; MTEL (29.4%), largest U.S. operator of radio paging systems; as well as Skylink Corporation, North American Mobile Satellite, and Mobile Satellite Inc., which together owned 12% of AMSC.

William Garner, AMSC's Chief Scientist, commented: "When AMSC was formed, each of the original applicants brought its own vision of the business and the technology specifications. Technical issues concerning satellite launch and operation have been resolved. But there's still diversity of opinions concerning issues like product positioning, primary target markets, and distribution channels." By 1992, the major owners had invested about $140 million in AMSC. Total projected investments through 1995 were about $500 million, with the bulk of additional funds coming from bank debt and, some time before launch, an initial public offering of equity.

Most FCC licenses are restricted to a specific application. But AMSC's license permitted a wide range including air, sea, and land communications and authorized AMSC to operate up to three satellites whose coverage area is indicated in **Exhibit 1.** Each satellite (being constructed by Hughes and with the first scheduled for launch in late 1994) would have an operating life expectancy of 10 to 12 years and at least seven-fold greater transmission power than existing communications satellites, allowing complementary earth terminals and antennae to be smaller and potentially less expensive than dish antennae and other current satellite technologies. Further, each satellite had capacity for up to 2,500 channels, depending on the type of antenna used and the bandwidth allocated.

To provide "full redundancy" in the system, AMSC and Telesat Mobile, Inc. (TMI), the Canadian mobile satellite services operator, signed an agreement in 1990 to build and deploy identical satellites, each serving as back-up for the other. Mr. Pemberton noted that this partnership provided other benefits: "Joint procurement of the ground segment of operations streamlines the bidding process and reduces costs for both firms. The same is true of end-user terminal development and procurement. And we provide uninterrupted service to U.S. customers calling or traveling to Canada."

Mobile Communications Market

In 1990, cellular, paging, and two-way radio services and equipment generated $9 billion in revenues with forecasts indicating a $32 billion market by 1999. One observer noted: "Mobile communications demand is driven by a desire for more productive use of transit time; improved scheduling and logistics; reduced information float; a need for emergency information and services; and, for many users, the comfort of convenient access to communications abilities." A 1990 study identified certain major markets for mobile communications services (see **Exhibit 2**). Serving these markets in 1992 were a variety of terrestrial- and satellite-based vendors. *Terrestrial-based systems* included:

• Specialized mobile radio systems used FM frequencies to transmit voice, data and fax messages. Vendors included Motorola (a leading manufacturer of radio, phone and other electronic equipment), whose Coverage-Plus service targeted regional short-haul trucking carriers; and MobileData (a subsidiary of Ericsson Communications), whose major customer was National Car Rental's 400 dealerships. In 1990, U.S. companies operated over 1 million specialized mobile radio terminals, paying about $500 million in access fees. Heaviest users included police departments, the armed forces, and taxi companies. AMSC's technology had superior transmission capabilities and coverage compared to existing mobile radio systems.

• Air-to-ground systems provided passenger phone service (via high-frequency radio transmissions) between airplanes and ground terminals. This service, initiated by GTE in 1984, generated over $20 million in revenues for the firm by 1991. But consumer acceptance had lagged expectations due to inconsistent transmission quality, high prices and, generally, availability of only one phone aboard each plane at inconvenient, public areas. In 1992, less than 2,000 aircraft were equipped with such phones, but GTE was taking steps to convert its system to digital technology (which would improve transmission quality) and to increase the number of phones aboard airplanes. Compared to satellite service, air-to-ground systems had inherent limitations, including scope of coverage, capacity constraints, and transmission quality.

• Personal Communications Networks (PCNs) involved handheld cordless phones as an alternative to pay telephones connected to local telephone exchanges. By 1992, the FCC had awarded more than 40 licenses for PCNs to companies such as AT&T, Bell South, and Motorola. Projected usage costs of such systems were $100 for necessary equipment and $10 per month service charges with nominal or no per-minute charges. PCNs being tested in 1992 were limited to voice communications and to outgoing calls within a 600-foot range of the base stations. However, PCNs were potentially compatible with satellite-based systems.

- Cellular Phone Service grew rapidly in the 1980s:

	1984	1987	1989	1990	1991	(Estimates) 1992	1993
Subscribers (in millions)	0.10	1.2	3.5	5.4	7.7	10.4	13.5
Penetration	0.04%	0.5%	1.42%	2.16%	3.07%	4.11%	5.30%
Monthly bill ($/subscriber)	240	145	101	91	94	91	89

Cellular telephones, about $4,000 per unit in the early 1980s, were often well below $1,000 by 1992. FCC rules specified two cellular companies in each geographical market; by 1991, all 306 U.S. metropolitan statistical areas (MSAs) had cellular service as did about half of the 428 rural statistical areas, together covering about 50% of the continental United States and 85% of telephone households in the country. However, the capital costs of cellular systems made them uneconomical in low-population areas (see **Exhibit 3**). For U.S. rural counties with fewer than 10 people per square mile, projections indicated the following:

Year	Rural Population	% Without Access to Terrestrial Cellular	# Without Access to Terrestrial Cellular
1991	57,200,000	60.0	34,300,000
1992	57,400,000	57.3	32,900,000
1993	57,700,000	54.7	31,600,000
1994	58,000,000	52.0	30,200,000
1995	58,300,000	49.3	28,700,000
2000	59,700,000	36.0	21,500,000
2005	61,200,000	26.8	16,400,000

Nationally in 1990, the occupations of cellular users were: Professional (18.1%), Managerial (15.8%), Homemaker (12.5%), Sales (11.3%), Foreman/Craftsman (11.3%), Technical (9%), other (22.1%). In rural counties, where income levels were generally lower than in MSAs, occupations of cellular users were: Foreman/Craftsman (19%), Retired (19%), Laborer (16.7%), Clerical (9.5%), Sales (7.1%), Owner/Proprietor (7.1%), other (21.6%).

"Roaming" (calls made outside the range of a subscriber's cellular system) was important to many cellular users but often difficult and unreliable due to handoffs among cellular systems. In addition, charges for placing calls while roaming varied from $.60–$1.00 per minute, plus a daily roaming fee of $2–$5 per cellular system utilized while roaming, plus whatever long-distance charges the caller incurred. An AMSC executive noted:

> Our service can complement cellular by offering customers seamless roaming coverage in the United States and Canada, including remote areas that have no cellular system and probably never will. This can reduce churn for cellular firms, generate more airtime, and attract new customers from the fringes of their coverage areas. AMSC's value-added applications can also offer cellular-carrier partners an opportunity for product differentiation in both urban and rural areas. Estimates indicate that over 10% of cellular revenues already come from roaming calls and that a third of all roaming fees are untraceable and uncollected by the subscriber's cellular carrier. We see provision of seamless roaming as generating the bulk of our revenues and cash flow.

Satellite-based systems for mobile communications included a variety of vendors.

- Qualcomm focused on trucking firms with a two-way data communications package launched on other organizations' satellites. The firm had more than 20,000 installed terminals generating about $30 million in revenues. However, the satellites and frequencies utilized by Qualcomm terminals (which cost about $4,500 each) limited transmission capabilities in cities, heavy-foliage areas, and during periods of severe precipitation; and its technology did not allow for provision of high-speed data or voice communications.

- INMARSAT, the exclusive supplier of maritime mobile satellite services since 1982, was a consortium with more than 60 country members. INMARSAT's mandate was to provide global communications services for safety at sea via a network of satellite terminals on ships and coastal stations. Each member country named one company as its "signatory." The U.S. signatory was Communications Satellite Corporation (COMSAT). INMARSAT was barred from providing nonmaritime services but in 1992 was petitioning member countries to revise its charter and allow provision of such services. An industry observer commented:

> INMARSAT has the technical infrastructure to provide global, mobile, two-way voice and data communications. But its performance reflects its governance structure. INMARSAT inherited COMSAT's satellite network in 1982, but enlisted just over 15,000 customers in the next decade. It's maintained its price levels despite big price decreases throughout the telecommunications industry during this period. Also, the AMSC satellite would be much more powerful.

All of the above vendors (and AMSC) utilized satellites in geosynchronous orbit. Other firms had plans for low-orbiting satellite systems.[1] One was Iridium, a $3 billion system proposed by Motorola which (at its projected completion date of 1997) would consist of 77 satellites providing global cellular phone coverage and some data services. In 1992, Iridium was still in the "proof of concept" stage and FCC authorization had not yet been obtained. But Motorola was pursuing multiple international agreements and partners for the concept.

AMSC ORGANIZATION

In 1992, AMSC was organized as indicated in **Exhibit 4**. Before joining the company in 1990, Mr. Pemberton's experience included marketing positions at IBM, president of Monroe Systems for Business, and president of Los Angeles Cellular Telephone Company from its establishment to full operations. He commented:

> I've had repeated, successful experiences in building start-up organizations. Hiring good people and giving them sufficient scope are crucial in these situations. This is especially true for AMSC. We have large revenue opportunities, aggressive growth plans, and changing demand patterns in what is still an embryonic area of telecommunications. This means we must be flexible. At the same time, our investment decisions often come in chunks of $100 million or more and affect all areas of our operations. Right now, for example, we must make important product policy decisions while establishing distribution channels, building system components, and creating user awareness and demand. That requires effective communication between Technology, Engineering, Finance, and Marketing—not easy to do when each area is running full tilt.

AMSC's business plan called for 600,000 subscribers (generating about $400 million in revenues) by 1999—the year AMSC projected its first satellite would reach capacity. Utilizing capacity on the satellite owned by TMI (AMSC's Canadian partner), total revenue and subscribers would peak at about $600 million and 950,000 in the year 2001, when AMSC planned to launch up to two additional satellites in accordance with its FCC authorization. Sales and Marketing, headed by Christopher McCleary, was responsible for meeting the firm's revenue goals and developing relationships with distributors. Mr. McCleary noted:

[1]In geosynchronous orbit, a satellite orbited 22,300 miles above (and at the same speed as) the Earth, giving the effect of being stationary. Three geosynchronous satellites orbiting around the equator can provide worldwide coverage. Low-orbiting satellites are 400 to 600 miles above earth in elliptical orbits, cannot handle substantial data transmissions, and at least 20 must be launched to provide worldwide coverage. But low-orbiting satellites can be smaller, less costly to launch, and communicate to smaller earth terminals.

Our key issues at this point are prioritizing the many opportunities out there, and then aligning AMSC product and channel capabilities as we learn more about these opportunities. While the basic satellite infrastructure has been chosen, specific service features will vary depending upon the nature of the terminal, whether or not we directly offer packet-switched data capabilities or allow third parties to provide these services, and other aspects of the ground system—whose suppliers and details are still being worked out. Meanwhile, we in Marketing daily learn more about end-user, reseller and partnering opportunities, as well as the implications for desired service features. It's a complicated, iterative process with few precedents and no rule-book.

To segment market opportunities, AMSC had created three product groups: MSAT Telephone, MSAT FlightNet, and MSAT PrivateNet. McCleary noted that "while market positioning, product features, promotion and distribution plans are still evolving, these groupings provide a framework within which these decisions can be made."

MSAT Telephone consisted of 10 planned service offerings (see **Exhibit 4**). For these services, AMSC would provide end-to-end mobile phone service to the public telephone network, which would complete the connection. Major services included MSAT Mobilephone (intended for customers in rural areas unserved by cellular systems) and MSAT Cellular Roaming (which would provide seamless roaming coverage to cellular subscribers as well as low-speed data and fax capabilities). The AMSC mobile phone (under development in 1992, with 14 manufacturers having signed agreements to submit potential bids) would be a dual-mode phone with a projected cost to AMSC of about $1,500. With the phone, a call would automatically be processed either via that subscriber's cellular system or (if the caller were not in range of a cellular system) via AMSC's satellite. AMSC anticipated that Mobilephone and Cellular Roaming would account for the bulk of capacity utilization on its first satellite and 70% or more of annual revenues through 2001. These projections assumed that, due to higher service and equipment costs, only one in fifty cellular or radio-paging subscribers would upgrade to MSAT Mobilephone or MSAT Cellular Roaming. McCleary noted that "The Cellular Roaming service focuses on an easily-identifiable group: cellular subscribers. But Mobilephone has many potential segments and we need to identify the best ones for marketing efforts and channel development."

MSAT FlightNet consisted of voice and data services including air traffic control, airline operations, and airline administrative communications. This product group addressed AMSC's license obligation to provide priority safety-related satellite services for the aviation industry and the Federal Aviation Administration (FAA), whose existing data network would be integrated with AMSC's system. FlightNet target customers—major airlines and the FAA—were projected to generate about $25 million in annual revenue for AMSC by 2001.

MSAT PrivateNet offerings would allow a customer to lease channels and configure them to its unique mobile voice and/or data communications requirements. Target markets included law enforcement agencies, fleet management operations, and developers of private telephone networks for public and private enterprises. AMSC managers saw two types of potential PrivateNet customers: Integrated End Users (large organizations with special internal communication requirements such as the FBI or Federal Express) and Value-Added Service Providers (firms that would repackage and market AMSC satellite capacity in conjunction with their own communications services). McCleary noted that "PrivateNet marketing requirements are applications-intensive and technically-driven. This differs from Flight-Net or MSAT Telephone services which will be marketed as 'on demand' products where AMSC develops and operates ground segment facilities. We therefore have a separate marketing effort for PrivateNet." AMSC projected about $50 million in annual revenues from PrivateNet customers by 2001.

The products described above would be AMSC's "full service" offerings, available after satellite launch in mid-1994. Prior to launch, AMSC had developed a "first service" program via leased capacity on the COMSAT/INMARSAT satellite. First Service was intended to develop pilot programs, identify applications, gain operations experience, build awareness in relevant segments, and secure initial customers for Full Service operations. An executive commented: "A satellite involves about $150 million each for the launch vehicle, the spacecraft, and ground facilities. Historically, there has been a 12% failure rate at launch. Once in orbit, a satellite is a 'wasting asset' with a lifespan of about 10 years; each minute of unused capacity is revenue gone forever. We need as much business as possible from the minute our own bird is in the sky."

First Service offerings were limited to two-way, low-speed (600 bits-per-second) messaging capabilities as compared to the voice, fax, and 2,400 bps messaging capabilities currently planned for Full Service. For First Service, AMSC had targeted transportation companies (for vehicle transfer and messaging services), law enforcement agencies (for remote data transfer), and energy companies (e.g., oil rig communications), among others. In addition, Marketing personnel were promoting first-service offerings to potential end users (see **Exhibit 5** for excerpts from a brochure for StarDrive, a first-service offering for trucking applications); and Value-Added Service Provider agreements had been signed with firms such as Rockwell International and Westinghouse to sell first-service (and, later, full-service) offerings with their own communications services. AMSC had constructed a network operations center at its Washington, D.C. headquarters and began generating revenues from first-service customers in April 1992. But the company expected operating losses during the first-service phase. An executive noted:

> First Service demonstrates our viability to investors and potential customers; establishes relations with companies whose support will be

important during Full Service; and generates applications knowledge. Also, most end users don't know and don't care whose satellite is providing the service pipe—and that's good and bad news. The danger is that we establish Full Service expectations but provide First Service capabilities, or we inadvertently position AMSC in terms of First Service applications and so undersell and underprice our post-launch opportunities. We must balance the need to establish pre-launch visibility in the marketplace with the need to maximize post-launch capabilities.

Product Development

Development of specific services involved three groups: Systems Engineering (reporting to Mr. Garner, the Chief Scientist), Engineering & Operations, and Sales & Marketing. Systems Engineering was responsible for the technical infrastructure of AMSC's system and initial specifications development. Engineering & Operations was responsible for ground and network operations (including terminals). Sales & Marketing was responsible for identifying end-user and reseller needs, applications development (with Engineering & Operations), and (with Finance) pricing of service offerings. An executive commented:

> Systems Engineering looks at the capabilities of our satellite technology and the rich chunk of bandwidth allocated to us under the FCC license. Engineering & Operations looks at the issues involved in actually providing services, and is concerned with the costs, maintenance requirements, and ongoing operating implications of planned and potential services. Sales & Marketing looks at the diversity of applications and target markets possible, and is concerned with maximizing revenues and signing up customers and resellers.

Brian Deobald, manager of Market Analysis, elaborated on product development issues:

> A satellite has limited capacity and a finite lifespan. What combination of voice, data, and/or fax-messaging transmissions would represent our best use of the circuits? What markets and applications have the strongest demand for mobile satellite services and at what price levels? Technology trade-offs complicate these decisions. For example, there's an inverse relationship between the size of the antennae on mobile phone terminals and the total number of useable channels on the satellite: smaller antennae (which consumers desire) require more satellite power which, in turn, reduces the number of available channels. Similarly, high-speed data applications reduce the number of channels available for the basic MSAT phone offerings.

An engineering manager commented:

The protocols on which our system is based give us wide scope for applications development and customization. But everyone out there has different application requirements, and our per-application development costs are significant: you must learn about the customer's business; develop the application; develop the software; maintain it; and integrate it into ground operations. Marketing keeps generating possibilities. But we simply don't have the money or engineering resources to chase all possible applications. That's one reason we offer satellite capacity for others to operate applications-driven switches.

Leslie Borden, general counsel, noted that in addition to software and engineering costs the costs of obtaining regulatory approval for many application possibilities were high. "Marketing brings back opportunities that are within our coverage area and technological capabilities but exceed the bounds of the current license," she noted. "An issue at this point is whether we should build what we can sell, or sell what we can build quickly and efficiently."

A marketing manager commented: "Getting and keeping customers means provision of market-relevant applications. Also, bringing costs down on the mobile phone requires mass production volume demand, and that requires diversity of applications." Another marketing manager noted: "At this point, we have the system's technical design but not the specifics of terminal and ground operations. So, we bring broad concepts to the marketplace and then bring back specific customer and reseller needs and opportunities; in turn, this should feed into the interdependent product-policy, target market and distribution channel decisions we face."

Finally, one executive noted:

> An issue is whether we should be primarily a wholesaler or integrator of mobile satellite services. With MSAT Telephone and Cellular Roaming services, we provide wholesaling functions with the cellular carriers retailing the service to end-users. But many other applications, especially data, move us more in the direction of acting as systems integrator to commercial, governmental or consumer end-users. The latter activity has higher selling and development costs, but also more value-added and potentially much higher pricing of available channels.

Pricing

Pricing of specialized applications and for PrivateNet capacity would vary by application, contract length, and amount of capacity required. AMSC's business plan projected an average price of $180,000/channel allocated to PrivateNet applications.

Users of AMSC's core on-demand services such as MSAT Telephone and Cellular Roaming would pay a monthly access fee and a per-minute airtime charge. Unlike cellular, AMSC's airtime charges would include any domestic long-distance charges. Under AMSC's business plan, an Authorized Service Provider (in most cases for the on-demand services, a cellular operator) would manage billing by receiving call records from AMSC and integrating the charges into the customer's regular cellular bill. ASPs would receive 35% of the subscriber's access fee and a monthly service charge, and remit charges to AMSC at wholesale rates.

In early 1992, AMSC hired a firm to conduct research in areas without cellular coverage and in cities surrounded by areas without cellular coverage. Over 75% of those participating in the study (i.e., those deemed eligible based on screening criteria such as minimum household income, stated potential interest in cellular service wherever traveling, and/or existing cellular usage thresholds) expressed very high interest in satellite phone service and could justify purchase either with economic criteria, the ability to be accessible at all times, or the need to receive emergency calls. Via a conjoint analysis exercise, the research indicated that the per-minute charge was the most important factor for those contacted (with little consumer interest at charges of $2/minute or more); monthly access fees and cost of phone were equal in importance (accounting for about 25% each of the purchase decision vs. 37% for per-minute charges); and phone type (car phone vs. car-and-portable capabilities) was the least important factor for those surveyed (accounting for 12% of the purchase decision). The price ranges which appeared to optimize AMSC's revenues for on-demand services were: c. $1,500 for the cost of the phone; $30–$45 in monthly access fees; and $1.00–$1.50 in per-minute charges. **Exhibit 6** provides data from this research as well as sample comments from focus-group participants. The table below compares AMSC's Mobilephone and Cellular Roaming services at $35/month access fees and $1.25/minute charges versus average cellular and radio-paging rates in 1992:

	Cellular Carrier	Radio Paging	AMSC: MSAT Telephone	AMSC: MSAT Cellular Roaming
Equipment cost	$200–$1,500	$130 (local) $300 (national)	$1,500–$2,000 (dual-mode	$1,500–$2,000 portable phone)
Monthly fee	$35	$11 (local) $30–$54 (national)	$35	$35
Per-minute charges	$.62–$.99	NA	$1.25	$1.25
Long-distance charges/minute	$.20–$.90	NA	0	0
Roaming fee	c. $3/day	NA	0	0

An AMSC manager noted: "MSAT Telephone, targeted at rural areas without cellular coverage, can command a premium because of the greater need for mobile communications in rural areas and the versatility of our system versus cellular or paging." Another manager commented: "Cellular Roaming is targeted at cellular subscribers who frequently travel across cellular systems and/or to areas without cellular. Estimates indicate that the current average roaming time is 75 minutes/month for cellular subscribers who do roam, and would probably be higher if roaming were easier to do." Mr. McCleary noted that "Potential customers will be more familiar with mobile communications in 1994 than when cellular was launched; and we know many cellular users want better roaming capabilities. This should aid pricing and penetration rates for our services, especially in occupations where cellular usage is highest."

Distribution Channels

AMSC's marketing organization was comprised of 15 people (including support staff). Two managers were responsible for Market Analysis, one for Product Development, two for Marketing Communications (including advertising and public relations), three for development of distribution channels, and four for business development in governmental, rail, maritime and aviation sectors.

Managers responsible for AMSC's distribution channels were informally known as "road warriors" because, as one such manager noted, "We currently spend much of our time on the road contacting, persuading, and negotiating with a variety of firms for our Authorized Service Provider (ASP) and Value Added Service Provider (VASP) programs" (**Exhibit 7**). Projected distribution partners for the ASP program were mainly existing cellular carriers as well as specialized mobile radio operators, paging service operators, and agents that sold cellular phone service to companies, trade associations, and other groups. By 1992 AMSC had signed Memoranda of Understanding with 23 cellular carriers (including a number of the top-20 carriers) interested in offering AMSC's services,and was pursuing ASP agreements with other potential distributors. VASP agreements were targeted at firms that would lease capacity on AMSC's satellite for repackaging and resale through the VASP's facilities. VASPs would be used primarily for the PrivateNet services, but also for specialized MSAT Telephone applications in boating and aviation markets. An important element for many prospective VASP partners was their ability to use AMSC's satellite capabilities in conjunction with the high-speed data, voice and other communications services the VASP sold and customized for various vertical market segments.

An issue facing AMSC in 1992 concerned the nature of its indirect distribution channels. John Jameson, a marketing manager, outlined the situation as follows:

> We're currently focusing on cellular carriers, cellular agents, specialized mobile radio operators (SMRs), and paging carriers as ASPs. These channels represent a large addressable prospect base, and it is easy to identify the important players. But each has advantages and disadvantages.

Cellular carriers, offering AMSC as a complementary service, can provide seamless roaming capabilities. They bring sales and service knowledge of mobile communications, and can assume most of these channel functions with this target market. But this channel requires a high reseller margin from AMSC, doesn't penetrate many rural areas, and exhibits a wide range of retail equipment pricing which might cause consumer confusion in our nationwide coverage area as well as some resistance to spending an incremental $2,000 on a dual-mode phone. Also, some cellular carriers may see disincentives in promoting AMSC along with their primary lines of business since they receive a certain amount of roaming revenues with the current patchwork coverage arrangement.

Cellular agents reach many corporate users, and also bring established sales and service knowledge. But the financial strength of many agents is questionable; the reputation of the channel is not the best; and their market access is limited and may have topped out as cellular becomes better known.

SMRs such as dispatch services provide access to a unique customer base where there is a naturally high need for roaming capabilities. This channel also has good penetration of public safety and trucking segments, and the current equipment pricing in these segments will make a $2,000 AMSC terminal less of an issue. However, the wide diversity of SMR terminal formats will significantly increase our service costs and may preclude us from achieving the scale economies required to produce a terminal for $2,000 or less.

Paging carriers are generally entrepreneurs with a telecom background. They reach a different segment than cellular or SMR, and our service is a complement to paging. But despite a consolidation trend, this remains a fragmented channel, composed of numerous mom-and-pop operations with unsophisticated billing and service systems. Hence, both our selling and support costs will be much higher. In addition, paging equipment is small and highly mobile; this may require that we develop a portable phone for this segment.

Some managers believed that AMSC should augment these channels. Tim O'Neil, a marketing manager, gathered data about the distribution channels utilized by 10 manufacturers of mobile phones and found a range of resellers (**Exhibit 8**). He noted:

The channel evolution is toward retail, and it's important that we acknowledge this trend. In the mid-1980s, cellular carriers sold 60% of their customers via direct channels and 40% via exclusive agents. By 1991, 25% of cellular was sold direct, 40% via agents, and 35% via retail channels. Also, mass merchandisers such as Sears or Wal-Mart, specialty retailers such as Radio Shack, and radio service shops have much higher presence in rural areas than cellular, paging, or SMR operators. However, we have begun to notice conflicts between traditional cellular channels and retailers. The latter generally work on a higher commission per phone and lower monthly usage commission, and many retailers therefore offer phones at prices lower than the other channels.

Another manager cited potential competitive issues:

> A new venture called Celsat recently announced plans to offer mobile satellite services and, unlike us, plans to compete directly with cellular operators by specializing in low-cost seamless roaming and high-speed data applications. Celsat only recently filed its application with the FCC and may not get approval. But we can preempt this kind of competition, from Celsat or other satellite service providers, with an early and strong retail presence.

However, other managers noted that retail distribution would mean that AMSC would assume billing and receivables expenses for end users, physical distribution costs to retail outlets, significant support costs, and more variance in the sale and presentation of its service. In addition, as one manager noted, "The response of cellular carriers to our distributing through retail channels is uncertain. It could hurt our support with cellular carriers and might mean channel conflict that hurts our ASP program and reputation with end users."

High-Speed Data Decision

Management also had to decide whether to offer a low-cost, high-speed data service in addition to the voice and circuit-switched, low-speed, store-and-forward data services it currently planned. The technology in question was known as packet-switched data and differed from the circuit-switched method traditionally used. Dave Ross, a product manager, explained:

> Circuit-switched data transmission, like a voice conversation, requires that a full channel be dedicated to the user for the duration of the transmission. This method is ideal for voice and traditional data transfers. It is billed on a per-minute basis and provides good price performance for heavy voice and occasional data users.
>
> Packet data transmission uses additional hardware and software to "packetize" data and insert the packets into a single channel shared by multiple users on a near real-time basis. This technique is highly efficient for electronic messaging, database queries, and other short "burst" transmissions. Customers are billed on a per-message basis.
>
> Building and operating a hub with packet-switched capabilities was originally part of AMSC's business plan. But in 1990, we decided to focus on voice communications and leave high-speed data capabilities and applications to our VASP partners. Our initial research indicated that of some two million voice terminal users, about 30,000 were also data users, and we decided not to take on the capital investments and marketing costs for that kind of market. Now, we're rethinking that approach as we learn more about the breadth and potential growth of the market for efficient, high-speed mobile data communications.

In 1992, at least two radio-based data networks were being planned: the Ardis network (a joint venture of IBM and Motorola) and RAM Mobile Data (a venture backed by BellSouth Corporation). Neither network would also offer voice services. But in April 1992, eight cellular carriers (including McCaw) announced plans to offer packet-switched data capabilities as part of their services. A cellular industry spokesperson explained:

> Today, cellular carriers can carry data, but the price is relatively expensive because carriers must dedicate a voice channel for every data exchange. But packet-switching piggybacks on voice channels without interfering with voice calls. We plan to give our specifications to computer and communications companies in hopes of promoting a standard and encouraging low-cost mass production of the necessary data-transmission devices.

This spokesperson estimated the cellular carriers' costs of upgrading their networks at 5%–10% of the existing capital investment in cellular (an estimated $8 billion nationwide) and projected that 30% of cellular traffic would be data traffic by the year 2000. Many of the cellular firms hoped to begin offering such data services by late 1993 or early 1994.

In 1992, marketing managers proposed that AMSC offer packet-switched data capabilities as part of its full-service offering to subscribers. Mr. McCleary noted: "As laptop computer use grows and wireless modems are introduced, people's perceptions and use of mobile communications are changing rapidly. Just as cellular voice users now want seamless roaming abilities, so will mobile data users want faster, seamless data-communication abilities. But it will cost the cellular carriers hundreds of millions of dollars to augment their networks with packet-switched data, and they're likely to limit this to the larger urban areas. Augmenting our system with high-speed data abilities will make our roaming coverage even more valuable to cellular and other ASPs while expanding our addressable markets. Also, packet-switching yields orders of magnitude more users-per-channel than the 300 users-per-channel for cellular roaming." Under the proposal, AMSC's monthly access fee would increase from $35 to $50 for bundled voice and high-speed data capabilities.

Marketing managers had identified segments where high-speed mobile data capabilities were potentially valuable (**Exhibit 9**). They noted that "Cellular carriers' marginal revenues have declined over the past two years; they will increasingly seek applications-driven sales in vertical markets to bolster demand, and high-speed data will be important." Beverly Brosky, AMSC's director for Government Systems, noted that mobile data communications were important in many governmental sectors (see **Exhibit 10**), especially among law-enforcement agencies. She emphasized that "Most federal agencies have three-year budgeting cycles. So, expenditures for 1995 (when we'll have Full Service available) must be put in place now, and that means pursuing specific pricing arrangements, terminal specifications, and agency-specific applications—many of which require high-speed data." Lynn Miller, marketing manager for Maritime and Rail markets, noted that "Data and voice have a nearly 50:50 usage split in maritime markets, and high-speed data is important in maritime applications. It also has potential in rail and other transport markets. Amtrak, for example,is interested in high-speed data for on-board credit-card verifications, up-dating of maintenance and scheduling data, and other applications."

AMSC's estimated capital investments to provide packet-switched data would be about $10 million, including $6 million for construction of a packet-switched hub. Some managers questioned this approach. An engineering manager noted: "Providing packet-switched capabilities will add an estimated $200 to $300 to the retail price of the dual-mode phone, and constructing another ground-station hub further complicates network operations and maintenance costs, while running the risk of delaying Full-Service introduction. Despite its throughput efficiencies, moreover, packet-switching still poses a trade-off: satellite capacity dedicated to high-speed data is less capacity available for the basic voice services or other applications." Another manager commented: "Our Canadian partner, TMI, is building packet-switched data abilities into their system, because their user base makes it important to them. We can learn from their experience. Rather than spending time and money on high-speed data at this point, why not wait and see if the actual demand justifies the added expense?" Another executive emphasized:

> I see potential for channel conflict if we add packet data to our offerings. We're recruiting VASPs on the premise that they will continue to provide high-speed data services to their users via their proprietary systems and utilize our system to augment their applications with nationwide coverage. The good news about packet-switching is that we can offer users easy access to the public-switched network and our satellite for high-speed data transmission. But the bad news is that the VASPs may now view us as a threat, not a partner. Will they continue to offer AMSC as part of their total solutions package? Many VASPs have longer relationships with high-volume corporate customers than we do.
>
> Also, we may be underestimating the costs and difficulties of the marketing issues involved. High-speed data applications have traditionally involved direct sales to large organizations where customizing the customer interface is important. We're not set up to conduct this kind of account management program outside the PrivateNet arena, and that's part of the purpose of the VASP program. We have enough on our plate already, and should stay focused on providing voice, low-speed data and seamless roaming services.

In considering these views, Mr. Pemberton commented: "We have limited marketing resources, a clock ticking toward satellite launch in 1994, and capacity to fill and optimize both before and after launch. We must decide soon about packet-switched data. Should we make the required investments? What are the implications for our marketing programs? Are our current distribution plans adequate, and what implications does any decision about high-speed data have for the distribution options we are considering?"

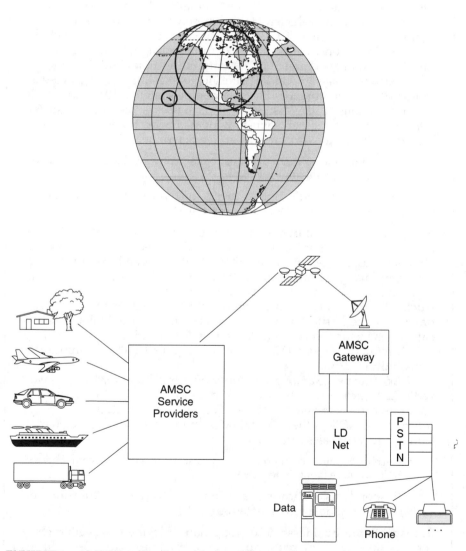

EXHIBIT 1 AMSC Satellite Transmission Coverage Area

EXHIBIT 2   **Markets for Mobile Transmission Services**

In 1990, AMSC hired Yankelovich Clancy Shulman (YCS, a market research firm) to identify markets for mobile communications services. YCS integrated information from industry sources with interviews and survey research.

Rural commercial business   1.2 million commercial businesses in 1990 located outside Metropolitan Statistical Areas (MSAs) owning or leasing vehicles. 50% of interviewed businesses have: 20+ employees, 2+ business locations, and annual sales over $1 million. On average, each business has: 9 cars, 9 vans/small vehicles, and 11 large trucks/construction vehicles. Half of these vehicles have a service territory range of 50+ miles from base. Major business categories include: services (25%), construction (16%), manufacturing (9%), retail/wholesale (17%), local government (12%), communications/utilities (9%).

Existing usage among 199 interviewees: cellular (17%), two-way radio (38%), citizen-band radio (9%), paging systems (10%), no mobile communications in vehicles (36%). Typical uses: scheduling/dispatch information (51%), other contact with manager/home office (45%), giving directions to work crews/service personnel (45%).

- Current mobile communications costs: Transceivers (average price) $1,017; average monthly fee $62.50.

Respondents indicating a need for voice-only transmission (68%), voice and data (18%), data only (14%).

Nonrural commercial business   500,000 businesses in 1990 with 20+ employees, owning or leasing vehicles and located in an MSA (14% of all businesses located in MSAs). 50% of interviewed businesses have: 100+ employees, 2+ business locations, and annual sales over $5 million. On average, each interviewed business has: 18 cars, 12 vans/small trucks, 5 large trucks/construction vehicles. Half of these vehicles have a service territory range of 50+ miles from base. Major business categories include: services (26%), construction (15%), manufacturing (20%), retail/wholesale (12%), local government (10%), communications/utilities (7%).

Existing usage among 199 interviewees: cellular (57%) , two-way radio (22%), car radiophones (6%), data messaging (2%), no mobile communications in vehicles (23%). Typical uses: scheduling/dispatch information (45%), other contact with managers/home office (66%), calling clients or sales calls (41%).

- Current mobile communications costs: Transceivers (average price) $976; average monthly fee $79.90.

Respondents indicating a need for voice-only transmission (58%), voice and data (36%), data only (6%).

Transportation business   3,500 long-haul trucking companies, charter bus lines, and intercity/rural bus companies with 25+ vehicles

(c. 5% of all U.S. transportation companies). 15% of interviewed businesses have 100+ employees, 33% have annual sales of more than $5 million, and 40% have 2+ business locations. Over 60% of these vehicles have a service territory range of 200+ miles from base and spend less than 20% of their time in downtown areas.

Existing usage among 99 interviewees: two-way radio (22%), citizen-band radio (33%), cellular (5%), paging systems (7%), data terminal messaging (2%). Typical uses: scheduling/dispatch (84%), route changes/directions (37%), emergency info on safety/weather/breakdown (43%), vehicle status report (47%).

- Current mobile communications costs: Transceivers (average price) $680; average monthly fee $60.

Respondents indicating a need for voice-only transmission (25%), voice and data (49%), data only (26%).

Private automobile Individuals using mobile communications in their automobiles (excludes vehicles owned by commercial businesses). In 1990, retail consumers owned c. 1.75 million cellular phones and 2 million citizen-band radios. About 50% of all cellular phones are purchased by retail consumers, although employers may pay for purchase cost and/or usage charges.

Existing usage: business (60%), personal communications (40%). Typical uses: office communications, scheduling, reporting to management, notification of travel delays.

Railroad About 47,000 locomotives, refrigerated cars, and passenger cars have electric power suitable for mobile transceivers, and an estimated 170,000 will have by the year 2001.

Existing usage: Locomotives are equipped with radio voice systems along heavily travelled routes. Refrigerated cars often equipped with data-only terminals. An experimental cellular system was begun in 1990 in the San Diego-Los Angeles and Boston-Washington routes. Typical uses: Locomotive engineer uses voice communications for safety/traffic management. Fleet managers use location communications to monitor conditions (e.g., temperature of refrigerator cars), idle stock, and route progress. Passengers use voice communications to access the public telephone network, largely for business uses.

- Current mobile communications costs:
  —Railfone: $1.50 connect + $1.50/minute
  —Position Location: $.05 - $.10 per message
  —Radio Service: railroad-owned and -operated systems

Aeronautical 3,900 U.S. airline jet aircraft, 60,000 corporate aircraft, and 20,000 large general-aviation aircraft operated in the United States. These high-value assets are operated nearly continuously in the airline and corporate areas, creating large communications potential.

Existing usage: All airline and corporate aircraft, and most general aviation aircraft, have VHF radios for air traffic control. All airliners have VHF voice and data communications for flight routing or weather data. About 30% of U.S. airline fleet has airfone passenger equipment.

- Current mobile communications costs:
  —Airlines: $.20/100-character message + $500/aircraft monthly fee
  —Passengers: $2.00 connect charge + $2.00/minute

Maritime   In 1990 there were 39,000 commercial transportation vessels and 128,000 commercial fishing craft registered with the U.S. Maritime Office.

Existing Usage: 525,000 VHF radios installed; 10,000 INMARSAT transceivers on large marine vessels throughout the world (c. 25% serve U.S. market).

- Current mobile communications costs:
  —Marine VHF radios: $350–$700 for equipment + $1/minute usage charges
  —Cellular phones: $600 for equipment + $100/month average usage charges
  —INMARSAT: $25,000+ for equipment + $2,400/month average usage charges

EXHIBIT 3 Top 17 Cellular Operators (1991)

Company (R) = RBOC	Total Subscribers	% of Total Subscribers	Total Served Population	% of Total Population	% Penetration
McCaw Cellular/LIN	875,500	16.57%	77,964,000	21.74%	1.35%
Southwestern Bell Mobile (R)	667,000	12.63%	32,050,000	8.94%	2.08%
GTE Mobilnet//Contel	666,000	12.60%	41,030,000	11.43%	1.62%
BellSouth Mobility (R)	663,199	12.55%	39,572,000	11.03%	1.68%
PacTel Cellular (R)	509,000	9.63%	35,597,000	9.92%	1.43%
Bell Atlantic/ Metro Mobile (R)	413,000	7.83%	26,856,000	7.49%	1.53%
Ameritech Mobile Comm. (R)	326,000	6.17%	17,103,000	4.77%	1.63%
Nynex Mobile. Comms. (R)	259,000	4.90%	25,819,000	7.20%	1.00%
US West NewVector (R)	209,700	3.97%	18,319,000	5.11%	1.14%
Centel Cellular	186,629	3.53%	13,825,000	3.85%	1.35%
Cellular Communications Inc.	105,500	2.00%	7,149,000	1.99%	1.48%
United States Cellular	57,300	1.08%	5,407,000	1.51%	1.06%
Vanguard Cellular Systems	54,800	1.04%	5,612,000	1.56%	0.98%
SNET Cellular	44,900	0.85%	3,575,000	1.00%	1.26%
Alltel Mobile Communications	44,000	0.83%	3,265,000	0.91%	1.35%
Comcast	43,000	0.81%	2,232,000	0.62%	1.93%
Century Telephone Enterprises	36,415	0.69%	3,323,000	0.93%	1.10%
Other Cellular Subscribers	122,112	2.31%			
Total	5,283,055		358,698,000		

Note: Total population exceeds U.S. population because each person may be served by two carriers.

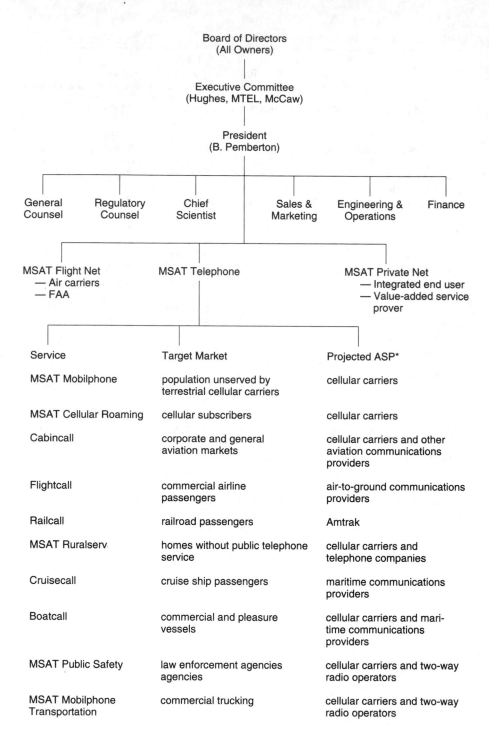

Board of Directors
(All Owners)

Executive Committee
(Hughes, MTEL, McCaw)

President
(B. Pemberton)

| General Counsel | Regulatory Counsel | Chief Scientist | Sales & Marketing | Engineering & Operations | Finance |

MSAT Flight Net
— Air carriers
— FAA

MSAT Telephone

MSAT Private Net
— Integrated end user
— Value-added service prover

Service	Target Market	Projected ASP*
MSAT Mobilphone	population unserved by terrestrial cellular carriers	cellular carriers
MSAT Cellular Roaming	cellular subscribers	cellular carriers
Cabincall	corporate and general aviation markets	cellular carriers and other aviation communications providers
Flightcall	commercial airline passengers	air-to-ground communications providers
Railcall	railroad passengers	Amtrak
MSAT Ruralserv	homes without public telephone service	cellular carriers and telephone companies
Cruisecall	cruise ship passengers	maritime communications providers
Boatcall	commercial and pleasure vessels	cellular carriers and maritime communications providers
MSAT Public Safety	law enforcement agencies agencies	cellular carriers and two-way radio operators
MSAT Mobilphone Transportation	commercial trucking	cellular carriers and two-way radio operators

*ASP = Authorized Service Provider

EXHIBIT 4   AMSC Organization and Product Groups (1992)

The only mobile communications system for the long haul.

*T*rucking companies throughout the United States have begun to recognize the need for better communications.

Faster delivery. Better fuel and fleet management. Quicker response to pick-up calls. Higher loaded-to-empty ratios. And fewer out-of-route miles. All are possible through the power of two-way mobile communications.

But with technology constantly changing, it's not easy choosing the right system for your needs.

Before you make a major capital investment, consider that what a system can do for you tomorrow is every bit as important as its bottom line impact today.

Only one mobile communications system provides the services you need now and the ability to deliver the advanced capabilities of the near future.

As an Authorized AMSC Service Provider, Rockwell Internationa will help its customers combine AMSC satellite communicanc services with the onboard monitoring capabilities of its futur generation TripMaster™ trip recorder systems.

Hughes Network Systems is providing the first vehicle terminals for use with the StarDrive mobile communications system. The lightweight antenna installs easily and has no moving parts

Introducing the StarDrive℠ mobile communications system from American Mobile Satellite Corporation.

The StarDrive mobile data communications system helps you improve operating efficiency, productivity, customer service, and profits by keeping you in contact with your drivers. Anywhere in the country.

As an open system, compatible with communications hardware and software from a variety of suppliers, StarDrive can integrate easily into your existing MIS network. Authorized AMSC Service Providers can help you take full advantage of our satellite technology. They can make StarDrive support many other systems you may already be using, such as computerized fuel management and cash-advance services.

More important, StarDrive is readily adaptable to the valuable services that will be offered in the near future: Two-way voice communications. Mobile fax. Access to public phone systems. Private networks. Complete remote vehicle monitoring. And more. All with full North American coverage.

EXHIBIT 5   Sample First-Service Offering: StarDrive

Respondents rated each factor on a 0 to 10 scale, where 0 is "Would Never Buy" and 10 is "Most Preferred." The table below shows the average for consumers in areas currently served/unserved by cellular phone service.

Cost of Phone	$1,000	$1,500	$2,000	$2,500	$3,000	
Served areas:						
% never buy	2.6	2.6	21	44.7	73.7	
Unserved areas:						
% never buy	8.8	20.6	38.2	58.8	76.5	
Monthly Access Fee	**$15.00**	**$30.00**	**$45.00**	**$60.00**	**$100**	
Served areas:						
% never buy	2.6	2.6	26.3	47.4	65.8	
Unserved areas:						
% never buy	2.9	2.9	17.6	35.3	67.6	
Flat Per-minute Fee	**$.50**	**$1.00**	**$1.50**	**$2.00**	**$2.50**	**$3.00**
Served areas:						
% never buy	2.6	21.1	23.7	34.2	44.7	60.5
Unserved areas:						
% never buy	0.0	8.8	23.5	44.1	58.8	76.5

Scale:	0	1	2	3	4	5	6	7	8	9	10
	Never Would Buy		Least Preferred			No Preference					Most Preferred

Sample Focus Group Comments (after responses to pricing levels):

"If the phone saves a couple of work-hours, it will pay for itself."

"In the Southwest, everything is spread out. A 300–400 mile round trip is normal, so using this service can save money."

"My son has diabetes. I would be willing to pay for this service just to have access to emergency medical service."

"For me, it's not a matter of making money, it's a matter of saving money. I build homes and a small error can easily cost $2,000–$3,000."

"I would need a portable phone because I am often out of range from my vehicle."

"I would not want to pay more than $_____ for the phone. Considering technological change, any phone will be out-of-date pretty quickly."

Source: Company-sponsored research.

EXHIBIT 7   ASP and VASP Programs

The *Authorized Service Provider Program* (ASP) grants a wholesale rate to third parties marketing AMS branded products. Third parties may market these products with end-user interconnectivity to the AMSC hub facility in Washington, D.C. Third parties continue to receive the wholesale rate as long as end users are on the system.

ASP provides mobile terminal equipment to customers from approved AMSC manufacturers; facilitates the installation and service of the mobile terminals; provides the end user with operations software, PC packages, or custom applications; responsible for billing, collection, customer service.

AMSC provides: vertical trade advertising support; product literature; technical consulting for ASP end users; trade show support; account referrals; recognition as Authorized Service Provider.

The *Value Added Service Provider Program* (VASP) allows third parties to lease capacity on AMSC space segment assets for repackaging and resale under the "third party's product identification," through the third party's interconnect facility. The VASP will construct and operate a VASP hub. At the time of MSAT deployment in 1994, the Value Added Service Provider will also operate a Feeder Link Earth Station.

VASP provides mobile terminal equipment to customers from approved AMSC manufacturers; facilitates the installation and service of the mobile terminals; provides the end user with operations software, PC packages, of custom applications programs; creates VASP branding for products; provides vertical trade advertising support; provides product literature and trade show support; responsible for billing, collection, and customer support.

AMSC provides technical consulting for VASP and end users; account referrals; recognition as AMSC Value Added Service Provider.

Network Elements	Responsibility		Responsibility	
	ASP	*AMSC*	*VASP*	*AMSC*
Space segment		X		X
Uplink to satellite		X	X	
Network operations		X	X	
Hub facility		X	X	
Terminals to end users	X		X	
Marketing and sales	X	X	X	
Customer service	X		X	
Billing end users	X		X	
End-user interface	X		X	
Product features		X	X	

EXHIBIT 8   Indirect Distribution Channels Utilized by Twelve Mobile Phone Manufacturers (% of manufacturer's U.S. sales, 1990)

	A	B	C	D	E	F	G	H	I	J	K	L
Appliance/home hardware	1.8	—	.1	6.9	—	1.2	.2	1.8	59.4	3.2	.4	13.3
Catalog showrooms	—	—	—	—	100	—	—	—	—	—	—	—
Food/drug stores	—	—	—	—	—	—	—	—	—	—	—	99.3
Electronic/video stores	3.8	6.4	.9	.8	.1	6.9	14.7	12.0	8.5	2.0	—	11.8
Mobile specialist	6.3	11.4	1.3	2.2	1.9	16.1	10.1	6.6	4.5	.9	2.0	4.5
Carrier	—	—	—	—	5.5	8.6	.1	.1	—	—	—	—
Mass merchandisers	4.1	—	.1	.1	6.7	78.6	1.2	1.4	5.5	.1	—	1.9
Computer/business stores	1.0	4.8	—	.1	7.1	1.8	.6	1.0	1.4	1.8	—	1.5
Department stores	—	—	—	2.5	—	38.4	—	40.2	—	1.0	—	—
Specialty camera stores	9.0	4.8	.2	8.0	12.9	6.1	6.1	31.6	13.8	.5	—	.3
Automotive parts/service	.2	4.3	.4	3.0	—	.5	5.3	1.0	74.7	.5	7.6	—

EXHIBIT 9   U.S. Mobile Data Market: Potential Market Segments

	Market Segments		Wide Area Mobile Jobs (in Thousands)
Field service	White collar	Computers, office equipment	236
Field service	Blue collar	Appliances, cable TV, utilities, elevators, heating and air conditioning	836
Transport	People	Taxi, limo, transit	197
Transport	Goods	LTL, courier, messenger	2,423
Public services		Police, fire, EMS, security	835
Field sales		Driver, real estate, scientific	1,621
Field sales	Services	Insurance, financial	243
Professional		Executives, reporters, medical, lawyers	2,440
Local service		Plumbers, electricians	1,440

EXHIBIT 9 (continued)

Mobile Data Benefits/Uses by Market Segment

	Computer-Aided Dispatch	Internal Database Access	Public Network Access	Fleet Monitoring	Remote Data Collection (telemetry)	Messaging and Electronic Mail
Field service	Real-time routing and scheduling	Access customer service records			Cost-effective meter reading	Provide field status to home office. Inform customer of status
Local trucking	Informed efficient dispatch	Customer records update				Efficient time-saving communications
Long-haul trucking		Customer records update		Fleet monitoring routing		Efficient time-saving communications Next assignment scheduling
Package delivery	Informed efficient dispatch	Package delivery trucking		Fleet monitoring routing		
Field sales		Information for price quotes, listings available	Stock prices public data access			Two-way messaging and paging Electronic Mail
Field professionals		Faster field reports, resource paperwork	Stock prices public data access			Two-way messaging and paging Electronic Mail
Public safety/ emergency services	Informed efficient dispatch	Driver or medical records		Vehicle location		

EXHIBIT 10   Federal Government Vehicle Fleets

Federal Government	Trucks & Tractors	Cars & Station Wagons	Ambulances	Buses	Total Vehicles
US Postal Service	134,338	9,531	0	14	143,883
General Services Administration*	44,407	53,432	234	2,840	100,858
Air Force	46,300	5,908	1,645	2,440	56,293
Army	34,147	9,407	1,108	2,770	47,432
Agriculture Department	27,169	3,937	1	43	31,150
Navy	25,029	3,213	684	972	29,898
Justice Department	4,308	12,706	10	137	17,161
Interior Department	12,574	1,666	11	109	14,360
Department of Energy	9,240	1,913	54	263	11,470
Treasury Department	1,419	7,943	0	13	9,375
Marine Corps	5,999	700	0	326	7,025
Civil Works, Corps of Engineers	5,894	838	1	19	6,752
Tennessee Valley Authority	2,281	1,495	11	0	3,787
State Department	1,825	1,122	11	0	2,958
Labor Department	1,205	328	12	34	1,579
National Aeronautics and Space Administration	987	157	13	11	1,168
Total	357,122	114,296	3,795	9,954	485,149

*Most vehicles are in Interagency Motor Pool and rented or leased to other government fleets. There is no duplication with other fleets listed.

Source: General Services Administration Report. Printed 1989.

Exhibit 10 (*continued*) Representative Sample of Government Agency MSAT Requirements

Agency	Current Equipment	Current Service Problems	MSAT Requirements
U.S. Coast Guard	INMARSAT/Comsat. Single Side Band.	Equipment & service too expensive	Marine vessels & aircraft, voice & data, mobile-to-mobile and mobile-to-fixed station.
Alaska	High-band VHF dispatch w/ repeaters; bases in each metro area.	Complete lack of coverage outside urban areas; no coverage for remote emergencies.	Mobile-to-mobile comm. and portable ground stations for remote applications. Want 3 base stations for: state troopers, major medical center, rural regional medical center.
Drug Enforcement Agency	415.5–419 MHz.	Poor quality voice; range & coverage; equipment parts, repair, & replacement.	MSS as a supplement to existing system. Voice communications.
U.S. Army Corps of Engineers	Microwave towers.	Coverage for remote areas and emergency situation, especially Alaska.	Comm. between Corps locations in CONUS. Real-time hydrologic information, early warning system for dam failures and floods.
Department of Energy	152–174 MHz. Simplex, repeaters.	None except for coverage during emergencies.	Emergency voice communications directly to Regional Office (HQ).
U.S. Forest Service	160–174 MHz-half duplex, repeaters.	Unreliable comm. for remote sites; long setup time; channels not always available or of poor quality.	2-way voice & data communications from remote sites using aircraft, land mobiles, and portables. Latitude and longitude transmission from aircraft.
National Communication System	Defense Switched Network; Nationwide Emergency Telecomm System (NETS)–conceptual.	Depends on commercial comm. system; survivability of system; compatibility of systems.	Emergency/crisis communications. Overall requirements definition and sat. survivability studies. Coding and encryption for MSS.
Federal Bureau of Investigation	Two-way dispatch radios, 162–174 MHz and 406–420 MHz. MW repeaters.	Mobiles go out of normal range of field division radio comm. systems.	Remote vehicle comm. to field division offices and FBI HQ; field division office to FBI HQ; location and tracking of beacons.
Immigration and Naturalization Service	160–169 MHz. MW will replace 408–419 MHz linking sites. Motorola and GE.	No radio support for investigators outside of urban areas.	Basic voice and digital communications.
San Bernardino County Sheriff	150 MHz. VHF used for administration. Dedicated and shared repeaters.	Lack of coverage in desert areas.	Emergency; search and rescue. Not day-to-day law enforcement.

Case 9

Dendrite International

In July 1993, John Bailye, president of Dendrite International, was considering changes affecting Dendrite's customer base. Bailye commented:

> Dendrite is currently a leading sales automation supplier to pharmaceutical firms. We have been unique in this marketplace, offering a global product that is customized to local market needs and backed up with in-depth customer service. But in the United States, 80% of pharmaceutical sales reps are now supported by automation systems of one kind or another. Other developments may reduce the size of pharmaceutical sales forces in the United States, Europe, and Japan.

Among the issues raised by these developments were the best means of ensuring Dendrite's future growth and possible changes in account management procedures.

This case was prepared by Professor Frank V. Cespedes and Research Associate Marie Bell as the basis for class discussion rather than to illustrate either effective or ineffective handling of an administrative situation. Certain company data, while useful for discussion purposes, have been disguised.

COMPANY AND INDUSTRY BACKGROUND

John Bailye had been a partner of Foresearch, an Australian company that provided market research services to pharmaceutical firms operating in Australia and southeast Asia. During the early 1980s, government regulations in many of these countries affected drug pricing and physicians' incomes. Bailye recalled: "Doctors had less time to see sales reps but reps continued to be measured on the number of calls they made, which is still standard practice in the industry. Meanwhile, the introduction of laptop computers offered a vehicle for improving sales productivity." Bailye established a division called Dendrite,[1] which in 1985 developed software to assist with call planning and reporting tasks. After a one-year pilot with an Australian firm, financial support for Dendrite was provided by a chemical company.

In 1987, Bailye and 12 employees moved their families and Dendrite headquarters from Sydney, Australia, to Warren, New Jersey. Bailye recalled:

> In trying to sell our product to major pharmaceutical firms, we soon found that they wanted a visible commitment in the United States, the single biggest market in the industry. We chose New Jersey because many pharmaceutical firms are headquartered there and because the Unix system we use on our main computer was developed by AT&T's Bell Labs, which is also in New Jersey. We therefore felt this area would provide well-trained technicians.
>
> But we knew little else about what we were getting into. It probably is hard for most Americans to realize how complex and different this country is. Our early days were tough: we had no credit background, little cash, and our families were adjusting to new ways of doing things. We also learned that, in the United States, it is not the product alone that matters. You must present a credible total organization to be given a real business opportunity.

In the United States, Dendrite was the ninth vendor supplying sales automation software to pharmaceutical firms. "All of these firms were of similar size and financial standing," Bailye noted, "so competition was fierce but relatively even." In 1988, however, Dun & Bradstreet (a $4 billion firm operating in a variety of information services markets) acquired a competitor, Sales Technologies, Inc. (STI), which soon dropped product prices and promoted itself as the only viable long-term option for corporate customers. "Customers started to compare this new 'giant' with other 'start-up' vendors and new business moved to STI," Bailye explained. "Dendrite was too new in the market to have credibility, despite the fact that our technology was better and, unlike STI, focused on the sales tasks of pharmaceutical reps. We also lacked the financial resources to wage a price war.

[1]A dendrite conducts impulses from a nerve cell to central nerve fiber.

Change was necessary and eventually involved all elements of organizational structure, market positioning, and technology applications."

Management first reassessed its primary target market. It decided that pharmaceutical firms were still the best market for Dendrite. "These firms are large, profitable, driven by sales productivity requirements, and among the earliest to adopt sales automation," noted Bailye. "The industry also comprised the core of our applications knowledge and working relationships." To distinguish itself, Dendrite decided to become a global supplier of both software and service to pharmaceutical firms. Martha Cleary, vice president of Planning, commented:

> This was an audacious decision for a small firm. In this industry, sales automation software had been supplied on a "turnkey" basis, leaving the customer to operate the system after its installation. We decided to introduce and enhance the concept of outsourcing, whereby Dendrite provided continuous support to maintain and operate the technology and service the needs of client sales reps through help line, training, and facilities management services. This strategy required that we provide full-service facilities in countries which, together, represent 75% of pharmaceutical salespeople.
>
> We had to make many changes simultaneously: redesign the software for multinational application; refinance the company to allow for expansion; restructure marketing programs to emphasize recurring service income, which was necessary to attract capital; and adopt new costing methods, since a key issue in running a service business is managing many unpredictable costs.

Management raised funds from venture capital firms and, by 1991, had established subsidiaries in Belgium, England, France, Germany, Italy, Japan, and Spain in addition to its offices in Australia, New Zealand, and the United States. This expansion was aided by Dendrite's product development strategy. About 80% of the programming code was "core code" which Dendrite then customized to local market needs and company specifications. One executive emphasized:

> Developing this core code took four years and over $5 million in funds from a cash-constrained company. But it's the generic engine which allows us to move into new markets more quickly and cost effectively than competitors. For example, we were able to enter Europe with 300,000 lines of core code which meant that we had to write an additional 100,000 lines for each local market. Competitors must start from scratch and each line is a potential "bug."

Dendrite's sales, less than $250,000 in 1987, were more than $23 million in 1992 (**Exhibit 1**), about 60% from software licensing and product customization fees and 40% from service, maintenance, and facilities management agreements. Projected sales for 1993 were $33 million. In 1993, more than 15,000 sales reps at 40 companies in 11 countries used

Dendrite systems. Commenting on the company's growth, Bailye remarked:

> A number of big pharmaceutical firms found that the risks associated with installing sales productivity tools are reduced with a single vendor as opposed to different vendors in each country. And the risks for customers are considerable: when 3,000 reps can't or won't use a system installed at a total cost of $15 million or more, that bends careers in Sales and IS at these firms. We were fortunate that, during this period, our major competition sold standardized systems installed without comprehensive service, and so many of these systems weren't utilized.

Product and Pricing

Vendors providing electronic territory management (ETM) and other sales automation systems multiplied in the 1980s. Productivity gains from such systems varied widely. The biggest impact generally resulted from a reallocation of time from administrative to selling tasks (an average 25% decrease in administrative tasks, according to Dendrite client studies) and from better targeting and territory management (2%–9% sales gains, according to Dendrite client studies). Bailye described "an evolution in field automation during the past decade":

> Product development among vendors has begun to take two distinct paths. Some firms focus on more intensive tools for sales efficiencies, while others seek diversity of functionality—i.e., to provide the means for improving information linkages between Sales and other functions in client companies.

Dendrite's product was a mix of software and services which, in a typical application (see **Exhibit 2**), could be briefly described as follows. Sales reps carried a laptop or notebook computer (purchased by the client company), which contained a database of a given rep's territory data (physician profiles, call histories, etc.). Each night, reps phoned the host computer and communicated their activities for reporting purposes. In turn, the system allowed reps to:

- Access a database concerning current and potential customers including physicians, hospitals, pharmacies, HMOs, etc. Information included basic data such as names and phone numbers as well as data about drug prescribing patterns which was collected by third parties, processed by Dendrite on its host computer, and "downloaded" through phone lines to the rep's laptop.
- Develop targeted lists of high-potential customers, and integrate these lists into a call plan that could be discussed with field managers.
- Record most sales-related activities such as number and type of sales calls, time spent in training or district meetings, and vacation or sick days.
- Send and receive messages via electronic mail with anyone else on the system, and also produce personalized letters and administrative documents.

- Use programs that provide quantitative tools useful in analyzing customer data and tracking progress against quarterly or annual objectives.

Sales managers received reports (weekly or monthly, depending on client preference) from Dendrite about the data continuously collected by the host computer. Field managers could also query the host database directly and produce their own reports. "They can compare the calling activities of different reps," a Dendrite manager noted, "or telemarket to all physicians to whom presentations on a particular drug were made the day or week before. We find that the capability spurs new marketing ideas at clients." Headquarters managers also received reports and could query the database. "Corporate sales managers," explained a Dendrite executive, "often use the data for redeployment purposes or to cross-reference their data with third-party information."

Dendrite's software was sold in two parts: the Base system (which provided the fundamentals required to manage call reporting) and various Added Value Modules (for advanced applications where territory-planning and optimization models were provided). Service involved a dedicated client team composed of customer service personnel at Help Centers (located in Dendrite offices) as well as technical service personnel who assisted clients in customizing, implementing, and maintaining the system.

Depending upon the configuration purchased, pricing involved a license fee, maintenance and support agreement, and service contract (see **Exhibit 3** for examples). The initial license fee was a one-time charge, ranging from $250,000 to over $1 million for the use of Dendrite's software. Maintenance and support agreements involved annual fees to maintain and customize the software, and provide a predetermined number of enhancements. Service contracts covered ongoing facilities management and other services provided by Dendrite's client teams. In the United States and Japan, Dendrite's service pricing was based on the number of system users, and ranged from $300 to $2,000 per user annually; in Europe, where pharmaceutical sales forces were smaller, service contracts were often quoted as a fixed annual fee.

Customers incurred other costs for ETM projects, including the purchase or upgrade of computers for salespeople and communications linkages between the host computer and corporate systems. Typical total costs for implementing an ETM project in a large pharmaceutical firm in 1993 might be $8 million, of which 35% was for Dendrite products and services and 65% for other products and services required to operate the system.

Competition

Including the hardware, forecasts indicated a worldwide $900 million market for ETM by 1995. In 1993, the majority of ETM sales were from hundreds of vendors offering generic, stand-alone software packages which retailed for $100–$400 per unit. These systems allowed a diligent user to collect and maintain information on customers, but were not designed for any specific industry or for integration with other parts of a firm's management system.

The latter capability was available from vendors who offered integrated systems that sold for $1 million or more. Some of these vendors (like Dendrite) specialized in an industry or vertical segment, and others sold across industry segments. In 1993, most were serving 5,000 to 10,000 representatives on their systems. In the pharmaceutical industry, Dendrite's major competitors in this category were STI, Walsh International, PharmaSystems, and Cornet. Dendrite's management believed that key success factors in integrated systems were service support and product flexibility (i.e., the ability to modify database structures to accommodate specific client requirements and subsequent ability to integrate with other client information systems). Management believed that Dendrite offered much higher levels of service than its competitors and, with the exception of Cornet, greater product flexibility. In addition, Dendrite was currently the only supplier with an ETM product developed for the Japanese Kanji language.

STI had estimated 1992 sales of $48 million from ETM systems used in industries including consumer packaged goods and petrochemicals. In pharmaceuticals it held a 40% share of installed reps in the United States. D&B also owned IMS, a supplier of market data to the pharmaceutical industry. In 1992 in Europe, STI began offering IMS data on its ETM system. However, STI had encountered lengthy delays in product development and implementation of its systems, some service problems, and had lost two major clients during the past 18 months. In late 1992 a number of top executives at STI were removed by D&B.

Walsh International, based in the United Kingdom, had sales of about $100 million, mainly derived from paper-based call reporting and data services for pharmaceutical firms. In 1990, Walsh launched an ETM system called PRECISE and by 1993 had automated about 5% of pharmaceutical reps worldwide. A Dendrite executive commented that "Walsh grew in the 1980s by acquiring call reporting companies in Europe and Canada, but they also have an office in Japan and claim to be producing a Japanese ETM product. Their main business is the sale and analysis of industry data, and they are a major competitor with IMS. They're in the process of converting their paper-based clients to PRECISE and often position the product as a 'give away' for clients buying their data. However, their ETM system is fairly rigid and does not currently lend itself well to integration with established client communication procedures and systems."

PharmaSystems (PS), based in the United Kingdom, was a newer company with a focus on ETM and management reporting systems. PS had entered the U.S. market in 1991 with venture backing from the British Coal Board. To date, PS had less than $1 million in sales and only one major client. But other firms had expressed interest in the PS system because it was compatible with a database called Express, which was also used in a market information system utilized by many pharmaceutical firms.

Cornet, based in the United States, had an installed base of about 13% of pharmaceutical reps worldwide, mainly derived from two large firms who licensed Cornet's software code for in-house development and customization. A Dendrite executive noted that, "strategically, outright sale of code can get your foot in the door; we did that with a large firm in 1988. But there is no recurring income and the cost of keeping the code current is high. Cornet will need to develop a product-service package in order to remain a player."

Phoenix, based in the United States, had an installed base of about 8% of pharmaceutical reps. The firm also offered direct mail, sample fulfillment, telemarketing, and market research services to pharmaceutical firms. In ETM, Phoenix offered a low-end product which sold for about $1,500 per year per user (including the handheld hardware unit), but had little potential for integration with other client information systems.

Dendrite also faced indirect competition from information services firms such as Andersen Consulting and Electronic Data Systems. These firms managed the design and installation of hardware and software systems, and had recently managed projects that affected sales and marketing information systems at some pharmaceutical companies. Further, some pharmaceutical firms developed their own ETM systems via in-house MIS departments.

Customers

Worldwide in 1993, there were about 200,000 pharmaceutical salespeople (and an additional 20,000 sales managers), 80% of whom sold in the United States, Western Europe, and Japan (**Exhibit 4**). In nearly all countries, pharmaceutical salespeople did not take orders; their primary task was to persuade doctors to choose their firm's product over that of a competitor.

The selling cycle for Dendrite usually required 18 months or more, during which time Dendrite's salesperson typically maintained daily telephone contact in addition to weekly on-site visits. "Ideally," a Dendrite salesperson noted, "we begin with the V.P. of Sales, who recognizes a productivity problem and delegates the issue to a direct report, usually the head of Sales Administration (responsible for sales reporting systems at the firm). The decision-making unit quickly expands from there, and often includes various users and commentators from Sales, Marketing, and IS." Another salesperson noted: "User groups help to define the business needs to be addressed by the system, while IS translates those needs into technical specs and possible connections with other aspects of the company's information infrastructure."

Following preliminary discussions with a prospect, Dendrite's salesperson arranged for a software demonstration and sought to have key decision makers attend full-day orientations about the system at Dendrite head-quarters. The goal was to familiarize the prospect about Dendrite's support capabilities and, as one salesperson commented, "to build necessary trust and credibility":

> Eighty-five percent of my time is spent face-to-face with client person-nel, ranging from sales reps to VPs of Sales and IS. They're investing millions in hardware and software that is very visible in their organi-zations. They want to know whom they're dealing with. I have been a pharmaceutical sales rep and field manager, and know what informa-tion the client's sales force wants. I also bring client personnel to meet our technical people, business managers, and customer service reps, and have them talk to the people that staff our Help lines.

Clients usually ranked vendors on the basis of ease of use, functional-ity, connectivity with other company systems, financial strength, and com-mitment to product development since an installed system involved continual maintenance and new technology applications. The "short list" of potential vendors generally included at least three firms. Also, while most pharmaceutical firms were interested in ETM systems, their goals often var-ied by geographical market.

In the *United States* (about 30% of worldwide pharmaceutical sales and 60% of Dendrite sales in 1992), pharmaceutical sales forces were among the largest in the world, ranging from 500 to more than 3,000 reps per firm. Sales reps called on medical personnel every four to six weeks to leave product samples and literature, perform service tasks, and (especially in private office segments) build relationships with prescribing physicians. A Dendrite manager explained, "U.S. managers are concerned with customer profile data such as prescribing patterns, medical specializations, and pa-tient volume. In evaluating field productivity, they tend to focus on call fre-quency as well as sales in the rep's territory for higher-margin products."

In *Western Europe* (32% of pharmaceutical sales), sales forces were gen-erally 100 to 200 reps in size, with the largest being 700. Government fund-ing of health care and large, managed-care organizations were common. Most of these organizations had established "formularies" (lists of ap-proved drugs from which their employee physicians could choose) and also restricted the activities of pharmaceutical reps with prescribing physicians. "In Europe," a Dendrite manager noted, "pharmaceutical reps generally see a given doctor once per year, always by appointment, and can only leave one sample. This places more marketing emphasis on advertising, direct mail, medical meetings and conferences, and on the information flows rele-vant to linking all people in the vendor organization who have contacts with managed care personnel." Bruce Savage, Dendrite's VP for Europe, commented:

> Europe requires more product customization due to language and regulatory differences by country. Also, European clients are more

price sensitive. It's often easier for a U.S. pharmaceutical executive to justify a budget request for a 2,000-person sales force than it is for the European executive to do this for a 200-person sales force. Postsale, we require about $1,300 per user to cover the personnel costs on our client support teams, and smaller sales forces mean fewer economies of scope in ongoing maintenance and service tasks.

In *Japan* (18% of pharmaceutical sales), sales force sizes were like those in the United States and, with fewer doctors, there was one pharmaceutical salesperson in Japan for every six physicians. Twenty U.S. pharmaceutical firms employed about 6,300 reps in Japan.

In the United States and Europe, physicians prescribed but did not dispense (or sell) drugs to patients. In Japan, physicians had historically combined prescribing and dispensing functions. Sales reps typically negotiated prices with individual physicians, who often received fees from pharmaceutical firms based on the number of prescriptions written. Many Japanese physicians also derived income from using free samples with patients and then submitting the prescription record to the government for reimbursement. Hence, abundant samples (often provided through allied wholesalers) were an accepted part of the selling process. In addition, most Japanese doctors worked in clinics or hospitals which required sales reps to wait outside to see the doctor. One result, a Dendrite executive explained, is that "social selling is very important in Japan. Reps develop face time with doctors by washing their cars, entertaining them, and running all sorts of errands. In turn, tracking these expenses is a key task for Japanese pharmaceutical firms. Daily call reports involve detailed information about the hospital, doctor, samples distributed, and any gifts or other expense-item tasks performed." Bill Magee, Dendrite's VP for Asia, added:

In the United States and Europe, our ratio of support staff to client sales reps is 1:200, but 1:100 in Japan due to the emphasis on personal service. We generally don't make money with a Japanese client until the second or third year. Also, while we're the only vendor with a fully operational Kanji system, there's a bias here toward doing business with Japanese-owned firms.

Market Developments

In 1992, spending on prescription drugs in the United States was about $50 billion and, as a portion of medical spending, had declined from 16% in the 1960s to 7% by 1990. However, U.S. health care costs had grown to over $900 billion by 1992, more than 14% of GNP. President Clinton had made health care a key issue in his campaign and had appointed a task force to draft legislation. The task force had singled out drugs for attention and, in mid-1993, was reviewing various options. While the eventual outcome of any government action was unclear, most observers believed that more managed care facilities were a likely outcome in the United States.

Managed care referred to institutions such as HMOs that limited a patient's choice of doctor and hospital(s), used centralized buying and formularies to lower product acquisition costs, and eschewed traditional fee-for-service physician compensation in favor of cost controls aimed at diagnosing and treating ailments with fewer tests and visits. By 1993, 56% of Americans in group health plans were enrolled in managed care networks, up from 29% in 1988. Forecasts indicated that, by 1995, 20% of prescription sales in the United States would be from pharmacies in managed care facilities and another 35% via contracts between retail pharmacies and managed care institutions that employ hundreds of staff physicians. One observer commented:

> Admission to the formulary will depend on physicians' input, but will be heavily influenced by administrators interested in price, cost-in-use, and added value services in addition to product safety and efficacy. Also, the many doctors practicing in both managed care and private-office settings are unlikely to sustain different prescribing habits for their patients. So a firm with products on the formulary also has access to another large market.
>
> Many managed-care firms are also developing information systems to track prescribing practices for each patient and physician and to develop therapy guidelines. Physicians who continually prescribe outside the guidelines will be questioned and may suffer economic penalties. Conversely, pharmaceutical firms will face greater demands for comparative data and cost-benefit information as a prerequisite for formulary admission.
>
> In this environment, pharmaceutical sales forces in the United States will be downsized. After R&D, the Sales organization represents the largest fixed asset investment of a pharmaceutical company. The targets for their activities will drop from 250,000–300,000 individual physicians to about 35,000 committees. The optimum size of the field force for a major pharmaceutical firm operating in the United States may be 400 to 700 reps, rather than 1,500 or more.

In Europe, managed care was already more common than in the United States, but pharmaceutical spending was a bigger portion of health care costs than in the United States. In response, many European countries were imposing price controls and other regulations. In early 1993, Germany imposed reimbursement regulations that resulted in a 27% reduction in prescriptions in the first month and a 32% reduction in the second. In the United Kingdom, there was a trend toward more centralized buying of health care products, including drugs. In response, noted one observer, "pharmaceutical firms in Europe may move toward even smaller, more specialized sales forces focused on a given product or therapeutic area."

In Japan in 1992, fixed-invoice pricing for pharmaceuticals was mandated and wholesaler rebating abolished. Under the previous system, wholesalers were reimbursed by manufacturers for supplying products to customers at prices below manufacturers' list price. Under the new system, manufacturers were barred from intervening in wholesaler/customer price negotiations. Japan also instituted caps on health care reimbursement, including drugs, and was moving toward the separation of prescribing and dispensing for pharmaceuticals. One observer commented:

> Sales reps can no longer discuss product prices and discounts with physicians, and more attention must be paid to wholesalers. They must place more emphasis on the therapeutic qualities of their companies' products. Reimbursement caps make Japanese clinics and hospitals more price sensitive, and the separation of dispensing and prescribing by doctors would alter pharmaceutical sales tasks. Samples become a less effective device for building relationships; product and market information becomes more pertinent; and pharmaceutical firms would also need to develop and coordinate distribution to more pharmacies and other drug suppliers. That may mean more reps.

Worldwide, there were fewer "blockbuster" drugs in the product pipelines of many firms. Of the 30 biggest selling drugs in the United States, for instance, 14 would be off-patent by the end of 1996, leaving billions in annual sales vulnerable to lower-priced generic competition. A Dendrite executive commented: "Pharmaceutical sales forces expanded in the 1980s, fueled by patented products whose margins made increased selling resources possible and desirable. But companies without such products are less likely to add to their already sizable distribution costs."

ORGANIZATION

Exhibit 5 outlines Dendrite's organization in 1993. Reporting to John Bailye were vice presidents for each geographical area as well as controller, planning, and technical services (responsible for new product development and support and maintenance of core code). Client teams in each country reported to their area vice president.

Sales

"We have two types of sales activities," noted one executive, "initial sales to clients and follow-on sales to existing accounts." Initial sales were handled by salespeople, all of whom had previous experience in the pharmaceutical industry, supplemented by the area vice presidents. Salesperson compensation involved a base salary, and a commission based on both the dollar volume of the contract and account profitability; sales commissions were paid only after the annual budget for that client team had been achieved, not when the contract was signed. Incentive compensation in 1992 averaged about 30% of the salesperson's total compensation. One salesperson commented:

In a customized software business, no two client situations are identical. Hence, we must be flexible in pricing, delivery dates, and the array of services and support we offer to clients in order to close a sale. This is especially true for a global supplier. Many corporate pharmaceutical executives want to negotiate pricing on a global basis. And for us, multiyear contracts in several countries are attractive. But their country managers are usually very protective of their autonomy. That means many changes in our system for each country at the same client. So, while we in Sales may negotiate a price that assumes standardized reports across a client's countries, postsale margins may suffer as many changes are required to get and keep the system in a country organization.

I ultimately can't control client demands, and this is a very competitive business where we tend to be the high-service/premium-priced supplier. Also, the selling process involves working across Sales, IS, and other client functions for a major capital expense which attracts board of director attention. I don't want to see a multimillion dollar agreement killed because of a quarrel about an additional $50,000 worth of applications or support service.

As well as managing client teams, Business Managers (BMs) were responsible for business development at existing accounts. Incremental sales were made by adding users to the system and/or application modules (priced on a per-user basis) as user feedback revealed additional client needs. A Dendrite executive noted: "Facilities management allows us to collect information about clients' changing business demands. The BM's task is to provide, from our range of modules, the applications most pertinent to their evolving concerns. They are in an ideal position to identify ongoing sales-enhancement tools."

Dendrite had 20 BMs in 1993. Most had a technical background and experience in operations or IS project management, usually outside the pharmaceutical industry. Their compensation involved a base salary and a bonus based on achieving financial and customer satisfaction goals (based on quarterly surveys of customers). Each client team was a profit center, and BMs were responsible for managing expenses. One BM noted:

Postsale, my major contacts are with the client's IS managers. I soon know more about their user needs than they do. For example, the field data we collect is very relevant to their Product Management and Market Research functions, and can also help Finance and Procurement manage supplies and other expenses. These areas often don't realize that Dendrite is a data and communications source. IS is very leery about vendor personnel approaching other functions and acts as a strong gatekeeper. A BM must be a good technical analyst in order to identify applications opportunities and then an accomplished diplomat in order to sell any opportunity to and beyond IS.

Meanwhile, my primary job is managing services for clients and account profitability for Dendrite. I'm usually brought in after price negotiations with the client and so "inherit" what Sales has negotiated. In an increasingly cost-conscious environment, Sales often agrees to provide applications, services, and delivery dates with less attention than I'd like to the costs, headcount, and deadlines involved. Most of my postsales time is absorbed by the efforts required to deliver on these agreements and still break even on the project.

Client Teams

Upon an agreement with a client, Dendrite formed a dedicated team responsible for customized applications, hardware connections, pilot testing, rollout, and then ongoing maintenance and management of the account (**Exhibit 6**). Team size was related to the number of users and ranged from 3 to 50 members, with an average of 22 people. Each team was headed by a BM and included Customer Support (CS) and Technical Support (TS) managers. Annual fully burdened costs for the BM, one TS rep, and one CS rep were more than $250,000, with additional costs for additional technical and service personnel dedicated to the account.

In the project phase, TS managers defined, customized, and installed the system on the client's hardware and computer network. TS also helped clients in purchasing equipment from vendors and managed Dendrite's leased-equipment program. After rollout, TS managers focused on system maintenance which involved system backups, communications support, data security, ongoing software enhancements, and 24-hour service for any hardware or system problems. In the project phase, CS managers developed system documentation, company-specific training materials and service manuals, and user training programs at client sites. One CS manager noted:

> The field reception of an ETM system is a function of how the client's corporate headquarters has "sold" the system, and we're there to help in this process. When it's been sold well, reps see the system as a tool that can help them, not a big-brother device to micro-manage their activities. Also, it takes about one month for a rep to use the system efficiently, and our role is to accelerate this learning curve.

After rollout, CS managers focused on the telephone Help lines dedicated to that client. Help lines were available to users from 8:00–5:00 P.M. daily (in each time zone) and in the United States averaged 400 calls per month per client. A CS rep explained that "Help line calls range from questions about software or malfunctioning power cords to requests for data. We receive training about the client's product line and, during rollout, quickly become familiar to the client's field reps. They will call to discuss marketing ideas, suggestions about reformatting a report, or other matters." In general, there was one CS rep and one TS rep for every 200 system users at clients.

Exhibit 7 outlines BM responsibilities. Before rollout, BMs worked closely with client IS and Sales Administration managers on system design, installation, and training. After rollout, BMs worked on ongoing customization, new or add-on modules to be incorporated in the system, and (with client IS managers) on evaluating the reception and effectiveness of the system.

One BM noted that "Clients basically want two things from the BM: that you really listen and care; and that you do everything else yesterday." Another noted that "As a rule of thumb, a cost-effective client team needs a minimum of 400 users. That makes European clients especially challenging from a P&L point of view. We have shared client teams, but that limits the levels and types of service you can provide." A third BM commented that "An ongoing issue in account management is guarding against 'service creep': most contracts negotiated with clients stipulate a flat fee per user, and clients have a tendency to ask for more and more services under this flat fee arrangement. If BMs were involved earlier in the sales process, we could identify this and try to price service more appropriately." A Dendrite executive commented:

> There's a shift in the BM's role from consultant during project development and installation, to service provider and account manager after rollout. The service role tends to be focused on daily firefighting tasks across a client's many field locations. These concerns make IS the key contact for BMs; and IS tends to focus on minimizing software bugs and hassles, not on business goals. Their measure of success is our product's technical performance, not productivity improvements or enhancements. In fact, for IS, enhancements run the risk of generating problems (for which they are blamed) and not just more sales calls or revenues (for which Sales or Marketing get credit). That's one reason IS managers don't like BMs talking to other departments.

CURRENT ISSUES

Commenting on Dendrite in mid-1993, Bailye said: "Technology and customer concerns are dynamic. New programming tools make it possible for six computer jockeys in a garage to reverse-engineer basic software and sell it more cheaply. The pharmaceutical industry is poised for a shift in many countries. Meanwhile, what we can do with our own product-service offering has also changed, and that raises fundamental strategic choices." Bailye was considering several alternative routes of potential company growth: into other markets besides pharmaceuticals, into other functional areas within pharmaceutical clients, or "deeper" into sales and marketing applications in the current target market.

Most sales automation vendors targeted multiple markets besides pharmaceuticals, including insurance, consumer package goods, and other industries that relied on large field forces to sell products. Some managers believed that Dendrite should also expand into other vertical markets. "We have both offensive and defensive reasons to do this," noted one manager.

"On the one hand, our software remains among the best for sales reporting and data dissemination, and specific formats can be customized for various industries. On the other hand, with fewer large pharmaceutical field forces available, the economics of our current market are changing. Also, the entry point for new vendors is typically smaller field forces, and we should expect increasingly heavy competition for pharmaceutical clients."

Estimates indicated that $10 million would be required to adapt core code and facilities management services to another industry's selling tasks, implying some time before a market entry would break even for Dendrite. This investment could be reduced substantially if development focused on stand-alone software with little or no support services provided by Dendrite.

Another possibility was to expand into other functional areas within pharmaceutical firms. One manager noted that "We are now the link between our clients' sales reps and their I.S. and sales administration managers. But the data we collect and disseminate has enormous cross-functional value for clients, and we can be the link between other departments and ongoing field sales and customer activity data. As sales force sizes decrease, we must evolve from a sales planning to a management information tool at clients." Another manager emphasized:

Both technological and customer developments support this strategy. Network technologies, which allow computers to share data, are spreading throughout industry, making cross-functional linkages more accessible. And, for pharmaceutical firms in particular, selling to big managed-care organizations will require better information links between field sales, national account groups, product marketing, finance, and distribution. We are now experts about a critical node in these evolving networks and should capitalize on our position.

Dendrite had under development a managed care module for its current system, and estimated additional core-code development costs of $2–$5 million depending upon the number of areas covered by a cross-functional approach. However, other managers wondered about the selling and service requirements inherent in this approach, and noted that competition would include multinational information consulting firms that were much larger than Dendrite and already had long-standing relationships beyond IS and Sales departments in clients.

A third option was to continue concentrating on sales applications and product enhancements that increased Dendrite's value to pharmaceutical clients. One manager noted:

The United States may be a mature market for sales automation, but not Europe or Japan. Also, some competitors are beginning to link with industry data providers, and we must continue to add value to our system through module applications and support. Pharmaceutical firms are very protective of their databases and there's a limit to how far they will let *any* vendor into their organization. To be successful, we must link our initiatives to sales automation because that's our base and identity in these firms.

Dendrite could develop many product extensions, including computer-based training modules, additional analysis and performance evaluation systems, multimedia applications that allowed for individualized sales presentations tied to on-line data sources, and use of current software for palm-sized computers expected to be introduced in coming years. Development costs for these enhancements were generally $1 million and often shared with current clients interested in expanding sales force applications.

Another issue facing the company was the coordination of Dendrite's sales and service efforts and possible changes in the role of the Business Manager. Many believed that the current arrangement immersed BMs in daily operations with little time to develop business opportunities. They proposed the addition of an Operations Manager to client teams, responsible for day-to-day technical and customer support issues. Costs of such a position would be comparable to those for the BM position. One executive commented:

> Growing an account requires a strategic rather than tactical focus, and contacts beyond IS and sales administration. Ideally, we would want two project teams: one for development/installation phases and one for on-going support. Now, however, the installation phase identifies the BM as the tactician who handles all the details and ties that person closely to IS, who doesn't want the BM "wasting" time with other functional areas. The Operations Manager position would free BMs from daily firefighting and allow them to sell to other areas at the client. It would also create a career path for CS and TS managers to become Operations Managers and subsequently grow into a BM role.

Others were uncertain about the impact of this proposal on service provision during the various phases from initial proposal to installation and ongoing operations. They argued for involving BMs earlier in the process, before contracts are signed. "If involved during the first draft of an agreement," said one manager, "a BM can impact the product configuration and deliverables, recognize the true costs of postsale service, and establish relationships with the other client personnel who get involved before a contract is signed but who tend not to interact with our client teams after the contract is signed." Still others questioned whether BMs had the skills or temperament required for selling new business. One manager commented: "People should do what they do best. BMs' strengths are in project management and fixing problems. Even with sales training, they will remain operations managers. And, given developments in our customer base, they will need to manage ongoing service and support costs even more tightly."

Reflecting on these options, John Bailye commented:

We are financing the business from ongoing operations and our venture backers will eventually look to reap returns on their investments via an IPO. Hence, growth remains important even as we face an environment where there are lots of forecasts but no certainties. Should we grow within the sales function across geographies, into other departments at global clients, or into new vertical markets? What are the implications for BMs and the organization of our account management activities? And how do possible changes at pharmaceutical firms affect current and future strategy? I want Dendrite working on those areas that will yield the best return over the long haul.

EXHIBIT 1 Consolidated Statements of Operations for Year Ended December 31, 1992 and Period September 1, 1991 (Date of Reorganization) to December 31, 1991 ($'000s)

	1992	1991
Operating revenues	$23,300	$4,853
Cost and expenses	20,953	5,647
Operating profit (loss)	2,347	(794)
Other income (expense):	(8)	(35)
Interest expense	71	7
Other	63	(28)
Income taxes:		
Reduction of income taxes from net operating loss carryforwards	286	—
Net income (loss)	$1,161	(822)

Consolidated Balance Sheets, December 31, 1992 and 1991 ($'000s)

Assets		
Current Assets:		
Cash and cash equivalents	600	874
Trade accounts receivable	5,063	1,762
Prepaid expenses and other current assets	669	479
Deferred tax assets	80	—
Total Current Assets	6,412	3,115
Fixed assets, net of accumulated depreciation	1,699	1,448
Intangible assets, net of accumulated amortization	2,106	2,688
Organization costs, net of accumulated amortization	2,106	2,688
Capitalized software development costs	895	30
	$11,204	$ 7,398
Liabilities and Stockholders' Equity		
Current Liabilities:		
Trade accounts payable and other current liabilities	$2,825	$1,464
Current installments of lease obligations	65	26
Current portion of deferred revenues	2,050	120
Current income taxes payable	270	—
Total Current Liabilities	5,210	2,710
Obligations under capital leases	41	31
Deferred revenues, excluding current portion	110	146
Deferred tax liabilities	435	—
Total Liabilities	5,796	2,887
Stockholders' Equity:		
Common stock, no par value	3	3
Retained earnings (accumulated deficit)	339	(822)
Equity adjustment for foreign currency translation	(445)	(94)
Less consideration to former stockholder of acquired business in excess of his basis in net assets sold	(1,364)	(1,364)
Total Stockholders' Equity	5,408	4,511
	$11,204	$7,398

EXHIBIT 2

SaleStar™ is a turn-key system of user-friendly software, hardware and support services that enables you to turn information management into increased productivity. Developed by Dendrite International, Inc., SaleStar™ is backed by the same focus on client service and support that has made Dendrite the leader in state-of-the-art electronic territory management systems for the global pharmaceutical industry.

FEATURES	BENEFITS
Call Planning	Enables sales representatives to improve productivity and performance by providing strategy to the call planning process.
Customer Profiles	Enables sales representatives to increase the productivity of every call by providing easy access to vital information (e.g., demographics, call history, pre- and post-call analysis, prescribing profile) on all their accounts.
Call Reporting	Enables sales representatives to easily and effectively track and communicate information from each sales call.
Customer Targeting	Easy manipulation of customer information enables sales representatives to target customers strategically based on a variety of criteria (e.g., best times to call, hospital department, affiliation, rating, call frequency, etc.)
Sample Tracking	Enables the home office to assess current and future sample needs, adjust marketing plans, determine how well a product is being received, and meet regulatory requirements.
Report Viewing	Provides sales representatives and managers easy and timely access to internal and third-party information such as product pricing, sales data and comprehensive management reports.
Third-Party Information	Provides sales representatives with up-to-date micro-marketing data on customer and industry profiles. (Information may be gained from several sources, including Scriptrac, AMA, SMG, and others.)
Expense Forms/Weekly Attendance	Enables sales representatives to spend more time on sales by making administrative reporting faster and easier.

FEATURES	BENEFITS
Meeting Planning & Recording	Enables sales representatives to easily and effectively plan, record and review information gained from peer programs, focus groups, or multiple customer presentations.
Electronic Mail	Provides managers and sales representatives with daily access to a reliable communication tool that doesn't depend on memos or telephone calls.

CUSTOMER SUPPORT SERVICES

Field User/Manager Support
Help Line
"How To" Instructions
Log-in Advice
Dendrite Log-in Reports
System Disk Request
System Utilities
Profile Q & A
Profile Addition/Deletion/Move
Correct Entry Error
E-Mail Support
Rep. Tracking
Call Tracking

Home Office Support
Reports QC/QA
Reports Distribution
Help Desk
Field Support–Home Office
Realignment Support
Client Meetings

Hardware Services
Field Hardware Support
Hardware Diagnosis
Hardware Replacement Request
Hardware Tracking

TECHNICAL SUPPORT SERVICES

System Administration–Hardware
    Daily, Weekly, Monthly Back-ups
    Communications Support
    Off-Site Storage
    System Security
    Laptop Support

System Administration–Software
    Transaction Processing
    File Structure/Source Code Maintenance
    E-Mail Administration
    Software Defect Resolution

Help/Screen File Updates

Processing/Dist. of Suite of Reports

Customer Support Services
    Error Correction
    Data Issues

Sales and Marketing Support
    Territory Realignments
    Third-Party Data Updates
    Data Extracts
    Reports Generation, Processing & Dist.

EXHIBIT 3 Project Pricing and Costs: Examples (in thousands, for twelve months ended December 1992)

"Small" = client with <400 users; "Large" = client with 1,500+ users

	Small	Large
Sales:		
One-time license fees[a]	—	—
Service fees	—	—
Customization	—	
Implementation	—	—
Software maintenance	—	—
Hardware support	—	
In-house publishing	—	—
Other	—	—
Total Revenue	$891.6	$3,244.0
Cost of Sales	$489.5	$1,753.2
Gross Margin	$402.1	$1,490.8
Gross Margin (%)	45.1%	46.0%
Operating Expenses:		
Repair/maintenance —	—	
Travel	—	—
Entertainment	—	—
Supplies/computer supplies	—	—
Personnel	—	—
Hardware support	—	
In-house publishing	—	
Overhead allocation	—	—
Total Expenses	$370.9	$962.6
Project Trading Profit	$31.2	$528.2
Headcount (Dendrite Client Team)	7.00	20.30

[a]These examples represent established clients. In year one of these projects, software license fees were 50%–60% of revenues.

EXHIBIT 4 Estimated ETM Market Size (1992)

	United States	Western Europe[a]	Japan	Rest of World	Total
Number of reps	44,000	70,000	42,000	44,000	200,000
Number of reps automated	35,331	5,683	2,760	N/A	43,774
Percent automated	80.3%	8.1%	6.6%	N/A	21.9%
Number automated by Dendrite	7,893	2,467	2,305	0	12,665
Number automated by other firms and internal sources	27,438	3,216	455	N/A	31,109

[a]Western Europe includes England, France, Germany, Italy, Spain and the Benelux countries.

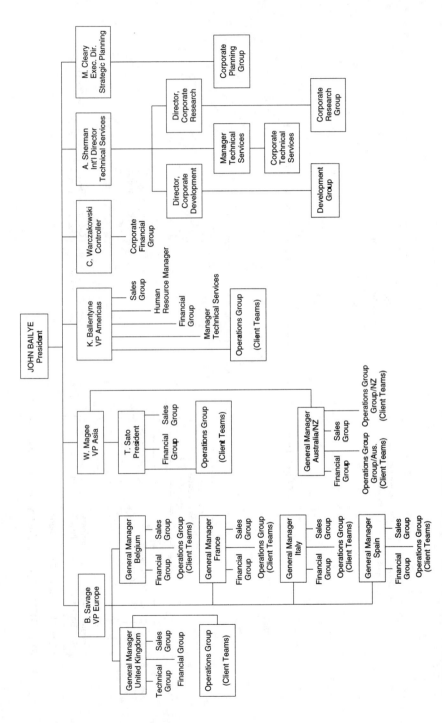

EXHIBIT 5 Dendrite Organization (1993)

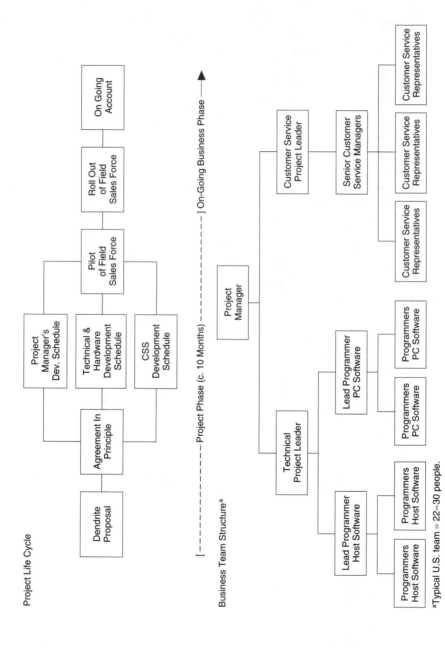

Project Life Cycle

```
┌──────────┐   ┌────────────┐   ┌──────────┐   ┌──────────┐   ┌──────────┐
│ Dendrite │   │Agreement In│   │Project   │   │Pilot     │   │Roll Out  │
│ Proposal │───│ Principle  │───│Manager's │   │of Field  │───│of Field  │
└──────────┘   └────────────┘   │Dev.      │   │Sales     │   │Sales     │
                                │Schedule  │   │Force     │   │Force     │
                                └──────────┘   └──────────┘   └──────────┘
                                ┌────────────┐                ┌──────────┐
                                │Technical & │                │On Going  │
                                │Hardware    │                │Account   │
                                │Development │                └──────────┘
                                │Schedule    │
                                └────────────┘
                                ┌──────────┐
                                │CSS       │
                                │Development│
                                │Schedule  │
                                └──────────┘
```

[— — — — — — Project Phase (c. 10 Months) — — — — —] On-Going Business Phase ⟶

Business Team Structure[a]

[a]Typical U.S. team = 22–30 people.

EXHIBIT 6 Project Life Cycle and Business Team Structure

314

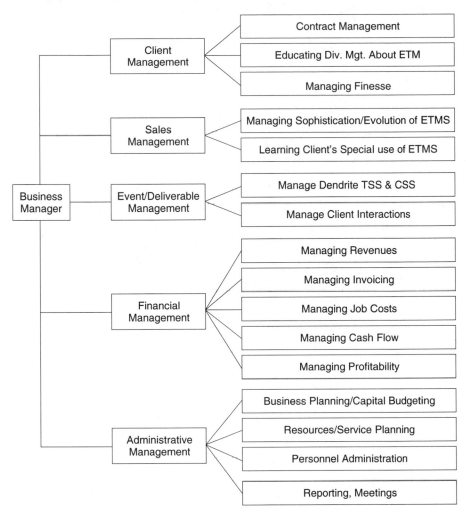

Note: TSS = Technical Support Services
CSS = Customer Support Services

EXHIBIT 7   Business Managers' Project Responsibilities

PART IV

Building and Maintaining Customer Relationships

Teamwork for Today's Selling

Listen to this account manager, responsible for building sales and a close relationship with a key customer, describe a recent conversation with a colleague: "I called our district manager in Phoenix and explained that I was preparing an important proposal for this big account, and would he please help with the part of it having to do with an account location in his territory. He reluctantly agreed, but I haven't seen anything yet, and he hasn't returned my last two phone calls. With friends like that—"

This is how the district sales manager sees it: "I've got monthly numbers to meet with limited time and resources. And I don't get paid or recognized for helping someone else sell. So I don't."

Now let's hear from the vice president of national accounts at a major telecommunications company: "We do about $3 million a year with Zembla [a large, diversified corporation] but that's peanuts compared with the potential. A big part of Zembla's strategy is their telecommunications network, which they've sunk millions into over the past decade. Last week their information systems czar called me to complain about our salespeople in two regions. They were trying to sell a discount service to a couple of Zembla divisions, and they were succeeding. He said that this subverted his company's telecom strategy, which requires high utilization of Zembla's

Frank V. Cespedes, Stephen X. Doyle, and Robert J. Freedman, *Harvard Business Review*, March–April 1989. ©1989 by the President and Fellows of Harvard College, all rights reserved.

network to make it operate efficiently. Attempts to sell some of his people off that network were causing a lot of friction in his organization. And in ours too, I might add."

Then there's the sales representative of a company where the proverbial 80% of revenue comes from 20% of the customers. She sells equipment to some of those large accounts, while other salespeople in another sales force handle related supply items to the same accounts (among others). She says: "Many customers want to coordinate their purchases of equipment and supplies because of the impact they have on their production processes. But equipment sales are usually higher priced transactions than supply sales, occur much less often, and involve contact with more people from more functions in the customer's organization. So you have more sales calls and a longer selling cycle, as well as different delivery and service requirements after the sale is made. I meet a lot with my supply brethren because, while we share all of our accounts, what's often not shared or clear are our individual goals."

A sales manager comments on his company's recent annual sales meeting: "Great resort, wonderful food, and the weather was terrific. Our senior VP of sales and marketing made his annual speech on teamwork. But that's not enough. Until teamwork becomes a daily part of operations, the occasional pitch for it is only lip service."

For many companies in the past two decades, selling has changed dramatically. Traditionally it was the vocation of a single energetic, persistent individual—"a man way out there in the blue, riding on a smile and a shoeshine," in Arthur Miller's memorable words. Now selling is often the province of a team composed of men and women who must coordinate their efforts across product lines (the products often made by different divisions and sold from different locations) to customers that require an integrated approach. Even when there is no formal sales team, moreover, it's often necessary to coordinate—as the vignettes at the start of this article show.

Mergers, acquisitions, and other changes in the business environment are forcing vendors in many industries to put greater emphasis on large customers with equally large and complex purchasing requirements. Conventional supermarkets, for example, accounted for about 75% of U.S. retail food sales in 1980. They will take in an estimated 25% in 1990; "super stores," "combination stores," and "warehouse stores" will account for most remaining sales. These chains possess the buying power (backed by sophisticated information systems) they need to insist on better service, lower prices, and a coordinated approach from their vendors, many of whom sell them multiple products through different sales forces.

Similar trends are evident in many industrial goods categories, where just-in-time inventory systems make customers aware of any discrepancies in prices, terms and conditions, delivery, or timely attention by vendors' salespeople in many buying locations. Internationally, the emergence of more multinational, even global customers places similar demands on many sales organizations—with distance, currency variations, and cultural differences in the vendors' sales force adding complications to the administration of these important shared accounts.

In these situations, selling depends on the vendor's ability to marshal its resources effectively across a range of buying locations, buying influences, product lines, and internal organizational boundaries. Coordination in these shared-account situations affects the company's expense-to-revenue ratio, ability to retain current business or develop new business at these accounts, and sales force morale and management. Yet, as the comments by salespeople indicate, coordination is not easy.

At four sellers of industrial goods we studied, only 11% of the salespeople involved in shared accounts were located in the same building, while 43% were in different sales districts and 7% in different countries. Of course, this dispersion erects time, expense, and scheduling barriers to coordination, and the problem is likely to get worse as many customers become more multinational in scope. Further, although development work on major accounts often takes years, one-quarter of the salespeople had been in their account positions less than five years. "It takes time to develop good working relationships on an account team," one sales manager explained, but account continuity is a recurring issue at these and many other companies.

In interviews, salespeople repeatedly cited more communication as the one thing that could most improve teamwork on shared accounts. In view of the distances and compensation involved, however, improving communication—especially the preferred mode, meetings—would raise these companies' marketing expense-to-revenue ratios to unacceptable levels. There is no doubt that a coordinated sales approach can be expensive. So, like any other expensive business resource, it should be employed where it will yield the highest returns.

Because the need for sales coordination depends on the complexity of the account, moreover, both large and small vendors face these issues. Large companies may enjoy scale advantages over the smaller competition, but they often have more products to sell and more layers in their sales and marketing hierarchies, making coordination among their salespeople difficult.

Smaller companies may have less bureaucracy than the big competition, but with fewer products and fewer resources they often base their marketing strategies on superior responsiveness to customers via customized marketing programs. Hence, this important source of competitive advantage for the smaller vendor raises the threshold of coordination required. Actually, our research showed that despite significant size differences among the various companies that we studied, the number of salespeople who must work together in shared accounts remained about the same at each company.

Our data and experience indicate three areas that are most important in sales coordination: compensation systems, the goal-setting process, and staffing and training issues that arise when shared accounts are an integral part of sales strategy.

COMPENSATION SYSTEMS

In sales management, you won't get what you don't pay for. One salesperson put it this way: "Teamwork reflects many elements. However, compensation is a foundation. An individual's belief that he or she is paid fairly spurs belief in the team concept."

Many companies have three types of teamwork situations:

1. Joint efforts on behalf of certain national or international accounts, in which all team members work exclusively with these accounts.
2. Headquarters national account managers (NAMs) or account executives coordinate with field sales reps; the NAM is dedicated to one or two accounts, but these accounts are among dozens or even hundreds that field sales representatives call on.
3. District sales managers' efforts affect important accounts that cut across sales district lines, but performance evaluations are based on intradistrict results.

To encourage the kind of teamwork required, a different compensation system may be appropriate for each type of sales rep and account situation. Flexibility is the key, and this often means complexity. Yet in big-account situations, many companies design compensation plans according to "keep it simple, stupid" criteria, however complex the sales tasks are. Top management then ignores important differences tied to account assignments and often rewards selling activity that neglects coordination at the customer.

If there are many salespeople calling on key accounts and teamwork is important, then a bonus based on total account sales often makes more sense than traditional, individually oriented incentive arrangements. Interep is the nation's largest radio "rep" firm; its salespeople in major U.S. cities call on ad agencies and advertisers to sell time on the more than 3,000 radio stations it represents. To avoid bureaucracy and maintain an entrepreneurial spirit, Interep's chairman, Ralph Guild, has spread the company's sales efforts among six different sales forces.

Mergers among big advertisers and ad agencies, however, have made customers increasingly receptive to a rep firm that can act as a coordinated supplier across various radio markets for different product categories. In response, Interep uses a team approach to selling that cuts across each sales force. A prime element is the compensation system. Unlike the plans at most other rep firms, where incentives are staunchly "Lone Ranger" in design, Interep has salespeople with shared-account responsibilities participate in a bonus pool based on the particular account's sales volume. The approach has been effective: Interep's sales are growing faster than the industry's, and according to market surveys, ad agencies generally view Interep as more responsive than competitors.

Another important compensation issue is the time frame employed. Sales efforts at big accounts often take months, sometimes years, to pan out. But compensation plans usually tie incentives to quarterly or annual snapshots of performance. The usual result, as one salesperson acknowledged, is this: "Because our compensation plan is short-term oriented, I put my efforts where there are short-term benefits. Also, many short-term sales goals can be met with a minimum of teamwork; the longer term results require the hassle of working with lots of other people." Bonuses for multiple-year performance, or for qualitative objectives like building relationships with certain account decision makers, can encourage team effort.

Sharing of sales credit is a nettlesome issue. Surveys of major account sales programs show that only a minority use credit splitting to help coordinate NAMs and field sales reps.[1] In shared accounts, split credits are often better than mutually exclusive credit decisions.

But not always. One sales rep noted how a common attitude toward split credits can fuel resentment and block teamwork: "Most salespeople feel that when the split is 50/50, they're losing 50% instead of gaining 50% of the incentive pay. A lot of time and energy is wasted arguing over splits."

Actually, a company can give full credit to those involved and still not (as many managers fear) pay twice for the same sale. The key is having a good understanding of the sales tasks involved and an information system capable of tracking performance so that shared sales volume can be taken into account when setting objectives. Consider an example: two salespeople last year sold about $500,000 each to individual accounts and about $500,000 to shared accounts. Their combined sales amounted to about $1.5 million. Two approaches to goal setting and credits are possible:

1. The employer sets targets and bonuses so that each person receives $25,000 for $750,000 in sales, with credit from shared account sales split 50/50. If each sells $500,000 in individual sales and $500,000 to shared accounts, each makes the $750,000 target and gets a bonus.

2. The employer pays a $25,000 bonus for $1 million of sales with all shared-account volume double counted and fully credited to both people. Each salesperson must then rely on team effort for about 50% of target sales, but each also receives full credit for team sales.

A participant in the first plan may reason that an incremental $250,000 in individual sales (perhaps developed at the expense of time devoted to the more complicated joint sales effort) could reach the $750,000 target. Consequently, he or she might decide to concentrate on individually assigned accounts, encourage the colleague to continue to work hard on the team accounts, and hope to gather those half-credit sales with little or no effort. Coordination and major account penetration are likely to suffer. Under the second plan, there is at least no compensation barrier to expenditure of effort on the more labor-intensive team sales.

Compensation alone won't harness teamwork if other control systems are out of kilter. But ill-defined compensation plans can thwart teamwork even when other control systems support coordination.

SETTING AND MEETING GOALS

Compensation means money. A less expensive way to foster teamwork is by clarifying goals—defining individual salespeople's main responsibilities and desired accomplishments (like opening new accounts, maximizing sales from existing accounts, and launching new products). When goals are unclear, selling can be frustrating because salespeople cannot know where they stand in relation to some standard. Good performance may appear then to be a random occurrence, independent of effort. This confusion can discourage effort, especially in those tasks that require working with other people.

[1] Gary Tubridy, "How to Pay National Account Managers," *Sales & Marketing Management,* January 13, 1986, p. 52.

Disseminating information about company strategy helps to clarify sales goals and the effort top management wants. Yet few companies regularly pass on information to the sales force about the company's objectives in its various market segments. Many so-called "strategic plans" do not make meaningful reference to the sales force's role in implementing strategy. Instead, the goals coming out of senior executive negotiations are usually kept secret because of fear that wide dissemination would unwittingly include competitors.

A strategy that does not imply certain behavior by the sales force, however, is often no strategy; it's merely an interesting idea. In the context of sales teamwork, moreover, competitive cost data are usually not what salespeople want; they need information about the company's goals in the marketplace, the nature of its potential competitive advantage, and their role in achieving those goals. Withholding this information is counterproductive. If salespeople are not selling in accordance with corporate goals, withholding information about strategy will not help, and if salespeople *are* selling in accordance with corporate goals, competitors will learn about them anyway.

One company we studied makes automatic testing equipment that is often bought to function as part of a total quality-control system at customer locations. Hence extensive customization for customers' production processes and information networks is necessary. These products are technologically dynamic and complex, demanding comprehensive product knowledge on salespeople's part. So the sales force is divided into product-oriented units.

The company holds semiannual sales meetings where the importance of integrated selling strategies is high on the agenda and where, in small groups, salespeople and senior executives talk about joint sales work and cross-selling activities on specific accounts. Top management considers these sessions as both an important input and output of strategic planning in a business where product development costs and an increasingly multinational customer base make account selection and incremental sales to major customers a key aspect of strategy.

In situations like this, where goal clarity and information about those goals are intertwined, managers might use the following checklist of questions to perform a quick audit of sales teamwork:

1. Do the goals spelled out to salespeople fit the company's strategic objectives? The compensation plan? One U.S. company, responding to the increasing globalization of its markets, began joint ventures with Japanese and German companies, realigned its product line and manufacturing operations at great cost, and established an ambitious "global account management" program. Quotas for the U.S. sales force, however, continued to focus on domestic accounts, and commissions were tied to domestic deliveries. Sales goals and corporate objectives were out of sync. Sometimes U.S. sales reps even tried to talk customers with foreign operations out of buying a product from one of the company's overseas operations! The frequent result: no sale at all.

2. Does the sales force understand the goals? Attention must be paid to "recommunicating" goals regularly—not least because the makeup of the sales force is always changing.

At IBM, account planning sessions spanning three to five days and often involving as many as 50 people have long been standard features of big-account management. The sales force discusses each account's business conditions and decision-making processes, and the staff concerned reviews all account applications, installations, and maintenance issues. The chief objective is an updated account plan for sales personnel.

Another goal is to acquaint people with the status of the account, including people in support roles. The impact on their morale and on the coordination of their efforts is an often overlooked, but crucial, aspect of sales teamwork. At one large medical equipment supplier, fast delivery is an important aspect of service to major hospital accounts. So account meetings include the truck drivers who regularly deliver to these accounts. "Knowing the warehouse," they can often make the difference in expediting a key customer's order.

3. Are the goals measurable?

Do the sales managers reinforce them? In most busy organizations, "that which is not measured does not happen," as one sales manager sardonically noted. Some companies respond to the more protracted and more complicated nature of shared-account sales by relaxing or ignoring measures. In such cases, the field salespeople often feel "We do the work, while the major account managers play golf and get the glory." It is precisely *because* shared-account sales demand sustained attention that measures are important. Without them, the pull in most sales organizations is toward the shorter term, individually assigned accounts.

Sales volume is only one measure of shared-account performance. Profitability, cross-selling, or new product introductions are often more appropriate measures, depending on the vendor's strategy.

Qualitative as well as quantitative measures may figure in evaluation of performance. At many investment banks, for example, a common source of data for evaluating individual performance at bonus time is input from colleagues via cross-evaluation surveys of collaborators on various deals. Account executives and product specialists may evaluate each other on certain criteria, including the other's contribution in marketing and service efforts for clients. These surveys keep account people sensitive to the coordination requirements of their jobs and keep managers aware of potential problems.[2]

STAFFING AND TRAINING

"I've worked alone 14 years in this territory," one field sales rep said, "and I prefer an 'I'll call you, don't call me' relationship with team players." A re-

[2]Robert G. Eccles and Dwight B. Crane, *Doing Deals: Investment Banks at Work* (Boston: Harvard Business School Press, 1988).

vamped compensation plan and an effective goal-setting procedure may change her attitude, but the odds are against it.

Teamwork in sales, as in sports and many other endeavors, is the sum of individual efforts working cooperatively toward a common goal. And just as most ballplayers play better in some conditions than they do in others, some hitting right-handed pitchers better and some left-handers, so do different salespeople perform better in some circumstances than in others. This has implications for account staffing. The sales rep we quoted should not be required or even asked to work in team-selling situations. The "don't call me, I'll call you" attitude won't help and may hurt in these circumstances. As long as her performance is acceptable, she should continue where she is.

A team process for recruiting is helpful for spotting such loners. At many companies, including Digital Equipment, interviews with team members are a crucial part of the hiring procedure. A team process is also useful for acquainting a prospect with account characteristics and corporate goals.

A perennial question for many companies that have key-account sales programs is whether to fill vacancies internally or hire externally. Most of the companies we looked at preferred to promote from within on the ground that understanding of the organization is more important and useful than general sales experience or even industry familiarity picked up at another vendor. Why? One reason is that shared-account programs place salespeople in positions where they have little authority over others who affect their performance on accounts. In such a situation, things get done through persuasion (helped by an informal reckoning of personal debits and credits), a knowledge of how the organization sets budgets and allocates resources, and a network of relationships cultivated over time. Outsiders, however knowledgeable and competent, are at a disadvantage in these areas.

At one company, a vendor of medical supplies, the account executive is called the "quarterback" of the company's resources for an account, and managers use the metaphor of a lens to describe the account manager's job: to bring into focus for a key account the company's resources in areas ranging from R&D and product development to distribution and customer service. Effective performance in this role calls for account executives who know internal systems as well as they know their accounts' buying processes and purchase criteria.

As sales tasks change, sales training should change too. In shared-account situations, product knowledge and generic selling skills (e.g., presentation expertise and time management) remain important, but the coordination requirements make other skills necessary as well. In major-account programs, salespeople usually work across product lines, often across sales forces and, increasingly, across country sales organizations that reflect different national cultures. Furthermore, line authority in these situations is often ephemeral, since coordinators, like NAMs and account executives, often have dotted-line relationships with other sales personnel. Team building is a crucial part of sales competence in these situations.

Yet, as one sales rep (echoing many others) noted to us, "All sales training I've ever seen in my company stresses development of individual skills, not teamwork. As a result, delegating responsibility and working with and through others are seen as weaknesses, not strengths, in our sales force."

Attention to team training is particularly important in companies with multiple sales forces, especially when they speak different technical or trade languages. Exposure to the other sales force's product line in training sessions can help. Mixed sales meetings encourage idea sharing across district or product lines and, equally important, build acquaintances among individuals who can later call on one another during an account crisis or opportunity.

A barrier to such training efforts is often not the money involved but the source of the money. Sales training is a significant expenditure at most companies—and, because the numbers usually do not reflect the cost of salespeople's time out of the field, a usually underestimated expenditure. But training budgets are often set according to district results or the performance of a particular sales group. The local managers who set the budgets naturally focus training on specific sales opportunities; they have little incentive to devote training to team efforts. A task for executives at many companies is to determine whether the method they use to apportion expenditures on sales training supports a goal of better sales coordination.

SITUATIONAL TEAMWORK

How a company thinks about improving sales coordination depends to a large extent on its products and the way it sells. Look at two organizations we studied, Company X, a supplier of automatic testing equipment, and Company Y, which sells business equipment and supplies.

While both handle large accounts where teamwork is essential, X sells technically complex and high unit-priced products, and Y sells technically simple products with lower unit prices. X has a small sales force and Y a large one. X's salespeople (mostly engineers) deal with long selling cycles and complex customer decision-making processes, while Y's salespeople (most without technical backgrounds) encounter shorter selling cycles and a more easily identifiable set of decision makers at their accounts. X's salespeople tend to place less emphasis on money (compensation systems, sales contests) and measurements (formal performance evaluation criteria) as control and coordination mechanisms than on "people issues" (relationships within the sales group and sales supervisors' skills). Y's salespeople tend to stress money and measurements as the key factors affecting teamwork.

These differences seem tied to the tasks facing salespeople at these companies and coincide with others' observations about the way task complexity affects the nature of the selling effort required.[3] The more complex the selling task, the more information must be exchanged between vendor and customer and the more information passed around among the vendor's salespeople working on a common account. Especially in technical sales situations, moreover, this information must be coordinated among people trained in certain core disciplines as well as in sales techniques. At the other extreme is the salesperson with the simple product whose mandate is a sim-

[3]Benson P. Shapiro, "Manage the Customer, Not Just the Sales Force," HBR September–October 1974, p. 127; and Barton A. Weitz, "Effectiveness in Sales Interactions: A Contingency Framework," *Journal of Marketing*, Winter 1981, p.85.

ple "go out and sell." Less information has to be transmitted between buyer and seller and among salespeople.

One inference to be drawn is that in complex sales tasks the initial selection of salespeople is more important. The technical skills required are expensive to obtain and keep honed through training; and the coordination skills necessary are more dependent on individual relationships. Where the sales task is less complex, however, requiring less information to be understood and communicated, "systems solutions" to coordination (mechanisms like compensation and measurement systems) are potentially more appropriate and respected by the sales force.

Organizations are often diligent in setting budgets, creating organization charts, and establishing other types of formal control systems. But they are often less attentive to the crucial but "softer" aspects of sales management. Sales managers in the companies we studied overwhelmingly stressed formal control systems (like compensation and quota-setting mechanisms) in their coordination efforts, while salespeople favored processes (like relationships with other salespeople and long-established company norms that aid or inhibit coordination). Sales managers are no doubt more comfortable with formal systems; they are easier to install and measure than initiatives aimed at nurturing process in the sales environment—and so easier to justify at budget-setting sessions. But in many situations, managers may be trying to address what salespeople perceive as interpersonal issues in teamwork with administrative "solutions."

While most top managers support teamwork, very few organizations actually focus on team effectiveness, and few managers get the process going on their own without the organization's support. As one sales executive commented, "Sales teamwork is ultimately a by-product of the organization and has to come from the top down. People in the trenches can be team players, but they need encouragement and incentives. Preaching teamwork won't work as long as senior managers' attitude toward the sales force remains at the carrot-and-stick level."

In seeking to make a sales organization more effective, however, it's important for management to keep aware of a key distinction: coordination doesn't necessarily mean consensus. That is, a team shouldn't approximate the dictionary definition of "two or more beasts of burden harnessed together." Years ago in *The Organization Man*, William Whyte skewered a certain pseudo teamwork that has a numbing and leveling effect on individual performance, creativity, and expression—qualities that are always vital in effective sales and marketing. But Whyte also missed the point: there are so many tasks in business that can only be carried on through groups. A sales manager with 20 years of experience put it this way: "You cannot legislate teamwork. It's an attitude that comes over the long term, and it's essential in a well-run sales organization. Despite this, there still needs to be plenty of room for individual success and achievement. Otherwise, teamwork becomes an amorphous concept that can lead a group to underachieve in harmony." Our suggestions can mean increased rewards for both the company and the individual salesperson.

Case 10

Astra/Merck Group

Speaking to the casewriters, Wayne Yetter, general manager of the Astra/Merck Group (A/M), commented:

> This undertaking is a greenfield approach to marketing in our industry: a unique opportunity to build a company based on the needs and requirements of the future, and without ingrained ways of doing things. We plan to revolutionize the pharmaceutical industry by being the best at linking patients and products.
>
> We also have short-term goals that are crucial: if we don't meet the level of sales called for in the agreement that formed this joint venture, the "counterrevolution" will probably be swift. But our eyes are on shaping a company that will lead the industry in the twenty-first century.

Matthew Emmens, vice president of Marketing & Sales at A/M, added:

This case was prepared by Professor Frank V. Cespedes and Research Associate Marie Bell as the basis for class discussion rather than to illustrate either effective or ineffective handling of an administrative situation. Certain data, while useful for discussion purposes, have been disguised.

Although many firms in this industry may not realize it, the future is now. The pharmaceuticals market has changed dramatically in the past decade and, even without the inevitability of government intervention or healthcare reform, is changing at an accelerating rate. Traditional methods are less effective as group buying makes obsolete the "pens, pads and pizza" of traditional detailing. Given these developments, our goal is to increase the potential **value** of our products by creating "pharmaceutical solutions" for customers. These solutions involve a combination of product, information, education and services. To accomplish this, we have had to build a unique process-driven organization without traditional walls.

In early 1993, executives at A/M were in the process of building their organization while evaluating interim results and the implications for future organizational changes.

COMPANY AND INDUSTRY BACKGROUND

In 1982, AB Astra (Astra) and Merck and Co. signed an agreement covering clinical trials, registration and marketing in the U.S. of new products resulting from Astra's research. During the initial years of the agreement, Astra received royalties on the sales of these drugs. This program of cooperation would pass into a new phase, however, if Merck's total sales of Astra products reached a "trigger" level of approximately $500 million over a 12-month period by December 31, 1993. If this sales volume were attained, Merck would be required to form a separate entity for its operation related to Astra products. In turn, Astra could buy a 50% interest in the new entity. Assuming Astra acquired this interest, Astra would no longer receive royalty payments and both firms would receive equal portions of the profit generated from the new entity. The joint venture would have an option on the majority of future pharmaceuticals resulting from Astra's research. In addition, the new entity would be allowed to solicit compounds from Merck and other institutions. Finally, the new company would report to a board of directors that had equal representation from both parent companies.

In the spring of 1993, Merck was marketing heart drugs (PLENDIL ® and TONOCARD ®) and a gastrointestinal drug (PRILOSEC ®) developed by Astra. TONOCARD was introduced in the United States in 1984, PRILOSEC in 1989, and PLENDIL in 1991. Until 1992, these products were sold only by Merck sales forces. In 1992, however, Merck decided to create a new entity, the A/M Group, to support Astra products even though the trigger level of sales had not yet been attained. Hence, in 1993, A/M's 490-person field organization was also selling the Astra products. One executive noted: "When the 1982 agreement was made, Astra had a small U.S. presence targeted solely at the hospital market and its financial position was weaker, while Merck was looking to augment the product portfolio it sells through its sales forces."

Merck & Co. had 1992 sales of $9.6 billion (**Exhibit 1**). Hailed as "America's most admired company" for a record seventh time in *Fortune* magazine's Annual Corporate Reputations Survey, Merck had also won a number of awards for developing innovative products and human resource programs. In the United States in 1992, Merck's 2,200 salespeople, 300 sales managers, and national account executives sold pharmaceuticals (including cardiovascular and gastrointestinal drugs) to hospitals, clinics, physicians, and other groups. In 1993, Merck's sales organization was a repeat winner of *Sales & Marketing Management* magazine's "Best Sales Force in the Industry" award, scoring highest in six of the survey's eight categories including "Recruiting Top Salespeople," "Quality of Training," "Opening New Accounts," "Holding Accounts," and "Reputation Among Customers."

AB Astra, founded in 1913, was headquartered in Sweden but more than 85% of its sales were from subsidiaries in 25 countries and through agents and licensees in another 100 countries. North America accounted for 13% of Astra's sales and, in the United States, Astra operated a sales force that sold anesthetics to hospitals and a 150-person sales force (established in 1991) that sold cardiovascular and asthma products to office-based physicians. Neither Astra sales unit in the United States sold the products carried by A/M. Between 1982 and 1991, Astra's sales increased 356% (compared to Merck's sales increase of 181% over this period), its earnings before taxes increased from 785 SEKm to 3,410 SEKm (334%), and its debt/equity ratio decreased from 85% to 34%. This performance had made Astra by 1992 the 28th largest pharmaceutical company in the world, based on sales (Merck was #1); and, according to an industry observer, "Astra now has the financial resources to build its own American operations, if it chooses to."

Products and Marketing Strategy

The products currently sold by A/M address two therapeutic areas: gastrointestinal (GI) and cardiovascular (CV) diseases.

GI included ulcers and inflammation of the esophagus. About 10–15% of the world's population have peptic ulcer—and a larger proportion have esophagitis—at some point in their lives. Research at Astra during the early 1980s resulted in a new therapy: inhibition of the enzyme acting as the "acid pump" in the body. PRILOSEC was the first drug on the market incorporating this therapy and, by 1993, had received regulatory approval in 60 countries and been prescribed for more than 25 million treatments. In the United States and Japan, about half the world's market for GI products, GI prescriptions had grown about 15% annually since the introduction of acid inhibitors. In the United States, PRILOSEC competed with drugs such as ZANTAC (owned by Glaxo and co-promoted in the United States by more than 3,000 Glaxo and Roche salespeople) and TAGAMET (see **Exhibit 2**). PRILOSEC had patent protection until the year 2000.

CV diseases included high blood pressure and angina pectoris (the heart does not receive enough oxygen), and is the most common cause of death and disability in industrialized countries. CV drugs, which included older agents called beta-blockers and newer agents known as calcium antagonists, formed the largest single product segment for pharmaceuticals, growing at about 10% annually over the past decade. PLENDIL, a calcium antagonist for the treatment of hypertension, was taken once a day and (unlike most other calcium antagonists) did not have any adverse side effects on the heart. In the United States, PLENDIL competed with a wide variety of CV drugs including PROCARDIA (sold by Pfizer) and CARDIZEM CD (sold by Marion Merrell Dow), and had patent protection until the year 2000. TONOCARD, an older drug developed by Astra, was used to treat certain ventricular arrhythmias (heart palpitations).

Commenting on A/M's product line, Mr. Yetter noted: "Astra has until 1995 to decide whether to take an equity position in A/M and, until then, it won't divulge what products in its pipeline might be suitable for A/M. Not knowing which drugs are in the pipeline, we must train our people for those we have today. But since A/M is a development and marketing entity, without a basic R&D function, we must also build an organization that, longer term, can sell products from a variety of sources in a number of therapeutic areas."

Yetter had started as a product manager with Merck in 1977 and, by the late 1980s, was vice president of Merck's Far East/Pacific operations. When he became general manager of A/M, he recruited Mr. Emmens, who had started as a sales representative with Merck and, by 1990, was a senior sales executive for one of Merck's U.S. field organizations. With others in the newly formed A/M Group, Yetter and Emmens developed a "Vision 2000" statement of A/M's basic philosophy and approach (see **Exhibit 3**). Emmens noted that a key part of A/M's approach was the ability to gather, focus, and disseminate relevant information to customers:

> Pharmaceutical companies ultimately provide two things: drugs and information. Customers always need information to treat patients: some need more medical information; others may need economic or administrative information. Information is what adds value to the products.
>
> But the traditional pharmaceutical firm has positioned itself to provide information that is narrowly focused on its products and in such a way that this information is perceived as a biased "pitch" by the customer. Samples and product literature become the focus of the interaction, not the treatment issues or broader objectives of the customer. Meanwhile, the proliferation of sales reps in this industry over the past decade has increased the noise level to the point where physicians, so accustomed to hearing the role-played sales pitch from reps, in turn role-play their responses even when no change in decision making is taking place.
>
> A/M has been conceived and developed as an information company in a different sense. This involves technology, training, specialization, and improved support capabilities intended to make customers more accessible and willing to look at initiatives that go be-

yond price and product. We really see this as a once-in-a-lifetime opportunity to build a better way of doing things and raise the standard
for marketing throughout the industry.

Market Developments

There are three types of pharmaceuticals. Ethical pharmaceuticals,
available by prescription only, were usually patent protected. Generic drugs
were low-priced, off-patent products, developed by firms with limited research and development functions and lower marketing costs than ethical
pharmaceutical firms. Over-the-counter (OTC) drugs were nonprescription
medicines sold direct to end-users. All three types of products might be present in a therapeutic area. As well as patented products in the GI area, for
example, OTC drug Pepto Bismol and generic drugs were also available.

Ethical pharmaceuticals accounted for 80% of industry sales and profits. In 1992, manufacturers of ethical pharmaceuticals allocated about 15%
of sales to R&D, 10–15% for manufacturing expenses, 20–30% on sales and
marketing and 10–15% on administrative and distribution functions, with
profit margins of 25–35%. Clinical trials accounted for about two-thirds of
R&D costs. Compensation for salespeople ranged from $40,000 to $60,000
annually and, including promotional and travel expenses, involved fully-
burdened costs of $100,000 to $200,000 per rep. Sales managers (who supervised five to 50 reps) typically earned more than $60,000.

According to a study by the Association of American Advertising
Agencies, in 1991, U.S. drug companies spent about $6 billion promoting
their products: $3.5 billion on "detailing" (the costs of salespeople and the
materials they use to inform health-care professionals about pharmaceuticals); $2 billion on sampling and various educational activities; $450 million
on advertising in medical journals; and $50 million on direct mail. One in-
dustry observer noted that heavy marketing costs were often associated
with new products: "product life cycles are shortening, forcing companies
to introduce products aggressively. You get one shot at a product launch
and must make the most of it. Ironically, some firms posting weak quarterly
earnings are those with the most productive new product flow."

In the United States, industry sales by customer segment/channel
were:

	1986	1992
Nonmanaged/Private-Office Physicians:	60%	43%
Preferred Provider Organizations (PPO):	5	15
Hospitals:	20	11
Mail-Order:	2	10
Medicaid:	6	9
Health Maintenance Organizations (HMO):	2	7
Federal Government:	3	3
Nursing Homes:	2	2

The 550,000 *office-based physicians* in the United States were the primary target for pharmaceutical firms. In 1990, about 70% of U.S. physicians were self-employed, while more than 20% were affiliated with at least one HMO or PPO. More than 35% of their revenues came from patients covered by government-funded Medicare (which did *not* include drugs in its coverage) and Medicaid (which *does* cover prescription drugs). Reps called on doctors every 4–6 weeks to leave samples and build a relationship based on product information, promotions, and personal contact. One industry observer described a traditional call on a private-office physician:

> On the first call, the rep often sees the doctor between patients and receives about 2 minutes of time. It takes 30 seconds to say hello and identify yourself, your company, and the product being promoted. The rep then gives a brief overview of the product and leaves samples and product literature. If time permits, the rep moves on to other products. Subsequent calls will involve more product literature, office supplies, food, and other gifts; hosting "educational" seminars at fancy spots is still a popular sales tool. Over time, sheer persistence and call coverage—and the fact that historically price was not the primary concern—developed a dialogue with the doctor. And once doctors prescribed a drug, they usually remained brand loyal.
>
> By contrast, calls on HMOs or PPOs are strictly by appointment with the director of Purchasing or a Formulary Committee of MDs and administrators. Detailed product information, about the therapeutic area and alternative medications, is necessary. Physician input is important but, given basic levels of safety and efficacy, the group's system economics often drive buying decisions.

Health Maintenance Organizations and *Preferred Provider Organizations* were forms of "managed care" that provided health care to enrolled members for a fixed payment. HMOs had enrolled about 15% of the U.S. population by 1990 and PPOs about 20%. Most HMOs offered a prescription drug plan to members and managed pharmaceutical costs by therapeutic substitution (use of another drug with nearly identical chemical formulation), preferred product programs, treatment protocols, and formularies (lists of approved drugs available to HMO physicians). In recent years, some HMOs had banned detailing of HMO physicians by pharmaceutical sales reps, and some had instituted "counter-selling" programs to persuade member physicians to prescribe formulary-listed drugs. A PPO was a contractual arrangement between a group of health-care providers and an insurance company to provide care at a negotiated price. Medical providers agreed to fees of 5–30% off customary charges in exchange for greater volume. About 50% of PPOs also offered prescription plans (for formulary-approved drugs) in 1992.

Mail-order firms provided an alternative to purchase and order-fulfillment at local pharmacies, and were utilized by many corporate, government, and retirement-association health plans. Mail-order firms purchased directly from the manufacturer (via the maximum quantity discount available) and dispensed a 90-day supply of medication instead of the typical 30-day supply, reducing transaction and usage costs. Hence, mail-order was best suited for medication used to treat chronic conditions which required frequent refilling of prescriptions (e.g., heart disease and ulcers). Mail order sales of pharmaceuticals, less than $100 million in 1981, were more than $2 billion by 1991. Most mail-order firms also had approved formularies, and some had "pharmacy benefits management" programs in which the firm's pharmacists contacted prescribing physicians to discuss less costly generic drugs or other alternative products in the therapeutic category.

"In reviewing market trends," noted Mr. Yetter, "we see three key areas of change that will alter the way pharmaceutical firms compete in the future."

Managed care institutions limited a patient's choice of doctors and hospitals, and eschewed traditional fee-for-service physician compensation in favor of cost controls aimed at diagnosing and treating ailments with fewer tests and visits. By 1993, 56% of Americans in group health plans were enrolled in managed care networks, up from 29% in 1988. Forecasts indicated that, by 1995, 20% of prescription sales in the United States would be from pharmacies in managed care facilities and another 35% via contracts between retail pharmacies and managed care institutions. Kaiser Permanente, one of the largest managed-care groups, handled drug buying in the following manner:

> In many Kaiser facilities, drug salespeople can't see Kaiser physicians during patient hours but must offer presentations at, say, lunchtime. Free samples go to the Kaiser pharmacy, not to doctors. Detailers may pitch only drugs already on the Kaiser formulary and must sometimes share the podium with a house pharmacist who boosts competing products.[1]

Government regulations affected pharmaceuticals in various ways. The so-called "Dingell Bill" significantly restricted the numbers and types of samples that could be given to physicians. Other regulations effectively limited many physician-directed incentives to less than $100 in value, while proposed regulations would restrict pharmaceutical promotional literature so that it more closely resembled product labeling. In addition, President Clinton had made health care a key issue in his campaign and had appointed a task force to draft legislation. The task force had singled-out drugs for attention and, in particular, recent price increases:

---

[1]"Drugmakers Get a Taste of Their Own Medicine," *Business Week* (April 26, 1993), p. 105.

	1990	1991	1992
Producer price index increase	5.70%	-0.10%	-0.10%
Prescription drug price increase	10.60	10.10	5.90

Source: U.S. Bureau of Labor Statistics and Prescription Pricing Report.

In response, ten pharmaceutical firms (including Merck) had offered to hold annual price increases to the rate of inflation. In 1993, moreover, this task force was reviewing various options, including price controls, the addition of drugs to Medicare benefits, and mandatory health-care plans that would extend Medicaid-type coverage to previously uninsured people.

Research and development costs in the industry had increased. A 17-year patent was granted to a firm when a compound was isolated and, typically, for every 10,000 compounds patented, clinical trials would be conducted on 100, and only one would actually gain approval. The costs associated with developing and bringing a drug to market, about $54 million in 1976, were an estimated $231 million by 1991. At the same time, the effective patent life had been declining in the United States, from about 16 years in 1960 to an average of less than 10 years by the 1990s. Of the 30 best-selling drugs in the United States in 1992, 14 would be off-patent by the end of 1996, leaving billions in annual sales vulnerable to lower-priced generic competition.

Mr. Emmens commented:

> These developments mean that the "customer" is shifting from the individual private-practice physician to large managed-care companies that, under pressure from the government, insurers and competitors, demand lower prices. Physicians will continue to be important, but their access to products will often be controlled by a strictly enforced formulary. This sets up a push-pull marketing environment: contractual agreements are needed to provide and maintain access to products that individual physicians then decide how and when to use.
>
> It also requires a redefinition of the sales function. Managed care committees are less persuaded by studies that demonstrate a product's scientific merit but ignore cost-effectiveness. Physicians themselves are becoming less affected by traditional promotional methods and are limiting their exposure to reps. Moreover, in the context of higher R&D costs and more price competition, many firms will be looking for new selling and promotional methods that are more efficient and effective than traditional methods.

ORGANIZATION AND MARKETING PROGRAMS

Exhibit 4 indicates A/M's organization in early 1993. "A/M is a development and marketing entity, not a research company," noted Yetter, "and we must capitalize on this difference. We've tried to organize from the customer inward and with multi-disciplined teams as the basic building blocks."

Development and Licensing

Development referred to the process of turning a chemical compound into an approved drug. Phase I was the preclinical phase where, via animal testing, a compound was demonstrated to work against a particular disease. Phase II involved studies of test patients. Phase III entailed large-scale studies which verified efficacy and dosage levels as well as any side-effects of the drug. Dr. Irwin Scher, vice president of Drug Development and Medical Affairs, noted:

> On the surface, regulatory requirements seem straightforward and, for a fee, contract houses will manage this for pharmaceutical firms. But the application of science to regulatory requirements is complex. The questions asked by regulators tend to change during the process of clinical trials, and experience in a therapeutic area helps to anticipate and shape the appropriate studies.
>
> At A/M, we expect development opportunities to come from smaller firms who lack the experience or resources to manage this process, and from non-U.S. firms who are attracted to the big U.S. market but also wary of the lengthy, expensive drug-approval process here. In this way, we expect to be a "compound magnet": a firm that takes products from multiple sources through development to marketing. Our advantage should reside in our therapeutic specializations and in the field's ability to get the attention of researchers and physicians in our chosen therapeutic areas.

Cheryl Rothwell, director of Licensing and Business Development, added:

> We have two basic licensing markets: pharmaceutical and biotech companies. Traditionally, pharmaceutical firms look for product trades, royalties, or co-promotion opportunities. Biotech firms often lack the experience and resources for clinical trials and large-scale marketing. Without R&D, we have no compounds to trade but prospective licensors won't be competing with in-house compounds going through the development process. In addition, we will have therapeutic specialties and a field force that should be more efficient and effective in business development.
>
> Another advantage should be our responsiveness to potential licensors. Industry-wide, the process takes 47–54 weeks from the initial phone calls between two firms to the actual contract negotiation. With clear objectives on a select number of therapeutic areas, we should be able to shrink this time to 6 months.
>
> In the year 2000, the products currently licensed from Astra go off patent, and generic competition usually means a 40–60% decline in

revenue for off-patent drugs. Based on my experience in the industry, moreover, I estimate that you can expect one development success for every 50 compounds that you license. Also, even if Astra does invest in A/M and we have access to their R&D, Astra works in a number of therapeutic areas besides GI and CV, and we will have little control over their research directions. My job is ultimately to ensure that we have appropriate products to sell.

Rothwell had created two positions within Licensing. "Licensing segment champions" were based in the field and responsible for identifying opportunities within a therapeutic segment. "Solutions integrators" at headquarters were responsible for analyzing the business case for a potential compound. This involved integrating the pertinent legal, regulatory, patent, and market forecasting issues that affected drug development and marketing. "We haven't started promoting our open-to-buy yet," noted Rothwell, "but I already receive about two calls per month from prospective licensors. However, there's a limit to the number of therapeutic areas that we can cover effectively, and we're still in the process of defining what those areas should be."

David Brennan, executive director of Marketing and Sales Planning, was a liaison with Licensing and Development groups. For this purpose, A/M had established Pharmaceutical Solutions Management (PSM) teams in its current therapeutic areas (GI and CV). PSM teams were comprised of representatives from development, licensing, marketing, sales, product sourcing, business research, distribution and information services. "The goal," noted Brennan, "is to develop a better cross-functional understanding of the business opportunity inherent in a product, the information and distribution requirements involved in serving different customers, and the ongoing concerns of users and physicians in a therapeutic area. This combination of development and marketing perspectives is unique in the industry, and is intended to develop our expertise, credibility, and (over time) product and service line in each area."

Information, Education & Services and Business Research

Information, Education & Services (IES) provided field units with information and support necessary to deliver pharmaceutical solutions to customers. This involved various patient and physician services sponsored by A/M and delivered at physicians' offices, hospitals, or HMOs (see **Exhibit 5** for examples) as well as more traditional promotional activities. Dorene Kronke, executive director of IES, noted that "we are building a repertoire of services here at headquarters, while decentralizing the design and use of services to field units":

In most pharmaceutical firms, the field must execute a very strictly defined detailing plan and doesn't have the autonomy to allocate its budget differently much less design and execute local programs. Here, we devote significant resources to developing IES opportunities that the field "purchases" in accord with its own analysis of specific customer needs and opportunities.

About half of current IES services are traditional industry promotions. But the other half are innovative ideas such as patient education videos, training sessions for clinical staff, seminars for physicians on financial management and reimbursement procedures, and vouchers for purchasing medical textbooks in our therapeutic specialties. At corporate we supply the expertise and contacts with third parties needed to develop a program, and then disseminate successful programs throughout the field organization.

Another IES responsibility is the information infrastructure upon which solutions-selling depends. For example, we provide field offices with desktop-publishing abilities and on-line access to the National Library of Medicine, a source of journal articles and other information. Most pharmaceutical firms won't spend money on such services, because marketing dollars are held by product managers who allocate budgets to product-specific promotions. IES is also a conduit for access to other parts of A/M that the rep may need in answer to a physician or administrator's question. The goal is to position our field reps as therapeutic specialists providing value beyond the cost-effective drugs they sell.

Each field unit at A/M had developed its own criteria for evaluating IES opportunities. One field manager noted that "our selling approach requires that we stay one step ahead in value-added service provision." An A/M salesperson commented: "Many firms give physicians or clinics research grants as a promotional device. But organizing a patient education evening with the physician or administrator can be more effective. Once the check is written, doctors forget who donated how much. But they remember which representative worked with them in educating patients about an illness or therapy. It reflects well on both the physician and Astra/Merck."

Business Research, headed by Diana Scott, handled market and customer research. Scott noted that "With pharmacies now tied to information systems, we can get detailed information about who prescribes how much of a product, our share in a category, trends in each territory, and who uses each product. We've invested in technology that makes this data easily accessible in the field." Scott also noted that this information played another role:

We're identifying new segmentation criteria that better capture customer needs and values in a changing environment. All customers want "effective" therapy, but the treatment context and outcomes vary. For example, organizations like the AARP (American Association of Retired Persons) are bigger forces in medical care and they value a drug's contribution to longevity; insurers and managed care organizations typically value a patient's return to the work force.

HMOs are a diverse group; some focus predominantly on medical and others on economic criteria in sourcing drugs. Identifying and responding to these differences are fundamental to our marketing strategy. Providing pharmaceutical solutions in large part means providing customer-specific information in an environment where cost containment forces different customers to focus on outcomes, not consumption, in different ways.

Exhibit 6 indicates preliminary segment descriptions based on initial research.

Planning and Distribution

Kenneth Murtha, director of Product Sourcing & Distribution, commented: "Sourcing and distribution are intimately linked in a company without a manufacturing operation, while distribution is a key sales support function in a company with customer-focused field units." In early 1993, A/M planned to work with one distributor (with multiple stocking locations) that provided products to 80 drug wholesalers who distributed products to hospitals, pharmacies, and other customer locations. Murtha noted that this channel structure differed from that of most pharmaceutical firms: "Merck, for example, has about 55,000 direct accounts in its U.S. distribution channel. Industry-wide, physical distribution accounts for 2–3% of manufacturers' sales. With a leaner channel and on-line links, we can shrink inventory and distribution costs to less than 1% of sales. I consider A/M to be analogous to Nike or other firms that, in effect, outsource manufacturing and distribution. We can be cash-flow driven because we're not asset intensive."

For field sales units, Materials Control distributed samples, product literature, and promotional items. Murtha explained that "efficiencies in this area are complicated by our decentralized field structure. Reps in each territory are developing customized ideas, and my organization provides the infrastructure for execution." Murtha also noted that the therapeutic areas handled by A/M were a key input to sourcing and distribution decisions: "Merck covers 27 therapeutic areas; A/M currently covers two. That explains a lot of the difference in channel structure. Depending upon how we expand across therapeutic areas or customer services, new channels may be necessary."

Robert Holmes, director of Strategic Planning, explained that "At A/M, like any pharmaceutical company, we generate revenue by the sale of pills. But unlike other companies, we believe that a customer focus, rather than a product focus, will lead to higher sales. Our approach assumes that value-added services will create a relationship that ultimately translates into better access to decision makers (a scarce resource in our industry) and better sales." Holmes also noted that, "in an increasingly managed-care environment, we need to get on the formulary and affect purchase criteria:"

Assume there are two drugs that effectively treat a disease state. Drug X requires 1 tablet/day for 4 weeks at $1.50/tablet, which equals $42.00. Drug Y requires 2 tablets/day for 8 weeks at $.90/tablet, which equals $108.00. Drug X is more expensive on a cost/tablet basis, but more cost effective from an outcomes perspective. That, in fact, is the case with PRILOSEC. It requires us to transform purchase criteria from a cost-per-tablet to a cost-per-outcome decision. PLENDIL, by contrast, has a lower cost-per-tablet than most of its competitors.

Longer term, we have three ways to grow. One is by therapeutic category; we're currently in CV and GI, but respiratory drugs are an Astra strength. A second route is by product source; we currently sell Astra products, but after the trigger is met, other firms are potential product sources. A third route is by market potential and customer needs; selling pharmaceutical solutions takes time and money, and we must identify segments that value our product-service bundles. Our goal is to maximize potential across all three dimensions without diluting our expertise and core competencies.

Field Sales

In 1991, A/M established three pilot "business units" (i.e., field sales districts). During 1992, this was expanded to 31 business units located throughout the United States. Each business unit was considered a customer support team and had the following personnel:

A *field director* was responsible for attaining sales objectives, directing the activities of business-unit personnel in the assigned geography, and developing business relationships with key customers. A *business manager* focused on large customers such as managed care or hospital buying groups in the geography, coordinated any national contracts with these customers, and handled other administrative issues. A *customer support manager* worked with IES on designing and sourcing needed information and support services. One or two *medical information scientists* (often MDs or PhDs in a therapeutic area) provided services to influential medical professionals, and served as medical/scientific trainers for field customer support teams as well as on corporate PSM teams. One or two *administrative assistants* provided office support. About 10 *pharmaceutical specialists* in each unit were the core field force, aligned by customer type (private practice, HMO, hospital, government) and responsible for attaining product sales objectives.

On average, each business unit had a total of 16 personnel. About 60% of business-unit personnel were from Merck, while the remainder were new hires, many from outside the pharmaceutical industry. Emmens commented:

> Two principles guide us. One is that specialists should not be isolated from other members of the field but contribute, through consulting and training, to the team effort and report to the same manager. The other is that how decisions get made—including micromarketing and resource allocation—is key to customer satisfaction and facilitated by

a flatter organizational structure. Unlike traditional pharmaceutical firms, we have no "region" and "area" managers concerned with implementing a standard detail and apportioning specialist resources from corporate. Instead, we've organized the company around teams of specialists, not the other way around. Each is a business unit, measured on contribution (not the number of pills sold, as in most firms), reporting directly to headquarters, and with the authority to allocate its budget and make decisions for its customers.

In the customer's eyes, the business unit *is* Astra/Merck—a locally operated business with technological and other links to our supply, distribution, and service capabilities. Conversely, localized budgeting, responsibility for the bottom line, and teams empowered to make and implement decisions should speed responsiveness and reduce management levels. Company infrastructure can be smaller and more focused on customers rather than internal auditing of activities.

Salaries and benefits of A/M field personnel were comparable to industry norms, but incentive compensation (about 25% of a new Pharmaceutical Specialist's total remuneration) was allocated differently: about one-third was based on A/M's attainment of national goals, one-third on business-unit attainment of goals, and one-third on individual performance in the assigned territory. Moreover, most pharmaceutical firms established daily call quotas for salespeople and required a set number of annual presentations about certain products to assigned accounts. A/M had no call or presentation quotas for field personnel. "These measures are in keeping with the team orientation," noted Emmens. "The new environment requires a group of specialists working together to provide a package of information and services that may not be directly related to short-term product promotion."

Anthony Zecca, an executive director of Field Sales, noted that "Empowerment isn't anarchy: there are still sales goals that must be met. But *how* those goals are achieved has been decentralized in order to optimize flexibility and commitment." A field director added:

I work with business unit teams to develop action plans, and spend about half my time (c. 125 days/year) in the field. When hiring people, I look for people with a science background: technical knowledge is helpful when you're building on therapeutic specialties. But an MBA is also helpful because, especially at managed care accounts, more of the purchase decision is handled by people with business (rather than medical) backgrounds. Relative to the traditional pharmaceuticals salesperson, our people must be more creative in analyzing and communicating cost-in-use (versus cost-per-pill) and then utilizing our array of services.

A Pharmaceutical Specialist, who had spent years in Sales with another firm before joining A/M, commented:

The traditional "detail" is product focused and rigid, because it's aimed at maximizing call frequency by getting through the litany of "indication, feature, price" as quickly as possible. Here, the sales approach requires multiple calls aimed at selling, not just specific products, but the vendor's capabilities in areas such as information services, ongoing knowledge of the therapeutic area, order fulfillment, and customer practice development. Traditional detailing means spending significant money on promotions and entertainment; here, we spend less on those categories and more on services.

CURRENT ISSUES

Speaking in early 1993, one executive commented: "Re-engineering is the current buzzword. But A/M goes beyond re-engineering because we're not revising an existing structure. We have a clean slate, and so more degrees of freedom. But we're also not a 'complete' company, and so must excel in our core components. In turn, excellence requires ongoing evaluations of the many initiatives being developed and, precisely because we're new and different, determining the basis for evaluations raises a number of issues."

One issue being considered in early 1993 was how to measure the productivity of A/M's pharmaceutical solutions approach. **Exhibit 7** provides data about the number of people in the largest U.S. pharmaceuticals sales organizations. One executive noted that "Traditional measures of sales productivity in the industry are dollar market share in the relevant product category; share of total prescriptions in the category and, on an annual basis, the number of new prescriptions. These remain important, and certainly our corporate parents evaluate selling efforts by these criteria. But our marketing strategy is aimed at longer-term 'quality' sales; we should look at our sales by prescriber type and customer segment. There's a hierarchy of influence in the medical market, and we aim to tap the influential but increasingly unaccessible parts of that hierarchy." Another executive commented: "It clearly costs more to establish a new sales and marketing organization rather than clone an existing model—perhaps two times as much. But we expect higher set-up costs to be offset by a smaller sales force and lower operating costs than industry norms."

Another issue concerned pricing policy. One executive noted that "An interesting issue is whether, and how, we price the value-added services that we provide to customers. Our approach seeks to change the pricing paradigm to a cost-per-solution rather from a price-per-pill basis. In a sense, this is similar to what Xerox did in the 1960s when it moved from price-per-copy to selling a machine bundled with service support. But customers are under significant cost containment pressures, and many competing products will soon be off-patent. Some feel that, given a choice between price or service, many customers will opt for a lower product acquisition price, and our pricing structure should reflect these choices."

A third issue concerned field management systems. A/M executives believed that the flatter sales organization and team approach improved communication and responsiveness. But the structure also eliminated the hierarchy that constituted the traditional career path for successful field personnel. One field executive noted: "We currently have a motivated group focused on building the pharmaceutical firm of the future. But about 35% of our Pharmaceutical Specialists are less than 30 years old, and more than 65% are less than 40. Career path is an issue in a flat organization that stresses specialties and relationships." A related issue concerned the bonus structure. One executive noted that the stress on national and business-unit objectives was intended to promote teamwork, and "we've seen that happen. Last year, for example, some business units loaned staff to other units that were not staffed sufficiently to meet market needs. That would never happen in most pharmaceutical firms, where each district (and each rep in each district) is ranked and bonuses paid accordingly. But the necessity to meet trigger provides a focused goal that helps teamwork, and thus far we've met our goals. In the future, with more generic drugs in our categories, national and individual business-unit goals may actually prevent people from attaining their bonuses even if they achieve their individual goals. The compensation system may then be perceived differently by people in the field."

Another issue concerned the longer-term implications of being a "compound magnet" on sales and marketing systems. One executive noted that "The CV and GI areas are increasingly crowded. In 1980, for example, there were 187 CV drugs on the market; by 1990, there were 373, and many big ones will be off-patent in a few years. To maximize our value to our owners, we must expand into other therapeutic classes." However, others believed that A/M should concentrate on its strengths in the CV and GI areas. One executive commented: "Our approach depends upon specialization. Our edge is in providing information pertinent to a therapeutic solution. If we license drugs across a variety of therapeutic areas, we may dilute that expertise and run the risk of looking like other pharmaceutical firms. Their reps have a little information about each of many products but no in-depth knowledge about any one therapeutic category." Another commented: "Specialization may sound narrow, but it need not be. Both GI and CV are big categories that are likely to get bigger as the U.S. population grows older."

All of these issues, moreover, had to be considered in the context of making the level of sales required to "trigger" the original joint venture agreement. At the end of 1992, achievement of "trigger" sales was still uncertain. A/M's 1993 sales would need to be 50% higher than 1992 sales in order to reach the sales trigger by the end of 1993.

EXHIBIT 1   Financial Information About A/M Parent Companies

Merck & Co., Inc., and Subsidiaries ($ in millions except per-share amounts)

	1992	1991	1990
Sales	$9,662.5	$8,602.7	$7,671.5
Income before taxes	3,563.6	3,166.7	2,698.8
Taxes	1,117.0	1,045.0	917.6
Net income	2,446.6	2,121.7	1,781.2
Earnings per share	2.12	1.83	1.52
R&D expenses	1,111.6	1,041.5	670.8
Net income as % of assets	24.1%	24.2%	24.1%

Percentage of Sales by Therapeutic Area (1991)

Cardiovasculars	48%	Ophthalmologicals	5%
Antibiotics	11	Vaccines	5
Anti-ulcerants	10	Other human health	5
Analgesics	6	Animal health/crop protection	10

AB Astra, Inc. and Subsidiaries (SEK in millions except per-share amounts)

	1992	1991	1990
Sales	15,568	12,501	9,420
Licensing income	704	573	412
Pretax earnings	5,120	3,410	2,507
Earnings per share, SEK	28.80	18.00	11.90
Return on equity	42.1%	33.9%	27.4%
R&D expenditures	2,488	1,967	1,573
Capital expenditures	1,967	2,117	1,054

Percentage of Sales by Therapeutic Area (1991)

Gastrointestinal	26%	Anti-infective agents	6%
Respiratory	23	Medical care products	2
Cardiovascular	20	Other products	8
Local anesthetics	15		

EXHIBIT 2 Product and Market Data (Sales [$] and Prescription [Rx] Data in millions)

	1991	1992
PRILOSEC	$205.4	$301.0
PLENDIL	15.5	23.9
TONOCARD	15.0	12.5

U.S. Market Data (1992)

PRILOSEC		
Total Market	$3,500	Rx: 58
ZANTAC	1,630	25
TAGAMET	584	11
PEPCID	342	6
PRILOSEC	301	4
AXID	242	4

PLENDIL		
Total Market	$2,700	Rx: 70.5
PROCARDIA XL	880.9	21.0
CALAN SR & Isop	542.0	15.5
CARDIZEM SR	262.8	6.0
CARDIZEM CD	202.8	4.6
PLENDIL	23.9	0.6

Estimated Worldwide Sales of Pharmaceuticals by Therapeutic Area

Therapeutic Area	1990 Sales ($bn)	Growth over Previous Year
Cardiovascular	$22.3	+16.3%
Gastrointestinal	21.2	+13.3
Antibacterials	15.8	+13.9
Central nervous system	14.1	+13.6
Respiratory system	10.5	+17.8
Musculo-skeletal	8.6	+15.3
Genito-urinary/hormone	7.3	+14.2
Dermatological	5.9	+12.4
Anti-cancer	3.5	+21.2
Others	18.9	+18.8
Total	$128.1	+15.4%

Top-Selling Pharmaceuticals in the United States

Product (Manufacturer)		Ailment Treated	1992 U.S. Sales ($ millions)	Year Patent Expires
ZANTAC	(Glaxo)	Ulcers	$1,734.6	1995
PROCARDIA	(Pfizer)	Hypertension angina	1,000.0	2003
MEVACOR	(Merck)	High cholesterol	1,040.0	1999
CARDIZEM	(Marion Dow)	Hypertension angina	922.0	1994
PROZAC	(Eli Lilly)	Depression	835.0	2001
VASOTEC	(Merck)	Hypertension	835.0	2000
TAGAMET	(Smith Kline Beecham)	Ulcers	647.5	1994

OUR MISSION
What business are we in?

To develop and provide pharmaceutical products and innovative services that are highly valued by our customers and consistently exceed their expectations.

OUR STRATEGIC INTENT
What competitive endpoint do we seek?

To *revolutionize the pharmaceutical industry* by being the best at *linking patients and products* through *unique, responsive, customer-shaped pharmaceutical solutions.*

OUR VALUE PROPOSITIONS
How will we add value to those with whom we do business?

- For our <u>customers</u>, we will *create customized health-care solutions that help them deliver optimal patient care.*
- For our <u>licensors</u>, we will *provide customized solutions* in addition to *unique "quids," rapid development, and innovative marketing and sales.*
- For our <u>owners</u>, we will *contribute to their overall financial objectives,* while *increasing their share of the U.S. market* and *providing a broadened portfolio of products.*
- For <u>each other</u>, we will *build and nurture a fun, high-energy team* that *rewards creative entrepreneurial action* and *realizes individual aspirations.*

OUR TARGET OUTCOMES
How will we know we have achieved what we intend?

- We will be *faster than other firms* in the industry in taking a new product *from clinical development into the hands of the patients.*
- We will be the *company "customers ask first"* by being the leading source of health-care information and services.
- Our marketing and sales organization will be *emulated by other pharmaceutical companies* and *recognized by customers and regulators as being the best in the industry.*
- We will be the *company of choice* when others wish to license their products.
- We will be the *best provider of pharmaceutical solutions* in targeted therapeutic segments.
- We will *consistently exceed industry norms* for growth and return on investment.
- We will *attract and retain the best people* and people having equivalent opportunities elsewhere *will choose Astra/Merck.*

OUR VALUES
What qualities do we care about?

Truth	...to customers, business partners, and employees grounded in ethics and integrity
Responsibility	...to provide valued products and services to patients and our customers, and satisfying work and career opportunities to our employees
Unity	...of purpose and belief that customers will determine our ultimate success
Support	...to customers through information, products, and employee excellence for the benefit of patients
Teamwork	...belief that teams are built by individuals contributing toward a shared vision

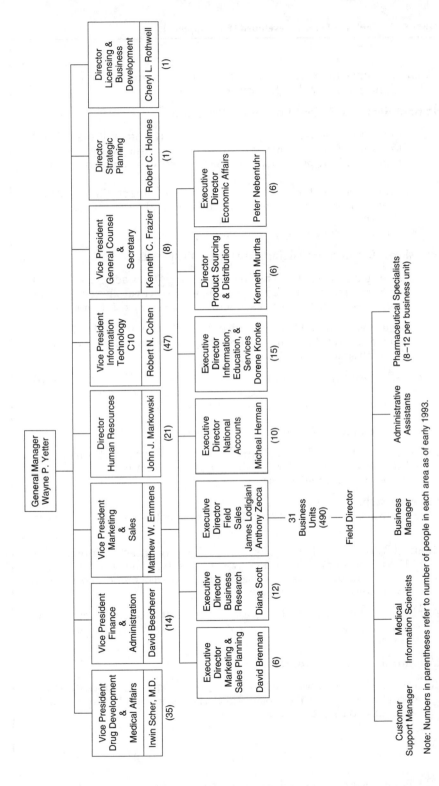

General Manager
Wayne P. Yetter

Vice President Drug Development & Medical Affairs
Irwin Scher, M.D.
(35)

Vice President Finance & Administration
David Bescherer
(14)

Vice President Marketing & Sales
Matthew W. Emmens

Director Human Resources
John J. Markowski
(21)

Vice President Information Technology C10
Robert N. Cohen
(47)

Vice President General Counsel & Secretary
Kenneth C. Frazier
(8)

Director Strategic Planning
Robert C. Holmes
(1)

Director Licensing & Business Development
Cheryl L. Rothwell
(1)

Executive Director Marketing & Sales Planning
David Brennan
(6)

Executive Director Business Research
Diana Scott
(12)

Executive Director Field Sales
James Lodigiani
Anthony Zecca

Executive Director National Accounts
Micheal Herman
(10)

Executive Director Information, Education, & Services
Dorene Kronke
(15)

Director Product Sourcing & Distribution
Kenneth Murtha
(6)

Executive Director Economic Affairs
Peter Nebenfuhr
(6)

31 Business Units (490)

Field Director

Customer Support Manager

Medical Information Scientists

Business Manager

Administrative Assistants

Pharmaceutical Specialists (8–12 per business unit)

Note: Numbers in parentheses refer to number of people in each area as of early 1993.

EXHIBIT 4 Astra/Merck Group

349

EXHIBIT 5   Examples of Locally Developed IES Components

"Contact" office refers to the A/M field business unit that initially developed the service with IES support.

Patient Services/Patient Education Programs

"Evening with a Dietitian"   (Contact: Kansas City)
- Discussion of diet for patients with GI or hypertension disorders
- Dietitian delivers program in a physician's office or at local hospital

Patient Education Seminars   (Contact: Philadelphia)
- Evening program held by nurse practitioners and/or nutritionists at local hospitals
- Each session covers a specific disease topic

Physician Services/Physician Education Programs

"Developing a Practice: Consulting Services"   (Contact: New Jersey)
- Arranging for experienced physicians with successful practices to advise newly trained physicians in setting up an office-based practice

"Partnering with State Health Services"   (Contact: South Chicago)
- Seminar for A/M customers on reimbursement procedures in conjunction with state health officials

Cardio-Pulmonary Resuscitation Certification   (Contact: Boston)
- Training programs conducted at local physicians' offices in conjunction with local American Red Cross or American Heart Association personnel
- Provide CPR certification and recertification

Business Consulting: "Networking"   (Contact: Minneapolis)
- Utilize databases and/or E-mail in order to contact physicians in other offices or clinics with similar needs

Patient Teaching Programs   (Contact: Akron, Ohio)
- Sponsorship of speakers specifically for patient teaching in various areas

Medical Information Fair   (Contact: Minneapolis)
- Held at a hospital to demonstrate A/M's available services for customers, including literature searchers, slide generation, lab services, and medical record capabilities

Analysis of Pharmaceutical Reports   (Contact: Akron, Ohio)
- Assisting customers in analyzing reports received from pharmacy management companies

Community Service Programs

"Domestic Violence Program"   (Contact: Boston)
- Speakers presented the topic to 75 attendees at a local hospital (MDs, nurses, and hospital president)

Drug Information Talks   (Contact: Houston)
  • Information on drug abuse for medical and paramedical personnel

Patient Education Materials   (Contact: Indianapolis)
  • Information about printed material and videos published by various associations and available at no/minimal cost (e.g., American Diabetes Association, American Heart Association, American Cancer Society, etc.)

EXHIBIT 6 Customer Segment Analysis Tools

Preliminary Segment Descriptions
Each segment may be characterized by its unique profile of needs and values.

Segment	Description
Medical Traditionalists	Members of this segment place great importance on patient-specific issues. They are not very interested in research or business issues (below average in both cases). They seek high-quality products and also value Educational Services. This segment also demonstrates an interest in developing loyalty to a product, company, or representative. They do not value an operating style that relies on procedures or controls. Physicians are the dominant force within this group, while HMOs, hospitals, and public facilities under-represented.
Health Care as a Business	This segment demonstrates above average interest in both patient and business issues. They rate costs as important, but rate patient satisfaction and quality management higher than the "Cost Conscious" segment. They are the least interested in partnering, but do value educational services. They seem to be less interested in opportunities to develop loyalty toward a product, company or representative. This segment represents those customers wrestling with the core health-care challenges and will likely be the most dynamic in terms of shifting needs and value. It contains the greatest balance among customer types, with physicians and hospitals nearing their representation in the overall market. Clinics, however, are significantly over-represented and HMOs have about half the share in this group as they do in the overall market.
Medical Thought Leader	Members of this segment have a greater than average interest in both patients and scientific research (particularly the latter). They have a much lower (below average) interest in business issues. They desire product quality most and are interested more in partnerships than educational services. Physicians and hospitals represent a higher percentage of this segment than of the population as a whole, while HMOs, clinics, and group practices are under-represented.
Cost Conscious	This segment is most focused on business issues. They view cost-per-pill as the most important issue and are the only segment that rated costs more important than other product attributes. They have little interest in research and the least interest in patient-related issues. They are somewhat interested in business services, but in general do not value educational services. Their interest in partnering is primarily related to contracts. HMOs make up over 36% of this segment, although they are only 13% of the total sample, and public institutions also play a greater role than in the general market. In addition, physicians are significantly under-represented, both as individuals and group practices.

EXHIBIT 7   U.S. Pharmaceuticals Sales Force Data

Company	U.S. sales ($ millions)	Size of U.S sales force 1992	% chg. from 1991	Managed care sales force 1992	Managed care sales force 1991
American Home Products Corp.	$3,338.0	3,250	NA	0	0
Abbott Laboratories	1,883.0	3,140	NA	NA	NA
Bristol-Myers Squibb Co.	3,258.0	3,000	(18.2)	0	0
Johnson & Johnson	2,793.0	3,000	NA	NA	NA
SmithKline Beecham	2,470.1	2,450	NA	NA	NA
Glaxo, Inc.	2,774.7	2,445	8.7	0	0
Merck & Co. Inc.	3,338.0	2,434	(9.9)	33	30
Pfizer Inc.	2,251.7	2,346	4.7	21	10
Schering-Plough Corp.	1,720.5	2,100	8.5	0	0
Warner-Lambert Co.	1,557.0	2,000	3.4	0	0
Ciba	1,878.0	1,600	8.9	0	0
Eli Lilly and Co.	2,704.2	1,600	NA	NA	NA
Marion Merrell Dow Inc.	1,965.6	1,500	(16.7)	0	0
The Upjohn Co.	1,613.8	1,500	5.5	0	0
Miles Inc. (pharm. & consumer)	1,061.7	1,397	3.5	14	11
Hoffman-La Roche Inc.	1,111.4	1,340	3.1	0	0
Rhone-Poulenc Rorer Inc.	656.5	1,249	24.3	7	0
Sandoz Pharmaceuticals Corp.	1,134.0	1,100	(8.3)	0	0
Syntex Laboratories Inc.	1,120.6	1,100	(11.3)	20	0
American Cyanamid Co.	795.8	1,025	25.0	25	20
G. D. Searle & Co.	744.3	1,000	47.1	10	10
Zeneca Pharmaceuticals Group	1,022.5	1,000	25.0	25	13
Procter & Gamble Pharmaceuticals	1,051.7	898	0.2	0	0
Burroughs Wellcome Co.	1,121.2	850	6.3	20	20
Hoechst-Roussel Pharmaceuticals	519.6	800	0.0	0	0
Sterling Winthrop Inc.	543.2	630	(3.1)	0	0
DuPont Merck Pharmaceutical	522.9	600	0.0	0	0
Organon Inc.	142.2	486	58.3	0	0
Berlex Laboratories	121.0	483	38.4	3	3
Forest Laboratories Inc.	215.0	450	12.5	0	0
Fisons Corp.	236.6	425	5.2	0	0
Carter-Wallace Inc.	287.3	395	8.5	0	0
Astra USA Inc.	143.8	350	40.0	12	10
Genentech Inc.	187.3	350	0.0	0	0
Knoll Pharmaceuticals	236.6	350	4.5	12	8
Solvay Pharmaceuticals	99.2	332	16.1	5	3
Block Drug Co. Inc.	205.5	308	(12.0)	0	0
Boots Pharmaceuticals Inc.	258.6	251	39.4	6	0
Amgen Inc.	521.4	225	2.7	0	0
Kabi Pharmacia Inc.	42.6	220	11.1	0	0
Ivax Corp.	221.3	214	0.9	0	0
Novo Nordisk	89.5	202	9.2	6	0

EXHIBIT 7   U.S. Pharmaceuticals Sales Force Data (*Continued*)

Company	U.S. sales ($ millions)	Size of U.S sales force 1992	% chg. from 1991	Managed care sales force 1992	Managed care sales force 1991
3M Pharmaceuticals	168.4	200	0.0	0	0
Fujisawa USA Inc.	182.6	159	(37.6)	0	0
Connaught Laboratories Inc.	21.8	117	(13.3)	5	5
Anaquest/BOC	211.5	109	36.3	0	0
Chiron Corp.	22.9	100	33.3	0	0
Serono Laboratories Inc.	147.5	93	10.7	5	3
ICN Pharmaceuticals Inc.	43.9	50	0.0	0	0
Alpha Therapeutic/ Green Cross	37.3	48	17.1	0	0
TOTAL	48,530.0	50,976	6.5		

Case 11

Hewlett-Packard Imaging Systems Division: Sonos 100 C/F Introduction

In August 1992, Cynthia Danaher, Marketing Manager for the Imaging Systems business unit (ISY) at Hewlett-Packard Medical Products Group, was considering issues raised by the upcoming U.S. introduction of a new cardiac imaging product. Ms. Danaher commented:

> Sonos 100 C/F (color flow) is an important product for us. Certain segments of cardiac imaging are expected to grow significantly in coming years, and the product is a chance to recoup lost ground in a key area. But the product also means new marketing requirements for ISY. Making the sales channel as effective as possible with this product, as soon as possible, will be crucial. And there are differing opinions about the best way to do this.

This case was prepared by Professor Frank V. Cespedes and Research Associate Marie Bell as the basis for class discussion rather than to illustrate either effective or ineffective handling of an administrative situation. Certain data have been disguised.

INDUSTRY AND COMPANY BACKGROUND

Hewlett-Packard, with fiscal 1991 revenues of $14.5 billion, manufactures and markets electronic products and systems for measurement and computation. The Medical Products Group (MPG) had 1991 revenues of about $900 million derived from a variety of product lines including patient monitoring systems, operating room systems, perinatal monitoring devices, and clinical information systems. ISY, a profit center within MPG, manufactured diagnostic ultrasound devices for cardiologists and vascular surgeons.

In a 1988 meeting with security analysts, MPG's stated goal was to be "the ultrasound company" on a worldwide basis. Key elements of the strategy outlined at that meeting included: a) leadership in chosen segments in terms of clinical contribution, technical performance, and quality; b) differentiated products; and c) lower costs. An important part of MPG's product policy was its commitment to upgradability. As one executive observed, "This allows customers to add new modalities to their existing equipment and the assurance of not obsoleting current systems in a market characterized by rapid technological change; and it provides MPG with substantial revenues from upgrades. In the past decade, we have provided over 20 product upgrades without obsoleting any of the systems we have ever sold to customers."

Ultrasound Imaging

Ultrasound imaging uses high-frequency sound waves (above the audible range) to create images of the body's interior. Sound waves transmitted through the body reflect off tissues of interest and return as an echo to the transducer (a device attached to the ultrasound computer system). The echo contains information about tissue characteristics, and can be electronically converted into two-dimensional images for medical analysis. Because high-frequency sound waves cannot penetrate bone or air, they are especially useful in imaging soft tissues and fluid-filled spaces such as abdominal organs, heart, pelvis, eye, thyroid, arteries, and fetus.

In 1992, the diagnostic ultrasound market was over $2 billion, with the United States accounting for 41%, Europe 33%, and Japan 12%. In the United States (see **Exhibit 1**), the market was divided into three broad groups of product applications: radiology (diagnosis of the kidneys, liver, pancreas, gall bladder), about 40% of the market; cardiology (heart diagnosis), 35%; and other (including OB/GYN and other applications). A high-end color ultrasound system could be purchased for $150,000 to $250,000 in 1992, while other imaging technologies such as cat-scans and magnetic resonance imaging units cost over $1 million and typically took much longer than the 30–50 minutes required for ultrasound diagnosis. The test could be completed in a non-invasive manner (nothing injected into the body) and without potentially dangerous exposure to radiation or agents with harmful side effects, permitting repeated tests over time with no risk to the patient. Ultrasound equipment also involved less training time for technicians, less downtime and service, and was in 1992 the only imaging technology that offered real-time display of moving structures such as the heart.

Echo-cardiography, a specialty in cardiology, used ultrasound to analyze the movement of heart walls, the presence of abnormal tissue, and (with color-flow capabilities) the direction and velocity of blood flow. Patient costs of $400–$700 per test in 1991 were currently fully paid by most U.S. medical insurance providers, and (depending upon patient demand) the addition of ultrasound equipment could generate substantial incremental revenues for a hospital, private practitioner, or group medical practice. However, a 1991 study found no evidence that hospitals added ultrasound systems and then "promoted" utilization of the machine. Both radiology and cardiology were specialties dependent upon patient referrals by other physicians. Heart disease remained the leading cause of death in the United States, and an aging population was expected to increase ultrasound usage in hospital and non-hospital settings.

Technology and Product Segments

Until the early 1980s, ultrasound equipment produced two-dimensional, black-and-white images using mechanical transducers. In 1981, Hewlett Packard entered the cardiology market with an electronic, phased array system. Over time, this technology increased the number of channels in the transducer from 48 to 64 to 128, increasing image quality in the process. In 1984, Irex (a subsidiary of Johnson & Johnson) introduced color ultrasound systems to the cardiology market, allowing for better detection of heart abnormalities. (By 1990, 40% of all ultrasound units shipped either had color or were color upgradable.) In 1986, MPG successfully combined Doppler technology with color for its high-performance cardiology systems. Doppler systems detect blood flow via frequency shifts reflected from moving blood cells; this allows medical specialists to monitor the direction and velocity of blood flow in the heart. In 1988, Acuson introduced Doppler color-flow capabilities for its radiology systems.

By 1992, Doppler color-flow was the standard in high-end ultrasound systems in both radiology and cardiology. But an industry observer noted that "Color flow technology is still at an early stage of development. A number of companies are working on new color-flow technologies that would allow for much improved tissue analyses. Three-dimensional imaging will become a commercial reality soon, especially in cardiology applications. And it's likely that some manufacturers will introduce 192 or 256 channel systems within the next three years. These developments increase the potential clinical applications of high-performance ultrasound systems."

The ultrasound imaging market was typically segmented by product performance across the two major application areas: radiology and cardiology. Radiology, about 45% of the worldwide ultrasound market, was considered to be the more profitable segment. Internationally, the market leader was Toshiba. But in the United States, Toshiba had a 9% market share while Acuson had a leading 44% share. In cardiology (35% of the worldwide ultrasound market), HP was the worldwide leader with an estimated 43% share in the United States.

High-performance products in 1992 were "full feature" systems, with color-flow and 96 or 128 channel capabilities providing superior image quality. List prices were $180,000 or more per unit in radiology and $150,000 or more in cardiology. In 1991, these products accounted for nearly 60% of radiology units sold in the United States (47% of cardiology units) and 75% of revenues (64% in cardiology).

Mid-performance products used either phased-array or older technologies, with 48 or 64 channels that provided images of lesser quality than high-performance systems. Mid-range radiology products sold for $130,000–$180,000 in 1991 and cardiology products for $90,000–$150,000. These products were about 18% of radiology units sold in the United States in 1991 (16% in cardiology) and 15% of revenues (17% in cardiology).

Low-performance products provided images of lesser quality and often lacked color-flow capabilities. In 1991, low-performance radiology products selling for less than $130,000 accounted for 23% of units sold in the United States and 10% in segment revenues; about 10% of these low-performance radiology products had color-flow capabilities. Low-performance cardiology products selling for $55,000–$90,000 were 37% of units sold in the United States and 20% of cardiology segment revenues; about 80% of these units had color-flow capabilities.

Customers

High and mid-performance ultrasound systems were generally purchased by hospitals or imaging clinics. Lower performance products were generally purchased for physician offices, out-patient settings and, except for some emergency room uses, other non-hospital settings.

In the United States, 2000 *hospitals* with more than 100 beds traditionally represented the core market for ultrasound systems. For cardiology systems, the buying process usually began when the cardiology department perceived a need for an ultrasound machine, based either on increased patient referrals, a planned extension of services, or a desired technology upgrade. The hospital's Chief of Cardiology was a key decision maker but required budgetary approval from hospital administrators. Based on the need determination, a group of vendors would be on the "short list" assembled for product and price evaluations. Product demonstrations were always required, and vendors' clinical specialists performed such demonstrations by conducting on-site tests at the prospective customer with cardiologists and sonographers (hospital personnel who actually operated the equipment). An MPG sales manager noted that "Both the sonographer's ability to produce a good image and the cardiologist's ability to read the image are skills that develop over time. Hence, user-friendliness is intimately tied to product performance."

Clinical specialists had extensive training and, at MPG, their fully-burdened costs were significant. For equipment typically purchased by hospitals, product demonstrations required specially-equipped vans to transport systems of 450+ pounds to the hospital site. Based on the demonstration, the cardiology department then narrowed the list to two-three vendors and submitted it (often but not always with a recommendation) to hospital administration for final approval. An MPG salesperson commented:

> Selling in the hospital market is a two-stage process and the buying cycle ranges from 3–12 months. In the first stage, I deal with the medical professionals: the cardiologists and sonographers. They are most concerned with image quality, product reliability, and service. I must establish relationships and awareness of our products' functionality and reliability with a number of people, and the product demonstration is crucial.
>
> The second stage is negotiations with administrators, who are more driven by price and cost issues. Fortunately, at $400–$700 per exam and with exams covered by Medicare, ultrasound is a revenue generator for hospitals with the right patient load. We have seen paybacks of five–nine months for hospitals that purchase $100,000+ ultrasound products. But much depends on the hospital's situation. For example, if a hospital is renowned for cancer treatment, they want the best available systems in that area and are more price sensitive with other equipment. If cardiology is their specialty, then performance is important.
>
> Another aspect of hospital buying behavior is the role of key accounts. A pyramid of influence operates in this market, with smaller and medium-sized hospitals often relying on larger research and teaching hospitals for technology cues. Therefore, maintaining a strong position in influential hospitals is critical.

About 13,000 cardiologists conducted tests in *non-hospital* settings such as group practices, health maintenance organizations, mobile health labs, and clinics throughout the United States. An MPG sales manager noted reasons why these physicians were interested in ultrasound:

> As in hospitals, ultrasound has been a proven revenue generator, with reimbursement for each test. Also, once referred to another facility for testing, there is a risk that patient will not return to the originating practitioner. Physicians in group practices that can perform these tests in-house are more likely to keep patients and generate future revenues, both from testing and future office visits. Finally, despite appointment delays, most physicians realize they are in a service

business and that patient inconvenience can be avoided with in-house testing.

The hospital cardiologist is a physician and administrator; the non-hospital cardiologist is a physician and business person. The latter are interested in image quality and reliability, but must be convinced that ROI from an imaging system will be greater than many alternative uses of their limited capital.

Non-hospital buying also required product demonstrations but the lower-performance equipment was less technically sophisticated, did not require a trained clinical specialist to operate, and demonstrations were often conducted by salespeople. If configured for a tabletop, smaller 120-pound ultrasound systems could be transported in the trunk of a salesperson's car. The demonstration was generally given to the cardiologist and an office nurse or receptionist (who often conducted the tests in non-hospital settings), and did not require the extensive post-demonstration evaluations and discussions conducted in hospitals. A salesperson commented:

> In hospitals, it's a longer-range consultative sale where technical knowledge is initially paramount. Outside the hospital, the selling cycle can be 30 days or less, and price negotiations are key from the start. Also, 60% of non-hospital systems are leased, and competitors often discount on a one-on-one basis with customers, not (as in the hospital market) with planned promotions. So, the salesperson must create financial packages and contact with Marketing (which controls product pricing) is more frequent and more important. At the same time, because the equipment is lower price, selling efficiencies are also important.

Regulations concerning reimbursement procedures had the potential to change the nature of demand for medical equipment. In 1983, a prospective payment system (PPS) for Medicare patients (40% of all hospital patient days) was mandated by the U.S. government. With PPS, hospitals were reimbursed for tests based on constantly up-dated national and regional costs, not on the individual hospital's costs. One result was slow growth for in-patient services at hospitals and growth in out-patient services conducted at both hospital and non-hospital locations.

Nonetheless, health-care expenditures climbed much faster than inflation during the 1980s, reaching $733 billion (12.5% of U.S. GNP) in 1991. Reforms in 1991 were aimed at extending PPS to capital purchases. Previously, capital-related costs for inpatient services were reimbursed 85% of what hospitals spent on equipment multiplied by the portion of total hospital days spent treating Medicare patients. Beginning in October 1991 (with a ten-year phase-in schedule), the government limited reimbursement for capital expenditures to a fixed amount dependent on the number of Medicare patients served by a hospital. An executive commented: "The new rules are very complex, and the 10-year phase-in means that many changes are likely once there is experience with the program. But hospitals face a new era of capital planning, and the uncertainty will probably slow their equipment purchases, especially at the high end."

At the same time, the government agency in charge of Medicare had announced an intention to adopt a new method of physician reimbursement. Previously, physicians had been reimbursed according to a system of "customary, prevailing, and reasonable" fees for a procedure. The essence of the new system was to base fee reimbursement on the time and effort physicians actually devoted to a medical procedure, with each procedure computed according to a complex formula. This system was to be phased-in starting in 1993 with payment for all services based on the new fee schedule by 1996. This announcement was greeted by intense lobbying by various medical groups, especially the American College of Cardiology and American Society of Echocardiography, who argued for modified payment schedules for their specialties. In 1992, the outcome of these efforts was uncertain. But some observers believed that, under the currently proposed rules, many physicians whose incomes would be reduced by the new fee schedule would seek to perform in their offices or outpatient clinics procedures they previously had performed in hospitals. One observer commented: "Many private insurers will eventually adopt the government's fee structure, and that will accelerate the impact. In the past, successful physicians left the business of owning and operating outpatient clinics to others and were satisfied with professional fees for their services. But that may change. More physician groups may operate their own outpatient clinics so they can recoup lost income and broaden their revenue base."

Competition

In the U.S. ultrasound market, MPG competed primarily with Acuson, Toshiba, and ATL in high and mid-performance segments and with Interspec, Biosound, and Vingmed in low-performance segments.

Acuson, founded in 1979 by a former HP engineer, shipped its first product in 1983. Acuson had concentrated on high-end radiology systems but entered the cardiology segment in 1988. In 1991, Acuson had $336 million in sales ($258 million in the United States), 67% from radiology and 22% from cardiology systems. This made Acuson the world's second largest ultrasound company and, with a 25% U.S. share, the domestic market leader. In the United States, the company had 75 salespeople, a 15% market share in cardiology units in 1991 (including share gains in 1991), and a much higher share in radiology.

Toshiba was the world's leading seller of ultrasound equipment, with 1991 sales of $380 million (about $64 million in the United States, 53% in radiology and 40% in cardiology). Toshiba entered the U.S. ultrasound market in 1985 and increased its share during the later 1980s. Toshiba's medical business had reported directly to Tokyo headquarters, but in 1989 Toshiba America Medical Systems became a separate company, with a product line focused on mid- to high-performance systems with prices below competing high-performance systems. Toshiba reportedly had the largest R&D budget of any ultrasound company (about $55 million in 1991), but had not been a leader in new technology. In 1991, Toshiba's radiology units showed little growth, but its U.S. cardiology sales grew from an estimated $17 million to $24 million.

ATL (Advanced Technology Laboratories) had $280 million in sales in 1991 (down from $287 million in 1990), 60% from the United States. More than 50% of ATL's U.S. sales came from radiology systems, 23% from OB/GYN ultrasound, and less than 10% from cardiology. In early 1991, ATL disbanded its cardiology sales force and transferred some of those salespeople to its radiology sales force. According to one executive, "ATL felt it did not have a competitive product for the hospital cardiac market and was experiencing little, if any, growth, in the non-hospital market with its older Ultramark 7 line." ATL lost six share points in cardiology in 1991, but was expected to introduce a new high-performance cardiology system in 1993.

Interspec had $41 million in worldwide sales in 1991, 65% from the United States and 95% from cardiology. After introducing its compact office market cardiology system in 1984, Interspec ranked among the top-10 U.S. ultrasound firms by 1986. Its 1990 annual report emphasized that the company would continue "to focus on the cardiology market segment while expanding technology into radiology and other specialized markets." Interspec's major products were the CX cardiology system for the private office market and the CX 200 for hospitals, both sold through a direct sales force.

Biosound, a single product company, competed in the low-performance segment of U.S. cardiology ultrasound. Its Genesis product, at $51,000, offered the lowest price in this segment, but with image quality and other features judged to be less than competing products. In 1991, Biosound had an 8% share in units (4% in revenues) in the U.S. cardiology market.

Vingmed was a Norwegian company, acquired by Interspec in 1987 and then sold to Diasonics in November 1991. Its major product, the CFM 750, was a feature-rich cardiology system that, at $80,000–$100,000/unit, was the highest priced and highest-performing system in the non-hospital segment.

The U.S. ultrasound market had witnessed major shifts in the market share rankings of leading competitors (**Exhibit 2**). Some market leaders in the 1970s had exited in the 1980s. Market positions also varied in cardiology versus radiology (**Exhibit 3**). In addition to the companies discussed here, moreover, units of corporations such as GE, Hitachi, Philips, and Siemens also sold ultrasound equipment, primarily high-end systems in both cardiology and radiology. Concerning the industry in 1992, an observer commented:

> Growth was high in the 1980s but slower in recent years, and R&D and marketing expenses have risen while prices have, in real terms,

remained flat or declined in some segments. Depending upon the impact of reimbursement changes, we may have too many manufacturers chasing too few customers over the next few years. That probably means more concentration among fewer manufacturers, each of whom seeks out new segments in order to grow.

IMAGING SYSTEMS DIVISION

HP's Medical Products Group was organized as indicated in **Exhibit 4.** HP entered the ultrasound imaging field in 1980 with its Model 77020 system meant for both radiology and cardiology applications. With only limited success in radiology, however, the company began to concentrate on cardiology in 1982 and soon became the acknowledged leader in this segment. ISY became a business unit profit center within MPG in 1981. In 1991, the majority of ISY's revenues were in the United States with an emphasis on cardiology systems.

Through much of the 1980s, ISY continued to improve the Model 77020 system, making numerous image quality enhancements and adding Doppler color-flow capabilities in 1987. All enhancements were made available to customers as field upgrades as well as new systems. In 1988, Acuson challenged ISY's leadership in the cardiology segment with the Acuson 128 XP, which offered 128 channels. ISY countered the same year with a product line consisting of three major systems: the SONOS 1000, a new high-performance 128-channel phased-array system; the SONOS 500, a re-vamped version of the older Model 77020 which was upgradable to the SONOS 1000; and the SONOS 100, a lower-cost, black & white, mechanical scanner for the non-hospital market. Deliveries of the SONOS 100 began immediately. Deliveries of the Sonos 1000 were shipped late and failed to meet quality expectations, requiring three revisions to achieve traditional HP standards and quality. Originally priced at $165,000/unit, the SONOS 1000 was selling for $130,000 by 1991. An MPG executive commented:

> The ISY culture had been technology-driven and R&D had failed to meet the competition. The initial euphoria over the SONOS 1000 rapidly evaporated. After a lengthy delay, products became available for side-by-side demonstrations (i.e., the same patient is "imaged" by competing systems, the primary measure of system performance), and high customer expectations were not met. An independent and fiercely confident sales force became defensive.
>
> In addition, the movement from a single high-end product to multiple products created positioning issues. Field people reported spending much time competing with our old system platform. R&D was in the center of the storm, working nonstop to close a performance deficit and improve product reliability at the same time they were adopting a new hardware environment. Concurrently, slower market growth, and

a difficult corporate financial situation in the late 1980s, put pressure on costs across all business units and functional areas at HP.

In 1990, MPG dropped the SONOS 500 designation for the Model 77025 and introduced an improved version as the SONOS 1000 Basic. In 1991, SONOS 1500 was introduced, with features and reliability judged to be the best in class. However, as a product manager noted, "Our initial problems with the SONOS 1000 allowed competition to establish positions and bracket us on the high-end and mid-range. This continues to challenge our positioning and product strategies. Also, cardiac imaging is now widely accepted, and applications continue to expand in various departments in hospitals. This challenges our ability to manage limited resources for divergent applications, while some lower-overhead competitors focus on specific applications."

ISY segmented the cardiology ultrasound market by product and customer type (**Exhibit 5**). Al Kyle, general manager of ISY since 1991, noted that "Acuson's entry into cardiology has focused on the high-end and performance-driven customers, while Toshiba has pursued the price/performance buyer. It's unclear if Toshiba is making money or if they care about profits at this point. But this competition is part of a transition we face in moving from a high-growth, technology-driven company to a slower-growth, market-driven, multiple product company with a more balanced focus on price, reliability and performance for different segments. This is difficult when you're facing cost pressures and many aspects of the organization are geared to competing purely on performance." In the United States, ISY sought to be the vendor of choice in all ultrasound cardiology segments. "Resource issues come into play," noted Ms. Danaher, "and a focus on cardiology is supported by our strong commitment to upgradability. But in a more mature market, the speed with which we execute this strategy is important."

ISY Marketing and Sales Organizations

Reporting to Ms. Danaher were managers for marketing communications (responsible for ads, direct mail, and product literature), technical marketing (responsible for customer engineering support), product management, and business development. Due to corporate budget constraints, a freeze on headcount applied across MPG marketing and sales units in 1992.

Product management included managers for all major markets and technologies. Mark Low, product manager for the Sonos 100, noted that "The roles and responsibilities of product managers vary. But the central role is to shepherd a product through development to introduction. This means working with R&D, engineering, and manufacturing on product definition, design, and specifications, as well as with these functions and sales on the marketing plan for the product."

Business Development, headed by Gary Abrahams, was the main liaison between sales and marketing, responsible for product training, competitive analysis, price exceptions, trade shows, national account support, and customer visits to the factory. (Customers who visited MPG's manufacturing plant included hospital consultants and purchasing group representatives, and such visits were seen as a strong closing tool by the sales force.) Mr. Abrahams noted that "We provide feedback about products from field groups to product management. Conversely, product marketing views us as a main vehicle for delivering messages to the sales force." Abrahams had been a district sales manager before becoming head of Business Development in 1990 (when Danaher moved from that position to Director of Marketing). He noted that "The field's assumption is that headquarters is out-of-touch, and you establish credibility by traveling with the sales reps, attending trade shows and conferences, sharing a drink, and finding other ways to establish a bond. That's important, because the essence of Business Development's job is to be the conduit and translator between the factory and the field. That often means presenting programs to the sales force in their terms, not in terms of product management's segmentation criteria."

ISY's sales force was one of eight sales groups within U.S. Field Operations, which reported to the general manager of MPG and was measured as a cost center. Four sales groups focused on patient monitoring systems; the others focused on healthcare information systems, clinical information systems, diagnostic cardiology, or ultrasound imaging. MPG estimated fully burdened costs in excess of $400,000 per salesperson. Since November 1991, the imaging group consisted of a national sales manager (Phil Kash, located in Atlanta), six district managers, 42 sales representatives, and a national support manager. The support organization involved eight "repair" districts and four "application" districts where customer engineers repaired equipment and clinical specialists performed product demonstrations and post-sale support.

During the past year, U.S. Field Operations had evolved from full-line sales representatives located in four regions, to the current organization, where sales units focused on different products sold by MPG's major business units. "This brought together sales and support units within the same district, improved customer focus, and increased our market share," noted Steve Swenson, U.S. Field Operations Manager at MPG. "It also eliminated a management layer." Before November, 1991 sales managers at MPG had overall sales goals and, according to Mr. Kash, "the focus within a region ultimately depended on an individual's familiarity with a product. Most had grown up selling our patient monitoring equipment, where the selling process differs significantly from imaging. You call on different hospital departments, and because patient monitoring equipment isn't a revenue generator, the selling process is more administrative." In that organization, moreover, ISY's Business Development group was directly involved in supporting, training, and (as Abrahams described it) "drumming-up attention for our product line in the field. Because there was no national sales manager focused on imaging, Cynthia and I became de facto sales managers, often speaking daily with district managers and sales reps about product matters, competitive developments, and sales tactics at an account."

Mr. Kash became imaging national sales manager (NSM) in November 1991. He had been with MPG for over 20 years, as sales representative and later an Area and Regional Sales Manager, and was part of MPG's ultrasound start-up team in 1980. He noted that "when imaging was in its infancy, we focused some district managers only on imaging and established leadership. But when growth slowed, imaging was pronounced a 'mature' business and those districts were rolled into the overall sales structure. The focus was lost and 'maturity' became a self-fulfilling prophecy. A major challenge when I became NSM was to have sales and service relearn a business they didn't know. I needed to instill a mentality that everybody sells. Service may fix systems but, especially in a business where support and upgrades are crucial, they also sell our capabilities to customers."

Mr. Kash also revised the sales compensation system. Traditionally, MPG sales compensation was 50% salary and 50% commission, based on dollar volumes sold. Each year, a target revenue quota was assigned to districts who translated this into a target income for the salesperson, who was guaranteed 80% of targeted income irrespective of actual quota achievement. "In the mid-1980s when growth was high," noted Kash, "most salespeople exceeded quotas and the guarantee was not an issue. But when growth slowed and Acuson entered the cardiology market, many salespeople failed to make quota yet still received 80% of targeted income. We needed more discipline and more incentive in a difficult market." Mr. Kash eliminated the targeted income guarantee and changed the compensation formula to 70% salary and 30% commission (based on dollar volumes of systems sold).

Reporting to Mr. Kash were district sales managers (DSMs) who received annual revenue and expense targets and assigned revenue quotas to imaging sales reps. Based on revenue targets, ISY Marketing paid to Sales a cost-per-order-dollar (which averaged about $.23 for a rep with a $3 million quota). This money became the basis for the annual expense budgets allocated to DSMs. One DSM noted that "I have two key responsibilities. The first is to support and motivate my salespeople. The second is to manage my business effectively by ensuring that quotas are met within budgeted levels. Budgets have tightened in recent years, and headcount freezes require cost-effective allocation of limited sales resources." The 42 imaging salespeople included former clinical specialists, but most had been full-line reps within the previous organization. In general, MPG salespeople were known for their technical selling skills. According to one manager, "Our orientation has been to focus on what systems can do for the patient and the cardiologist, and only secondarily on what ultrasound might mean for hospital revenues and administrators. The attitude is, the more on-site demonstrations, the more sales. That's an expensive approach which relies on demonstrable product performance superiority, but it's established our strong position in the top 200 hospitals."

Commenting on the recent sales reorganization, an ISY marketing manager noted that "We have a sales group targeted at the imaging business and Phil Kash is a born leader who is respected highly in the field." Another commented: "The new organization eliminates a layer in the field, but creates another layer between headquarters and the field. Roles and responsibilities are still unclear in some areas, metrics differ between marketing and sales, and the previous organization never really developed a clear process for resolving conflicts or differences." A third noted that "Sales, Support, and Marketing are reinvigorated, but the reality is many plans competing for the same resources. At the same time, the increasing breadth and complexity of clinical applications require closer, faster coordination among these groups." A veteran sales manager commented: "MPG's sales force has always marched to its own drummer. Only programs supported by the rank and file will succeed; programs thrust upon the sales force by top management are doomed to failure."

SONOS 100 COLOR/FLOW

The Sonos 100 B/W (black & white) was launched in December 1987 and targeted at the non-hospital segment of cardiology. It sold well for some months but was soon superseded by competing systems that offered color flow and annular or phased array capabilities. A salesperson commented:

> In 1987, Interspec was the leader in the non-hospital cardiology segment, but the market was looking to us for a product that would offer better performance with the service and security of the HP brand name. We had the opening, but ISY dropped the ball. When Sonos 100 was introduced, Interspec dropped its prices on existing systems and, less than a year later, introduced a color-flow product.

A marketing manager commented:

> Initially, the Sonos 100 was best-in-class, something our salespeople can relate to from their experience in the high-end segment of the market. But when the product was no longer best-in-class, it quickly lost sales attention. In addition, our sales force was not well equipped to tackle the non-hospital market.

ISY recognized the product limitations but was unable to devote resources to re-engineering the product until 1991, due to issues concerning the Sonos 1000 product, the development of the Sonos 1500, and Acuson's continuing threat in the high-performance cardiology segment. By 1992, however, the Sonos 100 had been re-engineered to provide color-flow technology, high reliability, and other features (see **Exhibit 6**), with product introduction scheduled for November, 1992. The U.S. non-hospital cardiac ultrasound market was an estimated $80 million in 1992, and Sonos 100 was targeted at the low and mid-level segments, estimated at about $40 million. Abrahams noted that the market was significant for MPG:

> Technical trends in ultrasound now make smaller systems important in the industry, as does the probable fall-out from reimbursement changes in health care. Also, the hospital market is flat; we need gains in non-hospital segments. Globally, moreover, the product is crucial. In the United States, MPG pursues a vertical strategy of providing a full range of cardiology products. Internationally, where there is less demand for high-end systems, we have a horizontal strategy of providing imaging systems across the price sensitive segments of cardiology, vascular, and radiology. In the United States, therefore, Sonos 100 fills-out an important price point and internationally it *is* the key cardiology offering.

In 1992, Mark Low became product manager for Sonos 100 C/F and developed a marketing plan with the following key elements.

Product. Sonos 100 C/F used mechanical arrays to produce two-dimensional color-flow images. "In product development," noted Mr. Low, "we decided that leapfrogging competition technologically would have delayed the product's introduction significantly (in a segment where we were already a few years late with color flow), and would have added manufacturing costs without contributing greatly to customer satisfaction in this segment."

ISY had conducted extensive clinical tests of Sonos 100 C/F against three competing products that currently accounted for over 90% of sales in the target segment. Based on the tests, user needs surveys, and personal interviews, each system was evaluated across categories weighted by their importance in the non-hospital ultrasound market. The categories were (in order of importance): performance, price, useability, reliability/uptime, range of applications, upgrade potential, features, and company image. With the highest possible score being 800, the results were: Interspec Apogee CX: 576; HP Sonos 100 C/F: 573; Vingmed CFM 750: 550; Biosound Genesis CFM: 479. Interspec's system had annular array technology and so scored slightly higher than Sonos in image quality and multiple applications. Vingmed's system had the highest performance rating but ranked low in useability. Biosound's product was the least expensive but scored poorly in performance and reliability. Sonos 100 C/F ranked equal or better than all other systems in color-flow abilities, and scored highest in useability, reliability, and company image. In addition to these firms, Acuson, GE, and Toshiba also sold some high-performance cardiology systems in the non-hospital market.

Price. Sonos 100 C/F would be priced at $55,000/unit. Competitors' comparably equipped systems sold for: Vingmed CFM 750, $82,000; Interspec Apogee CX, $68,000; Biosound Genesis CFM, $51,000. "We have high goals and a need to re-establish ourselves firmly in the non-hospital segment," noted Mr. Low. "So, we've priced the product as the best value in the class."

Promotion. Major forums for ultrasound product introductions were the European College of Cardiology and American Heart Association meetings. Sonos 100 C/F would be exhibited at both conferences in November. Marketing communications stressed that "The HP Sonos 100 C/F is an affordable color flow ultrasound system that enables the private office physician or internist to perform comprehensive cardiac as well as general diagnostic imaging conveniently and at low cost." A direct mail campaign was planned to the Sonos 100 B/W installed base of customers and a list of cardiologists supplied by the American Medical Association. Additional selling tools included product literature, a promotional video, and technical data sheets.

By August 1992, the outstanding issue was the nature of the distribution channel for Sonos 100 C/F. Interspec and Biosound (the #1 and #2 companies in this segment) each had about 20 direct salespeople in the United States, generating from $500,000–$1,000,000 in annual sales with an average of about $800,000 per salesperson. Field Operations management estimated their fully-burdened costs/rep at about $200,000 annually, which meant that their selling costs were 25–30% of sales. Ms. Danaher noted that, at ISY, "We have investigated a range of channel options, including dealers and adding new sales reps to focus solely on the non-hospital segment. But many dealers lack the clinical expertise and sales skills to deal with the product, while budget constraints make it impossible to add more salespeople. Therefore, the choice comes down to using the present direct sales channel or utilizing independent Manufacturers' Reps who focus on this segment. There are strong opinions on both sides."

Sales Channels

Of the 13,000 non-hospital cardiologists in the United States, five cities (New York, L.A., Chicago, San Francisco, Miami) accounted for 60% and 15 cities for 85%. Cardiology exams were also conducted in many small rural hospitals and clinics and by a number of the c. 50,000 Internal Medicine physicians in the country. A marketing manager noted that "An effective sales channel in this segment must reach geographically dispersed customers with a product that, because of its pricing, must be sold efficiently." Both Biosound and Interspec had used Manufacturers Reps (MRs), but (according to ISY sales executives) had switched to direct sales forces due to problems with MR turnover, the costs of training and monitoring MRs, and "customers' desires for a long-term relationship with the vendor. After switching to direct sales a few years ago, both firms doubled their sales volumes. The drawback is two-three years of investment in fixed selling costs with only a gradual return on investment."

Many ISY sales managers believed the Sonos 100 C/F should be sold exclusively through a direct sales force. "We now have a dedicated imaging sales force," said one manager, "which is well-trained and knows the full product line. They can offer a complete solution to any cardiologist interested in ultrasound. And, while non-hospital customers are price-sensitive, ultrasound equipment is a lot of money relative to their budgets; so they expect direct representation, especially when our key competitors are calling on them with a direct sales force." Another noted that "The Sonos 100 C/F is likely to be the most technically sophisticated and highest-priced product offered by an MR, who typically sells a broad range of diagnostic products. They work on commission and won't spend a lot of time developing a market or providing demonstrations and follow-up service. If this market is going to grow, we should leverage our skills in this area. ISY reps may need more training on negotiations, pricing, and reimbursement practices in the private-office market; but these skills can be taught. Loyalty to HP cannot." A DSM commented that "It's the sales force, not MRs, who can capitalize on any trade-up potential in the non-hospital market, especially since many of these cardiologists also work in the major hospitals where we're strong. Also, in a flat hospital market, more of my reps see the private-office market as a source of incremental revenues that's important in meeting quota."

Many marketing managers favored use of MRs for the Sonos 100 C/F. "The product has been designed for ease of use, and an MR is very capable of demonstrating it in the physician's office," noted one manager. "Also, most MRs who call on non-hospital accounts are former sales managers of the major companies, including Interspec and Biosound. They may not have the technical knowledge of our reps, but they're experienced salespeople with great negotiating skills and detailed knowledge of physician reimbursement procedures." Another noted that "The hospital and non-hospital cardiology markets are very different. Non-hospital customers don't care about our value-added services, and few are candidates for a trade-up. The time our reps might spend trying to sell a Sonos 100 to a private-office cardiologist could be better spent at a hospital account." A third commented that "Some DSMs want to retain the full line on the assumption that, if times get tough, they can allocate more effort to the non-hospital market. But product demonstrations are required in both markets, and reps needing to make quota will always treat the Sonos 100 at $55,000/unit as a second or third priority behind a Sonos 1000 at $130,000/unit or the 1500 at $190,000/unit."

In the industry, MRs were paid a 15% commission on equipment sold and most did not sell competing products within a category. The manufacturer also provided MRs with product training, inventory on consignment, and credit and collection services. When these costs were added, ISY marketing managers estimated the cost-per-order-dollar for sales through MRs at $.28–$.30. A sales executive noted that "MRs vary tremendously in their selling expertise and professionalism, and must be located, recruited, and supervised on an ongoing basis. To do this, you need at least one program manager devoted full-time to an MR channel. This raises the MR cost-per-order-dollar closer to $.40." A marketing manager commented that "The $.30 figure is a good one for MR sales. It includes administrative overhead and also factors in some pre-sale support costs that are utilized by direct reps in hospital accounts but are much less likely to be utilized at non-hospital accounts. Also, the bulk of MR costs are variable expenses."

Several MPG sales districts had utilized MRs in the past with varied results. "For the DSM," noted one manager, "an MR organization requires training, demonstration equipment, and commissions that come out of Sales' budget; and the MR is not under the direct control of the sales manager. For example, a DSM cannot, under current law, *require* a MR to write a sales plan or submit monthly forecasting. The result is that MRs were often treated as second-class citizens, without joint programs, qualified leads, telemarketing support, and easy access to demo equipment. The DSM would rather invest in the higher-end equipment than the low-end equipment used by an 'outsider'." Another executive stated: "ISY, as a profit center, may view the issue as an investment decision for a new product. But any decision must be implemented in the field, which is a cost center facing a tougher market and budget pressures."

Conclusion

The planning cycle at HP concluded on September 1 for a new fiscal year starting on November 1. Funding decisions for products, marketing programs, and sales channels would therefore be made soon. Ms. Danaher noted that "We have a limited window of opportunity with the Sonos 100 C/F and need to cover its market as efficiently and effectively as possible." A meeting with ISY product management, sales management, and general management was scheduled for the next week, at which Ms. Danaher and others would make recommendations concerning the Sonos 100 C/F introduction.

EXHIBIT 1   U.S. Diagnostic Ultrasound Imaging Market

Unit and Dollar Shipments
($ Value in millions: ASP = average selling prices in thousands)

Year	Equipment	Upgrades	Total $ Value	Total Units	Color Doppler Systems $ Value	Color Doppler Systems Units	Color Doppler Systems ASP
1980	$147	$3	$150	2,725	—	—	—
1981	217	2	219	3,785	—	—	—
1982	242	1	243	4,660	—	—	—
1983	268	1	269	5,350	—	—	—
1984	304	2	306	5,760	$2	10	$175
1985	339	11	350	6,550	7	40	175
1986	412	20	432	6,950	22	145	152
1987	505	35	540	7,475	134	925	145
1988	619	44	663	8,380	256	1,665	148
1989	722	79	801	8,975	467	3,040	154
1990	765	71	836	9,510	549	3,730	147
1991	813	95	908	9,950	621	4,485	139

Radiology and Cardiology Segments

Radiology Equipment	Units	ASP	$ Value	Cardiology Equipment	Units	ASP	$ Value
1990	2,245	$139	$311	1990	2,130	$111	$235
1991	2,305	138	317	1991	2,225	116	258
Upgrades				Upgrades			
1990	—	—	23	1990	—	—	43
1991	—	—	38	1991	—	—	50

Color-Flow vs. Non-Color Product Sales

Color-Flow	Units	ASP	$ Value	Non-Color	Units	ASP	$ Value
1990	3,730	$147	$549	1990	5,780	$37	$218
1991	4,485	139	621	1991	5,465	35	192

Hospital vs. Non-Hospital Segments (1991)

	Hospital	Non-Hospital
Radiology		
— $ Value of equipment sold (in millions)	$238	$79
— Units sold	1,515	790
— Average selling price (in thousands)	$157	$100
— Number of Installed Units	10,455	5,670
— Average number of annual scans/unit	1,100	800
— Total number of exams (in millions)	11.5	4.5
Cardiology		
— $ Value of equipment sold (in millions)	$176	$82
— Units sold	1,230	995
— Average selling price (in thousands)	$143	$83
— Number of Installed Units	8,350	6,940
— Average number of annual scans/unit	950	675
— Total number of exams (in millions)	7.9	4.7

Source: Industry Reports

EXHIBIT 2   U.S. Market Share Positions of Leading Ultrasound Manufacturers, 1983–1991

Company	1991	1990	1989	1988	1987	1986	1985	1984	1983
Acuson	1	1	2	2	2	3	6	6	—
HP	2	2	1	1	1	1	1	4	4
ATL	3	3	3	3	3	2	2	1	1
Toshiba	4	4	4	7	6	6	10	10	10
Diasonics	5	5	5	4	4	4	4	2	2
Aloka	6	7	7	6	8	11	—	—	—
GE	7	6	6	5	5	5	5	5	7
Siemens	8	8	17	15	—	—	—	—	—
Interspec	9	9	8	8	7	7	13	—	—
Hitachi	10	11	11	12	—	—	—	—	—
AI/Dornier	11	10	9	—	—	—	—	—	—
Biosound	12	12	13	9	10	9	8	8	8
Bruel & Kjaer	13	13	12	11	9	12	—	—	—
Teknar	14	14	14	—	—	—	—	—	—
Philips	15	15	16	16	—	10	8	7	5
Quantum	—	—	10	10	11	—	—	—	—
Kontron	—	—	18	17	—	—	—	—	—
JJU	—	—	—	—	—	8	3	3	3
Ekoline	—	—	—	—	—	—	—	—	6
Picker	—	—	—	—	—	—	10	9	9

	1991			1990		
Company	Rank	(Millions)	Market Share	Rank	(Millions)	Market Share
Acuson	1	$223	24.6%	1	$194	23.2%
HP	2	185	20.4	2	172	20.6
ATL	3	136	15.0	3	134	16.0
Toshiba	4	64	7.1	4	53	6.3
Diasonics	5	39	4.3	5	40	4.8
Aloka	6	38	4.2	7	35	4.2
GE	7	32	3.5	6	34	4.1
Siemens Quantum	8	25	2.8	8	22	2.6
Interspec	9	22	2.4	9	22	2.6
Hitachi	10	21	2.3	11	16	1.9
AI/Dornier	11	14	1.5	10	17	2.0
Biosound	12	13	1.4	12	11	1.3
Bruel & Kjaer	13	11	1.2	13	11	1.3
Teknar	14	10	1.1	14	9	1.1
All Others		75	8.2		66	8.0
		$908	100.0%		$836	100.0%

Source: Industry Reports

EXHIBIT 3

Leading Manufacturers of Cardiac Ultrasound Systems: U.S. Unit Sales & Market Shares, 1990 & 1991

Company	1991 Rank	(Units)	Market Share	1990 Rank	(Units)	Market Share
HP	1	960	43.1%	1	945	44.4%
Acuson	2	325	14.6%	4	250	11.7
Interspec	3	295	13.3	2	380	17.8
Biosound	4	180	8.1	6	90	4.2
Toshiba	5	175	7.9	5	115	5.4
ATL	6	130	5.8	3	255	12.0
GE	7	60	2.7	—	25	1.2
All Others		100	4.5		70	3.3
Total		2,225	100.0%		2,130	100.0%

Leading Manufacturers of Radiology Products: U.S. Unit Sales & Market Shares, 1990 & 1991

Company	1991 Rank	(Units)	Market Share	1990 Rank	(Units)	Market Share
Acuson	1	660	28.6%	1	560	24.9%
ATL	2	430	18.7	2	395	17.6
Toshiba	3	240	10.4	4	240	10.7
Diasonics	4	240	10.4	3	275	12.3
AI	5	125	5.4	5	145	6.5
Hitachi	6	115	5.0	6	120	5.3
Siemens Quantum	7	115	5.0	8	90	4.0
Philips	8	100	4.3	7	120	5.3
All Others		280	12.2		300	13.4
Total		2,305	100.0%		2,225	100.0%

Source: Industry Reports

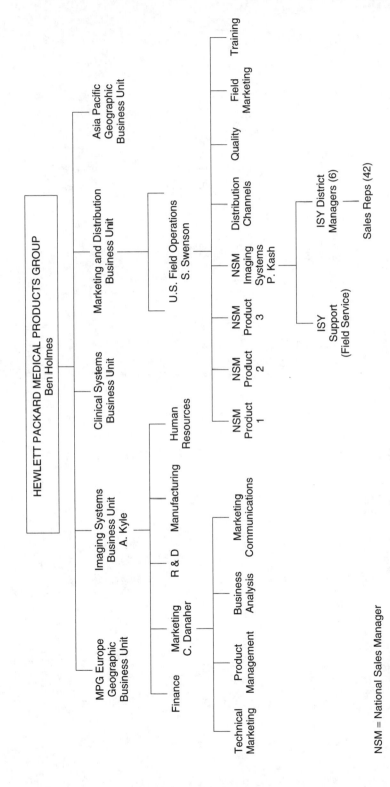

NSM = National Sales Manager

EXHIBIT 4 HP Medical Products Group: Organization Chart (1992)

EXHIBIT 5 Competing Product Offerings in U.S. Cardiology Ultrasound

Primary Target	Cardiology Products	Prices	Features	Sales Channels	Primary Competitors
—Urban Hospitals >400 beds	Sonos 1500		Phased array		
—Teaching Hospitals	Sonos 1000 Enhanced	> $150K	96 or 128 channel	Direct Sales Force	HP Acuson
	Acuson 128XP Xcelerator Toshiba SSH-140AC		Superior image quality Color flow, Doppler Annular or phased array		
—Urban Hospitals 200–400 Beds	Sonos 1000 Basic				
—Rural Hospitals	ATL Ultramark 9	$90–150K	48–64 channels	Direct Sales Force	HP Toshiba
	Toshiba 140A		Moderate image quality Color flow Doppler Mechanized, annular or phased arrays		
—Small Hospitals <200 Beds	Sonos 100			Direct Sales Force	HP
—Private Sector	Interspec Apogee	50–90K			Interspec Vingmed Biosound
—HMOs	Vingmed CFM750		48–64 channels		
—Group Practices					
—Mobile Units	Biosound Genesis		Acceptable image quality Color-flow or Black & White		
—Individual Practices					

HP SONOS 100CF Cardiovascular Imaging System

Technical Data

Features

Advanced HP color flow imaging delivers the sensitivity necessary to detect and characterize blood flow abnormalities in all cardiology applications.

Superior 2-D imaging provides high-resolution images of cardiac anatomy and fast-moving structures.

Image Frequency Shifting lets you change frequencies on the current transducer to provide the optimal combination of resolution and penetration.

Steerable PW/CW Doppler with a wide dynamic range accurately measures very small and distant flow measurements.

HP Colorization option improves contrast and discriminiation in evaluation of 2-D images, M-mode traces, and spectral Doppler displays.

2-D, M-Mode, and Doppler measurement capabilities for thorough cardiac ultrasound examinations and accurate diagnostic information.

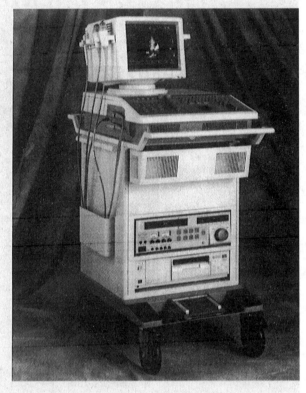

User-configurable analysis package lets you make comprehensive cardiac, vascular and obstetrical measurements and calculations.

Optional recording devices include Super-VHS VCR and color or black-and-white video printers.

EXHIBIT 6 HP SONOS 100CF Cardiovascular Imaging System

Case 12

Becton Dickinson and Company: Multidivisional Marketing Programs

In January 1990, Robert Jones, vice president of Sales for Becton Dickinson Division (BDD), received a phone call from John Kmetz, a BDD sales representative. Kmetz explained that Health Medical Center (HMC), a 435-bed teaching hospital, was evaluating the hypodermic products of a competitor, and was preparing to convert to that line based on cost savings potential. Kmetz also informed Jones of the following:

- HMC currently purchased BDD syringes and needles from a contract established with Allied Purchasing Group (APG), a large hospital buying group. However, HMC was experiencing severe financial problems, and the competitor had offered HMC a 15% discount off the price charged to HMC for hypodermics via BDD's contract with APG.
- HMC also purchased products sold by other BD divisions besides BDD.
- After consulting with his district and regional sales managers, Kmetz was recommending a 10% price reduction for HMC. However, he also noted that Ed Haire, BDD's director of Contract Sales, was concerned that this would undermine BDD's pricing structure with APG-member hospitals. Haire's initial re-

This case was prepared by Professor Frank V. Cespedes and Research Associate Laura Goode as the basis for class discussion rather than to illustrate either effective or ineffective handling of an administrative situation.

action was to let HMC convert to the competitor whose unproven product might not withstand conversion among end users. Haire indicated that, if the competing product did fail, BDD could protect its pricing structure within a large buying group and demonstrate the competitor's liabilities to other accounts.
- HMC expected a formal proposal from BDD in 10 days.

After speaking with Kmetz, Jones contacted Robert Flaherty, president of BDD. Jones noted that the size, prestige, and influence of HMC required a carefully planned response from BDD. Flaherty agreed, and noted that BD was currently running a program intended to develop multidivisional marketing efforts. He wondered if such an approach might help in dealing with HMC. Jones considered this a potentially attractive alternative to a price response, but was concerned that, with only 10 days available, time for preparing a multidivisional response was scarce. In addition, Jones was unsure of what levels of coordinated support he could expect from other BD divisions involved with HMC. Jones agreed to gather more information and make a recommendation to Flaherty about the HMC situation.

COMPANY BACKGROUND

Becton Dickinson (BD) manufactured products for health care professionals, medical institutions, industry, and the general public. The company was organized into two sectors—Medical (59% of 1989 sales) and Diagnostic (41%)—and 19 operating divisions. One executive emphasized that "our corporate structure is based on strategy units intended to achieve a strong focus on individual market opportunities. Many here firmly believe that this focus has helped each BD division achieve a leading or major share position in its market." (See **Exhibit 1**.)

Each division was a profit center with its own marketing and sales organization, national accounts program, distribution network, customer service department, billing and accounts receivables procedures, and warehousing facilities. One executive noted that "interaction between divisions has, historically, been minimal; and that has probably meant some inefficiencies and duplication. But there has also been responsibility, accountability, and a clear product-market focus with this decentralized approach. Increasingly, however, we must respond to customers seeking more efficient and effective approaches to their operating and service needs."

Market Trends

Among the most important trends in the hospital market during the 1980s was the growth of buying groups, or group purchasing organizations (GPOs). One impact was that primary decision-making authority for many major medical supply items gradually shifted (in part or in whole, depending upon the product and application) away from end-users of medical supplies to nonusers (purchasing administrators or materials management), and often away from individual institutions to centralized GPOs. As a result, BD operating divisions that previously dealt with distinct decision makers in separate hospital departments often experienced "overlap" in purchasing processes for their products at the group level. A single individual or committee within a GPO often became the primary decision maker for a range of BD core products.

Not all in the industry agreed on the value and future role of GPOs. Groups varied considerably in the benefits offered to their member hospitals and in the contractual compliance they could obtain from members. Indeed, as one BD manager noted, "an important marketing and sales task in this business is judging which groups will succeed, to what extent, and how to relate to the differences among groups. Especially in our product categories, there are large volumes at stake, and in these competitive sales situations you soon learn what the sports announcers mean when they talk about 'the thrill of victory and the agony of defeat.'"

Competitive Developments

BD competed with various suppliers of medical and diagnostic products, including Terumo Corporation, a Japanese firm that sold over 1,000 health care products worldwide. In the United States, Terumo competed directly against BD in several businesses including hypodermics, diabetes care products, I.V. catheters, and specimen collection. Although it (in most cases) offered prices significantly below established market levels, Terumo had achieved limited success in the U.S. market against individual BD divisions.

Terumo's recent activities were more significant in scope than anything attempted earlier. In 1988, Terumo had completed construction of a $70 million hypodermic plant in Maryland, with capacity to supply a significant portion of the hypodermic products used in the United States. Trade reports indicated that Terumo planned this to be the first of three major U.S. manufacturing plants, and that Terumo regarded hypodermics as especially "visible" products that could be used as lead items to establish stronger brand identity and distribution capabilities for other products slated to be manufactured at Terumo's other planned U.S. manufacturing facilities. In the months before opening its U.S. plant, Terumo dramatically increased its promotional spending, efforts to expand its distribution network, and its field sales organization (which increased to about 30 salespeople for hypodermic products and I.V. catheters by 1989).

While Terumo established plants in the United States, BD was completing a major hypodermic manufacturing facility in Singapore to better service the Far Eastern market. Worldwide in 1989, BD generated about 2.5 times the sales revenue generated by Terumo, and also held about double the unit share position for syringes and needles (both companies' largest single product category in terms of sales volume).

DEVELOPMENT OF MULTIDIVISIONAL MARKETING PROGRAMS

While BD management continued to regard a divisionalized corporate organization as the best approach for building and maintaining competitive position and financial performance, the company also began investigating in 1988 a multidivisional response to market developments and competitive threats. One senior executive explained that, implemented properly, such an approach could produce many benefits:

> First, we can better demonstrate BD's importance within an account. In many instances, our total sales with a hospital or GPO are large but "hidden" because those sales are spread across product lines sold by different divisions.
>
> Second, the appropriate approach can help to promote the many services that, as a corporation, we already provide to accounts. BD products are typically positioned as the top-quality brands supported by the broadest product line in the category (which facilitates ordering and usage by the customer), an intensive distribution network (which makes inventory-management tasks easier to handle and plan), end-user training by our sales forces, and other services. But many accounts focus on price and ignore these services unless there's a coordinated effort among divisions that sell to the same account.
>
> Third, this approach can also mean effective use of resources to develop additional value-added services and programs. This can be done through product bundling agreements and/or through the provision of order-processing systems or other services that might be prohibitive on the scale of any one division's business with an account, but feasible and attractive from a multidivisional perspective.

In early 1989, therefore, BD's CEO, Raymond Gilmartin, established a new operating group, Supply Chain Management (SCM), reporting to the CEO and charged with helping to better serve customers who contract with several BD divisions. The head of the new SCM group was Alfred J. Battaglia, who had previously been president of the specimen collection division. Battaglia described the group's mission:

> Supply chain management refers to activities which transport information and materials from our suppliers to our end users. At each step, modifications to the product and various services are what finally constitute the total value package a company offers to customers. SCM essentially provides leadership to an association of functional disciplines that, in total, manage these activities. The disci-

plines include corporate logistics, information systems, purchasing, EDI Service Products of various sorts, and corporate sales and marketing efforts.

SCM serves both internal and external customer groups. We try to coordinate different functional disciplines across divisions in dealing with external groups that work with a number of BD operating units; this would include many distributors, GPOs, individual hospitals, warehouse operators, and materials suppliers. Consolidated purchasing probably represents the greatest single short-term opportunity we have; but coordinated MIS and corporate marketing efforts are probably the biggest longer-term opportunities.

A key premise in our approach is that health care players at all levels of the supply chain are vitally interested in asset-management techniques and systems that can lower their total costs of obtaining and using needed products and services. Our ability to manage these activities across divisions can further differentiate our offerings and strengthen our relationships with end users, distributors, and suppliers.

Reporting to Battaglia were several managers responsible for aspects of multidivisional efforts. (See **Exhibit 1.**) In explaining the evolution of the SCM organization over the past year, Battaglia emphasized that the following concepts and issues had proven to be particularly important: the development and dissemination of market-segmentation and account-selection criteria for multidivisional efforts; a distinction between value-added and basic services; the continuing development of common information and communication systems; and the delineation of organizational roles and incentives for multidivisional marketing and sales efforts.

Market Segmentation

Identifying potential multidivisional-program accounts was a necessary first step. Mark Throdahl, BD's director of corporate planning, helped to develop many of the segmentation and account-selection criteria that informed SCM efforts. He explained that:

> Traditionally, we categorized customers by products and amounts bought from various BD divisions. That's the way we think, but not the way markets act. For multidivisional-marketing purposes, effective segmentation revolves around customer demographics (the account's size, location, and type of funding—for example, not-for-profit or for-profit hospitals); operating variables (the brands used in a product category and usage frequency); purchasing approaches (centralized or decentralized by department, channels utilized for various purchases, the frequency of purchase); and the technologies used (disposable vs. reusables). Without using such criteria to tailor our product and service offering to select accounts, we risk "averaging" our capabilities.

Using these criteria, the SCM group with marketing and sales managers from various divisions established a four-part "Profiling and Plan Development Process." Part one, account selection, involved identifying "important, susceptible, and/or vulnerable accounts" where a multidivisional effort was appropriate. At this stage, the goal was to distinguish between national accounts and key accounts, with the latter as the target for multidivisional efforts.

A *national account* was typically a hospital buying group with membership spanning several states; the group negotiated contracts in individual BD product categories. For such accounts, each division had national accounts managers (NAMs) responsible for sales of their division's products to these accounts, including negotiation of prices and terms with the account. NAMs reported to a divisional director of contract sales, responsible for administering contracts to the division's national accounts and reporting divisional sales to such accounts to corporate headquarters. Corporate then aggregated this data and might offer such accounts financial incentives, depending upon the total volume purchased by the account.

One executive described the program as "a package of separate divisional contracts, and in that respect it's probably representative of most national-account marketing programs. Such a program is vital in dealing with GPOs in the current industry environment. But it focuses on price discounts, and encourages only minimal interaction among the divisional NAMs." Allied Purchasing Group, the GPO through which BDD sold its hypodermic products to HMC, was a national account purchasing products from BD under incentive agreements. Like most national accounts, APG negotiated its agreement with BDD through a mechanism known as a Z contract, which provided for volume-based discounts in a product category.

A *key account* was an individual hospital that might belong to a GPO but that chose to seek an agreement directly with BD. These accounts were of sufficient size or importance to merit the additional time and effort required to generate, negotiate, and administer a multidivisional agreement. Throdahl noted that, "unlike a national account, these key-account programs do depend upon a high level of cooperation and communication among divisions. Often, key accounts are selected because of a competitive threat or opportunity best addressed by assembling different value-added services, rather than a price discount."

Part two of the Plan Development Process involved divisional input concerning the key account. One executive noted that "our multidivisional approach is division-based, rather than centrally administered. In our culture, it's important that the divisions maintain their autonomy and authority, and we believe this ultimately keeps us closer to our customers." An important step at this stage was development of a key account profile by regional sales managers (RSMs) from relevant divisions. One RSM described this as "a working document that captures information most pertinent to our position and the decision process at the account. It helps to define the framework within which an effective interdivisional action plan can develop."

The key account profile included a listing of important contacts in each department at the account, current product usage, individual RSMs' judgments about product potential at the account, the account's current group affiliation(s), distributors utilized, and preferred distributors (if any), as well as an assessment designed (as one RSM described it) "simply to generate discussion and some consensus about current risks and opportunities at the account. This assessment is made in terms of product categories, but it can generate suggestions about services that can help to minimize a given risk or maximize an opportunity."

The next parts of the account planning process involved development of a multidivisional action plan for the account. The goal, as one RSM noted, was to "translate the account profile into a specific tactical plan that spells out individual division and salesperson responsibilities with target dates for completion. You need that specificity in order to make the process real for our people in the field, who respond more to tactical moves than grand strategy plans at accounts." Another RSM noted two important criteria for an effective multidivisional effort:

> First, the key account profile must clearly specify our objectives via coordinated efforts. Second, the action plan must focus on resources and opportunities not available through individual divisional approaches: what can we accomplish more effectively together, rather than separately? I'm busy, and not a big believer in teamwork for its own sake; so I think it's important that synergy possibilities be spelled out and not assumed.

Another manager emphasized that "the whole approach won't work without closer coordination of sales and marketing managers at both the divisional and corporate levels":

> This approach requires sales to utilize classical marketing skills: customer needs analysis, segmentation variables, etc. Also, in implementation, this approach moves the selling situation from a conversation with a few department managers at an account to a more formal presentation where a number of high-level account personnel are present. Marketing, rather than sales, typically has the training and resource access to develop these presentations. Marketing, rather than sales, also typically has product-profitability data, which is key in risk-opportunity assessments, potential service initiatives, and the actual offering that is the output of multidivisional efforts.

Value-Added vs. Basic Services

An important goal of multidivisional efforts was achieving competitive advantage for BD through superior customer service. Battaglia explained that "We assume that price pressures in health care won't decrease during the coming years. Providing superior service while maintaining or even lowering operating costs will be the key to success." Throdahl added that "customer loyalty derives from value, which is a relationship between the quality of a vendor's offering and its price. In turn, that quality is composed of both product and service factors, and service factors become the edge as products and markets mature."

The SCM group distinguished between basic or expected services, and value-added or unexpected services. Basic services included fulfillment accuracy, on-time delivery, damage-free goods, efficient order-inquiry routines, effective sales representation, accurate invoicing, and efficient in-servicing of end users. Value-added services included custom-designed product labeling, customized quality-control recommendations for customers, deferred billing, priority order processing through dedicated order-entry specialists, JIT inventory management, extended warranty plans, and perhaps new services in areas such as waste disposal and risk management. Effective provision of the latter services often required multidivisional coordination.

Throdahl explained that "The ultimate rationale for these efforts is to focus our sales efforts, and the customer's purchase criteria, on total cost-in-use and away from price." He noted that BD field salespeople had traditionally sold to purchasing and end users rather than the administrative personnel likely to be most cognizant of total cost-in-use. "This represents an important training issue for us," he noted. Battaglia added:

> All the value-added programs in the world won't mean anything if our reps don't understand them, don't want to understand them, or can't use them. So this thrust must be supported by effective sales management, especially by the RSMs who are a key link in field motivation. Then, for the individual field sales rep, it means (among other things) knowing your account well enough so that you can operationalize the impact of cutting delivery time or order-transaction costs or the amount of product held in inventory. However, salespeople who have grown up in a different selling environment are not immediately comfortable with this type of selling effort. That's another reason we need closer coordination between sales and marketing people in multidivisional efforts.

Information Systems

Developing common information systems was cited as a key step in multidivisional efforts. "Many of the initiatives," noted Battaglia, "are increasingly information-based. MIS developments are creating opportunities for cost savings and services that differentiate traditional product offerings and supplier-distributor-buyer relationships."

At BD, each division had its own information systems with different product numbering schemes, order placement protocols, inventory tracking, billing, and financial systems. In 1989, SCM began a multiyear project aimed at instituting common product, customer, and vendor identifiers across divisions. "We need a common corporate database for account and product information," said one BD manager. "With this data, our position in contract negotiations is stronger; without it, field people in various divisions must spend lots of time in meetings, and that in turn can discourage efforts on multidivisional opportunities."

Naz Bhimji, director of Corporate Service Product Development, was responsible for computerized aspects of service development. He noted that, "My current focus is primarily the distributors: in this industry, they are a critical link in the supply chain." According to one industry report, "As much as 25%–30% of the cost in the [hospital supply] channel is redundant and could be eliminated if one were to start with a clean slate. But this requires a great deal of trust—a true "partnership"—between distributor, manufacturer, and hospital . . . [and] a heavy dose of technology to accomplish the exchange of data efficiently."[1] The same report, based on a survey of 950 hospitals and 150 distributors, estimated that reducing materials-related costs by $250,000 "can have the same bottom line impact for hospitals as $8.3 million in increased revenues because of the associated costs (in storage, handling, financing, etc.) and fixed reimbursement programs." But the report also noted:

> Materials management has not been a priority for hospital executives, who do not understand the costs involved or how large they are. Hospital management believes its costs are 15% of the total operating budget, whereas the range is realistically 25%–33%. (Meanwhile) product price is an important factor in a hospital's decision to look at value-added services. For instance, lower product acquisition cost was overwhelmingly selected as the top desired benefit [ahead of (2) better productivity, (3) better service, (4) increased revenue, and (5) better supplier relationships] . . . which may indicate that the hospital is not yet focusing on total delivered cost. This could trigger additional costs for the distributor or manufacturer in the investor stage.

Bhimji was developing a new electronic link (known as the Speed-Com® system) between BD and many of its distributors, which he described as "the first phase of a longer-range program." Phase one focused on electronic ordering and billing procedures. Suppliers of such systems claimed that vendors saved $.50 to $1.00 per purchase order line when the order was entered electronically versus by mail or phone. Phase two sought to replace increasingly time-consuming rebate mechanics with a net-billing approach (i.e., any rebates or volume-discounts already included in the billing on the basis of distributors notifying BD of product shipments). Bhimji noted:

> One impact is to minimize quarterly buy-ins (i.e., distributors buying higher volumes of a product that is being promoted in a given quarter

[1] Arthur Andersen & Co., *Stockless Materials Management* (Health Industry Distributors Association, 1989).

and then stocking that product in various shipping locations). This will lower distributors' warehousing costs and working capital requirements, and improve their cash flow. It lowers our shipping costs and helps to smooth-out costly surges in our warehousing and manufacturing; it also lowers our administrative and order-transaction costs by providing a single order point for different divisions' products. And it enables the end customer to select a distributor of choice—i.e., one who, via this link, can lower the hospital's inventory levels and operating costs.

Speed-Com, by providing data on dealer inventory status and end-customer demand across product categories, also built the foundation for phase three, an automatic replenishment system among BD, distributor, and user-customer. The goal was to provide, based on dealer forecasts of end-user demand and inventory targets needed for reaching agreed-upon service levels, an "orderless" system that would replenish dealer inventory on a regularly scheduled basis. "Such a system can lower total cost-in-use," noted Bhimji, "at equal or improved service levels for all the players involved. For distributors, it minimizes intermediate inventory levels, improves order-entry accuracy, and waives order-minimum requirements; for users, it means better, guaranteed levels of service at lower administrative costs; and for BD, it can mean the ability to use our increasingly automated manufacturing capabilities to respond quickly and economically to changes in demand patterns." He added that these initiatives were both "necessary infrastructure *and* motivation for multidivisional efforts."

Sales and Marketing Organization

By January 1990, the sales and marketing structure for multidivisional efforts had evolved to include managers at both the corporate and divisional levels. This structure, noted Battaglia, reflected both resource constraints and "a philosophy that the key account program will ultimately be driven by the divisions with coordination help from corporate."

At corporate headquarters, Noah Gresham was appointed corporate director of sales with responsibility for both national account and multidivisional key account efforts. Gresham had been in BD sales positions for nearly two decades:

Neither I nor anyone else at corporate can require divisional support. We essentially work across a number of dotted-line relationships with the field. But our support from Ray Gilmartin has been vocal and clear, and that helps to create an atmosphere in which divisional support is easier to obtain. My goal is to build a sales system that can respond to multidivisional opportunities more proactively. Divisional salespeople naturally have their own interests in mind first, and too often a multidivisional initiative is introduced at the last minute. It's harder to marshal resources and support under those circumstances.

Reporting to Gresham were Phil Deelo, corporate national accounts manager Midwest (a new position created in September 1989), and John Gormally, director of corporate national accounts (a position Gormally assumed in November 1989).

Deelo's responsibilities were to assist divisions in developing multidivisional agreements and providing Corporate support, when possible. He participated in key account profiling sessions, assisted on sales calls, and served as a liaison between divisional sales personnel and corporate sales management. He noted that "I've worked as an RSM in two BD divisions and I believe in decentralization: competitive positions differ, and good salespeople come in different shapes, sizes, and approaches. But I also believe in corporate sales efforts, because we often don't maximize our opportunities across divisions."

When Deelo's position was created, it was also decided to establish a new sales office in Chicago which, in addition to Deelo, would house the midwest RSMs from seven divisions: BDD, Acute Care, Deseret Medical Systems, Microbiology, BDVS, Labware, and Diagnostic Instrument Systems. Each RSM had previously been located in a separate divisional sales office. "The shared office," he explained, "makes busy field people think in multidivisional terms and deal with one another on a daily basis." Deelo also noted that it required attention to physical and interpersonal details:

> The RSMs had previously worked out of their homes and divisional offices. In terms of travel time, therefore, a centrally-located office in Chicago had different implications for different RSMs. We were also careful to make sure that everyone involved got exactly the same amount of office space; and when it came time to allocate the corner office, a double random drawing was held.
>
> These details are important because they help to set a tone. Multidivisional efforts represent a change, and that always means some anxiety. And especially in sales, coordinated efforts tend to increase fears that others might infringe on one's turf and disturb existing account relationships that may have taken years to nurture. We want to encourage positive attitudes and the sharing of information; we don't need or want any political issues tied to status considerations.

As director of corporate national accounts, Gormally worked with division NAMs that called on GPOs. Each division's vice president of sales set goals for his or her NAMs in terms of annual sales volumes, margins, and allowable incentives. Gormally had no authority over such decisions but did have some input via meetings with the NAMs and divisional sales management. Gormally also had direct responsibility for seven national accounts.

Gormally had worked in various sales positions for over 11 years in four different BD divisions. He noted:

> [I]n my current position, my primary customers are the NAMs in various divisions, and that's as it should be: the account manager ulti-

mately has real knowledge of what an account wants, not corporate. In my position, you 'win' when you get various NAMs to buy into decisions that affect cross-divisional positions at their accounts. My job is to keep this big-picture perspective in front of them and, when possible, coordinate efforts. This is very different from my previous positions in sales, where I always received short-term feedback based on relatively clear performance measurements.

At the division level, multidivisional sales efforts focused on two positions: the lead regional sales manager (lead RSM), and the corporate national accounts field manager.

The lead RSM served as the central coordinator for multidivisional agreements. He or she organized the account-profile and account-planning sessions, led the effort toward successful implementation of the plan, and typically served as the primary account contact for matters concerning a multidivisional agreement. (See **Exhibit 2**.) A multidivisional agreement (or contract) was defined as a customized offering by two or more divisions to designated key accounts with an emphasis on value-added service programs rather than financial incentives (although the latter were not excluded from these agreements). Any financial incentives in a multidivisional agreement were to be funded pro-rata by the participating divisions and paid to the account by the division represented by the lead RSM. Pricing and terms for products were negotiated by the participating divisions with input from the lead RSM.

The lead RSM might come from corporate, but was typically expected to be a divisional RSM and to perform multidivisional activities in addition to his or her ongoing sales management responsibilities. Gresham explained that the lead RSM was "typically the person from the division with the most to gain or the most to lose at a key account. That provides the incentive to assume the role and make the required efforts as team facilitator and coordinator with the account." This approach was initiated at a companywide sales meeting in March 1989 where RSMs from different divisions were organized into teams to discuss and plan for multidivisional efforts. During the two-day meeting, these teams selected certain accounts as the pilot targets, generated key account profiles and action plans for each account, and designated a lead RSM to coordinate multidivisional efforts with a given account. During the remainder of 1989, these plans were refined and steps at implementation were made. RSMs who participated in these sessions and subsequent efforts had a variety of opinions about the process:

> The account-planning sessions are very important because they force people into thinking specifically about the role of our various contacts in an account, segmentation issues, and risk/opportunity assessments. Initially, each divisional RSM had its own divisional agenda primarily in mind. But continued meetings tend to promote a healthy give-and-take among RSMs.

*　*　*　*　*

Each session involves a full day and typically a two-month lead time to get a date on the schedules of 4 to 6 busy sales managers. Also, different divisions have different conceptions of marketing and sales, and some divisions seem to think that multidivisional marketing is great if *they* define the rules.

* * * * *

In our company, interdivisional communication was not perceived as important. Few RSMs had common past experiences on which to build, despite selling to many of the same accounts. Back at the division, moreover, the lead RSM can be perceived as an ambivalent figure. Especially when a product has a high share position with an account, there's a feeling in some divisions that the lead RSM may sacrifice too much for multidivisional efforts.

* * * * *

This new process creates expectations about working together and a system of informal debits and credits among RSMs. Still, in many accounts, I have spent years sweating for business in an increasingly tough marketplace. Now, somebody from another division, with less at stake than I have, has influence over my plans and contact with my account. You wonder if they're as committed as you are to making things happen at that account.

The lead RSM was eligible for a $200 cash award when he or she successfully signed a key account agreement. The incentive was increased to $250 for the second agreement, and $300 each for the third and any subsequent agreements. In addition, any sales or marketing managers that played an "active role" on the key-account team were eligible for a cash award of one-half that awarded to the lead RSM. The determination of "active participation" was made by the lead RSM, while the incentive awards were funded by corporate.

The position of corporate national accounts field manager (CNAFM) was created in October, 1989 to formalize multidivisional responsibilities performed by certain senior sales executives in addition to their normal divisional sales activities. The initial appointees to this position were 5 RSMs and 2 NAMs from different divisions and geographical regions. They were expected to devote approximately 10% of their time to the CNAFM role, which included participation in key-account sales and marketing training programs and participating as lead RSM for at least one key account. Those appointed as CNAFMs were nominated by their respective divisional presidents, given a $1,500 salary increase, and were eligible for the incentives available to lead RSMs and key-account team members described above. Gresham noted that "Externally, some customers simply want to deal with someone whose business card indicates that he or she is a corporate representative. This is especially important at the levels where multidivisional agreements get signed. Internally, the position is a way of developing a cadre of people who have this experience and formal responsibility for thinking about corporate objectives. Also, managers appointed as CNAFMs help to give multidivisional efforts credibility within their respective divisions and, through training efforts, act as facilitators for a new selling approach."

These sales positions were complemented by a number of marketing positions focused on multidivisional efforts. In 1989, Bette Weber was appointed corporate marketing manager, a new position whose responsibilities included working with divisional sales and marketing personnel on programs supporting key account activities; conducting training sessions intended to enhance divisional understanding of BD's key account programs; and providing corporate marketing analyses and support in specific account situations. Weber identified four "tiers" of buyers at accounts—CFO, materials management, purchasing, and end users—and noted that much of her work is aimed at "moving our presence up to CFO and materials management levels." She noted that both sales and marketing input were important in such efforts because "sales and marketing hear with different ears; each has ongoing access to information and experience not immediately visible to the other."

Commenting in early 1990 on multidivisional marketing efforts, Battaglia noted:

> Our structures and systems for interdivisional marketing are evolving. The goal is increasing sales *and* our customers' awareness of BD's service value. We want to provide services that customers value and pay for, and that we as a corporation can provide especially effectively. In different ways, both the national and key accounts programs are aimed at marshaling resources to do that.

During the past year, Battaglia and others in the SCM group had spoken at a number of corporate and divisional meetings throughout BD. **Exhibit 3** provides a graphic that SCM managers had found useful in general explanations of how the value-added services concept related to BD's various sales efforts and its ultimate offering to customers.

HEALTH MEDICAL CENTER

HMC was a leading teaching hospital in the southeastern United States. Most other health care providers in the area regarded HMC as an innovator in health care training, medical procedures, and use of medical devices. As a customer, HMC also had a reputation as a "renegade" institution: it was a member of two other GPOs in addition to APG, and continually shopped among these GPOs for the best price and terms in a product category. In 1989, HMC had begun purchasing BDD syringes and needles via the BDD-APG national account contract, after previously purchasing these products via an individual contract signed directly with BDD.

In addition to BDD, four other BD divisions sold significant amounts of product to HMC, through separate sales and distribution efforts and a variety of separate contracts. However, BDD had the most substantial presence in the account, with previous year's sales of $256,000, of which $216,000 was needles and syringes. **Exhibit 4** provides a brief description of the five BD divisions that sold to HMC, their major product lines, primary contacts at hospitals, and contracting mechanisms with accounts such as HMC. **Exhibit 5** outlines current BD product usage at HMC as well as estimates of potential sales volume represented by HMC in a product category. **Exhibit 6** indicates the BD sales personnel responsible for HMC; consistent with BD's decentralized operations, there were five sales representatives (and five different sales management organizations) responsible for sales and service to HMC.

HMC was facing a severe budget deficit. State funding had been slashed, and HMC had instituted expense reduction measures, including the indefinite layoff of over 100 hospital personnel. Overall responsibility for expense reductions rested with Stan Delaney, vice president of financial services (see **Exhibit 7**), whose plan included $175,000 in expense reductions from materials management. He asked Phil Robinson (administrator of financial services) to implement this reduction with Judy Koski (director of materials management). Of the $175,000 required reduction, Robinson recommended that $100,000 come from medical supply costs. Koski agreed, and gave Joanne Wilson (purchasing manager) the responsibility for determining how to save $100,000 on medical supplies.

According to John Kmetz (the BDD sales rep at the HMC account), Wilson accepted the assignment with reservations:

> Wilson felt that Koski (her boss) underestimated the difficulty of saving this much money. Koski had never really gotten involved in any activities related to purchasing medical supplies, and Wilson was also somewhat peeved that she, as the purchasing expert, was not consulted earlier about this decision. Nevertheless, Wilson recognized the pressures being placed on Koski and, knowing that she had little choice, accepted the assignment without mentioning her doubts.

Wilson first analyzed the hospital's usage rates and costs for its top ten supply products. To do this, she solicited the help of Ted Barber, general manager of City Surgical, HMC's largest distributor, which supplied 80% of its medical supplies. Barber had previously been HMC's director of purchasing, and Wilson had reported to him. According to the BDD salesperson, City Surgical had "a very strong lock" on the supplies business at HMC.

Competitor's Response

In conducting her analysis, Wilson noted that syringes and needles were the second-largest medical supply expense item at HMC. Not long before, moreover, she had been visited by a Terumo salesperson (along with a distributor sales rep from one of City Surgical's local competitors), who encouraged her to evaluate Terumo's new hypodermics line. HMC had used Terumo's IV catheters, blood collection needles, and arterial blood gas kits for a number of years. At the time, however, Wilson was not ready to undergo the end user turmoil required for a hypodermics product evaluation. Such a process typically took 3 to 4 months and involved testing at nursing stations, the filling out of numerous forms by various hospital personnel, and meetings among the hospital committees involved in a major evaluation. But given her recent expense-reduction task, she decided an evaluation might now be warranted.

In considering an evaluation, Wilson first asked Barber if City Surgical could supply Terumo syringes and needles to HMC. Barber said he could, and would assist in in-servicing HMC if it decided to switch hypodermics brands. Kmetz noted that:

> City Surgical is a Terumo "Plus" distributor, so Barber can earn higher margins on Terumo's product versus BDD at current volumes. However, City Surgical is also part of BDD's Advantage Distributor Program, where it's eligible for financial incentives if it surpasses previous year's unit sales of BDD's products and agrees not to "actively" convert a BDD account to a different brand. Also, Terumo's hypodermics line was introduced to Wilson via a competing distributor. So, my perception is that Barber was definitely interested in the prospect of supplying their line, but was cautious in voicing support of Terumo at the account.

Barber then arranged a meeting among Wilson, himself, and Terumo personnel. Along with Terumo's local sales rep, Terumo's northeastern sales manager and national sales director flew in to attend. At the meeting, Terumo personnel demonstrated the "special" features of Terumo's new syringe, but Wilson noted that she had seen similar features on samples of BDD's new syringe. When the discussion turned to price, Terumo guaranteed a 15% discount off HMC's current pricing for BDD hypodermics. (Terumo managers knew that HMC purchased these products off the APG contract, and set their prices 15% below the contract price. At current volumes, this meant a $32,000 savings in hypodermics expenses for HMC.) The meeting ended with Terumo personnel inviting Wilson to tour Terumo's new U.S. manufacturing plant. Wilson declined, but expressed her pleasure at the invitation and their "attentive recognition of HMC's importance and current financial difficulties."

Wilson agreed to set up a Terumo hypodermics evaluation at HMC. She knew that, if successful, a switch would mean that she had attained one-third of her expense-reduction goal. She also knew that BDD hypodermics commanded strong loyalty among end users at HMC, and that conversion to a new brand would be a major undertaking. But she felt that, given the hospital's financial situation, purchasing had more power to implement this type of change.

Wilson's next action was to present Terumo's hypodermics line to HMC's evaluation committee (composed of managers from different administrative and clinical departments) in order to determine which departments would conduct the evaluation. It was decided that anesthesiology, pediatrics, and pharmacy would participate.

BDD Response

When the evaluation was initiated, Kmetz detailed for Wilson BDD's product line breadth, in-service support, and unblemished record of high product quality in hypodermics. However, Wilson explained her expense-reduction goals and indicated that HMC would convert to Terumo if the evaluation were successful. But Wilson did agree to give Kmetz access to the evaluating departments and to give BDD an opportunity to retain the hypodermics business if equal cost savings could be offered.

During the final stages of the evaluation process, Kmetz intensified his efforts to retain the business. He demonstrated that Terumo could not supply all the needle and syringe items offered by BDD, and that buying these items off the APG contract would increase HMC's costs by $7,000 (thus reducing the purported cost savings to $25,000). Kmetz also explained BDD's inability to undercut the APG contract. Wilson said she understood the situation, but stated that only an equivalent price discount would suffice, and repeated her plans to complete the evaluation and convert to Terumo's line if necessary.

By January 1990, the evaluation was completed: HMC's evaluation committee approved Terumo for use and then turned the decision over to the standards committee which, after a review of the product, also approved Terumo's hypodermics line for use at HMC.

Kmetz then consulted with Ed Haire (BDD's director of contract sales) and Wally Joyce (the BDD district manager to whom Kmetz reported). Both emphasized the dangers and potential consequences of undermining a contract with a large GPO, but also felt that HMC was too important an account to lose, especially at a time when Terumo was aggressively seeking sales for its new hypodermics line at prestigious teaching institutions. Kmetz noted that, "I see an opportunity to save this account: we have a good relationship there with end users, and it may be possible to retain the business with a 10% price reduction."

Current Situation

After speaking with Flaherty (president of BDD), Jones (BDD's vice president of sales) contacted Kmetz and Joyce about the possibility of a multidivisional approach to the HMC situation. He explained that HMC could become a key account and that interdivisional programs and services could provide cost savings equivalent to, or more than, that represented by Terumo's lower price, while maintaining BDD's pricing on its APG contract and perhaps solidifying its position with purchasing influences at levels higher than Wilson. He found that both Kmetz and Joyce were concerned about what they termed this "change in direction." "Wilson expects a formal proposal from us in 10 days," noted one. "This account has clearly expressed its desire for a straight discount," said the other, "and we risk any chance of saving the business by introducing a new, unproven approach in such a tight time period."

Concurrently, Jones and Marty Hart (BDD's RSM in the southeastern region) contacted relevant personnel at the other BD divisions involved at HMC. The following summarizes the reactions and information they received from those divisions:

BD's *Acute Care* division (BDAC) had considerable business with HMC as well as a strong field relationship with Wilson and others in purchasing. Their primary products at the account were surgical blades/scalpels and surgeon's gloves. This represented two of BDAC's eight major product lines, and thus the potential existed for significant sales increases at HMC. David Pulsifer, BDAC's president, also indicated that he had long known Barber (City Surgical's president) and agreed to call Barber in order to clarify the distributor's position. After a phone conversation, Pulsifer reported that Barber said, "I've done business with BD for years and would prefer to keep them as the primary hypodermics supplier to HMC. But I've also got to protect myself if that account decides to switch to another brand." Pulsifer expressed his division's willingness to participate in a multidivisional effort at HMC.

Deseret Medical (DM) division had been acquired by BD in 1986. Pam Mason, Deseret RSM, explained that the division only had the IV catheter business in the anesthesia department at HMC. "We have a good relationship with key anesthesia personnel, including the department director," Ms. Mason noted. "But we do not have a strong overall presence in the account and my field rep reports that at least one important decision influencer there—the IV therapy supervisor—has been difficult to deal with."

Mason also explained that, six months earlier, she had personally been involved in trying to get HMC to adopt Deseret's new Insyte catheter product, which was made with proprietary materials and had features that significantly reduced usage complications in many applications. HMC had evaluated Insyte and found it acceptable in all areas except neonatal and pediatrics, where end users preferred current products. "Without usage in these key departments," she noted, "Deseret can't demonstrate a significant cost savings to HMC. In addition, this account currently doesn't measure certain usage costs where Insyte is particularly cost effective." Mason stated that she welcomed the opportunity to work on a multidivisional agreement with HMC, "especially if it contains incentives helpful in placing this new product there."

BD VACUTAINER *Systems* (BDVS) sold blood collection tubes and needles. Jeff Williams, BDVS's RSM, explained that this division had long had "a solid, well-entrenched position at HMC with tubes, but we don't service their blood-collection needle business. Our relations with key lab personnel are very strong, and purchasing has historically had little involvement with blood-collection products. In fact, our divisional sales strategy is to solidify end user brand preference for BDVS products and keep purchasing out of this process." Williams expressed the concern that a multidivisional effort at HMC would increase purchasing's involvement in blood-collection buying decisions, and said his position was "noncommittal" with respect to BDVS involvement in such an approach.

BD's *Microbiology Division* (BDMS) sold products used by various hospital and commercial labs to diagnose infectious diseases and determine proper therapy. Harry Henderson, an RSM at BDMS, noted that the division had a strong position at HMC for one of its major product lines, prepared plate media. He further noted that, in recent years, BDMS had been able to raise its prices on these products with little impact on sales volumes or buyer resistance:

> First, we have an outstanding product whose quality is widely recognized; second, our salespeople deal exclusively with end users who view product quality as the paramount issue in this medical application. This is especially true at a research and teaching institution like HMC. By contrast, most other BD divisions must work, at least in part, with purchasing personnel for whom price is a priority.

In light of these differences, Henderson reported that BDMS was "concerned" about a multidivisional program at HMC.

Jones and Hart also spoke with sales and marketing personnel in other divisions, and found a variety of opinions. A district manager commented: "HMC is not worth the time and effort of an interdivisional approach. They have historically shopped among buying groups and vendors; they're interested in price, not service." A sales representative said: "I'm concerned about which distributor gets the benefit of any multidivisional agreement we might reach. City Surgical hasn't been important, or particularly supportive, for sales of my product line. There are other distributors to HMC that I'd want to see rewarded by any multidivisional approach."

An RSM (who was not involved with the HMC account) described the proposed approach as "a too-little-too-late attempt to rescue BDD from a tough situation." Another RSM noted that: "For years, I've worked to solidify our division's position at that account. Then, with a multidivisional approach, people from other divisions are formatting my plans and programs. Those RSMs don't know much about my previous efforts, and I'm uncomfortable when other people are dealing with my contacts and customers."

A product manager from one division involved with HMC strongly supported a multidivisional approach: "There are many opportunities there for cross-divisional services, especially in logistics, order entry, and waste disposal." At corporate headquarters, Gresham expressed his willingness to become actively involved at corporate and divisional levels to help secure needed resources and support. Similarly, Deelo, while not responsible for accounts in the southeastern region, also volunteered to help where appropriate and to provide information concerning previous multidivisional agreements that might be useful in thinking about the HMC situation.

After these meetings, Jones requested Kmetz to contact HMC in order to gauge possible receptiveness to a multidivisional proposal that would emphasize a product and service package intended to deliver cost savings in excess of those represented by Terumo's hypodermics discount. Kmetz then spoke with Wilson and reported that "Joanne seemed apathetic about the possibility, but did not reject the idea outright. She reiterated her request for a price equivalent to Terumo's offer, and said she still expected a BD proposal by the following week."

Conclusion

Jones spoke again with Flaherty. Both agreed to set up a day's meeting with personnel from the various divisions involved with the HMC account. Attendees would include the five division presidents, sales directors, relevant RSMs and sales reps, as well as Gresham and Deelo. "Bob," said Flaherty to Jones,

> I'd like to use that meeting as a way to fashion a multidivisional proposal for HMC, and I'd like you to think about what's involved in getting required support from other divisions. As far as expenses are concerned, I'm happy to have BDD act as the lead division and accept the incremental expenses in this situation. However, if you think that a multidivisional approach is not feasible in this situation, and that BDD's best bet is a price response, then let me know that as well.

EXHIBIT 1   Operational Structure—Becton Dickinson Medical and Diagnostic Sectors

MEDICAL SECTOR	
—BD AcuteCare	—BD Pharmaceutical Systems
—BD Canada	—BD Polymer Research
—BD Consumer Products	—BD Medical Gloves
—BD Critical Care Monitoring	— Deseret Medical
—BD Division	—Ivers Lee
—BD Infusion Systems	

DIAGNOSTIC SECTOR	
—BD ACCU-GLASS	—BD Labware
—BD Advanced Diagnostics	—BD Microbiology Systems
—BD Diagnostic Instrument Systems	—BD Primary Care Diagnostics
—BD Immunocytometry Systems	—BD VACUTAINER Systems

Note: "BD" is used above to abbreviate Becton Dickinson

EXHIBIT 1 *(continued)*

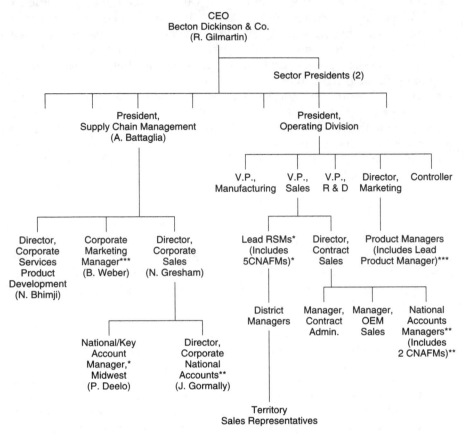

Legend: Asterisks indicate liaison activities between corporate headquarters and operating divisions for multidivisional sales and marketing efforts.

*   = Deelo (NAM, Midwest); corporate national account field managers (CNAFMs); lead regional sales managers

** = Gormally (Director, corporate national accounts); divisional national account managers (NAMs)

*** = Weber (Corporate Marketing Manager); divisional lead product managers

EXHIBIT 2 "Lead RSM" Role in Multidivisional Key Account Program

1. *Identification of Key Account*

   - A potential account is usually identified by a division or divisions who are under competitive pressure *or* see new business opportunities *or* we wish to solidify a strong position.
   - The lead RSM may come from the initiating division *or* may be the corporate national account field manager *or* the corporate national account manager—midwest region.
   - Lead RSM polls all appropriate divisions for level of interest.
   - Lead RSM reviews survey of responses and communicates "go or no go" decisions to all RSMs.

2. *Developing the Key Account Profile, Plan and Proposal*

   - Lead RSM schedules a RSM team meeting.
   - Team completes key account profile, action plan, and preliminary proposal, including appropriate input from marketing.
   - Team members secure value-added offering and pricing approvals from their division management.
   - Corporate national accounts is consulted prior to finalizing the proposal. This requirement is satisfied if either the corporate national account field manager or corporate national account manager—midwest region is involved because they are expected to communicate routinely with corporate sales.

3. *Interfacing and Negotiating with Key Accounts*

   - Lead RSM sets up meeting between customer and selected team members.
   - Proposal is submitted to customer, discussed and customized to meet the customer's needs.
   - An additional RSM meeting may be needed to address customer modifications.
   - The modified proposal in the form of an agreement or contract, is submitted to the customer for signature by lead RSM.

4. *Managing Key Accounts After the Multidivisional Agreement is Signed*

   - Schedule an implementation planning meeting with customer management and our participating divisions. Agree on contract implementation plan.
   - Each divisional RSM team member should submit divisional implementation plan to lead RSM.
   - Each divisional RSM team member should submit divisional implementation plan to lead RSM.
   - Lead RSM to review contract progress quarterly with the customer.
   - Quarterly implementation status report sent to RSM team by lead RSM.

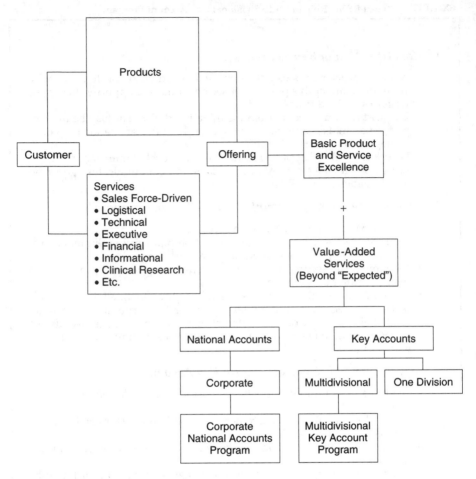

EXHIBIT 3   Overview

EXHIBIT 4 Description of Five BD Operating Divisions

Division	Major Products	Primary End Users	Primary Decision Influencers	Distribution System	Contracting Mechanism	# Sales Reps
BDAC	—Blades —Surgeons gloves —Scrubs —Preps —Suction	—Scrub nurses —Surgeons —Circulating nurses	—Purchasing groups —Purchasing managers —Or supervisor	—Broad (except for Beaver line)	—Direct sell, contract with customer	98
BDD	—Hypodermic syringes/needles —Insulin syringes —Disposal products —Exam gloves —Thermometers	—Nurses —Doctors —Pharmacists	—Purchasing groups —Purchasing managers —Evaluating committees —Distributors (non hospital)	—Very broad	—Hospital direct sell, contract (Z) —Nonhospital limited contracts	100
BDMS	—Prepared plated media —Dried culture media —Manual sensitivity disks —Anaerobic systems —Rapid manual tests	—Microbiologists	—Microbiology dept. —Pathologist —Purchasing groups (limited)	—Select	—Direct sell, contract (Z)	75
BDVS	—B.C. tubes —B.C. needles —SST tubes	—Hospital labs —Commercial labs	—Purchasing group —Lab managers —Department supervisors —Phlebotomists	—Broad/focused	—Direct sell, contract (Z)	54
DM	—IV catheters	—Nurses	—Purchasing groups —Head critical care nurse —Anesthesiologist —IV therapist	—Broad	—Direct sell, contract (not Z)	72

BDAC = Becton Dickinson Acute Care Division
BDD = Becton Dickinson Division
BDMS = Becton Dickinson Microbiology Systems
BDVS = Becton Dickinson VACUTAINER Systems
DM = Deseret Medical Division

EXHIBIT 5 Health Medical Center—Becton Dickinson Product Usage

Division	Product	BD Product Used in Medical Center?	Annualized Current or Potential $ Sales (000)
Becton Dickinson AcuteCare	—Arterial Blood Gas Syringes/Kits	No	$31
	—BARD-PARKER Surgical Blades/ Scalpels	Yes	17
	—E-Z SCRUBS	No	50
	—EUDERMIC and SPECTRA Surgeon's Gloves	Yes	40
	—Suction Canisters	No	40
	—Suction Catheters and Kits	No	34
Becton Dickinson Division	—BD Brand Fever Thermometers	Yes	$22
	—BD Brand Pharmacy Products	Yes	7
	—BD Brand Syringes and Needles	Yes	216
	—BD Brand Technique Needles	Yes	7
	—TRU-TOUCH Vinyl Examination Gloves	No	40
Becton Dickinson Microbiology Systems	—Prepared Plated Media	Yes	$53
Becton Dickinson VACUTAINER Systems	—MICROTAINER Brand Microcollection Tubes	Yes	$5
	—SST Brand Serum Separation Tubes	Yes	4
	—VACUTAINER Brand Blood Collection Needles	No	11
	—VACUTAINER Brand Blood Collection Tubes	Yes	21
Deseret Medical	—ANGIOCATH IV Catheter	Yes	$40
	—E-Z Sets	No	15
	—Epidural Tray	No	30
	—INSYTE IV Catheter	No	45
	—PRN	No	15

BDVS	BDAC	BDD	BDMS	DM
B. Brown Director, Sales	J. Schofield Director of Sales	R. Jones V.P. Sales	P. Ferrigno Director Sales	H. Nicholas V.P. Sales/Marketing
J. Williams RSM	B. Hancock RSM	M. Hart RSM	H. Henderson RSM	P. Mason RSM
R. Giardino Sales Rep	T. Pilkington Sales Rep	J. Kmetz Sales Rep	M. Papagano Sales Rep	A. Carr Sales Rep

EXHIBIT 6   Divisional BD Sales Structure Responsible for Health Medical Center

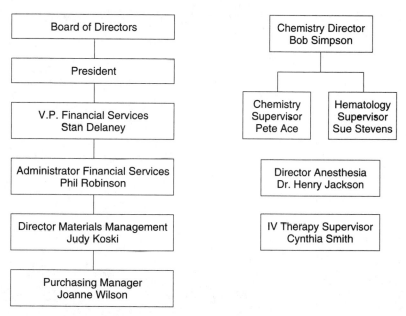

EXHIBIT 7   Health Medical Center Organizational Chart